*Philosophers in Depth*

Series Editors: **Stephen Boulter** and **Constantine Sandis**

*Philosophers in Depth* is a series of themed edited collections focusing on particular aspects of the thought of major figures from the history of philosophy. The volumes showcase a combination of newly commissioned and previously published work with the aim of deepening our understanding of the topics covered. Each book stands alone, but taken together the series will amount to a vast collection of critical essays covering the history of philosophy, exploring issues that are central to the ideas of individual philosophers. This project was launched with the financial support of the Institute for Historical and Cultural Research at Oxford Brookes University, for which we are very grateful.

Constantine Sandis and Stephen Boulter
Oxford

*Titles include*:

Alison Denham (*editor*)
PLATO ON ART AND BEAUTY

Edward Feser (*editor*)
ARISTOTLE ON METHOD AND METAPHYSICS

Philip Goff (*editor*)
SPINOZA ON MONISM

Leonard Kahn (*editor*)
MILL ON JUSTICE

Arto Laitinen and Constantine Sandis (*editors*)
HEGEL ON ACTION

Katherine Morris (*editor*)
SARTRE ON THE BODY

Charles R. Pigden (*editor*)
HUME ON MOTIVATION AND VIRTUE

Sabine Roeser
REID ON ETHICS

Henrik Rydenfelt and Sami Pihlström (*editors*)
WILLIAM JAMES ON RELIGION

Daniel Whiting (*editor*)
THE LATER WITTGENSTEIN ON LANGUAGE

*Forthcoming titles*:

Alix Cohen (*editor*)
KANT ON EMOTION AND VALUE

Pierre Destree (*editor*)
ARISTOTLE ON AESTHETICS

David Dolby (*editor*)
RYLE ON MIND AND LANGUAGE

Brian Garvey (*editor*)
J. L. AUSTIN ON LANGUAGE

**Philosophers in Depth**
**Series Standing Order ISBN**   **978–0–230–55411–5 Hardback**
                                 **978–0–230–55412–2 Paperback**
(*outside North America only*)

You can receive future titles in this series as they are published by placing a standing order.
Please contact your bookseller or, in case of difficulty, write to us at the address below with
your name and address, the title of the series and one of the ISBNs quoted above.

Customer Services Department, Macmillan Distribution Ltd, Houndmills, Basingstoke,
Hampshire RG21 6XS, England

# Aristotle on Method and Metaphysics

Edited by

Edward Feser
*Pasadena City College, California, USA*

First published 2013 by
PALGRAVE MACMILLAN

Palgrave Macmillan in the UK is an imprint of Macmillan Publishers Limited,
registered in England, company number 785998, of Houndmills, Basingstoke,
Hampshire RG21 6XS.

Palgrave Macmillan in the US is a division of St Martin's Press LLC,
175 Fifth Avenue, New York, NY 10010.

Palgrave Macmillan is the global academic imprint of the above companies
and has companies and representatives throughout the world.

Palgrave® and Macmillan® are registered trademarks in the United States,
the United Kingdom, Europe and other countries

ISBN: 978–0–230–36091–4

This book is printed on paper suitable for recycling and made from fully
managed and sustained forest sources. Logging, pulping and manufacturing
processes are expected to conform to the environmental regulations of the
country of origin.

A catalogue record for this book is available from the British Library.

A catalog record for this book is available from the Library of Congress.

# Contents

# Acknowledgments

I want to thank Stephen Boulter for commissioning this volume and Constantine Sandis and Melanie Blair for helping to bring it to fruition. I thank the contributors to the volume for delivering such a fine collection of essays. And I thank my beloved wife Rachel and our dear children Benedict, Gemma, Kilian, Helena, John, and Gwendolyn for tolerating the many hours I spend in my study working on projects like this one.

# Notes on Contributors

**Robert Bolton** is Professor of Philosophy at Rutgers University. He is the author of *Science, Dialectique et Ethique chez Aristote* (2010), and author or editor of numerous books and articles on Aristotle's methodology, epistemology, and psychology, and on other aspects of ancient philosophy. He is a former Rhodes Scholar and research fellow of the Centre National de la Recherche Scientifique, Paris.

**Stephen Boulter** is Senior Lecturer in Philosophy at Oxford Brookes University and the author of *The Rediscovery of Common Sense Philosophy* (2007). His research focuses primarily on topics in metaphilosophy, methodology, and metaphysics, with special interest in biology and the Aristotelian tradition. His second monograph, *Metaphysics from a Biological Point of View*, is due out with Palgrave Macmillan in 2013.

**David Charles** is a Research Professor of Philosophy at Oriel College, Oxford, specializing in ancient philosophy. His two books, *Aristotle's Philosophy of Action* (1984) and *Aristotle on Meaning and Essence* (2000), compare and contrast Aristotle's views with those of recent writers on these topics. He has edited a collection of essays by several authors entitled *Definition in Greek Philosophy* (2011), bringing together studies of Plato's, Aristotle's, and post-Aristotelian views on definition, meaning, and essence. He has written a series of articles on aspects of Greek and contemporary philosophy and is currently examining Aristotle's distinctive account of the psychological. He has been a visiting professor at several universities in the US (Brown, Rutgers, UCLA) and at Tokyo Metropolitan and Venice Universities.

**Edward Feser** is Associate Professor of Philosophy at Pasadena City College in Pasadena, CA. He is the author of *Aquinas* (2009) and four other books and editor of *The Cambridge Companion to Hayek* (2006) and has published numerous academic articles in philosophy of mind, philosophy of religion, and moral and political philosophy.

**Lloyd P. Gerson** is Professor of Philosophy at the University of Toronto. He has published widely on ancient philosophy, and his books include *Knowing Persons: A Study in Plato* (2003), *Aristotle and Other Platonists* (2005), and *Ancient Epistemology* (2009).

**Gyula Klima** is Professor of Philosophy at Fordham University, New York. He specializes in medieval and contemporary logic and metaphysics. His books include *Ars Artium: Essays in Philosophical Semantics, Medieval and Modern* (1988); *John Buridan: Summulae de Dialectica*, an annotated translation with a philosophical introduction (2001); *Medieval Philosophy: Essential Readings with Commentary* (2007); and *John Buridan* (2009). He is also the director of the Society for Medieval Logic and Metaphysics, and the editor of its *Proceedings*, as well as editor of the series *Medieval Philosophy: Texts and Studies* at Fordham University Press.

**Kathrin Koslicki** is originally from Munich, Germany. She received her undergraduate degree in philosophy from SUNY Stony Brook in 1990 and her PhD in philosophy from MIT in 1995. Since then, she has held various positions at universities throughout the US; since 2007, she has been an Associate Professor of Philosophy at the University of Colorado-Boulder. Her interests in philosophy lie mainly in metaphysics, the philosophy of language, and ancient Greek philosophy, particularly Aristotle. In her monograph, *The Structure of Objects* (2008), she defends a structure-based, neo-Aristotelian theory of parts and wholes.

**E. J. Lowe** is Professor of Philosophy at Durham University, UK, specializing in metaphysics, the philosophy of mind and action, the philosophy of logic and language, and early modern philosophy. He is the author of several books, including *Kinds of Being* (1989), *The Possibility of Metaphysics* (1998), *The Four-Category Ontology* (2006), *Personal Agency* (2008), and *More Kinds of Being* (2009).

**Fred D. Miller, Jr.** is Professor of Philosophy and executive director of the Social Philosophy and Policy Center at Bowling Green State University and Research Professor at the Center for the Philosophy of Freedom at the University of Arizona. He is author of *Nature, Justice, and Rights in Aristotle's Politics* (1995) and co-editor of *A Companion to Aristotle's Politics* (1995), *Freedom, Reason, and the Polis: Essays in Ancient Greek Political Philosophy* (2007), *A History of the Philosophy of Law from the Ancient Greeks to the Scholastics* (2007), and *Reason and Analysis in Ancient Greek Philosophy* (2012). He is also Executive Editor of *Social Philosophy & Policy* and Assistant Editor of *The Philosopher's Index*. He is currently preparing a translation of Aristotle's *De Anima* and *Parva Naturalia* for Oxford University Press.

**David S. Oderberg** is Professor of Philosophy at the University of Reading. His most recent book is *Real Essentialism* (2007), and he has published widely in metaphysics among other areas.

**Christopher Shields** is Professor of Classical Philosophy at the University of Oxford and a Fellow of Lady Margaret Hall. He is the author of *Order in Multiplicity: Homonymy in the Philosophy of Aristotle* (1999), *Classical Philosophy: A Contemporary Introduction* (2003), *Aristotle* (2007), *Ancient Philosophy: A Contemporary Introduction* (2011), and, with Robert Pasnau, *The Philosophy of Thomas Aquinas* (2003). He is the editor of *The Blackwell Guide to Ancient Philosophy* (2002) and *The Oxford Handbook of Aristotle* (2012). Forthcoming is *Aristotle's De Anima, Translated with Introduction and Commentary*.

**Allan Silverman** is Professor of Philosophy at the Ohio State University. He is the author of *The Dialectic of Essence* (2002) and numerous articles on Plato and Aristotle. In addition to his research in ancient philosophy, metaphysics, and ethics, he is a fellow of the Mershon Center for International Security Studies, where he works on citizenship.

**Tuomas E. Tahko** is a post-doctoral researcher at the University of Helsinki, working mostly on metaphysics and its methodology. He is the editor of *Contemporary Aristotelian Metaphysics* (2012) and author of more than a dozen articles.

**Stephen Williams** is Fellow and Tutor in Philosophy at Worcester College, Oxford. He is co-editor with Sabina Lovibond of *Identity, Truth and Value: Essays for David Wiggins*. He has written principally in philosophical logic and the philosophy of language and is currently writing a book on homonymy.

# 1
# Introduction:
# An Aristotelian Revival?

*Edward Feser*

Modern philosophy began with a rebellion against the Aristotelianism of the Scholastics and has, to a large extent, always been defined by it. To be sure, even in the work of the early moderns, the rejection of Aristotelian ideas was not always thoroughgoing. For instance, the Scholastic holdovers in the systems of Descartes and Locke are well-known, and Leibniz was keen to synthesize as much of previous thought as he could. But the obsolescence of the core doctrines of Aristotle's metaphysics and philosophy of nature – such as hylemorphism, the theory of act and potency, and the doctrine of the four causes – would eventually become something like settled wisdom in post-Cartesian Western thought.

In recent decades, there has been within academic philosophy a small but growing challenge to this anti-Aristotelian near-consensus. The revival of Aristotelian themes in ethics in the work of thinkers like Alasdair MacIntyre (1981), Martha Nussbaum (1986), Philippa Foot (2001), and Michael Thompson (2008) is, of course, well-known. But neo-Aristotelian ideas have been getting attention even in the philosophy of science and in metaphysics. In the former discipline, there is the "new essentialism" of writers like Brian Ellis (2001, 2002) and Nancy Cartwright (1992, reprinted in 1999). In the latter there is the revival of the notion of causal powers and the manifestations toward which they are directed in the work of thinkers like George Molnar (2003), C.B. Martin (2008), and John Heil (2003). (Not that these developments are entirely independent. See Mumford 2009 for a useful overview of the history and themes of both lines of thought.)

There are also, in general metaphysics, the revival of interest in Aristotelian conceptions of substance, essence, and the like in the work of writers like Kit Fine (1994a, 1994b) and E.J. Lowe (2006); and in Aristotelian teleology in writers like John Hawthorne and Daniel Nolan

(2006), Andre Ariew (2002, 2007) and Thomas Nagel (2012). Even a full-throated Aristotelian-Scholasticism is not without representatives in contemporary analytic philosophy (Haldane 2002; Oderberg 2007; Novak, Novotny, Sousedik, and Svoboda 2012).

While it would certainly be an overstatement to say that a full-scale revival of Aristotelianism is currently underway, it does seem that some of the various strands of thought alluded to are at least beginning to coalesce into something like a self-conscious movement. That, at any rate, is something one might reasonably infer from the titles and contents of the recent anthologies *Contemporary Aristotelian Metaphysics*, edited by Tuomas Tahko (2012), and *Powers and Capacities in Philosophy: The New Aristotelianism*, edited by Ruth Groff and John Greco (2012); and from major conferences like *Metaphysics: Aristotelian, Scholastic, Analytic*, held in Prague from June 30 – July 3 in 2010, and *Aristotelian Themes in Contemporary Metaphysics*, held at Boise State University in Idaho, from April 16–18 in 2011.

If there is such a movement underway, perhaps the present volume can contribute something to it. Though grounded in careful exegesis of Aristotle's writings, the book aims to demonstrate the continuing relevance of Aristotelian ideas to contemporary philosophical debate.

The first three chapters in the volume are concerned with the questions of what metaphysics is and what method is appropriate to it. In "The Phainomenological Method in Aristotle's *Metaphysics*," Christopher Shields considers the role that appearances (*phainomena*) – what *seems* to be the case – play, for Aristotle, in determining what *is* the case, whether in metaphysics or in other contexts. As Shields explains, Aristotle is committed to a "Principle of Phainomenological Conservatism" according to which the fact that something appears to be true provides considerable evidence for believing that it is true, though not infallible evidence.

Stephen Boulter's "The Aporetic Method and the Defence of Immodest Metaphysics" defends the traditional view that metaphysics is indispensible to philosophy, that at least some substantive metaphysical claims can be justified without appealing to science, and that some accepted interpretations of mature scientific theory can justifiably be rejected on metaphysical grounds. Central to his defence is an appeal to what Aristotle called "aporia" – real or apparent conflicts between claims that we have independent reason to accept, and which must therefore be resolved in some way.

In "Metaphysics as the First Philosophy," Tuomas E. Tahko addresses the question of what it is for metaphysics to be "the first philosophy" (as the Aristotelian tradition characterizes it), and examines its relationship to natural science. He considers the notion that metaphysics is "first" insofar as it deals with what is *fundamental* in the sense of being ontologically independent or not grounded in anything else, but argues that it is the notion of *essence* rather than fundamentality that is key to the priority of metaphysics.

The next several chapters examine some of the central notions of Aristotelian metaphysics – being, essence, substance, necessity, and the like. Robert Bolton's "Two Doctrines of Categories in Aristotle: *Topics, Categories,* and *Metaphysics*" argues that there are two different and incompatible doctrines of categories in Aristotle. Bolton maintains that this is not because of a development in Aristotle's thought, but instead reflects the different needs which these doctrines were intended to meet, in one case the needs of the practice of dialectic and in the other the needs and practice of metaphysical science.

In "Grounding, Analogy and Aristotle's Critique of Plato's Idea of the Good," Allan Silverman examines the ways in which Aristotle and some contemporary Aristotelians have spelled out the idea that some entities are grounded in more fundamental, foundational, or basic entities. He appeals to the notions of focal meaning and analogy, particularly as these are applied by Aristotle in explicating his notion of *energeia* or actuality and in critiquing Plato's Idea of the Good, as a way of making sense of grounding relations.

In Aristotle's thought, the notion of essence plays both a *definitional* role, specifying what it is for a thing to belong to a certain natural kind, and an *explanatory* role, accounting for why a thing has and must have certain properties. In "Essence, Modality and the Master Craftsman," Stephen Williams and David Charles consider why essence should play both roles, how the explanatory role figures in Aristotle's account of essence, and how essences might be said to explain why things of a kind necessarily have certain properties. In doing so, they make use of the notion of what the "master craftsman" or artisan uncovers about the natural materials he works with.

Gyula Klima's "Being, Unity, and Identity in the Fregean and Aristotelian Traditions" compares the understanding of the notions of being or existence, identity, and unity operative in post-Fregean logic and metaphysics, on the one hand, and in the work of Aristotelian thinkers like Buridan and Aquinas on the other. In Klima's view, precisely because these respective notions of being, identity, and unity are so different and address different questions, we are not forced to choose between them, and in any event we ought not to suppose that the post-Fregean notions are "the" right ones merely because they are modern.

According to the Aristotelian doctrine of hylomorphism, unified wholes (for example, organisms) are composites of matter and form. Substances, in Aristotelian thought, are taken to be ontologically independent in the sense of not being "said of" or "in" anything else. In "Substance, Independence and Unity," Kathrin Koslicki considers the apparent tension that exists between these doctrines insofar as hylomorphism might seem to make substances dependent on their matter and form, and explores some possible resolutions.

E. J. Lowe's "Neo-Aristotelian Metaphysics: A Brief Exposition and Defence" examines how a complete metaphysical foundation for modal truths can be provided by combining a neo-Aristotelian account of essence with Lowe's neo-Aristotelian "four-category ontology" of individual substances, modes, substantial universals and property universals. Lowe argues that such an account avoids any appeal to "possible worlds" and renders modal truths mind-independent but humanly knowable.

The next two chapters in the volume examine the relationship between Aristotelian metaphysical ideas and some key issues in modern science. In "Synthetic Life and the Bruteness of Immanent Causation," David S. Oderberg provides an exposition and defence of the Aristotelian doctrine that living things are distinguished from non-living things by virtue of exhibiting "immanent" causation, causation that originates with an agent and terminates in that agent for the sake of its self-perfection. He argues that life, so understood, cannot be given a purely naturalistic explanation, and argues against claims to the effect that synthetic life has been, or is bound to be, created in the laboratory.

Edward Feser's "Motion in Aristotle, Newton, and Einstein" considers whether the Aristotelian principle that *whatever is in motion is moved by another* is incompatible with Newton's principle of inertia, or has been falsified by Einstein insofar as the latter is sometimes held to have shown that change is an illusion. Feser argues that the Aristotelian principle (better expressed as the thesis that *any potential that is being actualized is actualized by something already actual*) is not only compatible with Newton's, but that there is a sense in which the latter presupposes the former; and that relativity at most affects *how* we apply the Aristotelian principle to the natural world, not *whether* it is applicable.

The final two chapters in the volume raise questions about ultimate explanation and Aristotelian natural theology. In "Incomposite Being," Lloyd P. Gerson examines Aristotle's notion of a divine Prime Unmoved Mover which just *is* perfect actuality without any potency, which is *thinking itself thinking of itself*, and yet which is in no way composite. Gerson considers the views of later Platonists who objected that thinking cannot be attributed to that which is incomposite, and discusses the difficulties facing possible responses to this objection.

Fred D. Miller, Jr.'s "Aristotle's Divine Cause" considers whether Aristotle's Prime Mover is supposed to be merely the *final* cause of motion or also its *efficient* cause, and if the latter, then what the relationship is between the Prime Mover's final and efficient causality. Miller examines various approaches to these issues that have been defended over the centuries, and concludes that the main interpretations all present difficulties.

# References

Ariew, André. 2002. "Platonic and Aristotelian Roots of Teleological Arguments," in André Ariew, Robert Cummins, and Mark Perlman (eds) *Functions: New Readings in the Philosophy of Psychology and Biology* (Oxford: Oxford University Press).

Ariew, André. 2007. "Teleology," in D. Hull and M. Ruse (eds) *The Cambridge Companion to the Philosophy of Biology* (Cambridge: Cambridge University Press).

Cartwright, Nancy. 1992. "Aristotelian Natures and the Modern Experimental Method," in John Earman (ed.) *Inference, Explanation, and Other Frustrations: Essays in the Philosophy of Science* (Berkeley and Los Angeles: University of California Press).

Cartwright, Nancy. 1999. *The Dappled World: A Study of the Boundaries of Science* (Cambridge: Cambridge University Press).

Ellis, Brian. 2001. *Scientific Essentialism* (Cambridge: Cambridge University Press).

Ellis, Brian. 2002. *The Philosophy of Nature: A Guide to the New Essentialism* (Chesham: Acumen).

Fine, Kit. 1994a. "Essence and Modality," in J. Tomberlin (ed.) *Philosophical Perspectives* 8: 1–16.

Fine, Kit. 1994b. "A Puzzle Concerning Matter and Form," in T. Scaltsas, D. Charles, and M. L. Gill (eds) *Unity, Identity, and Explanation in Aristotle's Metaphysics* (Clarendon Press: Oxford).

Foot, Philippa. 2001. *Natural Goodness* (Oxford: Clarendon Press).

Groff, Ruth and Greco, John(eds) 2012. *Powers and Capacities in Philosophy: The New Aristotelianism* (London: Routledge).

Haldane, John. (ed.) 2002. *Mind, Metaphysics, and Value in the Thomistic and Analytical Traditions* (Notre Dame: University of Notre Dame Press).

Hawthorne, John and Daniel Nolan. 2006. "What Would Teleological Causation Be?" in John Hawthorne (ed.) *Metaphysical Essays* (Oxford: Oxford University Press).

Heil, John. 2003. *From an Ontological Point of View* (Oxford: Oxford University Press).

Lowe, E. J. 2006. *The Four-Category Ontology: A Metaphysical Foundation for Natural Science* (Oxford: Oxford University Press).

MacIntyre, Alasdair. 1981. *After Virtue* (Notre Dame: University of Notre Dame Press).

Martin, C. B. 2008. *The Mind in Nature* (Oxford: Clarendon Press).

Molnar, George. 2003. *Powers: A Study in Metaphysics* (Oxford: Oxford University Press).

Mumford, Stephen. 2009. "Causal Powers and Capacities," in Helen Beebee, Christopher Hitchcock, and Peter Menzies (eds) *The Oxford Handbook of Causation* (Oxford: Oxford University Press).

Nagel, Thomas. 2012. *Mind and Cosmos* (Oxford: Oxford University Press).

Novak, Lukas. and Daniel. D. Novotny, Prokop Sousedik, and David Svoboda, (eds) 2012. *Metaphysics: Aristotelian, Scholastic, Analytic* (Frankfurt: Ontos Verlag).

Nussbaum, Martha. 1986. *The Fragility of Goodness* (Cambridge: Cambridge University Press).

Oderberg, David S. 2007. *Real Essentialism* (London: Routledge).

Tahko, Tuomas (ed.) 2012. *Contemporary Aristotelian Metaphysics* (Cambridge: Cambridge University Press).

Thompson, Michael. 2008. *Life and Action* (Cambridge, MA: Harvard University Press).

# 2

# The Phainomenological Method in Aristotle's *Metaphysics*

*Christopher Shields*

> —About all these matters, we must try to reach conviction *via* arguments, using appearances (*phainomena*) as witnesses and standards.
>
> *EE* 1216b26–29

## 1 Introduction

It is understandable that those wishing to characterize Aristotle's philosophical method have looked for guidance almost without exception to a passage in *Nicomachean Ethics* vii 1, where he prefaces his discussion of the puzzling phenomenon of *akrasia* (weakness of will) with an uncharacteristic methodological preamble. In this preamble, Aristotle contends, "We must set out the appearances (*phainomena*) and run through all the puzzles regarding them" (*EN* vii 1, 1145b2–4). Thereafter, having systematized the *phainomena* and re-interpreted or rejected those proving problematic, we may rest content: any proof we may wish for in this domain is already provided in this procedure (*EN* vii 1, 1145b5–7).

It is understandable that so many have turned exclusively to this passage for guidance – but also misguided. It is understandable not least because this is one of the very few overtly methodological reflections in the entire Aristotelian corpus. Still, ever since G. E. L. Owen's pioneering article "τιθέναι τὰ φαινόμενα" of 1961, scholars have over-taxed this single passage, massaging it to yield quite general methodological precepts that, taken in isolation, it simply cannot sustain. It is noteworthy, to begin, that scholars have developed different and incompatible interpretations of Aristotle's methodological preamble in *Nicomachean Ethics* vii 1, yielding, accordingly, different and incompatible characterizations of his overarching method.[1] In particular, they have developed different and incompatible interpretations of what we may call Aristotle's *phainomenological method* – his method of appealing to appearances (*phainomena*) – a practice we find throughout his corpus, though most pronouncedly in dialectical contexts.

We will come to a better appreciation of Aristotle's phainomenological method if, after having reviewed the limitations of the methodological passage of *Nicomachean Ethics* vii 1, we pose and answer a perfectly general question about Aristotle's appeals to *phainomena*: Why? Why should he pay special attention to *phainomena* – the things that *seem* to be the case – when he might instead begin directly by considering the *onta* – the things that *are* the case? After all, he holds that our ultimate goal as beings who by nature desire to know is to arrive at an unmediated knowledge of causes (*aitia*) and first principles (*archai*) which serve as the basis for all science (*epistêmê*) (*Met.* 980a21, 983a25; *Phys.* 194b18; *APo.* 94a20). With this as our goal, is it necessary (*dei*; *EN* 11145b2) to set out the appearances? Might we not dispense with the *phainomena* altogether in favor of a direct engagement with the *onta*?

To answer these questions, we do well to look beyond the methodological passage of *Nicomachean Ethics* vii 1, because it alone can hardly serve to settle questions of general method. When we look instead towards Aristotle's actual appeals to *phainomena*, particularly in the first philosophy of his *Metaphysics*, we see that a fairly clear and consistent picture emerges. Aristotle adheres to an evidentiary principle which we may call the *Principle of Phainomenological Conservativism* (PPC):[2]

- If it appears (*phainetai*) to a subject *S* as if *p*, then, in the absence of evidence to the contrary, *S* has grounds for accepting *p*.

That is, if it appears to *S* that *p*, then S has *evidence* for S that *p* is true – at least in the absence of countervailing evidence. The Principle of Phainomenological Conservatism is thus at once positive, in holding that *phainomena* look beyond themselves to *onta*, and negative, in being self-limiting: *phainomena* qualify as evidentiary but are not thereby guarantors of the truth. One may discern the principle at work in its positive guise in Aristotle's discussion of the Principle of Non-contradiction. Its self-limiting components emerge both clearly and instructively in Aristotle's combative attitudes towards sophistic treatments of matters impinging on metaphysical themes. As he candidly acknowledges, "sophistic and dialectic turn on the same class of things as philosophy." Yet, he insists, philosophy "differs from dialectic in the nature of the faculty required and from sophistic in respect of the purpose of the philosophical life" (*Met.* 1004a20). Philosophy differs from sophistic in part, it emerges, because sophistic relies upon an unreservedly and unsustainably enthusiastic reliance on *phainomena*: sophists suppose that *phainomena* secure something that they in fact, taken alone and unchecked, cannot: the truth.

The Principle of Phainomenological Conservatism, if correct, thus provides powerful reason to pay attention to the *phainomena*: generally speaking, without providing guarantees of any kind, *phainomena* track the truth. More to the point, whether or not it proves ultimately defensible,[3] if it is endorsed by Aristotle, then (PPC) provides a very good, even compelling, reason *for Aristotle* to recommend that we begin our philosophical chores by laying out the *phainomena*; it at the same time provides good grounds supposing that our philosophical chores do not end when we have managed to iron out such inconsistencies as the *phainomena* may present. We begin with the *phainomena* because we start with what is more intelligible *to us* (*gnôrimôteron hêmin*); but we end with what is more intelligible *by nature* (*gnôrimôteron phusei*; *APo.* 72a1–3), where what is more intelligible by nature may take us well beyond how things appear at the outset – and even, in some cases, beyond how they appear in the final analysis. In this process, we show ourselves guided by *phainomena* but hardly bound to them. There is, as (PPC) makes clear, no reason to presume that any truth that we can know is already somehow encoded in the *phainomena* with which we begin a given investigation. We should *not* think, then, that: "In fact, his method of first reviewing the *phainomena* is based on the assumption that some truth is hidden in them, whether they be sensory appearances or common opinions."[4] Rather, *phainomena* serve as evidence – and like other forms of evidence they may inform, commend or compel, but also, despite all that, may also mislead or misdirect. Still, Aristotle repeatedly and reasonably relies upon PPC: unless overridden, a *phainomenon* to the effect *that p* gives us grounds to judge *that p*.

Or so runs the argument of the present paper. After a preliminary set of linguistic observations intended to sort some features of the verb *phainesthai* (to appear), we reconsider the *locus classicus* for Aristotle's phainomenological method, *Nicomachean Ethics* vii 1, in order to show the limitations of this passage but then also, more importantly, to underscore the need for a broader investigation of Aristotle's involvement with *phainomena*. This involvement reveals his reliance on the Principle of Phainomenological Conservatism (PPC), which has a special role to play in his *Metaphysics*. The first phase of his reliance is positive: We find Aristotle appealing to *phainomena* in core passages in his

*Metaphysics*, including, instructively, non-sensory *phainomena*, such as those which count as evidence for such fundamental principles as the Principle of Non-contradiction. The second phase, by contrast, is restrictive: We find Aristotle sharply criticizing those who would suppose that the *phainomena are* the *onta*, that the way things appear simply are the ways things are. This second phase implies that Aristotle regards the first philosopher as invested in the *phainomena* but not beholden to them. This is, in fact, one crucial difference, perhaps *the* crucial difference, between the first philosopher and the sophist.

## 2   Appearing to be so and being so

The bare linguistic data regarding the word *phainomenon* are well-known to readers of Aristotle's Attic Greek, but bear recapitulating briefly. As a neuter present plural participle of the verb *phainesthai*, to appear, the word *phainomena* (sing. *phainomenon*) means just what the English phrases "things that appear" or "appearing things" or, more simply "appearances" mean. Like its English counterparts, *phainomenon* may mean many different things, depending upon its context of use, whether syntactic, circumstantial, pragmatic, or implicative. As a general syntactic rule of Aristotle's Greek, when used finitely with an accompanying participle, the verb *phainesthai* endorses what is being presented. (Compare the English: "Being brighter than all in the boys in her class, she appears to have had an easy time convincing them to see things her way.") When used with an accompanying infinitive, it is neutral as regards the question of endorsement. (Compare the English: "He appears to be unstoppable in the ring..." Here the speaker might or might not be endorsing the appearance, and so might comfortably complete the sentence with either: "...and that is why he is sure to win a gold medal." or "...but I predict that things will look very different when he finally goes up against a truly worthy opponent.")

Beyond that, there are different ways of organizing the meanings of *phainesthai*, whether or not it is used as a participle, just as there are different ways of organizing the meanings of "to appear" and "appearing" or "appearances".[5] For our purposes, the following non-exhaustive framework will prove most serviceable. First, as a general point about range, we may distinguish between perceptual and intellectual appearances:

- Perceptual: "If the strip appears red, then the solution is acidic." (Examples in Aristotle: *DC* 290a8–24; *Gen. et Corr.* 328a10–11; *DA* 428b24–25; *Parv. Nat.* 446a7–20, 448b123–15)

- Intellectual: "It appears that the four-color theorem can only be proven with the aid of a computer." (Examples in Aristotle: *DC* 270b4–15, 287b18, 303a20–24; *Parv. Nat.* 462b12–22; *Met.* 1009a8, 1004b19, b26, 1011b19)

Cutting across this first distinction, we may then distinguish a committal from a non-committal use:

- Committal: "Can you believe it? He appeared at the graveside wearing a loud pink Bowler. At a funeral!"
- Non-committal: "There appeared to be a woman in the passenger's seat, but it is difficult to be sure, because the car was moving very quickly."

Thereafter, again whether perceptual or intellectual, the commitment involved in the committal version, as already implied in the examples, may be positive or negative, in the sense of endorsing an appearance as accurate or as decrying it as inaccurate. These senses are all reasonably familiar, and, though some cases may be disputed, they all have reasonably clear instances in Aristotle.

The verb *phainesthai* (to appear) along with its participial form *phainomena* (what appears, or appearances) is thus remarkably elastic.[6] For examples outside of Aristotle, but of the same period, we may consider Plato. When asked whether courage is a virtue in the *Protagoras*, Protagoras can assent simply by saying, *phaineteai moi* (*Prot.* 332e, 333c): "It appears so", meaning, simply, "Yes." Elsewhere in Plato, in the *Republic*, Socrates can positively contrast the appearances (*ta phainomena*) with the things which "truly are the case" (*ta onta tê(i) aletheia(i)*) (*Rep.* 596e; cf. *Top.*100b24, *EN* 1113a24), where the clear import is that the appearances are not to be accepted as veridical. The first of the speakers is using the verb in positive non-perceptual sense; in the *Republic*, Socrates is using it in a negative non-perceptual sense.

In general, then, *phainomena* can be manifest to the senses or evident to reason; they can be endorsed, rejected, or merely reported. They can occur in sense perception, in memories, in dreams, in bouts of imagination, or in rarefied intellection. Sometimes we have grounds to accept them, and other times we have grounds to suspect or reject them outright; we can also entertain them non-assertorically, such that the question of endorsing or rejecting simply does not arise. Sometimes, arguably, the seeming-being distinction simply collapses, as in the case of sense data,[7] if there are any.[8]

Given that the Greek verb *phainesthai*, including in its participial form, has an array of syntactically- and contextually-sensitive meanings at least as broad as the English verb *to appear*, no appeal to *phainomena* is ever fully innocent. On the contrary, just as Owen contended, the word cannot be pinned down to a single, consistent meaning across all its applications. Still, as he also observes, "If there is more than one use for the expression *phainomena*, the uses have a great deal in common."⁹ One difficult question concerns just what this common core might be; Owen himself does not say.

## 3  The methodological remarks of *Nicomachean Ethics* vii 1

Owen motivated his observation regarding the multivocity of *phainomenon* in Aristotle by means of a criticism of Ross, who had offered a rendering of the word he found to be objectionable. The context of Ross's translation is precisely the methodological remark of *Nicomachean Ethics* vii 1 with which Aristotle prefaces his discussion of *akrasia*. In this passage, Aristotle seems to set out a three-stage process to effective philosophizing, according to which: (i) we begin by laying out the *phainomena* pursuant to a given subject of inquiry; (ii) we work through the difficulties and puzzles to which these *phainomena* give rise; and thereafter (iii) we rest with those *phainomena* which remain standing after our reflection. Thus, *phainomena* are present at every stage, remaining evidently even in the third and final stage. The passage in full runs, in Owen's rendering:

> Here as in other cases we must set down (*tithentas*) the *phainomena* [Ross: "observed facts"] and begin by considering the difficulties (*diaporgsantas*), and so go on to vindicate if possible all the common conceptions (*ta endoxa*) about these states of mind (*peri tauta ta pathê*) or at any rate most of them and the most important; for when both the difficulties are solved and the *endoxa* are left (*kataleiptai*), it would have been proven sufficiently (*dedeigmenon hikanôs*)' (*EN* 1145b2–7).¹⁰

In sum, when pursuing a topic of interest, we must first collect the *phainomena* and then sort through the problems pursuant to them. "And then?" asks Barnes. "And then,' he answers, "nothing: your philosophical task is over."¹¹

Indeed, from a certain perspective, Aristotle's advice might seem utterly unavoidable. One might naturally suppose that we are precluded from moving directly to things as they are, as opposed to how they appear, because such epistemic access as we may have to the *onta* of our world are perforce mediated by *phainomena*, conceived either as *onta*-as-they-appear-to-us or as the appearances encoded in our own subjective states, which thus stand between us and the *onta* we aim to know. From this perspective, we have no choice but to begin with appearances, because we must begin where we are, and wherever we are we are first and forever confronted with the *phainomena*; only thereafter, the assiduous work having been done, are we in a position to characterize the *onta* directly.

Indeed, and more stridently, according to some who adopt this perspective, no amount of hard work will suffice to allow us to grasp and characterize the *onta* directly: We must eventually end no less than begin with appearances, because we are *never* in a position to move beyond them, to know the *onta* immediately, without the intermediary of buffering appearances. Because we can never move beyond them, we are constrained to live within their circle: the *onta*, as they are in themselves, are permanently beyond our epistemic grasp. Aristotle's appearances, contends Nussbuam in this vein, "go all the way down."[12] This is why she regards Aristotle as an "internal realist" on the model of Putnam,[13] as holding roughly, that is, as Putman himself describes his view, that "truth ... is some sort of (idealized) acceptability – some sort of ideal coherence of our beliefs with each other and with our experience *as those experiences are themselves represented in our belief system* – and not correspondence with mind-independent or discourse – independent 'states of affairs'."[14] As applied to Aristotle, this would imply first that he does not hold to a correspondence account of truth, and then also that for him, truth simply consists in an idealized coherence of *phainomena*, with each other and with beliefs (*doxai*); the crucial thought would then be that we never move beyond *phainomena*, or, in general, beyond our representations of the world to an understanding of the world itself.

While neither Nussbaum nor anyone else has derived so sweeping a conclusion solely on the basis of *Nicomachean Ethics* vii 1, there has been a tendency among scholars, including Nussbaum,[15] to use this passage as a sort of springboard to a broader characterization of Aristotle's overarching method. Yet, lest we generalize too quickly on the basis of these isolated methodological remarks, we should allow that we have no grounds for presuming, at least not without strenuous argument, that Aristotle himself adopts this point of view across the broad sweep of his work: in dialectic; in practical science (*praktikê epistêmê*) including but extending beyond ethics; in the three branches of theoretical science (*theoretikê epistêmê*), namely, physics, mathematics, and first philosophy (*Top.* 145a15–16; *Met.* 1025b25, 1026a18–19, 1064a16–19, b1–3; *EN* 1139a26–28, 1141b29–32); or, for that matter, in the *Organon*, where Aristotle develops his theories of terms, propositions, and logic, including modal logic, as well as his general theory of scientific explanation. In most of these areas, Aristotle gives no indication that he supposes that the interface of mind and world is such that the *phainomena* with which we begin and end forever epistemically buffer the *onta* we seek to know.

On the contrary, it is noteworthy in this regard that when Aristotle, in two separate passages (*APo.* ii 19 99b15–34, *Met.* 981a21-b11; cf. *Phys.* 189a16; *DC* 306a6–17; *EN* 1145b2–28; *Met.* 1073b36), charts our course from ignorance to knowledge, he makes no mention of our interacting with the *phainomena*. In one of them, the last chapter of the *Posterior Analytics*, he contends that we begin in ignorance, perceive the world (*aisthansthai*), develop memories, gain experience (*empeiria*), acquire concepts, and eventually grasp first principles of various sorts by means of a kind of intellectual apprehension (*nous*). This general genetic story, whatever its merits or demerits,[16] omits altogether any mention of *phainomena*; it is rather a story of incremental information acquisition, inductive expansion, and eventual understanding. This process can – and evidently does in Aristotle's view – proceed without first coming to terms with something called the *phainomena*.

What, then, are these *phainomena* in *Nicomachean Ethics* vii 1? Here it is salutary to return to Owen's original criticisms of Ross. In making his case, Owen objected to Ross's rendering of *phainomena* as "observed facts" in the context of Aristotle's characterization of Socrates' approach to *akrasia*, that is, in the passage in which he dispenses his methodological advice. There, Aristotle contends that Socrates' denial of *akrasia* somehow contravenes the *phainomena* (*EN* 1145b2–5). But how precisely? Owen is surely correct to counter that Ross decides too much for the reader with his translation: Given the range of meanings of *phainomena* canvassed in the last section, one might hope for something more neutral than "observed facts".

Still, Owen is on far shakier grounds when mounting his case against Ross.[17] Owen notes that Aristotle insists that Socrates "plainly contradicts" (*amphisbêtein*; Owen's translation) the *phainomena* (*EN* 1145b23–28). Yet, a few pages later, this same Aristotle makes a rapprochement to Socrates, even to the point of endorsing his view (*EN* 1147b13–17).

If that is so, concludes Owen, *phainomena* cannot be "observed facts" but must be rather "what would be commonly said on the subject."[18] That is, as Owen understands the situation, Aristotle cannot hold that Socrates plainly contradicts the "observed facts" if he then also thinks that Socrates is, after all, correct about *akrasia*. Even so, suggests Owen, Aristotle is at liberty to suppose that Socrates can – and did – contradict what was *commonly said* about *akrasia*; that is why people found his view surprising or even paradoxical. Here, then, concludes Owen, the *phainomena* must be, more or less, the *legomena*, the "things said" and not "the observed facts" or even the things which appear to be the case – if, at any rate, "appearance" is here used with any kind of committal force.

Owen's argument is, however, much too quick. First, of course, is the complex question of just how close Aristotle's own view comes to Socrates' denial of *akrasia*; it seems, in fact, a good deal removed.[19] Waiving that worry, Aristotle might endorse the Socratic position on *akrasia*, even though he supposes that his approach contradicts more than what is commonly said about the topic. In Aristotle's view, Socrates' argument or account (*logos*; *EN* 1145b25) contradicts what appears to be the case about weakness of will, namely that we are most of us guilty of it at least on occasion. Socrates offers an account (a *logos*) according to which *akrasia* is meant to be impossible, but that account is not one that Aristotle can accept – even if the view he himself develops has partial overlap with Socrates' point of view in terms of the role of knowledge in structuring and directing behavior. Aristotle may suppose, for instance, that given the way things appear – indeed, given even the "observed facts" – Socrates' view overreaches insofar as it overspecifies the extent to which a revisionary moral psychology may contravene the *phainomena*. This, indeed, seems to be the point of Aristotle's saying that "Socrates campaigned against the account *in general*"; *Sôkratês men gar holôs emacheto ton logon*).

It might be, then, that Socrates' basic view is in Aristotle's mind rightly oriented but also importantly problematic, with the result that he supposes that it needs to be modified accordingly. This would be one way the *phainomena* might offer guidance: They provide evidence, but like other forms of evidence, they must be weighed and balanced against all other available forms of evidence.[20] In Aristotle's view, Socrates might be guilty of ignoring some positive evidence regarding *akrasia*; it does not follow that he, again in Aristotle's judgment, was wrong to restrict the force of the *phainomena* in view of countervailing considerations.

These remarks are not intended to exonerate Ross or condemn Owen. Rather, they are meant to illustrate how swiftly determinations about *phainomena* can become disputed when taken up in isolated, bracketed passages or contexts. When we consider such passages without an antecedent understanding of why we should bother with the *phainomena* in the first place, it proves difficult to determine just what sort of use Aristotle envisages for them. This holds true even of the methodological passage of *Nicomachean Ethics* vii 1. Again, if we wish to come to terms with Aristotle's attitude towards *phainomena* in this as in other passages, it is necessary to pose the question we have already posed: Why should we care about *phainomena* in this first instance?

The proposed answer, to repeat, is that we should look to the *phainomena* simply because they are evidentiary and for no other reason: *phainomena* are data which, other things being equal, provide grounds to accept various truths as truths, simply because things appear, however defeasibly, to be a certain way. When they are *endoxa*, as seems to be the case in the methodological passage of *Nicomachen Ethics* vii i, then the *phainomena* provide testimonial evidence: its being said *that p* by a suitable authority itself counts as evidence *that p*. We should not, though, overinflate the evidential value of *phainomena*, whether or not they are *endoxa*; they may be overturned by other forms of evidence, including even evidence provided by other *phainomena*. Once we appreciate that Aristotle's phainomenogical method proceeds along the lines of the *Principle of Phainomenological Conservatism* these more fine-grained worries about translation become manageable. In fact, they simply recede.

## 4   PPC in Aristotle's *Metaphysics*

One can see (PPC) at work in various of Aristotle's works, but nowhere more clearly than in his *Metaphysics*. For this reason, it is worth considering how the principle functions in Aristotle's *Metaphysics*, as a sort of special case, even though it is perfectly general across his philosophy. This sort of focused consideration also has the advantage of orienting the discussion of Aristotle's phainomenological method away from the undoubtedly important, but also permanently disputed methodological remarks of the *Nicomachean Ethics* vii 1.[21]

In a positive vein, we find Aristotle appealing to *phainomena* even in his defense of the Principle of Non-Contradiction (PNC) in *Metaphysics* iv 4. This principle he characterizes in this way: "For the same thing to hold and not to hold simultaneously of the same thing in the same respect is impossible" (*to gar hama uparchein te kai mê huparcheina adunaton tô(i) auto(i) kai ta auto*; *Met.* 1005b19–21). In the current context, Aristotle's discussion of this principle is instructive because in it he engages the question of how far the *phainomena* may be relied upon in metaphysical contexts, including those that are far removed from empirical inquiry (*empeiria*, and, in some contexts, *historia*; *Hist. An.* 491a13, *APr.* 46a29, *Part. An.* 646a9, *Gen. An.* 719a9–11, 741a14–16, 751a8–11). Although he never indicates that what seems to be the case must be the case, or that what is the case simply is what appears to be so (that *phainnomena* "go all the way down"), Aristotle makes clear that even if something's seeming to be φ is not at all the same as its being φ, still, something's seeming to be φ is, generally, a good reason for believing that it *is* φ. Indeed, in some contexts far removed from sense perception, appeals to *phainomena* are not only possible but positively inescapable.

Aristotle characterizes the PNC as unhypothetical (*anupothetos*) and as both the most secure (*bebaiotatê*) and most intelligible (*gnorimôtatê*) principle (*archê*) of all (*Met.* 1005b11–13).[22] He offers a kind of elenchtic argument for it, whose form and final force have been subject to debate.[23] For our purposes, it suffices to note that it is clear in outline that Aristotle contends that no direct proof for the PNC is forthcoming, since any such proof would inevitably feature the PNC itself as one of its premises. Still, as he argues, one may offer an indirect defense of this principle by entreating those claiming to deny it to signify (*semainein*) something, as they must do if they are saying something definite (*legein ti*), for instance *that the PNC is false*. One might be disposed to utter such a sentence for any number of reasons: because of the existence of paradoxes, [24] because one believes oneself in possession of counterexamples to the PNC, or simply because one is disposed to indulge in eristic for sport.

Aristotle considers the last two sorts of figures who oppose the PNC, noting that at least some of them are innocently confused. To such people, Aristotle offers one kind of response, but those who are obstinate for the sake of eristic must be forced (*Met.* 1005b25–34, 1009a15–30, and esp. 1011b3–6). He considers two sorts of such spirited opponents, and in so doing, appeals to *phainomena* in two distinct but complementary ways.

After laying out the core of his elenchtic defense, Aristotle advances a series of supererogatory objections against the PNC-deniers, to the effect that they: (i) abolish both substance (*ousia*) and essence (*to ti ên einai*) (*Met.* 1007a21–21); (ii) that they are committed to the view that all things are one (*Met.* 1007b18–20); (iii) that they also consequently deny the principle of the excluded middle (*Met.* 1008a3–7); (iv) that they are subject to self-refutation, if their denial is unrestricted (*Met.* 1008a7–34); (v) that they cannot fathom what truth and falsity are (*Met.* 1038a34-b2); (vi) that they are effectively plants, that is, that they have vegetative rather than rational souls (*Met.* 1008b2–12); (vii) that their actions, which observe the PNC, belie their protestations (*Met.* 1008b12–31); (viii) and finally that they forego the ability even to approximate truth, because this, too, presupposes the PNC (*Met.* 1008b31–1009a5).

The second of these objections contains an intriguing appeal to the way things seem. Aristotle argues:

> Further, if all contradictions are true of the same thing at the same time, then it is clear that all things will be one (*hapanta estai hen*). For the same thing will be a trireme, a wall, and a man, if it is possible to affirm and deny something of everything – as is necessary for those stating the argument of Protagoras. For if a man seems to someone not to be a trireme (*ei gar tô(i) dokei mê einai triêrês*), then it is clear that he is not a trireme (*dêlon ôs ouk esti triêrês*); but then, if indeed the contradictory is true (*eiper hê antiphasis alêthês*), he is also a trireme. The result will be that, as Anaxagoras said, all things are together, so that nothing is truly one (*Met.* 1007b18–26).

Although he does not use the verb *to appear* (*phainesthai*) in this passage, using instead the verb to *seem* (*dokein*), Aristotle is evidently making a point relying on a point about *phainomena*. He argues that if a man appears not to be a trireme, then plainly he is not; but then, if the contradictory predicate holds of him as well, it equally follows that he is not a trireme. So, too, for all other predicates, with the result, he urges, that "all will be one", that is, that there will be no plurality.

In this compressed contention, Aristotle is *not* arguing if one thing appears $\varphi$ and not-$\varphi$, it will *be* $\varphi$ and not-$\varphi$, but rather (i) that if one thing, a man, seems not to be a trireme, then it is clear that he is in fact not a trireme. (A different sort of anti-Protagorean argument, discussed briefly below, emerges first at *Met.* 1009a33-b4.) From this, it follows, *on the assumption* (ii) that all contrary properties obtain, that man will also be a trireme. The first premise (i) has an interesting double resonance. According to the argument of Protagoras, if $x$ seems to be not-$\varphi$ to S, then $x$ will be not-$\varphi$; so Protagoras is evidently committed to accepting (i), or at least a close relative of (i). In addition, however, Aristotle seems also to be asserting this premise himself, in *propria persona*, using his characteristic diction: if a man, as one would expect, seems not be a trireme, then "it is clear that he is not a trireme" (*dêlon ôs ouk esti triêrês*). In this case, something's seeming to be so provides powerfully good evidence, even psychologically overwhelming evidence, that it is so. Compare: "For if a man seems to someone not to be a Finn (because he is speaking Swedish), then it is clear to him that he is not a Finn."

This seems a much less stable inference, since the man might well be a Swedish-speaking Finn. Presumably, Aristotle selects this extreme sort of example at least in part because his opponents have, in this sort of case, especially good reason to contend that seeming is a good guide to being.

If that is so, then Aristotle is implicitly relying on what one might call *patent phainomena*, the sort of *phainomena* which provide overpowering, if defeasible evidence of the truth of what they present. Fantastical (though perfectly possible) stories aside, whenever it seems to someone that a man is not a trireme, then he also has extremely good evidence that he in fact is not a trireme. In the present context, the strength of the evidence plays a role in Aristotle's argument. For only having secured the conclusion that the man who seems not to be a trireme is in fact not a trireme can one move forward to say, as Aristotle does say, that if *indeed* the contradictory is also true (*eiper hê antiphasis alêthês*), then one must also conclude that he is equally at the same time also a trireme. This seems, then, a good example of Aristotle endorsing (PPC), the Principle of Phainomenological Conservatism. Its appearing to a subject *S* that x is not-φ, in this case that a man is not a trireme, already counts as evidence for *S* of x's not being φ, that the man is not a trireme. The argument equally relies upon the thought that if a man seems not to be a wall to *S*, then that, too, counts as good evidence for *S* that the man is not a wall. Again, on the assumption that contradictory predicates apply, then the same thing will be a wall and trireme and a man. Thus "will all things be one" (*hapanta estai hen*). The conclusion is *not*, then, that perception will be jumbled or that the Protagorean will be implicated in self-contradiction but is rather the metaphysically outlandish sounding contention (one, though, advanced in antiquity and beyond) that there is no plurality, that there is exactly one thing.

To the degree that that striking conclusion seems utterly unacceptable, then (PPC) makes yet another appearance in Aristotle's metaphysical method: that it appears that there is more than one thing equally counts as evidence for there being more than one thing. This is why the conclusion of the anti-Protagorean argument of *Metaphysics* iv 5 has, or is intended to have, the sort of force Aristotle invests in it.

The tight connection between seeming (*dokein*) and appearing (*phainesthai*) assumed in these remarks becomes explicit in Aristotle's next treatment of Protagoras, where he uses the verbs interchangeably, including in their participial forms. He argues that Protagoras is implicated in a denial of the PNC, because the bare fact of disagreement commits him to the view that *phainomena* are both true and false:

> If all seemings and appearances (*ta dokounta...kai ta phainomena*) are true, then everything must at the same time be true and false. For many people suppose things contrary to other people and think those who do not believe what they believe have false beliefs. Consequently, the same things must both be and not be. And if this is so, then all seemings (*ta dokounta*) will be true. (*Met.* 1009a6–13)

Since S thinks that *p* and sees that S' believes that *not-p*, if p's appearing true to S guarantees the truth of *p*, even while S' has a guarantor of its being not-true, then S will have reason to conclude one thing and then also its opposite. So, the same things will both be and not be φ. The proposition *p*, for instance, will be both true and not true.

There are, of course, various relativizing responses open to the Protagorean. Here, too, our goal is not to adjudicate disputes about the force of the argument, but rather to attend to its use of *phainomena*. First, it is to be observed, as already indicated, that seeming (*dokein*) and appearing (*phainesthai*) are used interchangeably in the course of the argument. Second, and more importantly, Aristotle is driving home the point that appearing and being do not collapse; indeed, neither appearing nor seeming is sufficient for something's being the case. If either were, then violations of the PNC would abound, a result he plainly regards as wholly unacceptable. This, then, reflects the restrictive aspect of his Principle of Phainomenol99cal Conservatism (PPC). Although something's appearing to be so provides good evidence of its being so, the evidence of appearance is no guarantor. The evidentiary force of *phainomena* is defeasible.

## 5   PPC and the abuse of *phainomena*

For this reason, Aristotle's discussion of Protagoreanism proves to be especially important – and in a way rather delicate for him – if he subscribes to PPC. If he thinks that *phainomena* are evidentiary, and if he implicitly allows that certain *phainomena* are compellingly evidentiary because of their being patent, then he himself must explain why *phainomena* are not guarantors of the truth. His discussion of Protagoras provides such an explanation. It shows that however evidentiary they may be, unfettered reliance of *phainomena* yields unacceptable results, including straightforward violations of the principle of non-contradiction. His discussion of various sophistic techniques provides a second, and distinct, sort of caution: If we are not prepared to balance *phainomena* against other *phainomena* and *doxa* (beliefs), and to appreciate that we cannot rely on individual *phainomena* atomistically, we cannot even distinguish first philosophy from sophistic.

This is a point Aristotle makes clear in his discussion of a sophistic paradox about Socrates and Socrates-seated:

> It falls to the philosopher to be able to investigate all things. For if this does not fall to the philosopher, then who will inquire into whether Socrates and Socrates-seated are the same things, or whether one thing has one contrary, or what contrariety is or how many meanings it has? And similarly with all other such questions. Since, then, these sorts of properties belong *per se* to unity *qua* unity and to being *qua* being – not to things *qua* numbers or lines or fire – it is clear that it falls to this science to investigate both what these things are [viz. unity and being] as well as what coincides with them. And those who study these matters at present go awry not by pursuing philosophical questions, but by failing to understand anything about substance, which is prior to other things.... An indication that this is so: dialecticians and sophists assume the same guise as the philosopher, for sophistry has only the appearance (*phainomenê monon*) of wisdom, and dialecticians do engage in dialectic about all things. Now, being is common to all things, and it is clear that they practice dialectic about all things precisely because of its being proper for philosophy to do so. For sophistic and dialectic focus on the same genus of things as philosophy, but philosophy differs from dialectic in the kind of power it has and from sophistic in its choice of life. Dialectic merely probes in areas where philosophy is knowledgeable, while sophistic gives off the appearance of being knowledgeable without in fact being so (*sophistikê phainomenê, ousa d'ou*). (*Met.* 1004a34-b26)

Philosophy and sophistic focus on the same genus of things; but only philosophy qualifies as a kind of wisdom. Sophistic merely gives off the appearance of being so.

Crucially, there is a sense in which the Sophists no less than Aristotle can claim to set out the appearances, and indeed can even be thought to engage in the second and third phases of the three-phase process recommended in the methodological passage of *Nicomachean Ethics* vii i. They "collect the *phaionomena*" and then also sort through them. Thereafter, they rest with those which remain standing. Consider the following, plainly sophistic argument: (i) Socrates and Socrates-seated appear to be one and the same; (ii) it appears that when two things are one and the same, what is true of the one is also true of the other; (iii) when Socrates-seated rises, Socrates-seated ceases to be; so, (iv) when Socrates-seated rises, Socrates ceases to be. The first premise seems correct: It *appears* that Socrates and Socrates-seated are one and the same. This is, even in Aristotle's terms, a *phainomenon*. The third premise is equally a *phainomenon*: It most definitely appears that Socrates-seated ceases to be when Socrates-seated rises. The second premise might reasonably be thought to be a simple appeal to a version of the Indiscernibility of Identicals, a principle Aristotle himself uses countless times. The result of its application to (i) and (iii), however, yields in (iv) something massively at variance with another *phainomenon*, namely that Socrates, who walks away when he rises, survives his standing.

If the sophistic argument seems vapid or patently fallacious, in the sense of resting on a simple equivocation, then it should be borne in mind that it comes close to being an ancient version of the so-called problem of *temporary intrinsics*, which many contemporary metaphysicians accept as sound.[25] One might accept (i) and (iii) and then feel compelled on the basis of (ii) to accept (iv). This is not, however, Aristotle's reaction. Instead, he accuses the sophists of failing to appreciate some highly technical claims rooted in his own category theory. They "go awry not by pursuing philosophical questions, but by failing to understand anything about substance (*ousia*), which is prior to other things...". One may debate how Aristotle understands this categorial insight to counter the sophistic argument,[26] as indeed one may dispute the success of his appeal in this regard. In the present context what matters, however, is the bare fact of the appeal. If we fail to temper appeals to *phainomena* by principles articulated only by first philosophy, then our appeals to them, however initially justified and appropriate, will prove abusive of the phainomenological method, and will lead us into falsehood. Crucially, then, Aristotle does not embrace the irenic attitude recommended by the second and third phases of the methodological remarks of *Nicomchaen Ethics* vii 1. He does not, that is, merely reconcile the *phainomena* and rest content. In metaphysics, as in other areas of philosophy, one assembles *phainomena* and sorts them. "And then?" "And then," shall we say, "nothing"? "Nothing, because our philosophical task is over."[27] In this passage Aristotle answers clearly, and to the contrary, "And then: category theory."

In the *Metaphysics*, we do not find Aristotle engaging in the three-stage process of collecting, reconciling, and ceasing. The appearances in metaphysics, as in other areas of philosophy, are real, and are evidentiary.

*Phainomena* must, however, be tempered by further philosophical considerations, including, as Aristotle makes clear in checking sophistic, category theory, which provides a framework for thinking about unity and being. Crucially, however, given the highly abstract character of the enterprise the *phainomena* tend not to be patent, or at least not innocently patent. It does appear that Socrates and Socrates-seated are one and the same; what is not so apparent is precisely *how* they are one and the same – and the sophists, when they trespass on the terrain of the first philosopher, need to rely upon a very specific sense of oneness to motivate their surprising conclusion. As against the too-swift seduction of sophistic, Aristotle counters that questions of oneness and unity in this domain concern the "sorts of properties [that] belong *per se* to unity *qua* unity and to being *qua* being." Consequently, *phainomena* in this domain prove delicate and must be handled in the demanding manner of the first philosopher.

## 6   Conclusions

Aristotle takes *phainomena* seriously. Indeed, in some passages, he seems to take them *too* seriously. That is why when we focus on the celebrated methodological passage of *Nicomachean Ethics* vii 1 without reflecting on Aristotle's practice of appealing to *phainomena* elsewhere, we are apt to overestimate the degree to which he regards himself as beholden to them. What is wanted, beyond reflection on his overtly methodological remarks, is an answer to a prior question, a question not so much as broached in the *Nicomachean Ethics* vii 1. This is the question, namely, of why we should dally with the *phainomena* at all, when our actual targets are the *onta*, the beings whose essences all human beings by nature desire to know. The answer is provided by PPC, the Principle of Phainomenological Conservativism: Something's seeming so is a good reason for believing that it is so.

A good reason for believing that something is so is not, however, also already a decisive reason for forming the judgment that it is, in fact, so. Instead, as the phainomenological method at work in Aristotle's *Metaphysics* attests, we often have good reason to forbear forming the relevant judgment: "We say that not every appearance (*phainomenon*) is true" (*Met.* 1110b1–2). The evidentiary value of *phainomena* is considerable, but like other credible witnesses, *phainomena* may sometimes fail to convince. Even so, Aristotle appreciates and exploits the tightly woven evidentiary connections between *phainomena* and theory. This is why he says, when speaking in an abstract context of the ingenerability of the primary body of the cosmos, "It seems our theory bears witness to the *phainomena* and the *phainomena* to our theory (*logos*)" (*Eoike d' ho te logos tois phainomenois marturein kai ta pahinomena tô(i) logô(i); De Caelo* 270b4–5). The witnessing of *phainomena* to *logos* enjoins phainomenological conservatism; the witnessing of *logos* to *phainomena* commends another, altogether more complex and delicate disposition to be essayed elsewhere.

## Notes

1. Some of these interpretations are discussed below in §III.
2. The name, but not the idea, of this principle derives from Huemer (2001), who offers a crisp formulation and defense of a related principle which he calls the Principle of Phenomenological Conservatism. Earlier, I had termed it simply "Aristotle's Phainomenalism," but that title proves misleading in its connotations. One further reason for aligning the names of these principles is that this will help show how controversial Aristotle's commitment to (PPC) is. That is, it may seem somehow trivial to commit Aristotle to the thesis that one should pay attention to the *phainomena* because that is the way things seem. In fact, though, (PPC) says much more, including that x's appearing to be φ is *itself* grounds for believing that x *is* φ. Those interested in the controversial character of Aristotle's principle, a matter left largely untouched in the current discussion, will benefit from discussions of Huemer's discussion of his related principle, even though Aristotle's principle plainly diverges in both content and context from Huemer's. See n. 3 for references.
3. For criticisms of a present principle of phenomenological convervativism, see BonJour (2004) and Littlejohn (2011). For a development and defense, see Huemer (2001) and (2007). As indicated in n. 2, the controversy surrounding Huemer's phenomenological conservatism helps underscore, first, the substantive character of Aristotle's acceptance of (PPC), but then also, independently, the epistemic role such a principle might reasonably be expected to play in a broadly realist metaphysics. See also §II for a discussion of Aristotle's realism in relation to the form of *internal realism* found in his writings by Nussbaum (1986).
4. Cleary (1994, 61–2).
5. Compare Barnes (1981, 491 n. 1), who divides the uses of *phainesthai* into: (i) a phenomenological ("he looks pink") *vs.* a judgmental sense ("he seems guilty"); and then also into (ii) a non-veridical ("he seems to be alive [but maybe he isn't]") *vs.* a veridical ("he is evidently guilty") sense. According to Barnes, the dominant sense at play in Aristotle's methodology is a sense at once judgmental and veridical (though, as illustrated, the sense of veridical in view is underdetermined).
6. The adjective and adverb formed off the verb, *phaneron* and *phanerôs*, seem always to be positive and committal, meaning, roughly, "evident" or "manifest", and "evidently" and "manifestly", though in at least one case also "'" or "frankly" or "openly"; as opposed to "surreptitiously" (*EN* 1145b15).

7. One need not, however, suppose that the distinction collapses only in the case of sense data. For another (putative) sort of instance, see Plato, *Theaet.* 166d1-e4.

8. In addition to the passages already cited, one finds Aristotle appealing or alluding to *phainomena* in all of these different ways, though, again, the force of some local instances might be disputed: *APo.* 81b23, 8a2–5; *DC* 297a2–6, 306a13–18; *Gen. et Corr.* 314b2–6, 325b15; *DA* 404a27–31, 427b2–3; *Part. Anim.* 642a18–21; *Metr.* 346a60–68; *Gen. An.* 742a17–19, 750a21–23, 760b6; *Met.* 986b27–23, 1009a6–1010a9, 1075b37; *Pol.* 1257b13, 1323a40; *Rhet.* 1402b23.

9. Owen (1961, 243) concludes that the word *phainomenon*, along, consequently, with various others words with which it tends to be paired, such as *epagôgê* (induction) and *aporia* (puzzle, or difficulty), is "ambiguous", primarily as between a linguistic and empirical sense. Evidently, then, according to Owen, the ambiguity is not the sort Aristotle recognizes as homonymy "by chance" (*apo tuchês; EN* 1096 b26). For doubts about the alleged related ambiguity of *epagôgê*, see Engberg-Pederson (1979, 301ff).

10. Owen does not complete this last clause in his (1961); I have added it. Compare Ross, including the last part of the passage (*OT, ad loc.*): "We must, as in all other cases, set the observed facts before us and, after first discussing the difficulties, go on to prove, if possible, the truth of all the common opinions about these affections of the mind, or, failing this, of the greater number and the most authoritative; for if we both refute the objections and leave the common opinions undisturbed, we shall have proved the case sufficiently."

11. Barnes (1995, 24).

12. Nussbaum (1986, 251).

13. Nussbaum (1986, 251).

14. Putnam (1981, 49–50; italics as found). Nussbuam locates Putnam-style internal realism to Aristotle in (1986, 257, 382). See Cooper (1988) and especially Davidson (1991) for discussions of the degree to which Aristotle, even as characterized by Nussbaum, can be seen to hold a version of internal realism recognizable in the writings of Putnam.

15. Nussbaum (1982, 267 n. 1) in fact misreports Aristotle as holding that the same method holds *epi tois allois*, rendered as "in all other cases" and says she is following Ross in so doing. Aristotle in fact says *epi tôn allôn*, which means only "in other cases" (cf. Demosthenes 8. 14), without any implication of universal coverage.

16. For a recent discussion which offers both a synoptic overview of the main interpretations of *APo.* ii 19 as well a fresh approach to its main contentions, see Bronstein (2012).

17. This point is made more fully and to good effect by Nieuwenburg (1999, 552–6). Although my own reasons for doubting Owen's contention are distinct from Nieuwenburg's, they are consistent with them and serve to augment his reservations.

18. Owen (1961, 144–55).

19. Kraut (2010) is rightly cautionary on this score: "Aristotle's agreement with Socrates is only partial, because he insists on the power of the emotions to rival, weaken or bypass reason."

20. Moreover, it is worth noting that Owen's own positive alternative certainly overcompensates. That is, Owen himself appears guilty of just the kind of

translational overreach of which he accuses Ross. Even if he is right that "observed facts" is too strong a rendering of *phainomenon*, Owen is not at all in a position to infer that the *phainomena* in question are the "things said"—the *legomena*. For Socrates might contradict a full range of *phainomena* without merely confuting the reports people offer about *akrasia*. It complicates matters slightly that Owen (1961, 114) unhelpfully suggests that the *legomena*, now regarded as *endoxa* "turn out as so often to be (a) partly matters of linguistic usage or, if you prefer, of (b) the conceptual structure revealed by language." (The identifying letters have been added by me.) Yet (a) and (b) are hardly a matter of indifference: (a) adverts to linguistic practice, (b) to the structure of concepts. Could Aristotle understand Socrates to contradict (b) even while—as Owen insists he does—endorsing Socrates' view?

21. Here, it is worth noting that in *no* other passage outside of *EN* 1145b3–5 does Aristotle speak of laying out the *phainomena*; indeed, he never even uses the exact linguistic formulation of Owen's famous title.
22. These characterizations are intensively discussed to good effect by Bailey (2006).
23. Wedin (2003) and (2004) offers a lucid overview of the logic of Aristotle's argument and its applications.
24. This is the approach advocated in Priest (2002).
25. For the locus classicus of the considerable discussion of this argument, see Lewis (1986, 202–5).
26. I consider this topic in some detail in Shields (forthcoming).
27. Barnes (1995, 24).

# Bibliography

Baily, Dominic. 2006. "Plato and Aristotle on the Unhypothetical," *Oxford Studies in Ancient Philosophy* 30: 101–26.

Barnes, Jonathan. 1981. "Aristotle and the Methods of Ethics," *Revue Internationale de Philosophie* 34: 490–511.

—— (ed.) 1995. *The Cambridge Companon to Aristotle* (Cambridge University Press).

BonJour, Laurence. 2004. "In Search of Direct Realism," *Philosophy and Phenomenological Research* 69: 349–67.

Bronstein, David. 2012. "The Origin and the Aim of *Posterior Analytics* II.19," *Phronesis* 57: 29–62.

Cleary, John J. 1994. "*Phainomena* in Aristotle's Methodology," *International Journal of Philosophical Studies* 2: 61–97.

Cooper, John M. 1988. "Review of Martha Nussbaum, *The Fragility of Goodness*," *Philosophical Review* 97: 543–564.

Davidson, Jack D. 1991. "Appearances, Antirealism, and Aristotle," *Philosophical Studies* 63 (2): 147–66.

Engberg-Pedersen. 1979. "More on Aristotelian *Epagoge*," *Phronesis* 24: 301–19.

Gigon, Olof. 1961. "Methodische Probleme in der *Metaphysik* des Aristoteles," in S. Mansion, (ed.) *Aristote et les problèmes de method* (Louvain: Publications Universitaires), pp. 131–45.

Hamlyn, D. W. 1990. "Aristotle on Dialectic," *Philosophy* 65: 465–76.

Huemer, Michael. 2001. *Skepticism and the Veil of Perception* (Lanham, MD: Rowman & Littlefield).

_____ 2007. "Compassionate Phenomenal Conservatism," *Philosophy and Phenomenological Research* 74: 30–55.

Irwin, Terence. 1988. *Aristotle's First Principles* (Oxford: Oxford University Press).

Kraut, Richard. 2010. "Aristotle's Ethics," *Stanford Encyclopedia of Philosophy.*

Lewis, David. 1986. *On the Plurality of Worlds* (Oxford: Blackwell Pubs.).

Littlejohn, Clayton. 2011. "Defeating Phenomenal Conservatism," *Analytic Philosophy* 52: 35–48.

Long, Christopher P. 2006. "Saving *Ta Legomena*: Aristotle and the History of Philosophy," *Review of Metaphysics* 60: 247–67.

Mansion, Suzanne (ed.) 1961. *Aristote et les problèmes de method* (Louvain: Publications Universitaires).

McLeod, Owen. 1995. "Aristotle's Method," *History of Philosophy Quarterly* 12: 1–18.

Nieuwenburg, Paul. 1999. "Aristotle and the Appearances," *Journal of the History of Philosophy* 37: 551–73.

Nussbaum, Martha. 1982. "Saving Aristotle's Appearances," in M. C. Nussbaum and M. Schofield, (eds), *Language and Logos* (Cambridge: Cambridge University Press) 267–93.

_____ 1986. *The Fragility of Goodness* (Cambridge: Cambridge University Press).

Owen, G. E. L. 1961. "τιθέναι τὰ φαινόμενα," in S. Mansion, (ed.) *Aristote et les problèmes de method* (Louvain: Publications Universitaires), pp. 83–103.

Priest, Graham. 2002. *Beyond the Limits of Thought* 2nd ed. (Cambridge: Cambridge University Press).

Pritzl, Kurt. 1994. "Opinions as Appearances: *Endoxa* in Aristotle," *Ancient Philosophy* 14: 41–50.

Putnam, Hilary. 1981. *Reason, Truth, and History* (Cambridge: Cambridge University Press)

Régis, L. M. 1935. *L'opnion selon Aristote* (Paris, J. Vrin).

Shields, Christopher. forthcoming. "First Philosophy First: Aristotle and the Practise of Metaphysics," in F. Sheffield and J. Warren, (eds), *The Routledge Companion to Ancient Philosophy* (Routledge).

de Vogel, C. J. 1961. "La method d'Aristote en metaphysique d'après Métaphysique A 1–2)," in S. Mansion, (ed.) *Aristote et les problèmes de method* (Louvain: Publications Universitaires), pp. 147–70.

Wedin, Michael V. 2003. "A Curious Turn in *Metaphysics* Gamma: Protagoras and Strong Denial of the Principle of Non-Contradiction," *Archiv für Geschichte der Philosophie* 85, 107–30.

_____ 2004. "On the Use and Abuse of Non-Contradiction: Aristotle's Critique of Protagoras and Heraclitus in *Metaphysics* Gamma 5," *Oxford Studies in Ancient Philosophy* 26: 213–39.

# 3

# The Aporetic Method and the Defense of Immodest Metaphysics

*Stephen Boulter*

## 1  Introduction

Do metaphysical questions have answers that are (i) truth-apt, (ii) non-trivial, (iii) tractable, but (iv) not provided by the sciences? For much of the last century, these questions received a resounding and (almost) unanimous "No" from the analytic community. But times have changed. The ongoing revival of interest in metaphysics within the analytic tradition itself is testament to the fact that many are now happy to answer each of these questions in the affirmative. But times have not changed that much. Most philosophers continue to eschew metaphysics, abandoning it to a small group of self-selecting enthusiasts who vigorously till the metaphysical garden in splendid isolation. The result is a curiously distorted picture of the state of metaphysics in the analytic tradition. Those who do engage in metaphysical reflection tend to be confident about its prospects, giving the impression that the analytic tradition has restored the queen of the sciences to rude good health; but a sociologist studying the philosophical community would soon discover that the circle of metaphysicians is small, isolated, and viewed with indifference or bemused puzzlement by their philosophical brethren.

That the circle of metaphysicians remains small is not surprising. Most philosophers go about their business with no overt engagement with, or apparent reliance upon, substantial metaphysical claims. And this is just as well, they say, because most remain to be convinced of the very possibility of metaphysics. As we shall see, there are many reasons for doubting the possibility of metaphysics. The most pressing grounds for concern on this score arise from the following Humean inspired dilemma: On the one hand, it is thought that if metaphysical questions can be answered at all, they are answered by the sciences or by conceptual analysis (or by some combination of the two) – and in neither case is there any substantial work for the metaphysician *qua* metaphysician.[1] But if metaphysical questions cannot be answered in either of these two ways, then the questions themselves are taken to be defective in some fashion, or perhaps merely verbal, in which case the only legitimate work to do in the area is to rid oneself of the desire to ask metaphysical questions.[2] Consequently, it is hardly surprising that most philosophers maintain that we can – and we must – do without metaphysics.

But what *is* surprising, given the revival of interest in metaphysics, is how little the current generation of metaphysicians has done to overturn this assessment of the necessity and viability of metaphysics. For if metaphysics is ever to be more than a minority interest – let alone restored to its central position within the discipline – this assessment surely cannot stand. So, drawing hope from "the first law to be inferred from philosophical experience", viz., that metaphysics always buries its undertakers[3], I present a case here for the necessity and possibility of what might be called *immodest* metaphysics.[4] The central theses are: (1) that metaphysics as traditionally conceived is indispensable to the philosophical enterprise; (2) that many non-trivial metaphysical claims can be justified without being "simply more science"; and finally (3) that accepted interpretations of mature scientific theory will occasionally have to be overturned on the basis of metaphysical reflection. All three theses are substantial, and all three will raise eyebrows. The first depends on a particular view of the philosophical enterprise to be sketched below. The second, pivotal, thesis requires updating and expanding upon Aristotle's aporetic method, wholly neglected in the recent "meta-metaphysical" literature. The third thesis emerges as a natural consequence of the first two. But before embarking on the defense of the three main theses of this chapter, it is best to begin with a brief account of the metaphysical project as traditionally conceived, and a catalogue of the standard challenges mooted in the literature regarding its viability.

## 2   The metaphysical project and its challenges

Metaphysics as traditionally conceived is the study of the most fundamental structure of reality. On this conception, a completed metaphysics would provide: (i) an ontology, i.e., a complete catalogue of the most general and irreducible kinds of entities included in the domain of our most unrestricted quantifiers; (ii) an account of the relations that obtain between entities of the various kinds; and (iii) an account of the "theatre" in which many entities have their being, namely, space and time. One further important point to note is that metaphysicians traditionally do not suppose this study to be straightforwardly empirical in nature, if only because it cannot be assumed without further argument that all that exists is in space and time – abstract objects being the obvious possible candidate. Consequently, the need to justify in a non-empirical fashion at least some claims concerning the fundamental structure of reality is built into the very conception of the traditional metaphysical project.

Given this conception of metaphysics, it is not surprising that many philosophers have wondered whether it is worth the candle. The following list is representative of the familiar kinds of worries philosophers currently express on this score:

1. Ontological relativists and post-modernists deny that there is a single fundamental structure to reality. If "reality" is a human construct, and variable from culture to culture, then metaphysics as depicted here is a subject without an object.

2. It has been argued that if metaphysics is to be possible at all it must be reconstrued as the study of the fundamental structure of *human thought* or *language*, not of reality itself, either because reality has no structure in and of itself (see 1 above), or because the only structure that is cognitively accessible to us is one imposed by our cognitive apparatus.

3. It has been argued that if there is a mind-independent reality whose structure is cognitively accessible to us (contra 1 and 2), the nature of that reality is discovered empirically. Consequently, if there is any metaphysical knowledge to be had, it is provided by the sciences in conjunction with conceptual analyzes, not by a distinct study called metaphysics.

4. If it is suggested, contra (3), that the structure of mind-independent reality is cognitively accessible to us via *non*-empirical means, the response is that non-empirical knowledge of extra-mental reality cannot be squared with the evolutionary history of our species. Epistemological naturalists insist that there is nothing in our evolutionary past to suggest that our species came under selective pressures that would lead to the emergence of the required cognitive faculty. The upshot of this naturalism is that appealing to one's *a priori* "intuitions" or reflections when developing metaphysics theories is methodologically dubious at best. But if metaphysical theories are justified empirically – the obvious alternative – then metaphysics is just more science (see 3 above).

Now on the basis of these sorts of considerations, a number of increasingly skeptical positions have been maintained. First, it is often concluded that warranted answers to metaphysical questions, when available, are provided not by metaphysicians *qua* metaphysicians but by the sciences and conceptual analysis (naturalism). If neither of these approaches offers an answer, two attitudes remain. One might still maintain that metaphysical questions have determinate answers but judge that one is never in a position to recognize the correct answer when it is lighted upon (skepticism). Or one might begin to suspect that metaphysical questions as traditionally conceived are defective in some fashion, and so lack determinate answers altogether (ontological anti-realism).[5]

This is a powerful set of objections to the viability of the metaphysical project as traditionally conceived. But there are quick answers to at least the first two objections. To the ontological relativists, post-modernists and neo-Kantian who would deny the viability of metaphysics on the grounds that there is no single fundamental structure to reality to be discovered by metaphysical reflection, the quick response is that this denial is itself based on metaphysical assumptions, and so the objections are self-defeating.[6] Objections (3) and (4) are altogether more pressing. But there are reasons for thinking that room must be made for the metaphysician *qua* metaphysician even by those who would sub-contract the discipline out to the sciences. Some of the more telling considerations are as follows:

1. The sciences cannot provide answers to metaphysical questions in any straightforward fashion, because the sciences do not as yet agree amongst themselves on metaphysical matters.[7]
2. Even if the metaphysician agrees to set aside consideration of abstract objects and focus entirely on the denizens of space and time, the assumption that the sciences can determine what actually exists in their respective domains unaided by metaphysical theory is arguably false. Empirical evidence counts in favor of the actual existence of X only if it has been established independently that X is possible. But establishing the possibility of X does not fall within the remit of the sciences. That is the business of metaphysics.[8]
3. Metaphysics can be subcontracted to the sciences only if there are good reasons to believe that mature scientific theories are at least approximately true representations of some aspect of reality. But it is not clear that this attitude vis-à-vis any scientific theory can be warranted in the absence of metaphysical commitments. For, as Duhem pointed out long ago, it is impossible, strictly speaking, to verify or falsify a scientific theory if one relies solely on empirical

evidence and logic. Now it is generally agreed that when the scientific community tests theories, it augments the empirical data and logic with what have been called "disciplinary matrices", complicated and usually implicit agreements regarding the background assumptions of the discipline.[9] But while the sociological aspects of the disciplinary matrices have been widely recognized and accepted, what has not been emphasized sufficiently is the metaphysical character of many of these assumptions.[10] The upshot is that an implicit metaphysics is involved in the choice to save or reject a scientific theory in the face of recalcitrant empirical evidence. Consequently, one cannot claim to derive a metaphysics from science for one's metaphysics determines which scientific theories one adopts.

It is time to gather the fruit of this section. The detractors of metaphysics as traditionally conceived fall into roughly three categories: (a) Those who think the philosophical enterprise can be prosecuted without recourse to metaphysical reflection; (b) those who deny its possibility; and (c) those who claim that we can arrive at warranted metaphysical claims but not thanks to the efforts of metaphysicians *qua* metaphysicians but thanks to the sciences. We have already seen that there is reason to doubt (c), and we will return to this topic in due course. Addressing (b) head on is the main challenge of this chapter. But addressing the Humean dilemma, the strongest challenge to the viability of metaphysics, is best left until a response to (a) has been provided.

## 3   The philosophical enterprise

The next step in this defense of metaphysics is to establish that there really is a role for metaphysicians within the wider intellectual economy, and within philosophy in particular. The necessity of metaphysics rests on two claims. First, that reflection of a distinctly metaphysical variety is called for in the treatment of problems of a very specific form. Recognition of this point is crucial if the metaphysical project is to be understood, and its claims evaluated appropriately. The second claim is that problems calling for metaphysical reflection are typical of the discipline of philosophy in general, and that to discuss the nature of these problems is to discuss the nature of philosophy itself. If these claims can be made good, then it follows that metaphysics is indispensable to the philosopher because metaphysics is the core discipline of philosophy. I begin then with an account of the particular kind of problem that calls for treatment by the metaphysician *qua* metaphysician. I have discussed the nature of such problems at length elsewhere,[11] so this discussion will be confined to a bald statement of its key claims.

I begin then with the general aim of philosophical activity in its broadest sense. The aim of the discipline throughout most of its history has been to provide a description and explanatory account of the nature of reality and the place of human beings within it. The idea, explicit in some and implicit in others, has been that knowing something about the nature of the world we live in, and something of our own human nature, is bound to shed light on what kind of life human beings should lead and what kinds of actions human beings ought to perform and which to avoid. It is for this reason that philosophy is always associated with the "Big Questions".

The second key claim regarding the philosophical enterprise is that philosophers *qua* philosophers do *not* provide the basic materials out of which "The Big Picture" is developed. If one is to understand the distinctive nature of philosophy one must begin by recognizing that a division of intellectual labor exists in the general intellectual economy between philosophy on the one hand and the sciences and truth-directed subjects of the humanities on the other. The contribution of the philosopher *qua* philosopher to the grand project is to draw on pre-existing materials derived from the special sciences, the truth-directed subjects of the humanities, as well as our store of pre-theoretical beliefs, and to *co-ordinate* this material into a coherent picture of human beings and our place in the Universe. It is this second-order task of co-ordination, lying outside the remit of any special science, which is specifically philosophical, and the problems encountered in the pursuance of this task are specifically philosophical problems.

Co-ordination problems arise when one notices a tension, real or apparent, between beliefs or lines of thought that one is otherwise inclined to accept – when a presupposition or entire line of thought from one special science, for instance, appears to clash with a belief from a distinct science, or theology, or common sense. The problem is that each line of thought is attractive and well-established within its respective domain, but the taking up of the one precludes, or at least appears to preclude, the taking up of (all) the others. The perennial free will/determinism debate provides a good example. This debate arises because a tension is noticed amongst individually plausible theses:

1. Adult human beings are appropriate subjects of reactive attitudes because they are free agents: we can, and sometimes do, act from free

choice, and so we can be held responsible for our actions (an assumption of pre-theoretical common sense, and our legal system).
2. If an action issues from free choice, then it is causally unconstrained (a natural interpretation of the presuppositions of free action according to common sense).
3. All occurrences, human actions included, are caused by antecedent occurrences (a presupposition of the sciences regarding phenomena above the micro-level).

The problem is that these individually plausible theses are at least *prima facie* inconsistent. The philosophical task is to determine what to make of this situation. Examples of such puzzles abound, and following Aristotle we can call them "aporia".[12] But the crucial point for present purposes is that aporia fall to philosophy, as opposed to a special science, if only because such puzzles usually do not arise *within* the domain of any special science but are due to a *prima facie* clash *between* first-order disciplines, or between first-order disciplines and common sense, and thus lie outside the competence of any first-order discipline. But the frequently inter-disciplinary nature of such problems points to the deeper fact that it is not first-order empirical work that is required for their resolution but a modification of our conceptual scheme with which we interpret the empirical data thrown up by the first-order disciplines.[13]

Now, if strictly philosophical problems or questions begin as and emerge from co-ordination problems as described above, then the following can be said about philosophical activity in general at the highest level of abstraction: The task of the philosopher *qua* philosopher is to give an account of the initial lines of thought that removes the appearance of contradiction, and so solves the philosophical puzzle. Solving problems of this sort is the *raison d'être* of the philosopher *qua* philosopher, and constitutes the philosopher's specific contribution to the general intellectual economy.[14] From this perspective all conceptual analyzes, second-order theory construction, argument development, analysis and critique, the careful drawing of distinctions – i.e., all the working philosopher's bread and butter activities – are best understood as means to this end, and they receive the tag "philosophical" because they can be used to this end.

Now if this is what a strictly philosophical problem looks like, and what success in philosophy consists in, then, again at the highest level of abstraction, resolutions of philosophical puzzles can take only a limited number of forms. After due consideration, the philosopher must either:

(A) Establish that the tensions in the initial lines of thought are merely *prima facie*, or
(B) Accept that the lines of thought form an inconsistent set.

Ideally the philosopher finds that the tensions are merely apparent, for this allows one to integrate the original lines of thought into the Big Picture without further ado. But many aporia involve genuine contradictions, and in such cases three less than optimal but unavoidable versions of (B) remain. If the philosopher is convinced that the lines of thought form an inconsistent set, she can maintain that:

B(i) *No totally satisfying account of the inconsistent set of propositions can be given; nonetheless none of the propositions should be abandoned.* At least two versions of B(i) are possible. A philosopher might take this position because she is convinced that we simply do not have enough empirical information to solve the problem at present. The recommendation is that one must live in hope that evidence will eventually come to light that will show one or more of the initial propositions to be false. In this case the aporia is thrown back to the first-order disciplines as being an empirical and not a philosophical matter. But a philosopher might also take this position on the grounds that the aporia is not solvable even in principle because she maintains that reality itself is not consistent (contradictory propositions can be true simultaneously). This line is open to those willing to admit that reality is not fully intelligible and that this fact must simply be accepted as a genuine feature of the intellectual landscape. Both versions of B(i) are failures in the sense that neither removes the aporia – albeit for very different, and in some instances, enlightening reasons. But it is also the case that both make substantial metaphysical claims, the first that reality *is* structured in such a way as to ensure its ultimate intelligibility (at least in principle), the second that it is not.

But a philosopher of a different temperament might choose a second version of (B). She might claim:

B(ii) *No coherent account of the inconsistent set of propositions can be provided, so all of the initial beliefs fall under suspicion.* One might take this view because all the lines of thought leading to the aporia are deemed upon reflection to concern domains beyond our cognitive competence. A philosopher might argue that we are prone to systematic error in these particular domains because of some feature of our cognitive apparatus. In these cases, the diagnosis is that our willingness to entertain beliefs beyond our cognitive competence is the source of the aporia, and we should refrain from entertaining such beliefs. But one might also maintain that the aporia arises because all the initially attractive lines of thought are committed to a similar false assumption. The suggestion here is that there is no in principle problem with our cognitive abilities in the domains under discussion, it is just that we have gotten off to an avoidable false start. The suggestion is that the removal of the common false assumption leads to the resolution of the aporia. The idea here is that the original propositions that constitute the aporia really were in tension (they could not be true simultaneously), but all were fundamentally misguided in some fashion. Both versions of B(ii) allow one to resolve the aporia but at a very high cost. Both require the rejection of the entire set of what had been deemed epistemically credible lines of thought prior to philosophical reflection.

A third version of (B) remains. After convincing herself that the aporia in not merely *prima facie*, the philosopher might claim that:

B(iii) *The aporia is to be resolved by modifying, qualifying or perhaps abandoning altogether* one or more *of the initial lines of thought.* This approach is most likely to be adopted by the philosopher who cannot bring herself to accept (A) – B(i–ii). That is, by the philosopher who maintains that not all philosophical problems are the result of conceptual confusions of some sort or another; that philosophers cannot be satisfied in all cases with the issuing of promissory notes; that it is methodologically more fruitful to proceed on the assumption that reality is intelligible until very strong arguments to the contrary are produced; and that it is methodologically more fruitful to proceed on the assumption that the various first-order disciplines are not subject to widespread and systematic error. The task for such a philosopher is then to establish in a principled fashion which of the initial lines of thought is to be saved and which sacrificed.

If space permitted, it would be helpful to provide further examples of aporias and of treatments falling into these various categories just identified. But perhaps enough has been said for present purposes.[15] While confident that the foregoing general account of the philosophical enterprise and the logical structure of philosophical problems does identify something fundamental about the discipline, I would not wish to suggest that every instance of philosophical activity will fit this model exactly. What I would claim for the account, however, is that it does capture the *focal* sense of the term "philosophy" inasmuch as strictly philosophical problems appear to begin life as co-ordination problems. This does not preclude the possibility that other sorts of problems and activities can rightly be termed "philosophical". But, to take another page from Aristotle's copy book, in the same way that one can speak intelligibly of healthy diets, healthy life-styles, and healthy urine because these are among the causes or indications of health within an organism, I would suggest that activities or problems are genuinely philosophical insofar as they emerge in the course of coming to terms with a co-ordination problem. In short, it is these co-ordination problems that provide the focal sense of the term "philosophy".

## 4 Aporia resolution

If this account of philosophy is taken seriously, then aporia resolution is the philosopher's principal occupation. And as just outlined, there are variations on four general stances one can take vis-à-vis any aporia. But how does one decide in a principled fashion which option is best in any given case?

In line with the respect accorded the first-order disciplines recommended by this understanding of the philosophical enterprise, in the first instance the philosopher ought to privilege the first, compatibilist, option. That is, the philosopher ought to assume that the aporia is merely *prima facie* until this proves untenable.[16] And there is no doubt that aporia do often arise because the theories or lines of thought that lead to the aporia are not properly understood. In these instances, an aporia can be resolved simply by doing one's homework, i.e., by making sure one knows what the theories are really claiming, and what their implications really are. In some cases, no specifically philosophical training or methodology will be required in order to resolve them because careful attention to the details of the initial material will suffice. In other cases, sophisticated forms of paraphrasing might be employed to show that a theory does or does not have a particular implication, and so does not generate an inconsistent set of propositions. Furthermore, in a large number of cases aporia arise from the failure to recognize certain distinctions. In such cases, the philosopher's knack of drawing the necessary conceptual distinctions proves crucial.[17]

But there is no guarantee that all aporia are merely *prima facie*. In such cases, no amount of background work or nice distinctions will help.

And if one is not prepared to abandon hope of philosophical progress (Bi), or the wholesale rejection of the first-order disciplines (Bii), then one must try to establish which of the initial lines of thought leading to the aporia is to be dropped (Biii). Rescher has developed one approach to this task.

## 5 Rescher's pragmatism

At bottom, the philosophical problem is knowing what to make of situations in which individually plausible theses are found to be incompatible. Rescher suggests a three stage approach. One begins by gathering all the data relevant to the aporia. This can be information gathered from the senses, memory, cognitive aids and instruments (e.g., telescopes, calculating machines, reference works) reliable witnesses, and the declarations of experts from any relevant discipline. Rescher's working assumption here is that one should accept this data as reliable "in the absence of specific indications to the contrary" (2009, p. 17). Second, one draws up an inventory of all the possible conflict-resolving options. The example of the free will debate mentioned above provides an illustration. If one decides that the tension is not merely *prima facie,* one is left with the following possibilities:

1. Reject 1 and deny that free choices are possible (hard determinism)
2. Reject 2 and insist that free actions can have a sufficient set of causes (compatibilism)
3. Reject 3 and insist that some events above the micro-level, including some human choices, are uncaused by antecedent occurrences (libertarianism)

The third and final step in Rescher's approach is where matters become problematic, viz., fixing on one of the identified conflict removing options. When deciding which of the logically possible solutions to adopt he says one must employ "guidance of plausibility considerations, subject to the principle of minimizing implausibility" (2009, p. 23). In short, one must "make the less plausible give way to greater plausibility" (ibid., p. 119). Of course, as it stands this amounts to little more than a restatement of the problem, for determining which option is most plausible is precisely the issue at hand. Rescher's suggested way forward begins with the observation that there are three distinct considerations that come to the fore in aporia resolution contexts. First, we value theses for which there is a great deal of empirical evidence, for such evidence provides a degree of confidence and security – a key cognitive desideratum. Second, we are not simply in the business of collecting facts; we want to understand the facts, and so we value theses with a high degree of explanatory power. Such theses tend to be far more general than individual empirical claims, and they tend to rely on core elements of our basic conceptual scheme. Finally, since the first two desiderata are in tension inasmuch as each comes at the expense of the other, one is also likely to seek a balance between security and explanatory power in a coherent system of beliefs that includes both empirical facts and an explanatory framework.

The question then, according to Rescher, is which of these desiderata to emphasize on any given occasion. Rescher's advice is to consider the context. He writes: "All in all...the rationale for a particular mode of prioritization lies in the specific goal and purpose of the domain of deliberation at issue. Just this essentially *pragmatic* consideration must be allowed to determine the correlative principle of prioritization" (ibid., p. 139). But this advice is unsatisfactory for a number of reasons. First, frequently there is no single domain involved in the case of aporia. Indeed, it is precisely because various domains are in conflict that the aporia arises in the first place. And these domains are likely to have different goals and purposes. Second, even if there were a single domain at issue, it is not clear that Rescher's advice addresses the problem at hand. The problem was to find a way of distinguishing the more from the less plausible. But identifying a goal or purpose for a domain does not allow one to make this adjudication. So, while Rescher has a very clear view of the nature of the philosophical dilemma, he has yet to provide a principled way of making the less plausible give way to greater plausibility because the pragmatic method never really addresses the issue of relative plausibility at all.

## 6 Metaphysics and plausibility

It is here that one can begin to see why metaphysics as traditionally conceived is indispensable to the philosophical enterprise. If the focal philosophical task is aporia resolution, and if that means, in a significant number of cases, making the less plausible give way to greater plausibility, then some way of determining the plausibility of theories or lines of thought is required. Moreover, if both conflicting lines of thought are justified on empirical grounds (as they will be if they are scientific theories), then more empirical evidence is unlikely to help. It is more likely that a reinterpretation of the available empirical evidence is called for. And this is precisely what a metaphysical theory is meant to offer by suggesting alterations to our account of the fundamental structure of reality and our accompanying conceptual scheme. Moreover, if one has a respectable theory of the fundamental structure of reality, then one has something against which the plausibility of other lines of thought from the first-order disciplines can be measured. If a line of thought is compatible with a respectable metaphysics, then it can be deemed plausible; if not, then it is up for reinterpretation or possibly outright rejection.

And it is here that one also begins to see how it can arise that the humble metaphysician could potentially be called upon to correct the august scientist (although both hats can be worn by one and the same person). If two conflicting lines of thought happen to be scientific theories, and the conflict is not merely *prima facie*, then something has to give. And in these cases, the solution to the conflict will not be found within either of the conflicting sciences, and neither science can claim the authority to overrule the other without basing that claim on some extra-scientific judgments. Some appeal to plausibility considerations ultimately grounded in a metaphysical theory will be required to determine which of the sciences needs to be revisited with a critical eye. Thus the eye-catching immodesty of metaphysics as traditionally conceived stems ultimately from the fact that sciences can, and do, disagree amongst themselves, and because scientific considerations alone will not resolve conflicts of this sort.

## 7   The aporetic method

I have now sketched an account of philosophy which renders plausible the view that metaphysics is indispensable to the philosophical enterprise. Moreover, this picture makes sense of the idea that "mere" metaphysics could reasonably be called upon to overrule an accepted interpretation of scientific theory. It is now time to address perhaps the most pressing concern: providing a warrant for metaphysical claims. For even if metaphysics is necessary, our confidence in a recommended resolution of an aporia will only be as great as our confidence in the metaphysics on which it is based. And metaphysical systems abound. How is one to choose in a principled fashion amongst them? In particular, we need some way of determining when a metaphysical claim is warranted which (1) does not rely on empirical evidence alone; (2) does not rely on ultimately ungrounded intuitions; but (3) is consistent with what we know of the phylogeny of our cognitive systems. I believe it is here that the aporetic method comes into its own.

The first thing to note about the aporetic method is that it starts with aporia, not with a critical discussion of distinctly metaphysical claims *per se*. On this view of metaphysics, metaphysical reflection is only called for in order to resolve independently existing aporia. So, the first step for any would be metaphysician is aporia identification. Now, the rationale for this crucial first step is not merely that adherence to it keeps metaphysics in touch with the rest of the intellectual economy (a desideratum in and of itself). The method, when properly deployed, shapes one's metaphysical research. Thus, at the beginning of Book III of the *Metaphysics* Aristotle states that one must begin one's metaphysical reflections by familiarizing oneself with the standard puzzles or aporia. These aporia set the agenda for one's reflections, and one who is not aware of these is "like those who do not know where they have to go." Moreover, if one is not familiar with the standard puzzles, one will not recognize a solution if one happens to stumble across it – "a man does not otherwise know even whether he has at any given time found what he is looking for or not; for the end is not clear to such a man, while to him who has first discussed the difficulties it is clear."

Moreover, aporia constitute not just a budget of problems to be solved but also opportunities for discovery.[18] Aporia are not simply intellectual inconveniences that need to be tidied up. Aporia reveal the cracks and fault lines in our account of reality. These cracks show that our current picture is inadequate (something one might otherwise miss) while also suggesting where the inadequacies lie, thus prompting research in specific directions.

An illustrative example will help. Einstein's discovery of the Special Theory of Relativity appears to have grown out of his reflections on the perceived tensions between lines of thought he accepted.[19] For present purposes, we can leave the details as to how these tensions arise to one side and focus only on the logical structure of the problem confronting Einstein. The first line of thought, derived from Newtonian mechanics, asserts that the laws of mechanics take the same form in all inertial frames. The second, derived from Lorentz's interpretation of Maxwell's laws of electricity, magnetism and optics, asserts that there is an inertial frame in which the speed of light is constant regardless of the velocity of its source. The problem is that these two lines of thought lead to a contradiction – namely, that the speed of light is and is not constant across all inertial frames – *if* one also accepts the Newtonian law of the addition of velocities *and* one rejects the ether concept. Now, the law of the addition of velocities had always been considered obvious by Einstein and others. And the ether concept, while central to the Lorentz interpretation of Maxwell, had become suspect in Einstein's eyes. He was thus faced with a classic aporia. Einstein's breakthrough came when it occurred to him to question the apparently obvious law of the addition of velocities (the only option left on the table if one refuses to abandon the other elements of the aporia). He began to consider the implications of abandoning this law, asking what reality would have to be like if this law were in fact false. He realized that rejecting the law would require a new analysis of the concepts of time, simultaneity and length. With this new analysis in hand, Einstein was able to resolve the aporia and maintain that the speed of light is constant in every inertial frame of reference. But the key point for present purposes is that it would probably never have occurred to Einstein to revisit the concepts of space and time in this way if this had not been suggested by the aporia before him. The moral of the story is that aporia can guide one's metaphysical reflections by posing very specific questions of the following general form: If the tensions in an aporia are not merely *prima facie*, then what must reality be like for these individually warranted but incompatible lines of thought to appear plausible? The suggestion, then, is that aporia set the metaphysician to work in the right direction with the reasonable expectation that a suitably able imagination will light upon a better picture of reality, a picture which will explain how a false theory could nonetheless appear compelling, and provide an alternative interpretation of the data leading to the aporia.

But metaphysicians have fertile imaginations, and they often produce very different pictures of reality in response to one and the same aporia. How does one adjudicate between them? The aporetic method itself suggests a test. Since the method assumes that the lines of thought leading to the aporia have genuine merit, *the least revisionary of the pictures is the most plausible*. This is not a matter of preserving for preserving's sake. The desire to conserve as many of the original lines of thought as possible stems from the respect accorded to the first-order disciplines implicit in the division of intellectual labor accepted by this account of the philosophical enterprise. For all its immodesty, the approach to metaphysics defended here takes it as a default position that the sciences are competent to run their own affairs, similarly with the truth-directed subjects of the humanities, similarly with the common man's ability to see his way through the tasks of daily life. It is only when tensions amongst these respectable lines of thought are noticed that there is any call for philosophy or metaphysics. And even then the initial hope is that the tension is merely *prima facie*. But if it should arise that the tensions are genuine, and a metaphysical theory is required for their resolution, then that theory is judged most plausible which preserves as many of the initial lines of thought as possible because *any* philosophical theory is indirectly supported by the evidence adduced in favor of the initial beliefs it is designed to accommodate. The more such lines of thought are preserved, the greater the degree of support the metaphysical theory enjoys. And if that metaphysical theory should, in turn, provide the key to the resolution of a range of other seemingly unrelated aporia, then the warrant for that theory becomes all the stronger in virtue of this happy "consilience of inductions".

To summarize: On the line taken here, a warrant for a metaphysical claim should take the following schematic form:

Step 1: Establish that $T_1 - T_n$ are respectable lines of thought from first-order domains.

Step 2: Establish that $T_1 - T_n$ form an inconsistent set of propositions (i.e., that the tensions are not merely *prima facie*).

Step 3: Construct a theory such that if it were true, then $T_1 - T_n$ would appear individually plausible despite the fact that $T_3$, say, is false.

Step 4: Establish that no other theory is available which preserves as many of the initial lines of thought while explaining how error entered the beliefs of competent authorities.

Step 5: On the basis of steps (1) – (4) conclude that the theory presented in step (3) is more plausible than any available alternative.

Step 6: On the basis of step (5) conclude that one is entitled to resolve the initial aporia identified in steps (1) and (2) by rejecting $T_3$.

Step 7: Test the theory introduced in step (3) further by considering other aporia. If that theory allows for similarly smooth resolutions of other aporia then that theory increases in plausibility.

Now I submit that this approach to the justification of metaphysical claims meets several key desiderata. First, if one has completed steps 1 and 2 in any particular case then it would appear that there is a job in the intellectual economy that falls to the philosopher, and that in discharging this duty it will be necessary, on occasion, to appeal to a metaphysical theory. Second, metaphysical theories generated in accordance with these steps appear to be rationally warranted without being just more science, or being grounded in mere "intuitions", so the

Humean dilemma has been circumvented. Finally, there has been no need to postulate cognitive faculties that cannot be squared with our evolutionary past. The aporetic method as sketched here relies on no such dubious faculties and is entirely consistent with epistemological naturalism. I conclude then, contra current orthodoxy, that immodest metaphysics is both indispensible to the general philosophical enterprise, and a viable project to boot.

## 8  Some objections to the aporetic method

In closing, it is worth considering briefly some likely objections. The aporetic method as such has not been discussed in the contemporary meta-metaphysical literature, but one obvious criticism is that it is simply a variation on the standard "battery-of-criteria" approach employed by mainstream metaphysicians. It might reasonably be thought that the aporetic method simply forwards yet another criterion, in this case a theory's ability to preserve more initial lines of thought from first-order domains than any other.

But in reply, one can say that this criterion has a claim to being a "master" criterion, not merely one of several competing criteria without a clear hierarchy to be found amongst them. After all, this criterion is tailored precisely to the intellectual task aporetic metaphysicians have set themselves. Here the wider purpose of metaphysical reflection, i.e., aporia resolution, is critical in deciding how best to evaluate a metaphysical claim. Moreover, this criterion has a degree of objectivity lacking in many other cases. In the first place, it is not up to metaphysicians to decide what lines of thought are initially placed on the table. This is an objective matter based on states of affairs in the first-order disciplines. And while it might be difficult to individuate lines of thought, making it difficult to count how many beliefs have been preserved by a given metaphysical claim, securing agreement on which of two competing metaphysical claims is the more revisionary is usually fairly straightforward.

Some further objections to the aporetic method have been aired within the circle of Aristotelian scholarship. It has been objected, for example, that the best the method can produce is coherence amongst our beliefs. But coherence is not the same as truth; for it is logically possible, indeed it is a frequent occurrence, that a set of coherent beliefs contains elements that are false. So, goes the objection, the aporetic method cannot overcome skepticism.[20] The reply must be that this charge is largely true but beside the point. If one accepts that it is no part of the metaphysician's task to satisfy the sceptic, but rather to resolve aporia in the most evidence preserving fashion possible, then this charge can be accepted with equanimity. For the method does provide a means of adjudicating amongst competing metaphysical claims, and that is all that can reasonably be expected. To ask for more than this – in particular, to ask for deductive proofs from self-evident premises – is to judge metaphysics by the standards of mathematics. But if one maintains, as Aristotle rightly did, that metaphysics is a distinct discipline with distinct problems, methods and standards of evaluation, then its claims must be evaluated by its own lights, not those of a different discipline.

It is also frequently objected that the method as it appears in Aristotle relies on "intuitions". But, goes the objection, there is no philosophically acceptable reason to give credence to intuitions. In a closely related complaint, it is argued that this undue respect for intuitions generates an excessive conservativism which many deem inimical to the philosophical spirit. But while Aristotle might have been vulnerable to these objections, the method as reconstructed here is not. The point of departure of this version of the method lies in tensions in well-established lines of thought from the various truth-directed disciplines, including the special sciences. These lines of thought are not simply gut-level intuitions or well-entrenched speech habits. Of course, there will inevitably be appeal to what one finds plausible at some stage of the process, but the method does not take these intuitions as points of departure as is implied by the objection. And while the method is, no doubt, conservative in some important respects, it in no way encourages complacency since it enjoins upon the philosopher the task of actively seeking out aporia, an activity which by its very nature brings to light the shortcomings of accepted lines of thought.

A final concluding remark: I have addressed those who maintain that the philosopher can dispense with metaphysics; and a method has been presented which shows how metaphysical claims can be warranted without simply being more science. What I have not addressed directly is the anti-realist assertion that metaphysical claims lack truth-values. The reason for this omission is the belief that the attraction of anti-realism in metaphysics stems from epistemological concerns. I hope the temptation to anti-realism has been removed now that an alternative approach to providing warrants for metaphysical claims has been sketched. But many will still feel that there are metaphysical questions discussed in the current literature that simply cry out for anti-realist interpretation. I think these sentiments are often well founded. While I have been at pains to argue that metaphysics as traditionally conceived is necessary and possible, there is no doubt that much current metaphysical discussion is, at best, unhelpful. The reason for this, I submit, is that most metaphysical discussion is divorced from the task of aporia resolution. If there is a moral to thischapter, it is that only those metaphysical claims that offer a solution to an aporia are worthy of serious consideration. Metaphysical claims with no connection to an aporia should be ignored because it is unlikely that one will be able to get any purchase on them, and because they are serving no useful purpose. Here, at least, is common ground with the metaphysical anti-realist.

## Notes

1. I have in mind here the specifically Quinean recommendation of determining one's ontological commitments by expressing an accepted scientific theory in the language of first-order predicate logic and then committing oneself to those entities that must be admitted as possible values of bound variables if the theory is deemed true – making due allowances for possible recourse to paraphrases. Here, the heavy lifting is done by the scientific theory. Conceptual analysis has a similarly deflationary impact on the role of the metaphysician, and appears to provide only "trivial" or "internal" answers to metaphysical questions.
2. I agree with Sider that most contemporary forms of ontological anti-realism stem from concerns relating to epistemology. He suggests that current forms of anti-realism are "based on the desire to make unanswerable questions go away." These questions are deemed unanswerable because they "resist direct empirical methods but are nevertheless not answerable by conceptual analysis (2009, p. 419)."
3. Gilson (1937, p. 306).
4. By contrast with Hofweber's *modest* metaphysics. See his (2009).
5. Standard variations on this final theme emphasize the possibility that parties to an ontological dispute are talking past each other because they attribute different senses to key terms (the existential quantifier and the term "object" being prime candidates). It is also suggested that perhaps ontological claims are not statements at all, but merely prescriptions about how one should talk. One might also suspect that a subject or predicate term in an ontological statement is itself problematic in some fashion, rendering it impossible to attribute truth conditions to the statements in which it is embedded.
6. See Lowe (2001, pp. 3–8) for extended discussion.
7. In actual practice, many argue as though a hierarchy of scientific authority does exist, and so physics is given precedence over chemistry and biology, and the latter are privileged over, say, linguistics and psychology. But it is not clear that this hierarchy can be justified without appeal to some implicit metaphysical principles.
8. This argument is due to Lowe, (2001, p. 5). See also his (2007, p. 5). This is in line with a standard view that the sciences deal with the actual, while metaphysics deals with the necessary and the possible.

9. See, in particular, Thomas Kuhn's (1974).
10. See Duhem's *The Aim and Structure of Physical Theory* for a perceptive and detailed account of scientific theory shorn of metaphysical baggage.
11. See chapter 1 of my (2007).
12. Aristotle stated that an aporia arises "...when we reason on both sides [of a question] and it appears to us that everything can come about either way." This produces "a state of *aporia* about which of the two ways to take up" (*Topics*, VI, 145b16–20).
13. This view of the nature of what I am calling co-ordination problems is found in Ryle's (2002) *Dilemmas*.
14. These points draw heavily on Aristotle's *Metaphysics* (995a23–995b4).
15. For further discussion and examples, see Nicolai Hartmann's (1965); Boulter's (2007, Ch. 1); and Rescher's (2006, 2009).
16. I am using the term "compatibilist" here to describe attempts to resolve any aporia by showing that the propositions of the aporia are compossible.
17. Gary Gutting (2009) has recently argued that the philosopher's contribution to the general pool of knowledge is precisely the knowledge of distinctions. See also Ch. 4 of Rescher's (2006).
18. Here, I am disagreeing with Rescher, who writes: "Aporetics is...less a method of innovation than of regimentation: its task is not to engender new insights but to bring systematic order and coherence into those we already have (2009, 3).
19. This paragraph is heavily indebted to John Stachel's work on the origins of the Special Theory of Relativity (2002).
20. Irwin, (2002, p. 8–10), *Aristotle's First Principles*. Oxford: Clarendon Press. One closely related complaint is that the method cannot generate a warrant for full-blooded metaphysically realist claims, although those of the anaemic "internal" realist variety might gain some support.

## References

Aristotle. 1941. *The Basic Works of Aristotle*. McKeon (ed.) (New York: Random House).

Boulter, Stephen. 2007. *The Rediscovery of Common Sense Philosophy* (Houndsmill: Palgrave Macmillan).

Duhem, Pierre. 1977. *The Aim and Structure of Physical Theory* (New York: Athenium).

Gilson, Etienne. 1937. *The Unity of Philosophical Experience* (New York: Charles Scribner's Sons).

Gutting, Gary. 2009. *What Philosophers Know: Case Studies in Recent Analytic Philosophy* (Cambridge: Cambridge University Press).

Hartmann, Nicolai. 1965. *Grundzüge einer Metaphysik der Erkenntnis* 5th ed. (Berlin: W. de Gruyter).

Hofweber, Thomas. 2009. "Ambitious, Yet Modest, Metaphysics," in Chalmers, Manley and Wasserman, (eds), *Metametaphysics: New Essays on the Foundations of Ontology*. (Oxford: Clarendon Press).

Irwin, T. H. 2002. *Aristotle's First Principles* (Oxford: Clarendon Press).

Kuhn, Thomas. 1974. "Second thoughts on Paradigms," in F. Suppe (ed.) *The Structure of Scientific Theories* (Urbana: University of Illinois Press), pp. 459–82.

Lowe, E. J. 2001 *The Possibility of Metaphysics* (Oxford: Oxford University Press).

—— 2007. *The Four Category Ontology* (Oxford: Oxford University Press).

Rescher, Nicholas. 2006. *Philosophical Dialectics* (Albany: SUNY).

—— 2009. *Aporetics: Rational Deliberation in the Face of Inconsistency* (Pittsburgh: Pittsburgh University Press).

Ryle, Gilbert. 2002 *Dilemmas* (Cambridge: Cambridge University Press).

Sider, Theodore. 2009. "Ontological Realism," in Chalmers, Manley and Wasserman (eds), *Metametaphysics* (Oxford: Clarendon Press).

Stachel, John. 2002 "What Song the Sirens Sang: How Did Einstein Discover Special Relativity?" in *Einstein from "B" to "Z"* (Boston: Birkhauser), pp. 157–70.

# 4
# Metaphysics as the First Philosophy

*Tuomas E. Tahko*

> *And there are as many parts of philosophy as there are kinds of substance, so that there must necessarily be among them a first philosophy and one which follows this.* (Meta. 1004a4–6.)

## 1 Introduction

Aristotle talks about "the first philosophy" throughout *Metaphysics* – and it is metaphysics that Aristotle considers to be the first philosophy – but he never makes it entirely clear what first philosophy consists of. What he does make clear is that the first philosophy is not to be understood as a collection of topics that should be studied in advance of any other topics. In fact, Aristotle seems to have thought that the topics of *Metaphysics* are to be studied *after* those in *Physics* (Cohen 2009). In what sense could metaphysics be the first philosophy? Let me take the liberty of applying the technical jargon of contemporary metaphysics to answer: The first philosophy is an account of what is, or what it means to be, *fundamental*. Things that are the most fundamental are not *grounded in* anything more fundamental, they are *ontologically independent*. This does not necessarily mean that first philosophy attempts to list the most fundamental things, although this could be a part of the discipline. Rather, the study of fundamentality focuses on giving an account of what it is for something to be fundamental. So, first philosophy studies a certain type of *being* – the fundamental type, and it may also involve an account of which (kind of) things are, or could be, fundamental.

It is plausibly the task of "the second philosophy", i.e. physics, to determine which things are in fact fundamental, although, as we will see, this is not possible without a previous account of what fundamentality *is*. For instance, explaining the view according to which

49

elementary particles are fundamental requires a previous understanding of what it would mean for them to be fundamental. Of course, this is not at all how Aristotle would have put it, but many contemporary metaphysicians working on the currently popular topics of fundamentality, grounding, and ontological dependence explicitly refer to Aristotle as the ideological source of these notions (e.g. Schaffer 2009, Lowe 2011, Fine 2012, Koslicki 2012a, and Tahko 2012). In this chapter, I will explore the connection between Aristotle's conception of metaphysics as the first philosophy and the contemporary "neo-Aristotelian" accounts of the nature of metaphysics. However, I will suggest that it is in terms of the notion of *essence* rather than fundamentality, grounding, or ontological independence that we can best characterize the idea of first philosophy, albeit there are obvious points of connection between these notions. Metaphysics, it turns out, is the science of essence.

I will first outline the Aristotelian roots of first philosophy in section 2, presenting an overview of some important notions, such as *being, substance,* and *essence.* In Section 3, I will discuss some of the most influential neo-Aristotelian accounts with special attention to the manner in which they interpret the idea of first philosophy and *priority.* This will involve a brief analysis of the currently topical notions of fundamentality, grounding, and ontological dependence, all of which have been used to illustrate the (Aristotelian) notion of priority. Section 4 focuses on my own suggestion regarding the interpretation of first philosophy and metaphysics as the science of essence. Here, I will partly build on the work of E. J. Lowe and Kit Fine as well as my previous work on essence. I suggest that, despite some exegetical issues regarding Aristotle's own views about essence, we should consider essence to precede existence ontologically, that is, the essence of a thing is not dependent on the existence of the thing – all kinds of *possible* things have an essence. I conclude with a case study from theoretical physics, the case of the Higgs boson. This case study illustrates how the suggested understanding of essence ties in with natural science and provides some evidence of the ontological and epistemic priority of essence. However, I also wish to analyze the relationship between metaphysics and natural science, so the case study serves multiple purposes.

## 2 First philosophy in Aristotle

The role of first philosophy in Aristotle is certainly more complicated than I have acknowledged so far. Indeed, I do not think that it can be sufficiently explicated in terms of fundamentality, ground, or ontological dependence – even if these popular notions do have Aristotelian roots and are crucial for our understanding of metaphysics more generally. Rather, I think it is in terms of *essence* that we should understand the idea of the first philosophy, as I will explain in what follows. But let us first examine Aristotle's own view. This will turn out to be rather more challenging than one might think, because there are relatively few methodological passages in Aristotle, and in his *Metaphysics* in particular. There is, however, no doubt that it is the "science of being *qua* being" that Aristotle considers to be the first philosophy. The question, then, is how we should understand this rather obscure expression. In this section, I will analyze the idea of "being *qua* being", although my discussion should not be regarded as Aristotle exegesis. In particular, I am interested in explicating a modern understanding of first philosophy, with special attention to the methodological challenges that first philosophy – as a science of being *qua* being – will face.[1]

So, what is the science of being *qua* being? First, it should be noted that it is not "being *qua* being" that is the subject of first philosophy – the subject is "being", which is studied "*qua* being" (being as it is in itself) (Cohen 2009). This is to contrast first philosophy with (natural) science, which, of course, also studies being, but not as it is in itself, but rather with a particular end or purpose in mind. This particular end could be, for instance, countability, which falls within the mathematical sciences, whereas metaphysics studies all kinds of being on a much more general level. It is in *Metaphysics* G where Aristotle introduces being *qua* being, but we also find some detailed discussion in *Metaphysics* K. Perhaps the most illustrative passage for our current purposes comes from *Metaphysics* E:

> One might indeed raise the question whether first philosophy is universal, or deals with one genus, i.e. some one kind of being; for not even the mathematical sciences are all alike in this respect, – geometry and astronomy deal with a certain particular kind of thing, while universal mathematics applies alike to all. We answer that if there is no substance other than those which are formed by nature, natural science will be the first science; but if there is an immovable substance, the science of this must be prior and must be first philosophy, and universal in this way, because it is first. And it will belong to this to consider being *qua* being – both what it is and the attributes which belong to it *qua* being. (*Meta.* 1026a25–33.)

Here, Aristotle tells us that it is "substance" that first philosophy studies. Indeed, moments later he specifies that the question of being is simply the question of substance (*Meta.*1028b3–8). It is beyond the scope of this essay to explicate the Aristotelian notion of "substance" in any detail, but it is important to understand that substances are ontologically prior – this is a topic that I will return to in the next section.[2] Aristotle lists a number of different options for what it is to be a substance; the primary candidates are essence, universal, genus, and subject. I will focus on the first one, which I find the most interesting. The reason for this choice is mainly that I believe there to be good reasons to think that understanding substances as essences is the best way of accommodating the Aristotelian idea of metaphysics as the first philosophy in contemporary metaphysics. Let me first sketch Aristotle's own case for understanding substances as essences – he presents it in *Metaphysics* Z.4–12.

Regarding essence, Aristotle says: "The essence of each thing is what it is said to be in virtue of itself" (*Meta.* 1029b14). Do not be misled by the "what it is said" in this passage, for it is quite clear that Aristotle does not consider essences to be a matter of convention – compare this with the distinction between a nominal and a real definition, or essence, also familiar from Locke (cf. Lowe 2011). As Bolton (1976, 524) puts it, "A nominal definition *signifies* [...] the same thing that one type of real definition *displays* [...]; and that is an essence." Bolton (ibid., 515) also suggests that, for Aristotle, knowledge of existence typically precedes knowledge of essence, but I consider this to be debatable. Bolton's case is based on his reading of the *Posterior Analytics* (especially 93a16–24). For instance, Aristotle discusses whether someone could know what a goat-stag is, but denies that this is possible – even though one may know what the name signifies – since goatstags do not exist (92b4–8). However, as Demoss and Devereux (1988) have pointed out, there are passages even in the *Posterior Analytics* that suggest the issue to be more complicated. In particular, Aristotle says that in grasping that a thing *is*, we also have "some hold on what it is" (93a25–28). Demoss and Deveraux (1988, 150) take this passage to be evidence to the effect that nominal definitions refer to underlying essences. This seems plausible, as if we set aside the interpretational issues regarding the *Posterior Analytics* and look at what Aristotle says about essence in the *Metaphysics*, we can find a potential explanation for the conflicting interpretations.

The explanation, I conjecture, is that Aristotle holds only *species* to have essences (1030a11–17); and more importantly, that species are eternal (e.g. *Generation of Animals*, 731b24–732a1).[3] We can now see that, for Aristotle, there could never be an essence of a non-existent thing, such as a goatstag, for Aristotle thinks that *there could be no such thing*. Therefore, if we were to share the Aristotelian conception of species, we would indeed have to agree with him that there is no goatstag essence. Surely, only things that could possibly exist can have essences, and since there are no actual goatstags, Aristotle regards them to be impossible in this sense. Aristotle does not use these exact terms, but we can perhaps take Aristotle's notion of *actuality* to correspond with what I am here calling *existence*. Similarly, my use of *possibility* roughly corresponds with Aristotle's *potentiality*. Accordingly, we can formulate the idea at hand as follows: *actuality precedes potentiality*. It follows that this peculiar doctrine may be an artifact of the Aristotelian conception of species, although this brief analysis is hardly conclusive.

It is reasonable to assume that the Aristotelian conception of species is not widely supported by contemporary philosophers. Hence, for the purposes of adopting the central Aristotelian idea of metaphysics as the first philosophy, I suggest a deviation from the Aristotelian conception of species rather than the idea that essence precedes existence, which I believe to have independent appeal. In any case, the purpose of this essay is not exegetical – I merely hope to have established that there *may* be room for an interpretation of Aristotle which does not rule out the possibility of essence preceding existence.

In the next section, I will begin to establish a link between contemporary analytic metaphysics (with Aristotelian influences) and the Aristotelian idea of metaphysics as the first philosophy.

## 3 Fundamentality, grounding, ontological dependence, and essence

The four notions in the title of this section are currently receiving an abundance of interest in analytic metaphysics. They all have roots in Aristotle, and this is often explicitly acknowledged in the literature. For instance, here is Jonathan Schaffer on grounding and fundamentality:

> I will argue for the revival of a more traditional Aristotelian view, on which metaphysics is about what grounds what. Metaphysics so revived does not bother asking whether properties, meanings, and numbers exist. Of course they do! The question is whether or not they are *fundamental*. (Schaffer 2009, 347.)

Schaffer is firmly of the opinion that for Aristotle, metaphysics is about what is fundamental in the sense of not being grounded in anything else. It is natural to think of first philosophy as the discipline which studies the *ultimate* ground of reality. As we saw in the previous section, the Aristotelian notion of substance would appear to be fundamental in this sense. Fundamentality and grounding are interrelated notions, and they can both be further explicated in terms of ontological dependence.[4] However, the latter comes in a number of varieties, and we should be quite careful in our analysis of fundamentality and grounding with the help of ontological dependence. In particular, although some varieties of ontological dependence can be explicated in modal or existential terms, these are not sufficiently fine-grained in all cases, especially if we hope to make sense of Aristotelian priority. As Koslicki (2012b) observes, Aristotle's conception of dependence, at least in the *Categories*, is often described in modal and existential terms, i.e. all things necessarily depend for their existence on the existence of primary substances. But this may not be the most plausible manner to interpret Aristotle's views on ontological dependence. Indeed, Aristotle himself was not unaware of the various ways that ontological dependence could manifest itself (Corkum 2008, 75). So, although Aristotle can sometimes be seen to use a modal characterization of ontological dependence (for instance in *Categories* 14a30–35), this does not mean that such a characterization is always correct. In particular, it gives implausible results when applied to essence and existence. Corkum's recent account is helpful here:[5]

> Aristotle is generally less concerned with the question of what things exist than we might expect. His ontological concerns are typically with such questions as, given the things which we call beings, in virtue of what does each such thing have claim to this ontological status? For example, this is Aristotle's concern with respect to mathematical objects: the philosophical question is not whether such things exist but how they do: see *Meta.* 1076a36–37. (2008, 76.)

This type of reading has received plenty of support recently. For instance, Peramatzis (2011, 203 ff.) also argues that a non-existential reading of Aristotelian ontological priority is more plausible, and Koslicki (2012b) abandons the existential reading at the outset. Peramatzis further points out that the modal formulation of Aristotelian ontological priority can be grounded in the non-modal, essentialist characterization, i.e. the "how" question described by Corkum. This can be considered to further support the idea that essence precedes existence, as suggested in the previous section.

How does the notion of essence tie in with Aristotelian priority? According to Ferejohn (2003, 327), one of Aristotle's central concerns in the *Metaphysics* is to determine what the fundamental entities are, or *how* they are. Ontologically independent, fundamental entities are (primary) substances – of which *forms* are the key example. Here, we once again encounter essences, for Aristotle says that "By form I mean the essence of each thing and its primary substance" (1032b1–2).[6] On a related note, Tierney (2004, 7–8) specifies that the *ti esti* ("what it is") of a substance, i.e. the essence or form of a substance, is a metaphysical primitive. The significance of this observation lies in the fact that the Aristotelian notion of essence cannot be defined in terms of other concepts or in virtue of the necessary features of a thing (Tierney 2004, 8, fn. 23). Finally, I draw on Yu (2003), who asserts that "The identity of form and essence unambiguously shows that the contest for the title of primary substance is not between form (which is one subdivision of subject) and essence" (p. 97).

Essences have the status of primary substances in Aristotle and are hence a natural candidate for the subject matter of first philosophy. But note that essences are not the ultimate ground of reality in the sense that Schaffer talks about ultimate ground. Essences should be understood as answering the *ti esti* question, which may include an account of what grounds the existence of an entity, but essences themselves are primitive for Aristotle and are hence not grounded in anything else. In one sense, essences are certainly fundamental, but they are not fundamental *entities*; rather, they are a part of Aristotle's fundamental *ideology*, and in this respect the notion of fundamentality applicable to Aristotle may be closer to Sider's ideological fundamentality: instead of a mereological "bottom level", as with Schaffer's entity-fundamentality, we are interested in the *ideological* "bottom level" of Aristotle's ontology (cf. Sider 2011: vii). The notion of ideology has a Quinean origin; it concerns a theory's choice of primitive notions.[7]

There is a continuity between the Aristotelian, primitive non-modal conception of essence and the neo-Aristotelian characterization of essence popularized in particular by Kit Fine (e.g. 1994, 1995a, 1995b, 1995c), although there are surely some differences between Fine's and Aristotle's accounts. I will not concern myself with an analysis of these differences, for they have already been discussed extensively (e.g. Klima 2002, Peramatzis 2011, Koslicki 2012a, Corkum forthcoming). All I wish to conclude from this section is that it is legitimate to understand Aristotelian priority in terms of essence. This analysis is certainly related to those of Schaffer, Fine, Koslicki, and many others, but I lack the space to discuss their accounts in detail. Rather, I will proceed to present my own account of metaphysics as the first philosophy, drawing on the previous discussions and Lowe's work in particular.

## 4   The science of essence as the first philosophy

We now have the beginnings of an account of essence as the subject matter of first philosophy, so it is time to explicate the study of essence itself. The starting point of my proposed conception of essence is the idea that *essence precedes existence*. The picture that I will present is inspired by Aristotle – it might be called neo-Aristotelian – but the goal is not to be faithful to Aristotle. I hope to present what I believe to be the correct account of the role of essence in metaphysics and, as it turns out, this also provides a natural understanding of metaphysics as the first philosophy. Of contemporary accounts, Lowe's (who draws extensively on Fine in this connection) is perhaps closest to the one that I am about to present. Indeed, he coins the phrase "essence precedes existence" as follows:

> [I]n general, *essence precedes existence*. And by this I mean that the former precedes the latter both *ontologically* and *epistemically*. That is to say, on the one hand, I mean that it is a precondition of something's existing that its essence – along with the essences of other existing things – does not preclude its existence. And, on the other hand [...] I mean that we can in general *know* the essence of something X antecedently to knowing whether or not X exists. Otherwise, it seems to me, we could never find out *that* something exists. For how could we find out *that* something, X, exists before knowing *what X is* – before knowing, that is, *what it is* whose existence we have supposedly discovered. (Lowe 2008, 40.)

This conception of essence has a number of important ramifications, which ought to be stated explicitly. Firstly, essences themselves are not entities. The importance of noting this is highlighted by another central assumption, namely that all entities must have an essence. This is just to say that an entity must have a determinable set of existence, identity and persistence conditions, whether or not we know these conditions in full. Now, if essences themselves were entities, this would produce an infinite regress of a rather vicious sort, since essences themselves, being entities, would have to have essences, and so on. So, if a thing exists, it must have an essence, but to have an essence is simply to have a real definition. In fact, since I think that non-existent entities can have essences, we can say even more, namely, that every metaphysically possible entity must have an essence. I should also mention that I do not think that it makes sense to talk about the essence of something precluding its existence. Here is why: for a thing to be metaphysically possible, it must be possible that it *could* have existed. A thing whose essence precludes its (possible) existence is contradictory – I take it that a set of existence conditions which precludes existence altogether is impossible. Thus, goatstags, insofar as they *could* exist, also have essences. In many cases, we also know the essences of non-existent things.

A brief note about the connection between my understanding of essence and grounding is also in order. The essence of a thing is not meant to refer to the ultimate or fundamental ground of being of a thing. Rather, it just refers to *being*, i.e. what it is, or would be, for a thing to exist. The existence of a given thing can and will, of course, depend on the existence of other things, unless it is ontologically independent (and at least on one view, these facts about existential dependence may be grounded in the essence of the thing).[8] But essence itself should not be considered as the ultimate or fundamental ground of the being of the entity whose essence it is. I prefer to think of essence more as a statement of what the being of the entity consists in; its existence, identity, and persistence conditions. Depending on one's view, it may or may not be part of the essence of a thing that its existence is grounded in the existence of some fundamental things, that is, whether or not facts about what grounds what are themselves grounded in the essences of things. We do not need to settle these questions here though.

Lowe's account of essence is probably closest to my own, but there are some important points of difference between our views. The most crucial of these differences involves the relationship between essence and modality. I agree with Lowe and Fine on the ontological order of explanation between essence and modality. So do Aristotle and the majority of the commentators I have referred to above. But I consider the epistemic order of explanation to be debatable. Let me elaborate.

The ontological relationship between essence and modality that I subscribe to suggests that not all necessary truths about a given object $X$ are essential truths about $X$, but all necessary truths are grounded in essential truths (about something or other). This implies that essential truths about $X$ are a proper subset of the necessary truths about $X$, but even those necessary truths about $X$ that are not essential truths *about* $X$ are nevertheless essential truths about something. We can illustrate this with Fine's (1994) classic example of Socrates and his singleton: Socrates is necessarily a member of singleton Socrates, but this does not appear to be essential *for Socrates*. Rather, it is part of the essence of sets that they have their members essentially, and hence true in virtue of the nature of sets that Socrates belongs to singleton Socrates. This is the type of confusion about essentiality and necessity that Fine is attempting to weed out. Moreover, according to this view, essence is ontologically prior to modality in the sense that essential truths are more fundamental than modal truths. Finally, it is also important to note that on this view, we should *not* reduce essence to *de re* modal properties.

On the epistemic side, things are murkier. Lowe (e.g. forthcoming) is of the opinion that our epistemic access to essence is direct and *a priori*, and generally within everyone's capabilities. However, some (e.g. Oderberg 2007, 2011) would contest this and favor *a posteriori* access to essence; this approach is commonly associated with the idea that science discovers essences. There are good reasons to think that Aristotle himself would be more amenable to the latter line, although I should note that Lowe makes no claim to the effect that his view is the Aristotelian one. Indeed, even the essentialist tradition due to the work of Kripke and Putnam is perhaps more faithful to Aristotle in this regard. Be that as it may, I side with Lowe, at least to the extent that the science of essence must be an *a priori* discipline. Lowe (forthcoming) claims that the *a posteriori* essentialists are mistaken in their claim that we "discover" essences empirically. He considers the Aristotelian real definition, i.e. essence, to provide a type of formula for a thing or a kind of thing, which may or may not manifest in the actual world.

Where I differ from Lowe is on the nature of our *a priori* access to essence, as I consider it to be indirect. Specifically, I hold that we have direct *a priori* access to modal truths rather than essentialist truths. Further, since I take all modal truths to be grounded in essentialist truths, there is a necessary link between modal truths and essentialist truths. So, compared to Lowe's approach, I propose to reverse the epistemic order of essence and modality. I develop this account in detail elsewhere (Tahko ms. A); here, I wish to focus on a caveat for any account according to which modality is epistemically prior to essence. The caveat is that we must have some means to determine which of the necessary truths concerning an object are essentialist truths about that object. As the formulation of the relationship between essence and modality proposed above suggests, essentialist truths are a proper subset of necessary truths, and we need some criteria to identify this subset. Furthermore, the criteria that we use to determine this should not assume previous knowledge of essentialist facts, for otherwise the view would collapse into pure *a priori* essentialism.[9] This is, of course, familiar already from Aristotle, who holds that there are necessary, but inessential, properties called *propria*. *Propria* do not tell us what a thing is, i.e. they do not answer the *ti esti* question, or Corkum's "how" question (that is, how a thing exists).[10] However, it appears that for Aristotle this problem does not arise in a similar manner, for it is always (empirical) science that determines the real definition. I will offer the beginnings of a solution to this problem – call it "the problem of *propria*" – in what follows.

My solution begins with the assumption that we have *a priori* access to metaphysical possibility, and it is via this modal knowledge that we access the essences of all possible kinds of entities, whether they exist in the actual world or not. This process is empirically indefeasible in the sense that it only concerns *possibilities*. It is an empirical question, which of these possibilities correspond with the actual world. For instance, provided that Euclidean geometry is consistent, it is one possible scenario of what the actual geometry of the world could be like, among the other alternative geometries.[11] There is still a modal fact at play here, and it must also be grounded in essence. Since the picture at hand accommodates the essences of non-existing things as well, there is nothing strange about there being essentialist facts that ground non-actual geometries.

We can use Aristotle's own example – that of a goatstag – to illustrate the problem of *propria*. As we saw in Section 2, despite Aristotle's initial skepticism about anyone being able to know what a goatstag is, there are some suggestions in the *Posterior Analytics* to the effect that just being able to use the nominal definition of a goatstag entails there being some previous hold on what the thing in question is. I consider it plausible that this previous understanding consists of modal knowledge. Specifically, we are interested in the set of essential properties that could manifest in a thing like goatstag, were such a thing to exist. Of course, not just any combination of properties is possible, for some of these properties are mutually exclusive (e.g. round and square). We must first rule out the *impossible* combinations of properties, which delimit the space of possible kinds of objects to those that at least could have existed. It seems that even Aristotle himself considers goatstags to be possible in this sense, although we saw that because Aristotelian species are eternal, he would consider all things that do not exist to be impossible. Yet, if we can know what the name "goatstag" signifies, as Aristotle acknowledges, then it seems that at least *some* grasp of what goatstags are, or would be, is required. This is certainly the conclusion that Lowe's analysis suggests:

> To know something's essence is not to be acquainted with some *further thing* of a special kind, but simply to understand *what exactly that thing is*. This, indeed, is why knowledge of essence is possible, for

it is a product simply of *understanding* – not of empirical observation, much less of some mysterious kind of quasiperceptual acquaintance with esoteric entities of any sort. And, on pain of incoherence, we cannot deny that we understand what at least some things are, and thereby know their essences. (Lowe 2008: 39.)

According to this analysis, some knowledge of the essence of a goat-stag is needed in order to even understand what is being said when one hears someone talking about a goatstag. Lowe, (forthcoming, [17–18]) in fact, suggests that understanding *what a thing is* just means understanding the proposition that expresses the real definition of the thing. He does not say all that much about what propositions expressing real definitions are like, but it is not implausible that they list the existence, identity, and persistence conditions of things. Of course, in some cases, the existence conditions may not be satisfied in actuality – because the thing may not exist – but listing these conditions is a crucial part of expressing the essence of a thing.

The link between grasping the essence of a thing with *understanding* what a thing is, proposed by Lowe, rests on the idea that some previous knowledge of essence is required in order to comprehendingly talk about, say, goatstags. However, it does appear that there must be something more to essence than just the bundle of the existence, identity and persistence conditions of things, for how are we supposed to know which object a given set of such conditions is associated with?

Indeed, this the heart of the problem of *propria*. Specifically, what is it about a set of necessary properties that makes it the essence of a thing, when we know that there are *propria*, i.e. necessary properties which are not essential? A given member of a natural kind must have a certain set of essential properties to qualify as a member of that kind, but what determines the essence of the kind? Oderberg (2011, 97) introduces a unifying *a priori* principle, unique to each kind, in order to establish this link, but I have my doubts about this move. If each object is associated with a unique unifying principle, then the unifying principle itself is starting to look very much like the essence, and it is not at all clear to me that this helps in addressing the epistemic problem. Let me use another example to illustrate the problem and sketch a potential solution.

## 5   Case study: the Higgs boson

If you have not heard the news yet, the discovery of the Higgs boson was announced on July 4th 2012 by two independent teams working at

CERN in Switzerland. More information regarding the discovery is to be expected in the coming months and years, but at the time of writing, the situation is as follows:[12]

- A new boson has been discovered in the mass range ~125–126 GeV.
- This falls within the expected mass range of the Higgs boson.
- The Higgs boson was originally postulated in the 1960s to help to explain how particles get their mass.
- Actually, it is the Higgs *field* that would do this.
- Physicists knew already before the discovery that there is something like a Higgs field or fields that would serve this explanatory purpose.
- The only way to study this field, or fields, is to study the Higgs boson(s) (which is/are not directly observable either).
- The Standard Model of Quantum Mechanics predicts one type of Higgs, the Standard Model Higgs, but the discovered particle might not be the Standard Model Higgs; this depends on the particle's properties, such as spin.

In short, physicists knew that there must be something like the Higgs field which is responsible for the mass of things like W and Z bosons – elementary particles that had already been discovered. Physicists wish to study the properties of this field, which can be done by finding and studying the corresponding Higgs boson. The Higgs field might not be elementary; it could be composed of several other fields, each of which would have a corresponding Higgs boson. Many of the details will not matter for our purposes, but a few things are crucial. In particular, we know of a number of *possible* combinations of particles and fields that would explain our current empirical data.

What I wish to focus on is the relevance of the *existence* of the Higgs boson(s), while keeping in mind that the discovered particle might *not* be the Standard Model Higgs. We know that whatever the arrangement of elementary fields and particles is, they manifest themselves in such a way that we observe massive particles like W and Z bosons. Hence, we are primarily interested in an *explanation* for previous data, that is, we want to understand the mechanism which is responsible for the emergence of massive particles (i.e. the Higgs mechanism). To this end, it makes little difference whether the Higgs boson exists. The experiments at the Large Hadron Collider at CERN are designed to reveal us something more about the nature of the Higgs field or fields, and we already know of the existence of something like the Higgs field(s). Now it seems that at least one type of Higgs boson has been discovered, but at the time of writing it is unclear what its properties are. We know that it is a boson, and hence has an integer spin, but only a scalar boson (i.e. a boson with a spin of zero) could serve the postulated role in the Standard Model. All this was clear before any confirmation of the existence of the Higgs boson(s).

It is not difficult to see where I am going with this example. Firstly, I consider it a real-life example of how knowledge of essence can precede knowledge of existence. But it is more than that, for there is also an implicit solution to the problem of *propria* here. Specifically, how do we know that theoretical physicists are talking about the same thing when they debate the properties and the existence of the Higgs boson(s)? That is, how do we know that the properties are essential to that kind of thing instead of some other kind of thing, especially if we do not even know whether there is only a single Higgs, or several? There is certainly some common ground between the disputants, such as the Standard Model, but that is hardly sufficient to ensure that they are indeed talking about the same *thing*. In fact, I do not think that it is even necessary. Here is why: there are numerous *candidate essences* that are able to fulfill the explanatory role that the Higgs boson(s) play, and not all of them conform to the Standard Model. By the time you read this, we may already know whether the recently discovered boson is the Standard Model Higgs, but at the time of writing all these options were still open.

We have a reasonably good idea as to what would explain the empirical data that we currently have. Among other things, we have already observed W and Z bosons and other massive particles. It turns out that unless *something like* the Higgs field(s) is postulated, the Standard Model will have to be abandoned (at least in part). So, the need to postulate the Higgs field(s) stems from the conviction that the Standard Model must be saved. But the Higgs field(s) cannot be observed directly, nor can the Higgs boson(s): we can only infer its/their existence from decay products. So, we looked for evidence of the Higgs boson(s) via their decay products, and the existence of the Higgs entails the existence of the corresponding field(s). However, I suggest that it is the *explanation* – not the *existence* of something or other – that guarantees a common ground between physicists working on the Higgs.

When the search for the Higgs began, its possible mass range was fairly wide. The LHC ruled out chunks of it little by little, finally arriving at ~125–126 GeV. But all of the specific masses in the original range were possible (essential) properties of the kind of thing that we were looking for. I venture to suggest that we must have known what *kind* of thing would explain the data before we were able to systematically look for evidence for its existence. It could have turned out that it is a *merely possible* kind of thing, and it could still turn out that the Higgs field is not elementary and instead consists of a number of other fields. But even in this case, we had a previous grasp of the essences of the other possible kinds of things that would have explained the data, though no such things exist. So, the explanation we are looking for is connected with the kind(s) of thing(s) that occupies (or occupy) an appropriate explanatory role.

How does this help to solve the problem of *propria*? Well, since our epistemic access is to possible rather than actual essences, a crucial part of our inquiry is listing the different possible combinations of (logically compatible) necessary features which may or may not be unified into a genuine, actual kind. Ultimately, it is the task of empirical science to determine which of the candidate essences that we conjecture are actual essences, that is, which combinations of essential features make up genuine kinds. This is exactly what we see in the case of the Higgs boson(s): we had a list of candidate essences compatible with current empirical data, consisting of sets of necessary properties. What unifies these sets of necessary properties into kind essences is the explanatory role that they play in the context of the broader theory. The role of the Higgs field(s) is to give particles their mass, regardless of whether the Higgs field is elementary and whether there is more than one Higgs boson. This enables us to determine the candidate essences, i.e. the different combinations of properties that would enable the role that the Higgs field(s) play. The genuine, actual essences must be determined with the help of empirical evidence. Notice that I do not say *discovered*, because the role of the empirical work is merely to confirm which of the candidate essences are genuine. Hence, the problem of *propria* will ultimately be addressed by empirical science, but not without a prior study of the candidate essences. Importantly, this process is fallibilistic: We can only make an educated guess about which essences are genuine. Science determines whether we guessed correctly, but science is, of course, subject to revision as well. The existence of the Higgs boson has now been confirmed to 5.0 sigma significance, i.e. to a level of certainty up to five standard deviations. In statistical terms, this means a probability of less than one in a million that the observed phenomenon is produced by something else than the Higgs, namely statistical fluctuation. But, if further empirical information emerges, we can always revise the picture.

In sum, our epistemic access to essence is a piecemeal, complex matter, yet a necessary precursor of philosophical and scientific knowledge.

# 6  Conclusion

I trust that the reader has not lost sight of our original topic. The understanding of metaphysics as the first philosophy that I have presented rests on the idea that metaphysics is the science of essence. In Section 2, we saw that it is not unreasonable to attribute this view to Aristotle. Contemporary metaphysicians have different views about how to understand the relationship between essence and the now-popular topics of fundamentality, grounding, and ontological dependence, discussed in Section 3. I attempted to demonstrate that all of these notions can be tied to Aristotle and especially his discussion of priority, even if the contemporary discussion is not entirely continuous with Aristotle. In any case, the notion of essence has a central role here. What the science of essence amounts to is somewhat more controversial. I have only been able to provide a glimpse into the topic here, but I hope that this has been sufficient to motivate further research into this emerging field. I side with Lowe in that I consider essence to precede existence (ontologically), and in Section 4 I attempted to defend this idea, which may or may not be faithful to Aristotle. I make no exegetical claims in this regard, but as we saw, there may be some reasons to think that this idea can be reconciled with the passages in *Posterior Analytics* that are seemingly opposed to it. Finally, in Section 5, I took an example from theoretical physics to illustrate the science of essence as I understand it. We saw that even though the study of essence takes epistemic priority, the picture would not be complete without empirical input. This I believe to be a point in accordance with the Aristotelian line, as it is clear that natural science plays an important part in Aristotle's metaphysics.

One might perhaps object that the label "first philosophy" is not entirely accurate for the account I have presented, for metaphysics and natural science could be considered to be parallel, or to complement each other. But this would be to ignore the Aristotelian roots of the notion of "first philosophy", which, as I have demonstrated, are amenable to such an understanding. What makes metaphysics the first philosophy is its ontological as well as epistemic priority over natural science rather than complete independence of empirical science.

## Notes

I would like to thank Tommy Kivatinos, Kathrin Koslicki, and Mika Perälä for comments and discussion regarding many central topics of this essay.

1. For some discussion of these methodological challenges with actual Aristotle exegesis, see Ferejohn (2003).
2. See, for instance, Witt (1989), Scaltsas (1994), and Koslicki (this volume) for more discussion of the notion of substance.
3. See Bodnar (2012), and also Witt (1989, 144ff.) and Cohen (2009). I would like to thank Kathrin Koslicki for useful discussions regarding this issue. Some further support for my reading can be found from David Charles (2000), who discusses Aristotle's conception of species in much more detail (e.g. 2000, 25).
4. See the essays in Correia and Schnieder (2012) for a comprehensive overview of the topic.
5. However, see Corkum (forthcoming) for some more hesitant remarks on Aristotle's views regarding existence.
6. See also Yu (2003, 105ff.) and Wedin (2000, 197ff.) on the identity of form and essence.
7. I consider there to be a significant chasm between Aristotelianism and Quineanism, but in this case the Quinean notion of ideology serves an illustrative purpose.
8. For further discussion, see Dasgupta (ms.).
9. This is related to the problem of unifying a set of essential properties into, say, a kind essence: there should be something to hold a set of essential properties together in order to ensure that the essential properties of a given kind are always featured in the members of that kind. Oderberg (2011, 90) calls this "the unity problem", but sometimes it is also called "the problem of complex essences" (e.g. Dumsday 2010). Since my emphasis is slightly different, I will adopt another name for the (interrelated) problem(s): "the problem of *propria*".
10. See also Corkum (forthcoming, [17]), as well as Fine (1994) and Koslicki (2012a).
11. See Tahko (ms. B) for further discussion.
12. For a more comprehensive survey and future updates, see Matt Strassler's "Higgs FAQ", URL = <http://profmattstrassler.com/articles-and-posts/the-higgs-particle/360–2/>.

# References

J. Barnes (ed.) 1984. *The Complete Works of Aristotle, The Revised Oxford Translation* (Princeton: Princeton University Press).

I. Bodnar. 2012. "Aristotle's Natural Philosophy," *The Stanford Encyclopedia of Philosophy (Spring 2012 Edition)*, Edward N. Zalta (ed.) URL = http://plato.stanford.edu/archives/spr2012/entries/aristotle-natphil/.

R. Bolton. 1976. "Essentialism and Semantic Theory in Aristotle," *The Philosophical Review* 85 (4): 514–44.

D. Charles. 2000. *Aristotle on Meaning and Essence* (Oxford: Clarendon Press).

S. M. Cohen (2009) "Aristotle's Metaphysics," *The Stanford Encyclopedia of Philosophy (Spring 2009 Edition)*, Edward N. Zalta (ed.) URL = http://plato.stanford.edu/archives/spr2009/entries/aristotle-metaphysics/.

P. Corkum. 2008. "Aristotle on Ontological Dependence," *Phronesis* 53: 65–92.

_____ forthcoming. "Substance and Independence in Aristotle," in B. Schnieder, A. Steinberg and M. Hoeltje (eds), *Ontological Dependence, Supervenience, and Response-Dependence*, Basic Philosophical Concepts Series (Munich: Philosophia Verlag).

F. Correia and B. Schnieder. (eds.) 2012. *Metaphysical Grounding* (Cambridge: Cambridge University Press).

S. Dasgupta (ms.) "The Status of Ground," draft of November 2011.

D. Demoss and D. Devereux. 1988. "Essence, Existence, and Nominal Definition in Aristotle's 'Posterior Analytics' II 8–10", *Phronesis* 33: 133–54.

T. Dumsday. 2010. "Natural Kinds and the Problem of Complex Essences," *Australasian Journal of Philosophy* 88 (4): 619–34.

M.T. Ferejohn. 2003. "Logical and Physical Inquiries in Aristotle's Metaphysics," *The Modern Schoolman* LXXX, 325–50.

K. Fine. 1994. "Essence and Modality," *Philosophical Perspectives* 8 (Logic and Language), 1–16.

_____ 1995a. "Ontological Dependence," *Proceedings of the Aristotelian Society* 95: 269–90.

_____ 1995b. "Senses of Essence," in W. Sinnott-Armstrong, D. Raffman and N. Asher (eds), *Modality, Morality, and Belief, Essays in Honor of Ruth Barcan Marcus* (Cambridge: Cambridge University Press), pp. 53–73.

_____ 1995c. "The Logic of Essence," *Journal of Philosophical Logic* 24: 241–73.

_____ 2012. "What is Metaphysics?" in T. E. Tahko (ed.) *Contemporary Aristotelian Metaphysics* (Cambridge: Cambridge University Press), pp. 8–25.

G. Klima. 2002. "Contemporary 'Essentialism' vs. Aristotelian Essentialism" in J. Haldane (ed.) *Mind, Metaphysics, and Value in the Thomistic and Analytical Traditions* (Notre Dame, IN: Notre Dame University Press), pp. 175–94.

K. Koslicki. 2012a. "Essence, Necessity and Explanation" in T. E. Tahko (ed.) *Contemporary Aristotelian Metaphysics* (Cambridge: Cambridge University Press), pp. 187–206.

_____ 2012b. "Varieties of Ontological Dependence" in F. Correia and B. Schnieder (eds), *Metaphysical Grounding* (Cambridge: Cambridge University Press).

_____ this volume. "Substance, Independence and Unity."

E. J. Lowe. 2008. "Two Notions of Being: Entity and Essence," *Royal Institute of Philosophy Supplements* 83 (62): 23–48.

_____ 2011. "Locke on Real Essence and Water as a Natural Kind: A Qualified Defence," *Aristotelian Society Supplementary Volume* 85 (1), 1–19.

_____ forthcoming. "Grasp of Essences versus Intuitions: An Unequal Contest," in T. Booth and D. Rowbottom (eds), *Intuitions* (Oxford: Oxford University Press).

D. Oderberg. 2007. *Real Essentialism* (London and New York: Routledge).

_____ 2011. "Essence and Properties," *Erkenntnis* 75: 85–111.

M. Peramatzis. 2011. *Priority in Aristotle's Metaphysics* (Oxford: Oxford University Press).

T. Scaltsas. 1994. *Substances and Universals in Aristotle's "Metaphysics"* (Ithaca and London: Cornell University Press).

J. Schaffer. 2009. "On What Grounds What," in D. Manley, D. J. Chalmers, and R. Wasserman (eds), *Metametaphysics: New Essays on the Foundations of Ontology* (Oxford University Press), pp. 347–83.

T. Sider. 2011. *Writing the Book of the World* (Oxford: Oxford University Press).

T. E. Tahko. 2012. "In Defence of Aristotelian Metaphysics," in T. E. Tahko (ed.) *Contemporary Aristotelian Metaphysics* (Cambridge: Cambridge University Press), pp. 26–43.

_____ (ms. A) "The Epistemology of Essence," URL = http://www.ttahko.net/papers/epistofessence.pdf.

_____ (ms. B) "Euclidean Geometry and the A Priori," URL = http://www.ttahko.net/papers/euclid.pdf.

R. L. Tierney. 2004. "The Scope of Aristotle's Essentialism in the Posterior Analytics," *Journal of the History of Philosophy* 42 (1): 1–20.

M. V. Wedin. 2000. *Aristotle's Theory of Substance* (Oxford: Oxford University Press).

C. Witt. 1989. *Substance and Essence in Aristotle* (Ithaca and London: Cornell University Press).

J. Yu. 2003. *The Structure of Being in Aristotle's Metaphysics* (Dordrecht: Kluwer).

# 5

# Two Doctrines of Categories in Aristotle: *Topics, Categories, and Metaphysics*

*Robert Bolton*

## 1 Introduction

The aim of this chapter is to offer support for the view – one contrary to the main tradition represented by Alexander and most more recent commentators – that there are, in fact, two different sets and two different, and incompatible, doctrines of *categories* in Aristotle. I do not have in mind here any difference between the *Categories*, or the *Organon*, and the *Metaphysics*. Rather, both doctrines are present in the *Organon* and even in a single chapter of the *Organon*, *Topics* I.9. The proper explanation for this striking fact is not, as some would suggest, historical or developmental – that one doctrine came earlier in Aristotle's thinking, the other later. Nor is it, as others have suggested, that both doctrines need to be mastered to adequately employ dialectic, so that both are present in the *Topics*. Instead, as we shall see, one doctrine, for Aristotle, is precisely suited to the needs of the art of reasoning *kata doxan*, i.e. to the practice of dialectic, the other to procedure *kat' aletheian*, or to the needs and the practice of science, indeed of metaphysical science. I go on to consider a main question for this result, one whose proper resolution helps us to understand better Aristotle's scientific method overall and the special, if limited, role of dialectic in it. I begin by developing a problem for the interpretation of *Topics* I.9.

## 2 *Kategoriai* in Aristotle's *Topics*

At the beginning of *Topics* I.9 Aristotle tells us that "it is necessary" (*dei*) at that point in his discussion to provide a complete list of all of the kinds or classes (*gene*) that compose the *kategoriai*. (103b20–21) Thus, he continues:

> These kinds [that compose the *kategoriai*] are ten in number: what something is (*ti esti*) quantity, quality, relative, place, time, position, state, action and affection. (103b20–23)

The reason for the *necessity* for providing this complete list of *kategoriai*, for Aristotle's purposes here, is then immediately explained by him, quite precisely, as follows:

> *For* [i.e. the reason for the necessity for introducing these *kategoriai* here is that] an accident, a genus, a *proprium* (*idion*) and a definition (*horismos*) will *always* be in one of these *kategoriai* since all [dialectical] premises which employ them [i.e. all premises which employ an accident, a genus, a *proprium* or a definition as predicate] will indicate either what something is (*ti esti*), or a quantity, or a quality [of it] or something from one of the other *kategoriai*. (103b23–27; cf. b20–21)

Here, Aristotle tells us *why* it is necessary, here in *Topics* I.9, to list these *kategoriai*. As his remark reminds us, in earlier chapters of *Topics* I Aristotle has been describing the general nature of dialectical argumentation, and he has already restricted dialectical problems and premises to propositions (introduced in questions) in which either an accident, a genus, a *proprium* or a definition is ascribed as predicate to some subject. (I.4 101b17–36, 8 103b3ff) These *four* types or classes of things are, of course, known traditionally as the four *praedicamenta* or *predicables* because they are classes made up of the entities which can serve as predicates, or as things predicated of subjects, in standard dialectical discourse. In *Topics* I.9 then, Aristotle tells us further, in the passage just quoted, that whenever anything of any one of these four types of predicable is introduced and ascribed to some subject, what is introduced will also always be either what that thing is, or a quantity or a quality of it, or something from one of the other *kategoriai* just mentioned. This makes it unmistakably clear, to begin with, that the things which are "in" and thus *belong to* the *kategoriai*, as that term is used here in the opening lines of *Topics* I.9, are such things as particular accidents, genera and *propria* – for instance, so Aristotle offers us, the genus *animal* or the accident *white*. (I.4 101b30–31, 5 102b8) This makes it quite appropriate to follow those commentators who understand the *kategoriai* here as types of *predicates*, in the sense not of predicate *expressions* or other linguistic items, but of *things* which *belong to* subjects in the way in which accidents, genera and *propria* do. These entities, such as for instance the genus or kind *animal* or the accident *white*, are not linguistic items. Nor are they dependent as such on linguistic items, though they *are* suitable for introduction and treatment in language by means of them. We do not typically think of *definitions* as *entities* on a par with accidents, *propria* and genera. This shows us that the terms *horismos* or *horos*, both of which Aristotle uses here, are better translated as *definiens* or *definer* rather than as *definition*. Aristotle's examples, such as *pedestrian biped animal*, fit this construal. (I.4 101b30–31.) The kind *pedestrian biped animal* is as much a non-linguistic entity as is the kind animal. The term *definition* will thus be used here in this sense of a definer.

   This interpretation of what the members of these *kategoriai* are follows Aristotle's own earlier usage in *Topics* I where he describes an accident, a genus, a *proprium* or a definer as a *kategoroumenon*, i.e. as something which can be predicated of or attributed to something or other. (See I.8 103b8, I.5 102b20; cf. *Int* 7 17a38f) On the other hand, the alternate suggestion of some that the *kategoriai* introduced here at the beginning of *Topics* I.9 are types of *predication*, or other linguistic items, not types of things predicated or predicables, does not easily fit with this since particular accidents, such as the white color attributable to some particular horse (I.5 102b7–9), clearly are not examples of predications or other linguistic entities.[1] (Linguistic entities, e.g. predications, are, of course, themselves things, e.g. actions or speech acts, and as such entities in the category of action (*poiein*), but they are hardly the only things categorized in *Top* I.4–9).

   However, if the ten *kategoriai* here are ten types of *things* attributable to subjects, just as the four classes of so-called *predicables* are, then the question immediately arises as to how *this* doctrine of ten *categories*, as Aristotle explicitly labels it, is related to doctrines found in the work we call the *Categories*, particularly the doctrine found in Chapter 4 of that work, where we are also famously introduced to a very similar, but not identical, list of ten types, again, apparently, not of predication, or other linguistic items, but of *things* (*onta*), Aristotle says, that may be treated in discourse. (1b25–27 with 2 1a20ff). But before we move too quickly to address that issue, it is crucial to be completely clear on what the *role* is of the doctrine of the ten categories listed at the beginning of *Topics* I.9, and on what the necessity for it is for Aristotle's purposes there, since if its role and the need for it there turn out to be quite different from those of the ten types of things listed in *Categories* 4, that will clearly be important for assessing the relation between the two texts and the doctrines that they present.

As we have already noted, the doctrine of the ten categories introduced at the beginning of *Topics* I.9 is explicitly presented as a *necessary complement* to the doctrine of the predicables. It is the latter which is Aristotle's real object of concern throughout I.4–9 as one can easily see, for instance, from a comparison of the opening of I.4 (101b11–19) with the conclusion of I.9. (103b39–104a2) The importance of the doctrine of the predicables is, of course, that the whole of traditional skilled dialectical practice, as Aristotle codifies it in the *Topics*, depends on the mastery and application of this doctrine. As we have already seen, Aristotle says that every dialectical premise (*protasis*) and problem (*problema*) *reveals* or *indicates* (*deloi* or *semainei*) either a genus or the definition, or a *proprium* or a contingent accident, of some subject. (I.4 101b17–25, 8 103b3ff; cf. 5 102b4ff)

He does not mean by this that to qualify as a genuine dialectical premise a proposition must introduce the *true* genus, or definition, of some subject, since genuine dialectical premises may be false. (I.1 100a25ff, VIII. 11 161a28) He means, rather, that each such premise or problem put forward in dialectic is standardly *understood to introduce* something from just one of these four kinds of predicable by the participants in the given dialectical encounter. So, to discuss any question or *problema* dialectically, e.g. whether pleasure is choiceworthy or not (I.11 104b7), one must first determine what kind of predicate or predicable this *problema* indicates or is understood to introduce. Are we concerned with the question whether choiceworthiness is an *accident* of pleasure, or a *proprium* of pleasure, or its *genus*, or its *definition*? We must first settle this before we can proceed to deploy the various dialectical *topoi*, or lines of skilled dialectical examination and argument, catalogued in *Topics* II-VII, since these are centrally geared to the discussion of a question when understood in just one or another of these four specific ways. The need for, and thus the *role* of, the doctrine of the ten categories introduced at the beginning of *Topics* I.9, then, is to aid in guiding discussion on that basis. If we then ask why, for Aristotle, the doctrine of ten categories here *is* necessary for the implementation of the doctrine of the predicables, he gives us his answer by way of examples. For instance, as he goes on immediately to indicate, if we can learn that an answerer in a dialectical discussion who undertakes to defend the claim that pleasure is something choiceworthy intends to defend this as a claim as to *what pleasure is* (*ti esti*) and thus to attribute to it an item from the first category, of *ti esti*, then we know that he is either making a claim about the *genus* of pleasure or about its *definition* or *definer* and further dialectical discussion can proceed accordingly. As Aristotle says:

> For, each such thing [predicated of a subject in some dialectical problem or premise] indicates *what it is* [and so introduces an item from the category of *ti esti*] either where something is said of itself [i.e. where something is said of the *same* thing, as when a definition of the thing is offered],or where the *genus* [of something] is said of that thing [as when color is said of white]. But when something [e.g. color] is attributed [as predicate] to some *different* thing [such as a body, not a color], it does not indicate what it is but rather a quality or a quantity [of it] or something from the other *kategoriai* [i.e. other than the category of *ti esti*]. (I.9 103b35–39)[2]

So, one can use the fact that some answerer intends to say, e.g., *what* pleasure *is*, and not simply what it is like or how it is related to other things, in maintaining that it is something choiceworthy, to help decide which predicable is in question – namely either genus or definition – in order to know how to proceed further to deal with that claim in the practice of dialectic. The appeal to predicates which do or do not indicate *what* something *is* to identify genera or to disqualify items as genera or ingredients in definitions, or as full definitions, is found very often later in the *Topics*. (See, e.g., I.8 108b22, IV1 120b21ff, IV.2 122a3ff, IV.6 128a13ff, VI.3 153a15ff, VII.3 153a15ff.) Similarly then, Aristotle indicates, if the answerer means not to say of something what that same thing is, but only to characterize by use of a predicate some *different* thing and thus to say only what that thing is like (*poion*), or how it is related to something or to attribute to it some entity from one of the other categories of things that are predicated, other than *ti esti*, then we will know that it is a *proprium* or an *accident* of a certain sort that is in question as predicate in the proposition at hand and we can again continue accordingly. (103b37–39. See also II.2 109a34-b12,II.8 114a13–25.) So, the *necessity*, as Aristotle puts it, for the doctrine of categories as it is introduced at the beginning of *Topics* I.9 derives from the special need for its use to assist in determining what predicable is in play in a given dialectical encounter and to guide discussion on that basis since this is all important if that encounter is to proceed in the dialectically appropriate way.[3] Aristotle may well be thinking that his categorical notions here of what something is, what it is like, or where it is are much more generally intelligible than the more abstruse notions of *proprium*, genus etc., so that these more easily understood categorical notions can be used in dialectical encounters, in ways he indicates, even with members of a general or lay audience, to help channel discussion toward the appropriate predicable. (Cf. VI.4 141b15–19, I.2 101a25–34.)

It is also very clear from the passages quoted above that the classification or sorting of entities into the ten categories, or types of things predicated, listed at the beginning of *Topics* I.9, does not involve a *unique* assignment of any such entity to just one category, but only an assignment with respect to some particular proposal or question for investigation at hand. As Aristotle's own examples make plain, *color* could be introduced in some dialectical problem or premise in order to indicate *what something is*, e.g. what kind of thing white is. (103 b31–33) But color could also clearly be introduced to say what something is like or what sort of quality it has, as when we say that color belongs to a certain body or surface. (b35–39, IV.1 120b12ff at b21ff. Cf. II.2 109a34ff) In the former case, where we say that color belongs to white, color would typically be understood as an entity from the category of *what something is* (*ti esti*), but in the latter case, color would typically be understood instead as an entity from the different category of *quality*. That is, when we say that color belongs to some body, we need not, and normally do not, mean by this that the body *is* a color (though some materialist who thinks that colors are bodies might mean this). We mean that the body *has* color, or is (a) colored (thing).[4] But still it is color, an entity just from the category of quality, that we introduce in order to express what the body is like and what quality it has, just as it is color that we introduce in order to express what something is when we say that color belongs to white, where in this case, however, color is an entity from, and only from, the different category of what something is. So, entities are only identifiable as belonging to, or as bringing into play, one or another of the ten categories listed at the beginning of *Topics* I.9 by appeal, at least in part, to someone's particular intention or to some context of discussion.

Thus, to consider some of Aristotle's examples, if some answerer in a dialectical discussion is maintaining for instance that a certain medicine is good, where this is intended by him to introduce some *quality* of the medicine, or what the medicine is like, then in his claim *good* will indicate or signify a quality, even if the goodness of the medicine is in fact a healing *action* of the medicine not a *quality* of it. (See I.15 107a3–12; cf. VII.1 152a38–39) Or if some answerer maintains that color happens to belong to blue, where color is introduced by him to indicate what blue is like, then color indicates a quality of blue for purposes of that discussion, even if in actual fact a color is *what* blue *is*. (See II.2 109a34ff.) Similarly, if some answerer maintains that all objects of belief are, as a kind, *things that are (onta)*, meaning to indicate *what* objects of belief *are*, and their genus, then *being* or *thing that is (to on)* signifies, for purposes of that discussion, a genus and something in the category of *ti esti* or what something is, even if not all objects of belief are things that are and even if being is not a genus. (See IV.1 121a20ff and further below.) That the answerer is wrong that objects of belief are, as a kind, things that are, and wrong even in supposing that *to on* is a genus, does not affect the fact that, in his claim, *to on* signifies a genus and something in the category of *ti esti*. We need to know this to know just how to try to show dialectically, by use of the *topoi* that concern the appropriate predicable, that his claim *is* wrong. We only show that it is wrong by the proper dialectical standard given that it indicates what something is and a genus in this claim and this is determined in large part by the intentions of the answerer.

These various features and aspects of categorical assignment and membership are quite appropriate to Aristotle's purposes in the *Topics* since, unlike a science or special discipline, including metaphysics or linguistics, dialectic is not restricted in what it may properly consider in any way, either to what is true, or to actual things of a certain specific type or types that are actually related in certain fixed ways, or even to actual things at all. (See IV.1 121a20ff) That the same entity, e.g. color, can on one occasion properly be introduced to express, whether truly or falsely, what something is and on another occasion to express, whether truly or falsely, what something is like is quite suitable to the practice of dialectic. More generally, the practice of dialectic, as Aristotle conceives it, presupposes no positive scientific or specialized doctrine, either metaphysical, linguistic, or otherwise. Aristotle tells us, in *Rhetoric* I.1 for instance, that:

> [Dialectic] concerns the sorts of things which it is, in a certain way, common to absolutely everyone to know and which are based on no *specialized knowledge (aphorismene episteme)*. (1354a1-3, Cf. *SE* 11 172a11-b4)

## 3   Metaphysics in the *Topics*

However, there is one further passage in *Topics* I.9 which might seem to go against the results we have reached so far. In illustrating how entities from the category of *ti esti* can be introduced in dialectical propositions to indicate the genus or definition of something, Aristotle makes the following remarks:

> It is right away clear that someone who indicates [by the predicate which he introduces in some premise] *what something is* will also indicate [by the subject which he introduces in using that premise] sometimes a substance (*ousia*), sometimes a quantity, sometimes a quality, sometimes something from one of the other *kategoriai*. For [to take an example], when a [particular] man is set before someone, and he says that the thing set there *is* a man or an animal, he expresses [by use of his predicate] *what it is* and also indicates [by his subject] a *substance*. But when a white color is set before him and he says that the thing set there is white or is a color he [again] expresses *what it is* but also [this time] indicates a *quality*. (103b27–33)

Although the interpretation of the details of this passage is subject to various disputes it is at least very natural to take it that Aristotle again offers us here, very explicitly, a list of *kategoriai* in the sense not of types of predication, or of other linguistic items, but of kinds of entities, entities such as a man and a color, a list which now, however, includes substances, qualities, quantities, etc. A particular man, for instance, is here taken to be a substance, while white and also color are taken to be qualities. (Cf. IV.1 121a7–9) On this reading, a real subject such as Socrates will *indicate* or *signify*, i.e. will be a sign or indicator of the presence of, a substance while an entity such as the real kind man will signify or be an indicator of a case of what something in fact is. (Things, for Aristotle, as well as names or thoughts, may signify, or be signs or indicators of, other things. *Mete* II.4 361a28, *HA* IV.8 533a11; cf. *APr* II.27 70b7ff.)

It is also very natural to take it that Aristotle is here supposing that it is not anyone's intent or understanding that fixes, either initially, for purposes of discussion, or otherwise, what type of thing it is that is designated, e.g. by the term "the thing before me," or by the term "Socrates", when someone affirms, say when facing Socrates, that the thing before him is a man or that Socrates is a man. The thing in question in either case is a *substance*, an ontologically primary reality, like it or not. Similarly, what is designated by the term "color", when someone says that a certain color before him is white, or is a color, is a *quality*, like it or not. Moreover, each entity in question is *uniquely* a substance or a quality, etc., quite independently of the context of discourse. *Color,* for instance, is not a *quality* as attributed to one sort of thing, e.g. the sea, and a different category of thing altogether as attributed to blue. Color is a quality, and nothing but a quality, not sometimes a quality and sometimes what something is as opposed to a quality. That is, in this passage from *Topics* I.9 Aristotle appears to be introducing a metaphysical doctrine, even one called here a doctrine of categories, seemingly identical to the one that he is often supposed to have on display in the *Categories* itself, as well as in various passages in the *Metaphysics* and elsewhere (e.g. in Z.1 1028a31–34, 4 1030a17ff, 9 1034b7–19, L.4 1070a33ff; cf. *Phys* V.1 225b5–8). On this doctrine of categories, all of the entities that there actually are, or at least all of the entities of a suitably simple sort that there are, fall objectively and uniquely into just one of the fundamental kinds or categories of what there truly is – substance, quality, quantity (*Cat.* 4 1b25ff) In *Categories* 8 (10b17f), though not in fact earlier in the work, it appears that these very kinds are explicitly called *categories*, just as they are here in *Topics* I.9 (103b29).[5]

But even if this very natural reading of this passage in *Topics* I.9 (103b27–33) is correct (and I am very strongly inclined to think that it is correct), this does not conflict either with the remarks about categories with which Aristotle opens *Topics* I.9 or with the remarks about the scientific and ontological neutrality of dialectic which he makes elsewhere. For in this passage, so I would suggest, Aristotle is simply *illustrating* the ontologically neutral remarks with which he opens *Topics* I.9. He has made it clear there that all predicates which are intended by answerers in dialectical discourse to introduce or indicate anything from any of the classes corresponding to the four predicables will also be properly understood by them to indicate either what something is or its quality or its quantity. This is a logical or methodological remark concerning standard dialectical distinctions and procedure, one which derives from what would be generally accepted as a basis for the practice of dialectic, by Aristotle and by others in his philosophical community. Aristotle then goes on to illustrate this remark, in the passage just quoted (103b27ff), by showing how familiar predicates from the predicable *genus* (for instance, *animal* as applied to certain substances such as a particular human being), and *color* as applied to certain qualities such as white, are all standardly taken to indicate what something is. (Cf.103b36–38) He later proceeds to bring out, as we have seen, how typical entities from the predicable *accident*, such as *white*, or *color* as attributed to things other than colors, are standardly taken to indicate a quality or what something is like as opposed to what it is. (103b35–39 with IV.1 120b12ff.)

In giving these examples, Aristotle is not here introducing or presupposing, as a necessary basis for the practice of dialectic, the biological doctrine that the true *genus* of humans is *animal*, and not, for instance, some kind common to all living things, or one common to all material things.[6] This is just a widely familiar view about the genus of humans or about what a human is, which Aristotle can use to effectively illustrate his methodological point. Again, when Aristotle says by way of example in *Top* I.4, that the definition of *man* is *pedestrian biped animal* (101b30–31), he is not presupposing as a rule of or as a necessary basis for dialectic any biological, or even non-biological, doctrine concerning the definition of man. We know, in fact, from *Parts of Animals* I.3 (643b9ff) that Aristotle himself can regard this as a totally inadequate definition by division of the species man. He is, again, only illustrating his rules for the practice of dialectic with a familiar but, for him, perhaps quite faulty example. Similarly then, when Aristotle says that a *man* or an *animal* is *what* a certain *substance* such as a particular man *is* and that a *color* is *what* a certain *quality* such as white *is*, he is not presupposing as a basis for dialectic any doctrines such as are found in *Categories* 2–9, for instance the doctrine that individual human beings are substances, or primary realities, and the doctrine that entities such as white or color, or good or virtue, exist only as non-substantial attributes of such substances and not, say, as substantial Platonic forms or as mere appearances produced by the interactions of the only true substances, namely atoms. He is just drawing for illustrative purposes on the contents of a certain familiar metaphysical doctrine of categories of being, in fact the one found in the *Categories*, in order to help clarify his main methodological claim, made in developing the doctrine of the predicables, that the entities introduced when someone purports to give the genus (or definition) of something in dialectical discussion will indicate *what* the thing *is*, whether that thing happens to be, for instance, a substance or, for instance, a quality, as familiarly sometimes understood.

There is no guarantee even, in *Topics* I.9, that the metaphysical doctrine of categories of being to which Aristotle alludes, according to which, for instance, particular humans are substances and, as such, primary realities, is one which he himself accepts. As we have already noted, in the *Topics* Aristotle can uncritically illustrate claims which he makes about the practice of dialectic with doctrines which he does not accept. In *Topics* V.7, to take another example, Aristotle says that for destructive purposes, you can show that being at rest is not a *proprium* of man by pointing out that being at rest belongs to the Platonic form (*idea*) of man (*autoanthropos*) only *qua* form and not *qua* man. (137b3–13, cf. VI.3 140b2ff) Here Aristotle is not committing himself to the existence of a Platonic form of man. He is only illustrating how to make a certain type of move in dialectic, a move which one might use in arguing, for instance, against a Platonist who holds that there is such a form and who holds that things which apply to a form *qua* form need not, and in some cases cannot, apply to participants in that form. So, the most that we can infer from *Topics* I.9 is that there is a doctrine of categories of being that Aristotle expects his main readers or hearers to be aware of according to which these categories are substance, quantity, quality, etc., and according to which individual human beings are substances and only substances, and colors, and color, too, are non-substantial qualities, and only that, of such substances, a doctrine sufficiently familiar so that Aristotle can use it to effectively illustrate his methodological remarks. The *Topics* tells us nothing definite about Aristotle's own philosophical views on the categories of being or their contents, and thus it cannot serve as the basis for any conjectures about the development or lack thereof of Aristotle's own metaphysics.

## 4   Two doctrines of categories in Aristotle's *Topics*

From our discussion thus far, then, it is clear I believe – again, contrary to Alexander and the main tradition which he represents – that there are in fact two quite different doctrines, and sets, of categories, each labeled as such, introduced back-to-back in *Topics* I.9.[7] The first is a logical or, better, a methodological doctrine, introduced specifically as a necessary aid in the implementation of the doctrine of the four predicables, a doctrine which tells us that the four sorts of entities attributed to or attributable to subjects in standard dialectical discourse, whether these be real existing kinds or not, fall into ten types, although a given predicate may fall into different types or categories on different occasions of its use so that it may thereby bring different predicables into play on different occasions. This doctrine is metaphysically neutral or, better, it is metaphysically neutral enough, so that it can be agreed to and used by all or most significant parties to the dialectical discussion *of* metaphysical or other disputes, as the methodological material in the *Topics* must be. (See I. 14 105b30–31, quoted below.) The second doctrine of categories in *Topics* I.9, however, is a non-methodological highly controversial metaphysical doctrine to the effect that there are ten ultimate real kinds into which the fundamental things that there actually are can be uniquely sorted, including the kind substance, or primary reality, to which particular human beings and particular horses paradigmatically belong. This second doctrine is not sufficiently neutral or uncontroversial to form a part of the necessary methodological equipment of or basis for dialectic. As with many other controversial doctrines introduced in the *Topics*, it is only alluded to for illustrative purposes and is not put forward as an ingredient of or a necessary presupposition of the positive methodological teaching there. From its introduction, we can infer that this metaphysical doctrine was a familiar enough one to his intended audience, at least by the time that Aristotle made his last additions to the *Topics* as we have it, but no more. (Cf. *SE* 34 183b16ff.)

It is, perhaps, infelicitous of Aristotle, from our point of view, to use the same word, *kategoriai*, in *Topics* I.9 and elsewhere, in describing each of these two quite different doctrines. But he is not writing with the interests or preoccupations of present day philosophers and scholars in mind but rather, chiefly, with the interests of his own in-school readers and hearers in mind, and we can easily suppose that, under his instruction, they would not have been confused.[8] There is a close parallel to this worthy of note in Aristotle's treatment of another topic, begging the question. As he indicates in *Topics* VIII.13 (162b31ff), this time more explicitly, this involves two quite different doctrines with two quite different purposes, depending on whether one is dealing with dialectical argumentation or with scientific argumentation. (Cf. *APr* II.16 64b28ff) The same is true with "categories". One might speculate as to why, in *Topics* I.9, in order to illustrate the uses in dialectical discussion of entities from his first category, of *ti esti*, Aristotle introduces a quite different set of categories where the first category is not *ti esti* but rather is substance. Given the likely fact that Aristotle used the *Topics*, like many other treatises, as the basis for lessons and discussion, one might well conjecture that his aim, at least in part, just was to generate some puzzlement and to provoke questions which would enable him then to clearly explain how different the two sets of categories are and what their different uses are.

This account is further confirmed by a later passage in *Topics* IV.1, where Aristotle again introduces, though this time without using the word *kategoriai*, the same categories of being as in his second list of categories in *Topics* I.9 – substance, quantity, quality, relative and "the others." (120b35ff) Here again, his main concern is to make another general methodological point concerning the proper use of the predicables in the practice of dialectic. This is that one cannot properly introduce as genus and species, in the case of some species one is trying to define, items which are not "in the same division" (*diairesis*). (b35) Rather, he says, "the genus must fall under the same division as the species." (121a5–7) He then illustrates, and clarifies, this methodological point with examples, as follows:

> If the species is a substance (*ousia*) so also is the genus, and if the species is a quality, the genus is also a quality. For example, if white is a certain quality so also is color. The same is true for the others. (121a7–9)

Here, Aristotle must be alluding to a familiar view according to which there is a set of firm "divisions," not now of particulars at all since they do not figure in divisions, but only of the definable species and genera of entities, a set of divisions into substances, quantities, qualities, etc. Here again, color belongs uniquely to just one of these divisions, namely *quality*, not sometimes to the category of quality and sometimes to the quite different category of what something is, even as applied, as here, to white. Since substance, quality, etc. are here described as "divisions" it is clearly suggested that, on the view in question, they are divisions *of* something, namely of some higher kind; and it is hard to see what this higher kind could be other than *being*. In fact, as we have already seen, later in this same chapter, *Topics* IV.1, Aristotle speaks uncritically, in rather a Platonic vein, of *being* as a single kind that applies to everything that is. (121a21–22) In other texts, however, as we know well, Aristotle rejects the idea that being is a kind or genus, either of a Platonic or non-Platonic sort. (*Met* B.3 998b24; cf. *APo* II.7 92b12ff, *SE* 11 172a13–15) One might try to show from this that the *Topics* offers us Aristotle's early metaphysical doctrine on which he accepts the view that *being* is a single *genos* or kind, a view which he later rejected. But this would be a very hazardous inference indeed, since the *Topics* itself, shortly later, also puts forward an argument *against* the suggestion that being is a kind or genus. This argument is that if being were a genus it would have to be the genus of everything so that every other kind will be a species or sub-kind under being. If so, then what is *one* would have to be a sub-kind under being and so *one* would have to be less widely predicated than being, which is clearly absurd. This sample argument, whatever its merits may be, is used to conclude that no characteristic which applies to everything can be a kind or genus. (IV.6 127a25ff)

The implication to be drawn from this is not that in the *Topics* Aristotle's own metaphysical views are in total confusion, or that the *Topics* contains strata from different periods of Aristotle's metaphysical development, or that it contains spurious material in need of excision. The implication, rather, is that the *Topics* tells us nothing at all about Aristotle's own metaphysical doctrines or development, given the nature of the treatise. Aristotle can introduce many familiar, but sometimes highly controversial, metaphysical doctrines, including the doctrine of categories of being found in the *Categories*, and various elements of the Platonic theory of forms, in order to illustrate the methodology and the uses of dialectic without necessarily being committed to any of them. As he says in *Topics* I.14:

> For philosophical purposes one must deal with these things [premises and problems] in accord with truth (*kat' aletheian*), but for purposes of dialectic [e.g. here in the *Topics*], by reference to standing opinion (*kata doxan*). (105b30–31)

## 5 Categories in Aristotle's *Categories* and *Metaphysics*

When we come to the *Categories* on the other hand, as we have already begun to see, the role of the special doctrine of categories presented there seems clearly to be quite different from that of its alternate in the *Topics*. To begin with, there is no doctrine of predicables there to which the doctrine of categories there is a necessary complement, and the different classes of entities introduced are not introduced as needed to aid in the implementation of the doctrine of the predicables. In Chapter 2 of that treatise, we are presented first with four types of things that may be "expressed without combination." (1a16ff) There is no suggestion that this might include non-existent things; the things in question are all "things that are." (*onta*, 1a20) Nor is there room for variation, at any stage that interests Aristotle there, in the class, among the four, to which a given uncombined entity belongs. Each of these things that are, according to *Categories* 2, is either (i) *said* of a subject but not *in* any subject, or (ii) *in* a subject but not *said* of any subject, or (iii) both *said* of a subject and *in* a subject or (iv) neither *said* of a subject nor *in* a subject. The text later asserts that the fourth of these classes objectively contains just the primary substances, and that the other classes objectively contain "all the other things." (5 2a11ff, 2a34ff) In Aristotle's scheme here, the same entity *color* can be both *in* a body and *said of* white. (2 1a28f) But, despite this, color is, in each case, an entity from the same category, namely quality. In the scheme of the *Topics*, too, as we have seen, color may be introduced to indicate what something is like and also to indicate what something is. But there, in the two different cases, color is in the two different categories of quality and of what something is. In the *Categories*, color may be predicated of something in just two possible ways, either when that thing is a color (= when color is *said of* it) or when it has a color (= when color is *in* it). In the *Topics*, however, i.e. according to traditional dialectical practice, color can be predicated of something in four possible ways – as contingent accident, genus, *proprium*, or definition.

To try to translate one of these schemes into the other is misguided; they belong to different endeavors. To illustrate: The capacity for pleasure, or for pain, is *in* humans by the lights of the *Categories* (cf. 9 11b1f); but this is neither a contingent accident, nor a *proprium*, nor the genus or definition of humans – though one could of course propose it as such for dialectical discussion. (Necessary, and thus non-accidental, attributes may be neither *propria* nor genera nor definitions of their subjects.)

In *Categories* 4, as we have noted, we are again treated to a presumptively exhaustive and mutually exclusive list of types of things that may be "expressed without combination": substances, quantities, qualities, etc. No entity is in one context one of these types of things, in another context another. Moreover, there is, in the *Categories*, no single type or category composed of the entities that indicate *what something is*. The species and genera of substances, which indicate what they are, belong just to the category of substance but no other species or genera do. (2b29ff) The other species and genera, which indicate what the things other than substances are, belong just to the categories other than substance. Further, *pedestrian biped animal*, taken as a definition, belongs in the category of *what something is* in the *Topics* but in no category in the *Categories*, since it is a type of compound entity and is not "expressed without combination." The category of substance, in the *Categories*, includes, as primary items, particular individuals such as Socrates. But neither the first category nor any other, in the *Topics*, includes such entities. From these things it is abundantly clear, once again, that the doctrine of the ten types of things that are, in *Categories* 4, is not only a quite different doctrine, with a quite different role or function than the logical or methodological doctrine of the ten types of predicates that one can invoke as predicables and attribute to subjects in dialectical propositions, found in *Topics* I.9, but also that these two doctrines of categories are in fact strongly inconsistent. They categorize the same entities in quite different and incompatible ways. Yet another doctrine in the *Categories* that is too controversial to be a basis for or a presupposition of dialectic is the doctrine that there is nothing contrary to a substance. (5 3b24ff) Plato's primary substances, his forms, such as the forms of the good the beautiful and the large, clearly have contraries, and are presented by Plato as such for distinct metaphysical purposes. (See, e.g., *Rep* V 476a, VII 524cff.) From these things, we can now easily see further that the attempt, made already in ancient times and recently revived by some scholars, to give to the *Categories* the title *Introduction to the Topics*, or to treat it as such, is well off the mark.[9] The metaphysical doctrine of categories of things that are which Aristotle takes up most of the *Categories* to expound is no part of, or introduction to or basis for the methodology of dialectic which it is Aristotle's stated aim to expound in the *Topics*. (I.1 100a18ff)

Nevertheless, one might still try to argue that the list of categories found at the beginning of *Topics* I.9 is not ultimately different from the other list of ten types of entities found also in I.9 and in *Categories* 4, for the following reason. As we have seen, in the first list in *Topics* I.9 the first category is *what something is*. Later in I.9, and in *Categories* 4, the first type or category of entity listed is *substance*. The other entries in the two lists appear, at least, to be the same. If Aristotle believed that it is all and only the substances which count as *what* anything *is*, then the two lists could turn out to coincide. There is no indication at all in the *Topics* or *Categories* that Aristotle believed this. Rather, it is clear both in the *Categories* and in the related illustrative material in the *Topics* that the category of substance paradigmatically includes particular humans and other animals, which definitely are not there what anything is, as well as their species and genera which alone there do indicate what they are. (*Cat.* 5 2a11ff, *Top.* I.9 103b27ff, IV.1 120b35ff) So those texts provide no basis for collapsing the two sets in *Topics* I.9 into one and in fact, as we have seen in detail, they cannot be consistently combined. Even the two sets of categories other than the first are not the same since entities belong uniquely to these other categories in the second set, the one found also in the *Categories*, but not uniquely to these other categories in the first set. But if we look further, at *Metaphysics* Z, it can seem, and it has seemed to some, as though Aristotle perhaps may think there that it is all and only the substances that strictly count as *what something is*. Aristotle opens *Metaphysics* Z in the following way:

> What is (*to on*) is so-called in many ways... For *what is* sometimes indicates what something is, i.e. some *this* (*ti esti, kai tode ti*); sometimes a quality, or a quantity or one of the other things so predicated. But while *what is* (*to on*) is so-called in all these ways, it is clear that, of these, it is that case of what something is which indeed indicates a substance (*ousia*) that *is* in the primary way. For when we say what *sort* of thing (*poion*) some *this* is, we state for instance that it is good or bad, but not that it is three feet long or a man. But when we say *what* it [i.e. some *this*] *is* we do not say that it is white or hot or three feet long, but that it is for instance a man or a god. (1028a10–18)

Now one might argue, as some have, that in this passage Aristotle in effect introduces the two lists of categories or kinds from the *Topics* and *Categories* – namely, *what something is*, quality, quantity, etc. on the one hand; and *substance*, quality, quantity, etc. on the other – and he identifies them, since he indicates that the class of substances and the class of cases of what something is are the same. [10] However, it is not in fact clear that, in this passage, Aristotle does restrict cases of what something is to substances. To do that, he would have to say, or imply, that one cannot properly say *what* any quality *is* or introduce anything that designates a quality to say *what* anything *is*, contrary to what we find in the *Categories* and in *Topics* I.9. But Aristotle does not say, for instance, that one cannot introduce a predicate such as white or color to say what *anything* is (which would contradict his example in *Topics* I.9 103b31–33). All he says here is that one cannot introduce a qualitative predicate such as white or color to say what some *this* is. (The subject of *estin* in 1028a17 is *tode*, carried over from a15.) If qualities are not *thises*, as according to the doctrine of the *Categories* they are not (5 3b10ff), then it does not follow that one cannot use such qualitative predicates to say *what* a quality *is*.

Also, when Aristotle says that "it is that case of *what something is* which indeed indicates a substance that *is* in the primary way," he does not say or imply that the category of things which are in the primary way, i.e. the first category, includes just or only cases of *what something is*. He says that certain cases of what something is belong to this category but he does not say that they are the only things which belong to this category. What he says does not rule it out that the primary substances of the *Categories* such as particular human beings, which are *thises* but *not* what anything is, also belong to this category. Later in Z.1 itself, Aristotle says that particular substances of the sort that walk and sit "*are* primarily without qualification." (1028a20–31) If this is not to contradict what we find earlier in the chapter, Aristotle cannot mean to imply earlier that only cases of what something is belong to the category of the things that are in the primary way, namely the category of substance. More importantly for present purposes, as we have noted, Aristotle does not even say earlier that *all* cases of *what* anything *is* belong in the first category, the category of primary realities. Rather, he says only, in his most precise formulation, that the cases of what something is "*which indeed indicate a substance*" belong in the first category. (1028a14–15) This allows that if there are any cases of what something is which do not indicate a substance, i.e. what a substance is, then they will not belong to the first category.

The language which Aristotle uses here in Z.1 is, in fact, very close to the language which we have seen him use in *Topics* I.9 where he says that that "someone who indicates *what* something *is* will sometimes [also] indicate a substance, sometimes a quantity, sometimes a quality, etc." (103b27ff) That is, expressions like "that case of what something is which indeed indicates a substance" (1028a14) are used by Aristotle to mark off one subset of cases of *what something is* from others. So, rather than implying that he wants to restrict all cases of what something is to occupants of the first category, the one composed of primary realities, Aristotle seems to be implying in Z.1 that it is only a certain subset of cases of what something is that belong to this category, namely those that indicate or are properly applied to "a substance."

This same perspective is also found in Z.4. There, too, Aristotle distinguishes different types of cases of what something is, those that belong to "a substance and a *this*," those that are applicable to quantities, those that are applicable to qualities, etc. (1030a17ff) He does also go on to suggest there that those cases of what something is which are applicable to a substance and a *this* are cases of what something is of a primary and unqualified type, so that while we *can* say what a quality is, we do not thereby say, of anything that is, what it is without qualification. (a21ff) This might tempt some to try to argue that in Z.4 at least Aristotle finally collapses the two sets of categories in the *Topics* and *Categories* into one by restricting the first category, i.e. the substances, to the cases of what something is without qualification. But there are at least two major difficulties with this. First, while Aristotle does clearly say in Z.4 that cases of what something is in the primary way only belong *to* substances (1030a21–23, 27–30, b5–6), he does not clearly say that these cases of what something is *are* the substances and the only substances. It is left open, at the least, in Z.4 that among the substances *to which* cases of what something is of the primary type belong are particular human beings such as Socrates and Callias. Later in Z, in fact, Aristotle is quite happy to say that these particular entities are substances, of one type, and, as such, he can hardly mean, in Z, to exclude them overall from the first category. (Z.11 1037a24–30) That these entities are not *primary substances*, in some sense of this expression, in Z (11 1037a28), does not show that they are not substances, and thus members of, and only of, the first category, according to Z.

However, and most importantly for present purposes, whatever one might say after full study of *Metaphysics* Z, for which there is hardly space here, this sort of attempt to argue that in Z Aristotle finally collapses the two lists of categories found in *Topics* I.9 and *Categories* 4 into one ignores, once again, the purpose or role of the first list in *Topics* I.9 as a part of the methodological equipment of dialectic. As noted earlier, by contrast with this the doctrine of *Categories* 4–5, like the second list of categories in *Topics* I.9 and like *Metaphysics* Z itself, involves very highly controversial metaphysical claims, claims not accepted by most, if any, of Aristotle's main philosophical peers. Aristotle could not mean, ever, to want to make this doctrine of categories, or any related doctrine to which he may have come as a metaphysician in, say, *Metaphysics* Z-H, a part of the methodological basis of or equipment for dialectic since the latter, as we have seen, needs to be restricted to what is sufficiently neutral to serve as common ground to all or most disputants on all topics of dialectical discussion, metaphysical and otherwise. There is no reason to believe, from Aristotle's texts, that he ever came to have any reservations about the suitability of the original list of categories in *Topics* I.9 *for this purpose* – as a basis for and a necessary part of the equipment of dialectic. In his philosophical lexicon, *Metaphysics* D, where Aristotle is explaining standard uses of various philosophical notions, he gives the same metaphysically neutral list of "types of categories" (*schemata tes kategorias*) as he offers at the beginning of *Topics* I.9 and later in, e.g., *SE* 22 178a4ff. (D.7 1017a22ff; cf. E.2 1026a35-b1, *APo* I.22 83a21–23) Whatever development Aristotle's metaphysics itself may or may not have undergone, the *Topics* and its special methodological material on categories does not provide us with any part of it. In a word, the first doctrine of categories presented in *Topics* I.9 has *and retains* a role and a suitability for use in the practice of dialectic, especially in the implementation of the doctrine of the predicables, that is unaffected by any development or lack of development in Aristotle's science of metaphysics. This emphasizes for us, once again, how inappropriate it is to see the *Categories* and its special metaphysical doctrine of categories as any sort of introduction to or presupposition of the *Topics*. It is perhaps possible that, of the two doctrines of categories which make their appearance in *Topics* I.9, one was developed, historically, earlier than the other. But it is also possible, even likely, that, in Aristotle's own hands, the two doctrines were developed or refined together over time, more or less simultaneously, given their important and quite different uses in the two different modes of inquiry – *kata doxan* and *kat' aletheian* – both of which Aristotle had a long-term interest in developing and articulating. (*SE* 34 183b15ff)

## 6   Dialectic in the *Categories*

There is one final ground, however, worth surveying, from which someone might still object to the attempt here to sharply separate

Aristotle's objectives, and thus his two doctrines of categories, in the *Topics* and *Categories*. Some might argue that the *Categories* itself is in fact written from the same perspective as the *Topics*, that is, from the dialectical standpoint, so that on that ground it is not fruitless to try to conjoin the doctrines that we find in the two works and not so absurd for early editors to give the title, *Introduction to the Topics*, to the *Categories*. Though commentators seem largely to have ignored this, if we look carefully at the way Aristotle formulates the main claims of the *Categories* it is indeed quite striking how much of this is directly presented as what "is said" (*legetai*) or as what "is held." (*dokei*) This, of course, is language that Aristotle standardly uses to introduce *endoxa* or those noted opinions or "things that are held" (*dokounta*) that have credibility, *prima facie*, in dialectic. (*Top.* I.1 100a29-b23; VIII.1 156b20–23, VIII.5–6) Consider, for instance, the following highly important passages from *Categories* 5:

That which is *said to be* a substance (*ousia legomene*) most strictly, primarily, and most of all is that which is neither said of any subject nor in any subject, for instance a particular man or a particular horse. Substances are *said to be* secondary to which, as their species, the things *said to be* primary substances belong, both these species and the genera of these species. (2a11–16)

It is because the primary substances are subjects for all of the other things, and all of the other things are predicated of them or are in them, that they are *said to be* substances most of all. (2b15–17)

It is plausible that, after the primary substances, their species and genera alone should be *said to be* secondary substances. For they alone, of things predicated, make clear the primary substance. (2b29–31)

Every substance *is held* (*dokei*) to signify some *this*. As for the primary substances it is incontrovertibly true that they signify some *this*, since what is made clear is indivisible and one in number. But as for the secondary substances, while they appear similarly, from the form of the expression, to signify some *this* – when someone says "man" or "animal" – this is not in fact true. Rather, they signify a sort of qualification since the subject is not one, as a primary substance is, but man and animal are said of many things. (3b10–18)

*It is held* (*dokei*) that a substance does not admit of more and less. (3b33–34)

*It is held* (*dokei*) to be most of all distinctive of a substance that what is the same and one in number is able to receive contraries. (4a10–11)

While not every significant claim in the *Categories* is explicitly introduced in this fashion, as what is most of all said or held, enough of
importance is so introduced as to strongly suggest that what Aristotle
aims to do there is not so much to give his own views, at a certain stage
of his thinking, on certain metaphysical topics as simply to present what
is, most of all, *said* and *held* on these topics.[11] On this basis, one might
then infer that the *Categories* is best understood as written from the
dialectical perspective so that the argument offered above for putting
some distance between the objectives of the *Categories* and the *Topics*
on the subject of categories is undermined. On this basis, one might
also argue, further, that just as the *Topics* cannot be used to determine
Aristotle's own views on metaphysical subjects, or to chart his metaphysical development, the same is true of the *Categories*.

To evaluate these proposals it will be best to begin by attending to
the ways in which Aristotle's mode of inquiry in the *Categories* is, arguably, *not* dialectical. In *Topics* I.2, Aristotle details for us just two ways in
which dialectic is to be used in philosophical inquiry. First, he says, it
can be used "to raise difficulties for both sides" of any disputed issue in
some area of investigation from the dialectical standpoint, that is from
the standpoint of what is held (*dokei*) and, in particular, of what is more
noted or accredited (*endoxoteron*) than some claim being questioned,
and especially from the standpoint of what is noted or accredited most
of all (*endoxataton*). Secondly, dialectic has a special philosophical use,
Aristotle says, to critically examine proposals for primary principles, such
as basic definitions, in a given science or discipline. (101a34-b4, with
VIII.5–6 and *SE* 34 183a37ff, *APo* I.19 81b18ff) We find neither of these
things much in play in the *Categories*. Little is even offered as a primary
principle or definition of any of the basic notions or subjects introduced;
and the few statements that are, or that one might argue are, definitional
in character, are not in general subjected to critical examination. There
is just one place where this clearly occurs, namely in *Categories* 7, where
Aristotle worries over how to properly define a *relative*. (8a28-b24) On
the whole, the *Categories* simply lists main views or doctrines on certain
matters with little attempt to distinguish principles from derived truths,
and there is no special focus on the examination of principles.

Equally, there is little in the *Categories* that counts as the raising of
difficulties for both sides of disputed questions. In most cases, Aristotle
does not even bother to list the disputes. In *Categories* 5 where, as we
have seen, he tells us what is *said*, or what is *held* most of all about
substance, he omits even to mention much of what is held, as we can
easily see if we compare *Categories* 5 with *Metaphysics* Z.2 where Aristotle

is also explicitly listing what is held (*dokei*) about substance. (1028b8ff) Most of what we find in Z.2 in Aristotle's catalogue there of what is held about substance is not mentioned in the *Categories*, much less critically examined. (See Z.2 1028b16–27, cf. L.1 1069a28–30.)

It is illuminating, in this connection, to compare Aristotle's treatment of substance in the *Categories* with his well-known treatment of incontinence (*akrasia*) in *Nicomachean Ethics* VII.1–4. There, just as in *Metaphysics* Z.2, Aristotle begins by listing a full range of what is held (*dokei*) and said (*legetai*) about incontinence and related states. (*EN* VII.2 1145b8ff) He then goes on, as *Topics* I.2 says one should in a dialectical investigation of a philosophical subject, to raise difficulties (*aporiai*) for "the things that are said." (*ta legomena*, 1145b20–1146b8) This mode of procedure is strikingly absent from the discussion of substance in *Categories* 5. There is one passage there (quoted above) where Aristotle considers both sides of one issue and offers a correction of one thing that is held, when he argues that the view that "every substance signifies some *this*" is false since it applies not to all substances but only to primary substances, because a secondary substance is not numerically one but rather is said of many things and, thus, is not a *this*. (3b10–18) And in one passage, Aristotle considers and rebuts a possible objection to what "is held to be most of all distinctive of a substance," when he argues that, despite what is also "held," *statements* unlike substances do not receive contraries when they, apparently, change from being true to being false. Rather, it is only the thing the statement is about which actually changes, not the statement itself. (4a22ff)[12] But there is nothing like a full presentation of the most significant things that are held about substance, nor any general review of the problems to which they give rise, of the sort that is expected in a dialectical inquiry, according to *Topics* I.2, and is begun in Z.2 and presented, concerning incontinence, in *EN* VII.1–2.

To see the full significance of this one special fact having to do with the relation between *Categories* 5 and Z.2 is noteworthy. In Z.2, Aristotle draws a clear distinction in his presentation between two different classes of things that are *held* about substance. He first lists the things that are held to be most evident. He says:

> It is *held* (*dokei*) that substance belongs *most apparently* to bodies so that *we say* that the animals and the plants and their parts are substances, and the natural bodies such as fire and water and earth, and everything of that sort, and also whatever things are either parts of these things or composed of them, either some or all, such as the heaven and its parts – stars and moon and sun. (1028b8–13)[13]

By contrast, however, with what "we say" and, as such, "hold" to be most apparent, Aristotle then goes on to list what is only "held by some" concerning substance. He continues:

> But it is *held by some* (*dokei tisi*) that the limits of bodies are substances, such as a surface and a line, and a point and unit, and more so than a body and a solid. Further, some do not think that there is any such thing [a substance] apart from perceptible things, but others think that there are eternal entities that are more in number and more real, just as Plato thought that mathematical objects and forms were two types of substance, and that there is a third type of substance consisting of perceptible bodies. And Speusippus thought there were yet more... (1028b16ff)

It is noteworthy that the things reported as *held* or *said* to be substances in the *Categories* come only from the first group listed in Z.2, not from the second. That is, all the things presented as held to be substances in the *Categories* are among the things that "we say" are substances "most apparently," according to Z.2, as opposed to the things that only "some," e.g. some renowned thinkers, such as Plato or Speusippus, say are substances.

The upshot of this is that while the *Categories* does not at all present us with a dialectical *inquiry*, into for instance substance, it does present us with a good deal, at least, of what we might expect to be left with as the *result of* such a dialectical inquiry. According to *EN* VII.1, the results that a proper critical inquiry into the conflicting things that are said or held on some subject should leave us with are the *endoxa*, the noted beliefs of the many and the wise – ideally all of the *endoxa*, but if not, when the *endoxa* are inconsistent, as they massively are on substance according to Z.2, then with most of them, and in any case with the most authoritative of them. (*ta kuriotata endoxa*, 1145b 2–6)[14] According to the *Topics*, the most authoritative *endoxa*, the ones that Aristotle refers to there as the *endoxotata*, are simply the things that are *held* (*dokounta*) most of all. (*SE* 33 182b37ff) He refuses to permit those special *endoxa* that are opinions of "the wise" but which conflict with common opinions, such as those listed in the second part of Z.2, even to be introduced as dialectical premises, i.e. as a basis for arguing to dialectical results. (I.10 104a8–12) Rather, how things stand with regard to these opinions must be settled only on the basis of premises that are more commonly accredited. (I.11 104b27–28, *Rhet* I.2 1356b28ff) Further, in *Topics* VIII, Aristotle describes an opinion as *more endoxon*, and thus more authoritative, than another in dialectic when it is more intelligible or better known. (*gnorimoteron*, VIII.5 159b13–16) He cannot mean by this that the more authoritative opinion in dialectic is what he standardly describes as what is better known *by nature* (*phusei*) since that would collapse what is more authoritative in dialectic into what is more authoritative in science. (*APo* I.2 71b29ff) On this basis, Aristotle could not exclude altogether the opinions of the wise that conflict with common opinions from the class of dialectical premises, or things one is entitled to argue from, since such opinions might well turn out to be what is better known by nature. Rather, then, Aristotle must mean to characterize what is more *endoxon*, and thus more authoritative in dialectic, as what is more intelligible or better known in the only other mode that he recognizes, namely *to us*. (*hemin*, 71b33ff; cf. *Top* VI.4 141b3ff, *EN* I.4 1095b2ff) So, if the *Categories* presents and leaves us with, as results, a good portion at least of the *endoxotata*, the *most* widely and firmly accredited views, about, for instance, substance, as Z.2 confirms it does, then Aristotle will be presenting there much of what a proper dialectical inquiry into substance would result in and leave standing as most authoritative without presenting us with the full inquiry that would lead to those results. The latter would include, for instance, an examination of the other conflicting *endoxa* about substance presented in Z.2.

This can be further confirmed from the discussion of relatives in *Categories* 7, where Aristotle is somewhat more open to presenting the variety of conflicting things that are held and more revealing of the mode of inquiry that has led him to his results than he is in other cases. His reason for this comes out at the end of that discussion, where he says:

> It is doubtless difficult to present firm results on such matters [concerning relatives] without having investigated them many times, but to have thoroughly aired the problems is not without value. (8b21–24)

Here Aristotle indicates for us that the kind of problem based inquiry of which we get our best glimpses in Ch.7, inquiry which Aristotle seems to regard as still most incomplete in the case of relatives, is the very kind which led him to his more settled results in the other cases as well. In Ch.7, Aristotle does more fully present conflicting things that are *held*, about relatives. For instance, he says that it is *held* that a relative occurs simultaneously with its co-relative. (7b15) But he goes on to correct this by reference to another thing that he says is also *held*, namely that one particular relative, the knowable, may well exist before its co-relative, knowledge, does. (7b22–27) Here, rather clearly, Aristotle is following the standard procedure in dialectic of correcting one *endoxon* by reference to another conflicting one that is more *endoxon*, i.e. more widely and firmly held, than it. This indicates for us how he has reached his results in the *Categories* overall.

This does not necessarily imply, of course, that for Aristotle the things that "we say" and "hold" to be most evident are in every case things that are explicitly so held by *everyone* or, at least, by more or less everyone whom we take to be sensible and competent for discussion. (See *Top* I.11 105a3ff, *Rhet* I.2 1356b35ff.) The view that the knowable can exist before the knowledge of it does no doubt has this standing. So, most likely, does the view that a kind such as *animal* has many members and is thus not a single thing one can point to (a "this") in the way a particular horse is; or the view that a particular horse is not any sort of attribute of anything but rather is a prime subject for attributes, some of which indicate what it is, some what it is like. But overall, the various views in question do, arguably, reflect very common, at least implicit, general ways of thinking about reality, even among those who would not employ all, or any, of the special jargon that Aristotle can use to articulate these general ways of thinking.

We can now go back to the questions which led us to investigate the status of Aristotle's results about substance in the *Categories*. If those results belong to the subset of those "things that are said" that would likely be left in place *after* full dialectical inquiry, as Z.2 indicates they would, then can we still say, as was argued earlier, that the material in *Topics* I.9 (103b27ff) that duplicates some of these results in the *Categories* is no part of what Aristotle could be committing himself to in the *Topics* where he is describing dialectic? The answer to this question is still "Yes." Although Aristotle's results in the *Categories* may have this status, as what is, or would be in the end, said and held most of all, they are also often highly controversial, as one can easily see both from the second half of Z.2 and from Aristotle's discussions of the views of his predecessors, on substance and related matters, in *Metaphysics* A and M. As noted earlier, most, if not all, of Aristotle's main philosophical peers would reject the main views on primary reality, or substance, put forward in the *Categories*, even if these views are most noted and accredited (*endoxotata*). So, if the aim of the *Topics* is to provide the machinery that can be and is generally agreed to by the main parties to major philosophical disputes, for use in the dialectical discussion and resolution of those disputes, it cannot incorporate, as a part of that very machinery, what is as highly controversial as certain of the views on substance found in the

*Categories* and, thus, in the second list of categories offered in *Topics* I.9. Rather, this material in the *Categories* and in *Topics* I.9 is what Aristotle expects those who agree on the rules in the *Topics* for dialectical discussion to come to as a *result of* such discussion, not part of what he expects them to accept or presuppose as a *basis for* that discussion. Of course, for the distinctions employed in the first set of categories in *Topics* I.9, such as those among what something is, what something is like, or how much of it there is, to be of use in dialectic there must be some commonly agreed-upon way of understanding these distinctions, one that is, and was, generally acceptable and available, at least to skilled participants in dialectic. And some suitably uncontroversial material that fits this description may well be found in the *Categories* as doubtless elsewhere (e.g. in *Met* D 10, 13–15, 20–21, or perhaps in some lost logical work or works). Also, some of it is clearly too generally acceptable to need writing down for dialectical purposes and much of it is simply in the air, as it were, in Aristotle's special philosophical surroundings. (Cf. *Top* I.10 104a6–7.) But there is too much in the *Categories* that does not fit this description for a chief aim of that work overall to be to provide such uncontroversial material.

## 7   The place of the *Categories* in Aristotle's thought

If this is the correct way to understand not only *Topics* I.9 but also the *Categories*, then it naturally leads us to a reconsideration of the old question: Does Aristotle change his views on the metaphysics of substance, as presented in the *Categories*, in the central books of the *Metaphysics*? We can now see that the answer to this question is obviously "No." The reason why the answer is *obviously* no is because the question incorporates a false presupposition. The question presupposes that the claims about substance in the *Categories* are, or were at some point, Aristotle's own views. But we can now see that we have no reason to make that assumption on the basis of what we find in the *Categories*. The *Categories* does present us with, for instance, what is most *endoxon* about substance or, in other words, with the way things stand on substance from the standpoint of what is and remains, after dialectical review, as best known and most intelligible to us. But it is Aristotle's conviction that what is best known and most intelligible to us on some topic may be, and is even likely to be, unclear and incorrect, and in need of revision from the scientific standpoint.

In a well-known passage in the opening chapter of the *Physics* Aristotle characterizes the things that are "evident and clear to us" on some subject, before proper scientific principles have been discovered, as "rather indistinct." (*ta sugkechumena mallon*, I.1 184a20–21; cf. *HA* I.6 585b34) He compares our understanding at this early stage of scientific inquiry to the understanding of a child who calls all women mothers and only later is able to employ the proper articulations and to adequately distinguish the two kinds. (184b3–5) Given this, it is not only possible, but even likely, that since the *Categories* presents what is best known to us (for instance, on the subject of substance), then, in Aristotle's own view, at least some, if not much, of it will require revision, or rejection, from a more scientific standpoint. This is why Aristotle can say early in Z.2, right after listing the things that are "held to be most apparently" substances, that he still needs to consider the possibility that "none of these things are substances." (1028b15) His scientific methodology, as we can see from *Physics* I.1, requires this, in view of the fact that this is only what is best known to us. So, for instance, when we find in the *Categories* (5 3a29ff, 7 8b15f), as also in the first section of Z.2, the claim that the parts of substances, such as the head and hands of an animal, are themselves substances, while this is rejected in, for instance, *Metaphysics* Z.16, there is no basis for saying that Aristotle himself has changed his views. Since this claim, as we can see from Z.2, belongs among the *endoxotata*, i.e. the things that are accredited by us most of all, about substance, it is properly presented in the *Categories*, just as at the beginning of Z.2, even if Aristotle did not himself accept it when he wrote the *Categories* and even if he then knows that it will require revision from the more scientific standpoint of Z.16.

This, however, should now lead us to ask finally what the point is of the kind of presentation that is offered to us in the *Categories* understood in this way – as an assembly of the *endoxotata* about substance, etc. – if it is not even, necessarily, Aristotle's own doctrine. Here again, the *Physics* gives us an answer. Aristotle tells us clearly there that in scientific inquiry generally "the natural procedure is to go *from* the things which are clearer and more intelligible to us *to* the things which are clearer and more intelligible by nature," namely to scientific principles. (I.1 184a16–18) He argues that this very procedure is "necessary" for finding true scientific principles. (a19) We find this same doctrine repeated in *Metaphysics* Z.3 (1029b3–12) where Aristotle uses it to justify concentrating his first attention on certain perceptible substances, as the things that are most of all "agreed" by us to be substances, in his search for the definitional principle as to what substance is. (1029a33–34, cf. *EN* I.4 1095a30ff) So, the point of the *Categories* is that it does what Z.3 and *Physics* I.1 tell us we *must* do as a first stage in scientific inquiry, namely to lay things out as they are best known and most intelligible to us as a prelude to looking for their principles and causes.[15] That, on the present account, is what the doctrine of categories in the *Categories* itself offers us, while the other doctrine of categories more proper to the *Topics* has, as we have seen, a very different objective.

As has often been noted, later in *Physics* IV.1–5, Aristotle offers us a good example of how he understands the natural procedure for inquiry introduced in I.1, in his well-known discussion of *place*. In IV.1–3, Aristotle first provides a preliminary account of the things that are held about place, together with a discussion of the problems to which such preliminary data give rise. Then in IV.4, he collects together certain data that emerge from his earlier discussion, as the starting point for his attempt to find, finally, the causal definitional principle which specifies *what place is*. He says:

> *What place is* should become evident in the following manner. Let us posit, concerning place, *whatever is held truly to belong to it* (*hosa dokei alethos huparchein auto(i)*) in its own right. *We do deem it correct* (*axioumen*), then, that a place is the primary thing encompassing that of which it is the place, and is no part of the thing; and, further, that its primary place is neither less nor greater than the thing, and further that its place is left behind by the thing [when the thing moves] and is separate from it; and, addition to these things, that *above* and *below* are applicable to every place, and each of the bodies by nature moves to and stays in its proper place and this makes it to be either *above* or *below*.
>
> It is with these things laid down that what remains should be investigated. We must try to conduct our inquiry so as to set forth *what place is* in such a way both that the difficulties about it are resolved and that *the things that are held* (*ta dokounta*) to belong to place do turn out to belong to it, and, further, so that it is evident what the cause is of the trouble and of the difficulties about it. For it is in this way that anything is best established. (210b32–211a11)

Here, Aristotle purports to tell us the best way to conduct any scientific investigation into what something is. First, we must collect together *hosa dokei alethos huparchein auto(i)*. This might mean "whatever is held about a thing that is in fact true of it," with *alethos*, truly, modifying *dokei*, is held.[16] But it is unlikely that this is what Aristotle means. To begin with, he does not collect here *whatever* is held that he takes to be true about place. There are very many such things found in his discussion in *Physics* IV.1–9 that he does not list here. He offers only a small selection of especially significant data. More importantly, as we have seen in *Physics* I.1 and in *Metaphysics* Z.2 and 3, Aristotle believes that it is only at the end of inquiry that we can effectively determine, among all of the initial data, which are genuinely true and which are not. In fact, there is at least one of the data listed here that he does not in the end accept, namely that above and below are applicable to *every* place. There is, for instance, nothing below the place of the material at the center of the earth for him. So this datum, at least, will require revision and he no doubt already realizes this when he sets it down here in his favored class. In going on to list his initial data in *Physics* IV.4, Aristotle does not use again the phrase *hosa dokei alethos huparchein*. He rather refers to these data simply as what *axioumen*, that is as what *we deem correct*. (210b34) Later, he refers again to the initial data simply as *ta dokounta*, the things that are held, with no further qualification. (211a9) These facts indicate that Aristotle means *alethos*, truly, to modify *huparchein*, to belong, in his claim. That is, by what *dokei alethos huparchein auto(i)* Aristotle means what is *held* to truly or most evidently belong to place or, in other words, to the *endoxotata* about place.[17] In a parallel context, in *De Anima* I.2, Aristotle begins his inquiry into the nature of the soul "by presenting the things that are most of all held to belong to it by nature." (*ta malista dokounth' huparchein auto(i) kata phusin*, 403b25)

These things indicate that in *Physics* IV.4 the special data about place from which Aristotle begins his investigation of what place is have the same status as the data about substance in *Categories* 5, and in the first half of *Metaphysics* Z.2. In Z.3, as we have also seen, Aristotle indicates that it is from data of just this sort that he intends to pursue his inquiry into what substance is, since such data constitute what is best known to us, and that is where any proper scientific inquiry should begin. (1029b3–12) So, in the *Categories* Aristotle presents us with data about substance of just the sort that he collects about place at the beginning of *Physics* IV.4.

If we want to see further, then, what the value of such a collection is, this section of the *Physics* is a useful place to look. After collecting his special data in IV.4, Aristotle goes on to investigate *what place is* by considering four main proposals. (The parallel to this in Z.3ff is hard to miss. See 1028b33–36) As he says, he is looking for that proposal from which it will *result* that the special *dokounta* about place are correct. In other words, he is looking for the proposal that best accounts for and explains the appropriate initial data. Later in the physical works, in *De Anima* I.1, he argues generally that this is the proper way to validate any proposed definitional principle in science, as opposed to dialectic, namely by showing that the definition best explains the appropriate initial data. (402b16–403a2)[18] So, for example, to return to *Physics* IV.4, the proposal that the place of thing is its form, in the sense of its shape (*morphe*, 211b7) or outer surface, can be defended, Aristotle says, since this would account for the generally accepted datum that the place of a thing encompasses it. However, the shape or surface of an object is a boundary that belongs to the object, so this proposal cannot account for the datum that the place of a thing is separate from it and remains when the thing moves. (211b5–14 with 209a31-b6, b17ff) Aristotle's own proposal by contrast, that the primary place of a thing is the inner-most motionless boundary of the surrounding object, not the outermost boundary of the thing itself, accounts for both of these data, or so he argues. (212a14–21) In like manner, then, the data on substance in the *Categories* should provide Aristotle with the basis for an inference to a definition of what substance is that best explains these data. The data in question, in either case, may not be the only data requiring expla-nation, and they may be subject to revision, but they will be crucial data according to *De Anima* I.1 and *Physics* IV.4.[19] Aristotle's discus-sion of place, then, illustrates clearly for us what the status and role is of the main data on the categories of substance, etc. presented in the *Categories*, by contrast with the alternate material on categories offered in the *Topics*.

## 8   Concluding postscript

It may have been observed that little or no attention has been paid here to a question that has much occupied students of Aristotle's doctrine of categories, especially perhaps from Kant onwards, namely: How did Aristotle *generate* his set of just ten categories? Scholars have proposed that the first list of categories in *Topics* I.9 suggests one approach to the generation of the categories, while the second list there, the one found also in *Categories* 4, suggests another. They have debated at some length whether the two approaches can yield consistent results. As we can now see, however, this debate has largely been based on the false assumption that there is just a single doctrine of categories in Aristotle with a single purpose. Once we understand that there are, in fact, two doctrines, each with its own aim, and once we see more clearly what these different aims are, it may be possible profitably to approach this old issue afresh.[20]

## Notes

1. For this alternate proposal, see, e.g., Brunschwig (1967, p. 13), and Frede (1987a, pp. 29–48). This alternative would require that there be a syntactically different predication relation, or different copula as it were, in play in the predication of a quality of some subject from that involved in the predication of a quantity of that subject. This is, in itself, highly implausible, and there are no direct signs of such a doctrine in Aristotle. For the record, in a seminar that I once attended offered by Frede and Paul Grice on the *Categories,* it was conceded by Frede that this raises a serious difficulty for the proposal in question, one which inclined him at that point to change his view. (If it be suggested that the multiple "predication" relations in question are not linguistic but ontological then that would introduce elaborate inappropriate metaphysical machinery into the bases for dialectic. On this, see further below.) For others who have held this view, and also for a thorough presentation, for which there is not space here, of the large variety of alternative proposals on many other points in the interpretation of *Topics* I.9 and its relation to *Categories* 4, see now especially Malink (2007). The present account takes a stand on most of these points, one that is recommended here, in no small measure, on the ground of its overall coherence.

2. Aristotle counts it as a case of something being said of itself, or said of the *same* thing (see the mss variant at 103b36), when a definition or genus of the thing is given. See *Top* V.5 135a10–12, VI.3 140b33–34 and I.7 103a23–27 with Alexander *ad loc,* III.1 116a23–27, IV.1 120b21ff and APo I.22 83a24ff. So, for instance, Socrates is the very same thing, not some different thing, which is a man; and man is the very same thing, not some different thing, which is an animal or a pedestrian biped animal.

3. In *Top.* I.15 Aristotle refers to the use of the categories listed at the beginning of I.9 to detect ambiguities, as a further aid in inquiry into definitions. See 106a1ff, 107a3ff, Cf. VI.2 139b19ff. It is a requirement for one type of thing to be the same as another, and thus suitable as a definer of it, that it belong to the same one of these categories as the other. See VII.1 152a38ff. This requirement can also be used in the detection of, or to help avoid, fallacies that turn on ambiguity or multiple definition in dialectical argument. See *SE* 22. So, these categories of I.9 also have these further closely related uses in dialectical practice centering on the predicables, especially definition. In the *Topics* the *differentia* is treated as *generic* in character and so as covered by the rules governing the genus. (I.4 101b18–19) So, the rules for the genus and, as such, for what something is, apply to all items in definitions, as these are understood in the *Topics,* both to genus and to differentiae, even though a differentia itself does not signify what its subject is except in company with the genus which, according to Aristotle, it implies or involves. (IV.2 122b16f, VI.6 144b16ff) See also the next note.

4. Here the predicate *colored* (thing) is not a simple entity, "expressed without combination." (See *Cat* 4 1b25.) So *colored* (thing) cannot figure in a classification of simple entities of this type in the way that *color* can. The same holds for a differentia such as *pedestrian* (thing) since for Aristotle a differentia always imports some suitable genus, e.g. animal, as noted above. (*Top* VI.6 144b16ff.) Aristotle does describe such a differentia as a sort of quality (*poion*

*ti*, IV.2 122b17), but it is not for him a quality of its subject, e.g. a pedestrian thing such as a man, but rather "always (*aei*) of its [implied] genus," such as animal. (IV.6 128a27) This does not mean that the genus animal is a pedestrian (not a flyer), but rather that being a pedestrian is always a way of being an animal. (VI.6 144b16ff; cf. *Met* Z.12 1038a9ff which represents this same dialectical perspective, and also Z.1 1028a 22–29) So (a) pedestrian = (a) pedestrian animal, and this is not a quality of, e.g., (a) man but a *ti esti* and a genus of it. (VI.6 144b22–23) This is why, in the *Topics*, differentiae, though they are not genera, are generic in character, as noted above, and do not constitute a separate predicable. Similarly, then, if (a) colored = (a) colored body then, though this, unlike (a) body simply, is not a *ti esti* of e.g. (a) stone, it is not a quality of (the) stone either, but rather a type of compound made up of a quality (here *color* not *colored* since the latter = colored body) and another type of entity (a body, or a substance in *Cat*). For the full relevance of this see further below. For an alternate treatment of differentiae and of entities such as *colored*, see Malink (2007) and earlier discussion referred to there.

5. At 8 10b17ff Aristotle speaks of quality and the "other *kategoriai*" such as, for instance, quantity, relative and place. He does not mention all of the kinds listed earlier in Ch.4 at 1b25–27, but it is just that list, from which the kinds he mentions come, that he is in the course of discussing in *Cat* 4–9 and there is no other list of such kinds earlier in the *Categories* that he could have in mind as the *kategoriai*. Moreover, the argument he produces at 10b17–25 is only adequate to his purposes there if it is the members of that list to which he is referring by the name *kategoriai*. He argues that if one member of a pair of contraries is a quality, the other member will be, too. So, he says, if justice is a quality, then its contrary, injustice, will be, too, *since* it is not either a quantity or a relative or a place, nor anything "from the other *kategoriai*." (b19) If Aristotle did not understand the list in Ch.4 to constitute the *kategoriai* to which he refers here, and if, for instance, he did not understand *substance* to be one of these *kategoriai* then, given the list in Ch.4, he would also need a separate argument that injustice is not a substance, in addition to the argument he provides, to be entitled to conclude that injustice is a *quality*. But clearly he feels no need for such an additional argument. At 8 11a37f, Aristotle does at least entertain the possibility that some entity might be both a quality and a relative; but not the possibility that it might be in one context the one in another context the other. For simplicity, this subtlety may be left aside here. The argument could easily be framed to accommodate it.

6. As Democritus held. See *Met.* H.2 1042b11–15.

7. See Alexander *in Top ad loc*, Ackrill (1963) and, recently, Smith (1997). For many others belonging to, and some opposed to, this tradition, see Malink (2007).

8. See further below on this matter. This is one of the places where it is useful to remember that, like most of Aristotle's extant works, the *Topics* was not published at a definite point by him but rather was used for in-school lessons and discussion, and was doubtless much revised over long time, as Aristotle himself indicates in *SE* 34 183b15ff.

9. For this view, see now Menn (1995). The history of this matter is reviewed in Frede (1987b). There is not space here to discuss the general problem of the unity of the *Categories*, a problem whose solution depends in any case, first of all, on determining what the aim is of Chs. 2–9. The comparison

with the *Topics* is essential toward that end. Also, the much discussed question as to how the categories were generated requires prior clarity on the matters considered here, matters usually ignored in that discussion. On this, see further below.

10. I have translated the phrase *ti esti kai tode ti* above (1028a11–12) in a way that gives support to this suggestion. There are other ways to translate it, e.g., as "what something is and [also] a *this*," but I am inclined to favor the above translation for reasons offered in Bolton (1995). The present discussion both draws on and further develops certain of the proposals in that paper. For an independently reached account that offers a somewhat similar approach on some points, see Matthen (1978). For further discussion, see, e.g., Frede and Patsig (1988).

11. Other passages in the *Categories* where Aristotle introduces material in this way, as what is said (*legetai*) or held (*dokei*), include: 1a1, 6, 12; 2a7, 3b36, 4a3–7, 4b14, 5a38; 5b1–9, 17–23; 6a1, 12, 26–35; 6a36-b11, 6b19–34, 7a23; 7b 15, 22, 24, 8a14, 8b26, 30; Ch.8 (frequently). Aristotle's meaning in many of these passages is often obscured by a tendency to translate *dokei*, etc. as "it seems," etc., as though the things in question, e.g. in *Cat* 5, are all put forward as things that seem so to Aristotle. But as we shall see below from parallel contexts in the *Ethics*, *Metaphysics* and *Physics*, the *dokounta* or *legomena* in question are not always things that seem so to Aristotle even though they are all things that are held in such a manner, he believes, as to demand attention. When Aristotle wishes to identify what "seems" so he has another, better and more accurate, word to use, *eoike*. See, e.g., Bonitz' *Index* 263b10ff. For the close association in Aristotle's mind of what *dokei* with what is *kata doxan*, i.e. is in accord with standing opinion, see *Apo* I.19 81b18ff.

12. In these passages Aristotle corrects one thing that is held by reference to another that is even more widely and firmly held. See below for further evidence for this reading of Aristotle's procedure. For Aristotle's uses of this procedure see also Bolton (1990, 1995) and earlier discussion referred to there.

13. Here, it is especially apparent that what Aristotle lists as *dokei* most evidently to obtain is not what "seems" most evident to him. Most of what he lists here he himself regards as clearly false. Rather, as he indicates, these are all things "we say," i.e. things that are very widely held, even if they do not seem so to Aristotle or various others.

14. For a detailed discussion of how Aristotle uses this procedure in *EN* VII.1–4, see Bolton (1991) and Reeve (1992) with references there.

15. Menn 1995 argues that the *Categories* cannot be a contribution to Aristotle's metaphysics because it is not concerned with causes. This is comparable to arguing that the *History of Animals* cannot be a contribution to Aristotle's biology because it is not concerned with causes. Its aim, as with the *Categories*, is to collect data presumptively in need of causal explanation prior to searching for the explanations. (See *HA* I.6 491a6ff.) Aristotle does use commonly understood language-based data in the *Categories* to get at features of, e.g., substances. But, *pace* Menn, this does not rule out a metaphysical or scientific interest. Aristotle famously does the same thing in e.g. *Met* G.1–2 and Z.1; cf. *Phys* IV.1–4.

16. See, e.g., Ross (1936) *ad loc.*

17. In the *Topics* Aristotle can use the term *dokounta* without qualification to designate those *endoxa* that are *phainomena*, i.e. those that appear generally to be so. (VIII.5 159b17–23)
18. Aristotle describes the initial data here as *ta sumbebekota kata ten phantasian*. (402b23–24) This does not mean, of course, the attributes that we might imagine the thing in question to have, but rather those that "are presented to us." (Hicks' tr.)
19. The most crucial data for Aristotle, as we shall shortly see, are all also perceptual data that make up experience (*empeiria*). So Aristotle holds that *endoxotata* in fact can and typically do also have this status. For development of this point, see Bolton (1987) and Bolton (1990) and further references there.
20. Earlier versions of this chapter were presented at sessions of the Los Angeles Area Colloquium in Ancient Philosophy and of the Midwest Seminar in Ancient and Medieval Philosophy. I particularly thank David Ebrey, Marko Malink, and Benjamin Morison for very helpful discussion of the issues.

# References

Ackrill, J. L. 1963. *Aristotle's Categories and De Interpretatione* (Oxford: Clarendon Press).

Bolton, R. 1987. "Definition and Scientific Method in Aristotle's *Posterior Analytics* and *Generation of Animals*," in A. Gotthelf and J. Lennox, (eds), *Philosophical Issues in Aristotle's Biology* (Cambridge: Cambridge University Press).

——— 1990. "The Epistemological Basis of Aristotelian Dialectic," in D. Devereux and P. Pellegrin, (eds), *Biologie, Logique et Metaphysique chez Aristote* (Paris: Editions du CNRS).

——— 1991. "Aristotle on the Objectivity of Ethics," in J. Anton and A. Preus, (eds), *Essays In Ancient Greek Philosophy IV: Aristotle's Ethics* (Albany: State University of New York Press).

——— 1995. "Science and the Science of Substance in Aristotle's *Metaphysics Z*," *Pacific Philosophical Quarterly* 76: 419–69.

Brunschwig, J. 1967. *Aristote: Topiques* (Paris: Les Belles Lettres).

Frede, M. 1987a. "Categories in Aristotle," in M. Frede, *Essays in Ancient Philosophy* (Minneapolis: University of Minnesota Press).

——— 1987b. "The Title, Unity and Authenticity of the Aristotelian *Categories*," in M. Frede, *Essays in Ancient Philosophy* (Minneapolis: University of Minnesota Press).

Frede, M. and G. Patsig. 1988. *Aristoteles Metaphysik Z* (München: C. H. Beck).

Malink, M. 2007. "Categories in *Topics* I.9," *Rhizai: A Journal for Ancient Philosophy and Science* 4: 271–94.

Matthen, M. 1978. "The Categories and Aristotle's Ontology," *Dialogue* 17: 228–43.

Menn, S. 1995. "Metaphysics, Dialectic and the *Categories*," *Revue de Metaphysique et de Morale* 100: 311–37.

Reeve, C. D. C. 1992. *Practices of Reason* (Oxford: Oxford University Press).

Ross, W. D. 1936. *Aristotle's Physics* (Oxford: Clarendon Press).

Smith, R. 1997. *Aristotle's Topics I and VIII* (Oxford: Oxford University Press).

# 6
# Grounding, Analogy, and Aristotle's Critique of Plato's Idea of the Good

*Allan Silverman*

In recent years, there has been a revival of interest in Aristotelian meta-physics. Among the prominent contemporary neo-Aristotelians one would include Gideon Rosen, Jonathan Schaffer, and especially Kit Fine, whose interest in Aristotelian approaches dates back at least to the 1980s. Doubtless, there are many differences among their respective views. But it is safe to say that all of them emphasize a relation of grounding or dependence that serves to mark some entities as funda-mental, foundational, or basic and other entities as derived or founded upon, or grounded in, the basic items. (A card-carrying Platonist myself, it strikes me as curious that pride of place is given to Aristotle in promoting the idea that there is this sort of dependence. Of course, Aristotle makes much of dependence in his critique of Plato whereas dependence is arguably less central to Plato's project. But more on the relation of Plato to Aristotle below.) Questions about whether certain items exist, for example, numbers, tables, minds, are secondary. "Of course they [numbers] do! The question is whether or not they are fundamental." (Schaffer, 2009, p. 346) Indeed, worries about existence are generally, though not entirely, dismissed as part of the Quinean and Carnapian orthodoxies against which these neo-Aristotelians set their sails. First one needs to determine the nature and number of grounding or dependence relations and how these relations, when they take funda-mental or basic entities as one relatum, yield the derived entities as the other relatum. In what follows, I want to examine some ways in which Schaffer, Fine and Aristotle think about grounding and dependence. In Section 1, I will focus on some problems arising from the manner in which the contemporary metaphysicians characterize their notion of ground. In Section 2, I will explore Aristotle's ideas of focal meaning and especially analogy, as developed in remarks on *energeia* in *Metaphysics* Theta and his criticism of Plato's Idea of the Good in *Nicomachean Ethics* I.6, in the hope that they may help us understand how to think about the relation between ground and the various grounding relations.

## 1  Dependence and grounding

Here is Schaffer's characterization of the view he attributes to Aristotle:

> Thus, on Aristotle's view, metaphysics is the discipline that studies substances and their modes and kinds, by studying the fundamental entities and what depends on them.

Putting this together, the neo-Aristotelian will conceive of the task of metaphysics as:

*Aristotelian task*: The task of metaphysics is to say what grounds what.

That is, the neo-Aristotelian will begin from a *hierarchical view of reality* ordered by *priority in nature*. The primary entities form a sparse structure of being, while the grounding relations generate an abundant super-structure of posterior entities. The primary is (as it were) all God would need to create. The posterior is grounded in, dependent on, and deriva-tive from it. The task of metaphysics is to limn this structure.

What of the method? A very general answer may be given as:

*Aristotelian method*: "The method of metaphysics is to deploy diagnos-tics for what is fundamental, together with diagnostics for grounding." (Schaffer, 2009, p. 351)

Schaffer's avowed model is Aristotle of the *Categories*. Aristotle's basic, fundamental unit(s) of being are the primary substances, namely Socrates, Secretariat, a rose. Schaffer makes no claim to be a scholar of Aristotle, so he offers a passage from Gill to illustrate what he aspires to emulate:

> In the *Categories* the main criterion [for selecting the primary substances] is ontological priority. An entity is ontologically primary if other things depend for its existence on it, while it does not depend in a comparable way on them. The primary substances of the *Categories*, such as particular men and horses, are subjects that ground the existence of the other things; some of the non-primary things, such as qualities and quantities, exist because they modify the primary substances, and others, such as substantial species and

genera, exist because they classify the primary entities...Therefore the existence of other things depends upon the existence of those basic entities. (Gill, 1989, p.3)

It is important to note a few features of Schaffer's picture of Aristotle's metaphysics. First, while he seems to think that all non-basic entities depend on the primary substances, he does not here distinguish the secondary substances, the species and genera that classify, to use Gill's word, the primary substances, from items in the other categories that are present in the primary substances, nor does he discuss the items that might be said to classify those items that are present in the primary substances, the universals in the non-substance categories. This is not to say that he does not appreciate that the relations between particulars in the non-substance categories and the basic substances, may well be different from the relations that connect the universals to particulars that fall under them. On the other hand, it is not clear whether he regards the way in which, say, quantities depend on primary substances to be the same or different from the way in which qualities depend on primary substances.

Second, Schaffer does not venture into the *Metaphysics* and its potential differences from the *Categories*. Thus, he omits (at least in this paper) any discussion of form and matter, actuality and potentiality, essence and accident, or the divine. Perhaps more saliently, he cruises quickly over the controversial notion of focal meaning or being and analogy or analogical being.

Third, and relatedly, Schaffer hesitates to address the status of the grounding relation or relations. While he insists that grounding should be taken as primitive and as an unanalyzable notion – "it is *the primitive structuring conception of metaphysics.*" (Schaffer, 2009, p. 364) – and while he thinks that grounding can be used as a primitive to analyze a family of useful structural concepts, that grounding may come in various species or kinds, he is undecided about the grounding relations themselves: "Surely they exist, so are they fundamental or derivative? I am undecided. If fundamental then they are conflated with substances. But if derivative there is a worrisome regress. A third option would be to redefine fundamentality to leave room for a third option....On this picture, grounding stands outside the priority ordering altogether, imposing structure on it." (Schaffer, 2009, p. 373, note 32)

There are at least two questions that bear on the status of the grounding relation. Critics and defenders of grounding recognize that the basic, primitive or metaphysically significant relation they appeal to, Grounding, with the capital $G$, embraces a species of small $g$ grounding relations.

Fine defends the primacy of a "distinctive kind of metaphysical explanation, in which explanans and explanandum are connected, not through some sort of causal mechanism, but through some constitutive form of determination." (Fine, unpublished, p. 1) He argues that there are three distinct forms of modality, metaphysical, natural and normative, and allows that there may be three distinct grounding or in-virtue-of relations corresponding to the modalities. Considering how to understand the relation between the generic notion of ground (Ground) and the three in-virtue-of relations, he offers two prospects: Either they might be defined in terms of a single generic relation, or the generic relation might be understood as some kind of "disjunction" of the special relations. "If there is a generic notion here, it is that which connects the modality to the corresponding explanatory relationship and that has no status as an explanatory notion in its own right." (Fine, unpublished, p. 4). Fine is inclined to the later option. This seems to open up the prospect that the Grounding relation is no longer to be accorded pride of place as primitive. Lacking any explanatory status, the work seems to be done by the three special explanatory relationships, the metaphysical, natural, and normative. Furthermore, there seem to be other (kinds of) relations, such as various reductive, emergence or supervenience relations, species, as it were, falling under the sub-genera of the metaphysical, natural, and normative in-virtue-of relations. If these various relations are realizations of the three special relations, then there is more reason to doubt that Grounding is doing any work at all, that is, any work that is not being done by the realizations of the three sub-genera.

For Fine, the different types of ground or in-virtue-of relations appear to align with the different modalities. It is unclear whether the essentialism that is key to his neo-Aristotelian picture aligns the different necessities with different conceptions of essence.

> Corresponding to the concepts of normative and natural necessity will be normative and natural conceptions of ground, which are to be distinguished from the purely metaphysical conception. The view that the normative is grounded in the natural is only plausible for the normative conception of ground and the view that the mental is grounded in the physical is only plausible for the natural conception. Since the grounding relation in these cases is not metaphysical, there is no need for there to be explanation of its holding in terms of the essentialist nature of the items involved. (Fine, unpublished, p. 54)

It seems that when the explanation holds in terms of the essentialist nature of the items, we are in the realm of the metaphysical. This leaves a great deal unspecified. When the items are mental entities, pain, or normative entities such as goodness, it might be queried whether they have essences, and if they do whether the sorts of explanations that appeal to those essences are metaphysical in-virtue-of their appeal to essences or whether they are normative or natural in-virtue-of the kind of item whose essences they are.

Leaving aside whether Grounding is doing any work, let us return to Schaffer's worry about the status of Grounding relations within metaphysical theory. This is an ancient concern, to which Plato draws attention early – in the *Phaedo* (100b-e) – and late – and *Parmenides* (129–34), and especially in the *Sophist*'s (254b-257) discussion of the greatest kinds. Having developed a metaphysics of Forms which are (Are) and particulars which participate, questions arise as to the status of the relation of participation that links particulars to Forms. Given the *Sophist*'s commitment to a Form of Being, it is not unreasonable to raise the same worry about the status of the relation of Being, the ontological counterpart to participation linking an essence to the Form, or other item whose essence it is. As I understand Plato, he opts for Schaffer's third option (*supra* p. 4), but with a twist: Being – Grounding – imposes structure on the priority ordering. But he thinks that the question of what sorts of features or relations ought to be treated as fundamental to a given theory should distinguished from the question of what entities are to be treated as fundamental. For Plato, Forms, souls and the receptacle might be the basic entities. Being and Participating would then be the fundamental relations, whose jobs, like Schaffer's Grounding relations, are to allow for the expansion of the ontology so as to include derived entities and to distinguish the different kinds and levels of beings. For Plato, "participants", too, exist, that is are *onta*, and thus he includes within the ontology material bodies, material particulars, and their images. (Some scholars will dispute this. Others would also include property-instances, the-large-in-Socrates.) Aristotle of the *Categories*, while accepting the same two fundamental relations, starts from different basic items, certain material particulars, and thus *derives* universals, Plato's Forms.

Worries about the status of Being and Participating, or of the specific grounding relations and the relation of the notion of Ground to them, evidence the difficulty that metaphysicians face in trying to incorporate the principles, relations and categories into the theory itself. Over the millennia, the branches of metaphysical inquiry have included a distinction between general and special metaphysics. The former would give one a detailed framework of the conditions and problems to be addressed by any proposed special metaphysics. Special metaphysics would then be the attempt to delineate a peculiar set of items and principles that satisfy the general conditions. In so far as questions about what one is doing when one engages in metaphysics deserve the title of "Metametaphysics", it would seem to be part of what traditionally has been the province of general ontology. Special ontologies would include Plato's metaphysics of Forms, self-moving souls, the receptacle and Being and Participating, and Aristotle's categorial account of substances, qualities, and so on, along with form and matter, and actuality and potentiality. General metaphysics might then, among other things, study the general question of the status of fundamental relations and their incorporation into the theory itself, as well as the various affinities between the receptacle, matter and potentiality, or *energeia* and self-moving soul, or essence, substance, form and Form, or affinities between different Grounding relations. (See Grice, 1989) Aristotle, it seems to me, engaged in both general and special metaphysics. Indeed, I think that a paradigm of general ontology is his effort to link the different special metaphysical items and, if they are elements in distinct special ontologies, different special ontologies through his accounts of the different senses of notions like cause, priority, and so on. (I aim not to imply anything linguistic or even conceptual through the use of "senses". For a primer, see *Metaphysics* Delta.) Of particular import here are his use of analogy and the phenomenon of focality or *pros hen* relations. Focality, or what Shields labels core-dependent homonymy (CDH), and analogy are ways of grouping objects that are members of a kind, as it were, but cannot be said to be synonymously the kind of thing they are and, perhaps, are not on a par with one another.

> CDH: *a* and *b* are homonymously F in a core-dependent way iff: (i) *a* is F; (ii) *b* is F; and either (iiia) the account of F in '*b* is F' necessarily makes reference to the account of F in '*a* is F' in an asymmetrical way, or (iiib) there is some *c* such that the accounts of F-ness in '*a* is F' and '*b* is F' necessarily make reference to the account of F-ness in '*c* is F' in an asymmetrical way. (Shields, 1999, p. 58. See pp. 124–6 for Shields' final account of the notion that relies on Aristotle's four causes.)

Schaffer takes Aristotle's account of the *pros hen* dependence of items in all the categories other than substance on the substances to be paradigmatic of his notion of ground. In these cases, the non-substances are not on a par with the substances, since the non-substances depend on the substances. Yet, all non-substantial beings seem to be treated on a par, since they all count as beings in so far as the account or accounts of what they are refer to the account of the substances on which they depend. If there is some one kind of substance to which all Schafferian derived beings are related in this or a suitably singular way, then they could all be beings in a *pros hen* fashion. On the other hand, if the issue concerns the different grounding relations and how they are related to each other, for instance whether they do or do not stand in some core-dependent relation to the Grounding relation, then the different grounding relations may yield different hierarchical arrangements of the various fundamental and derived beings. Perhaps it is clearer to consider how Fine's three in-virtue-of relations are united. If they stand in a relation of core-dependence, then, let us hypothesize, while the normative and the natural may be distinct from each other and from the metaphysical grounding relation, they may be related in a core-dependent manner on the metaphysical if somehow in giving an account of why each is an in-virtue-of relation, one must refer to the account of the metaphysical in-virtue-of relation.

It is easy to mistake the notion that items in non-substance categories depend on substances for the notion that non-substances lack essences, that is, that they are not definable. While strictly speaking, no particular is definable, whether Socrates or his pallor, both man and pallor are definable, which is to say that both have essences. In the case of the quality, Aristotle thinks that in saying what it is to be such, one will have to refer to the substance of which the quality is the quality. With respect to the substance, on the other hand, though (almost all) substances of course cannot fail to have qualities, in giving the definition no mention need be made of qualities (assuming that the differentia is not a quality). It seems to be unlikely that the different grounding relations are related in this fashion. To revert to Fine's three in-virtue-of groundings, while all may rely on the notions of essence and explanation, there is no obvious reference in the account of the normative to the account of the metaphysical. Might they be related in a different manner?

## 2  Actuality and the good

The argument of Aristotle's *Metaphysics* takes us from the search for causes and principles through the *aporiai* to the prospect for a single science of being and then to the prospect of different kinds of beings whose ordering potentially culminates in a distinct kind of divine substance. As we navigate the central books (and equally *Lambda*, were one to look that far), the priority or fundamentality of sensible substance, on which the *Categories'* account of dependence is based, seems to give way to the priority of form or soul. (It is not clear whether this is priority in the sense discussed in *Categories*.) The priority of soul or form over matter and composite in turn yields to an account in terms of potentiality and actuality, *dunamis* and *energeia*. While *Theta's* discussion of *dunamis* is obscure and controversial, there is no doubt that in the end, potentiality is dependent on actuality, that *energeia* or actuality is fundamental and prior in all ways in which priority is judged. It is all the more noteworthy, then, that in the crucial last chapters of *Theta*, the analysis of the ways in which items can be *energeiai* relies not on an account of synonymy or core-dependence, but on the concept of analogy. The various actualities – compare the various grounding relations or in-virtue-of relations – are analogously connected. What does that mean, and is there still a way to mark one or some as more basic than another?

It is not clear what Aristotle means by analogy. It seems, at bottom, a mathematical notion rooted in proportion. It holds among two (or more) pairs of things when as A is to B C is to D. Most recently Beere has investigated perhaps the star case of analogy, Aristotle's discussion of *energeia* in *Theta* 6 1048a35-b9; cf. 1046a4–11). (Beere, 2009, pp. 178ff) Analogy is used when one cannot explain how a concept applies univocally to all its instances. Moreover, it is used when the appeal to focality also comes up short. Thus, it would appear that there is no definitional or essential dependence that structures the various items that merit the term "actuality". There are, then, no primary actualities that all other types of actualities depend on in the manner in which complexions and diets, for instance, are healthy in so far as they depend on a fundamental notion of healthy bodies. In Beere's view, the fact that both straightforward synonymy and core-dependence fail to account for the unity of the items that are actualities shows that the dependence cannot be metaphysical.

> Nevertheless, it is compatible with this restriction that a certain class of cases in an analogical kind plays a special role for our grasp of the kind. For core-dependent homonymy, the dependence of the non-core cases on the core cases is an ontological, mind-independent dependence. It is not merely that our understanding of the derivative cases presupposes our understanding of the non-derivative ones. For instance, non-substantial properties depend, for their status as beings, on substances. In the context of analogy, one might allow that a certain case plays a privileged role for our grasp of the kind, without thinking that the other members of the kind depend on this case for their being members of the kind. (Beere, 2009, p. 187)

Since space is lacking to detail Beere's intriguing account of direct and indirect analogy, and since I want to look in greater detail at another famous case where Aristotle seems to suggest analogy may apply, namely his criticism of Plato's Form of the Good in NE I.6, let me highlight two features of analogy as Beere sees that notion developed in *Theta*. First, the notion of analogy as an aid to our (best) grasp of the unity of a kind seems altogether epistemological. As it unfolds, we are to look for a lucid account of the primary case of actuality, the house builder, and then come to understand the other cases on analogy with the primary case. This may well be the best way into an understanding of *energeia*, and it may explain why we classify different items as actualities, but it leaves open whether they are all, in fact, actualities of the same kind. (Compare Grice's worry that the meaning might be the same but different universals are introduced. (Grice, 1988, 186)) Second, if, as it seems, there is at a metaphysical level a primary actuality, to wit the prime mover, and if the primary case of the house builder exhibits a kind of actuality that is not itself the same as that of the primary actuality, we will need a careful account of how we are to move from the epistemologically primary to the ontologically primary. In short, we would need as detailed a logic (or metaphysic) of analogy as possible. Aristotle's never provides one, nor, to my knowledge, has anyone else. But perhaps we can make learn from Aristotle's use of focality and analogy in his argument with Plato over the good.

In Chapter 6 of Book I of the *Nicomachean Ethics*, Aristotle famously critiques Plato's Form of the Good. All three (neo-)Aristotelian accounts of dependency and grounding surface over the course of two Bekkar pages: the relation of the non-substance categories to substance; *pros hen* focality, that is core-dependent homonymy; and analogy. The opening argument declares that the Platonist does not posit Ideas of classes within which they recognize priority and posteriority. His first complaint is that things are called good both in the category of substance and in that of quality. Since substance is "prior in nature to the relative [or any other category] for the latter is like an offshoot and accident of what is, there could not be a common idea set over all these goods." (NE 1096a17–23) This first argument seems to suggest that where there is a priority scale the notion of goodness, say, simply doesn't apply. With regard to number, the argument seems to be that the Idea of Number, were there one, would have to be prior to the first number, which is impossible. So, there is no Idea of number. Correspondingly, were there an Idea of Good, it would have to be prior to the first/best good. Since Aristotle's case seems built on the claim that Plato does not posit an Idea of Number itself, and Plato, to most readers, does posit such an Idea, this argument seems flawed (But see Stewart, 1999, vol.1, pp. 77–81). His second argument:

> Further, since things are said to be good in as many ways as they are said to be (for things are called good both in the category of substance, as God and reason, and in quality, e.g., the virtues, and in quantity, e.g., that which is moderate, and in relation, e.g., the useful, and in time, e.g., ... clearly the good cannot be something universally present in all cases and single; for then it would not have been predicated in all the categories but in one only.

These are categorial (or definitional) complaints about the univocity of "good." This much-more-discussed argument relying on the semantic multiplicity of being and the categories may be only as good as the argument concerning the many ways of being. One question is whether the multiplicity of being is meant only as an example, or whether the multiplicity of good somehow relies on, or is dependent on, the many ways that being is said. Either way, it seems to most an obscure argument, and to many an unsuccessful one. Why should the goodness of items in different categories be so different that they cannot be understood under the single Form of the Good? One difficulty is that the account one might give as to why predication of goodness varies across categories should not yield multivocity *within* the category. Thus, Ackrill's appeal to different criteria or reasons for calling things good would fail to avoid this difficulty. (Ackrill, 1997, pp. 201–10) For instance, it is hard to see why "good" doesn't apply differently to the virtues and to colors, though both are qualities. But more worrisome, perhaps, to one trying to understand the debate between Plato and Aristotle is that it not only seems that Plato has no hesitations about thinking that categorically different things can bear the same property, he recognizes that there may well be different reasons for why they do. And that seems right. Just consider all the different things Socrates and his interlocutors call "beautiful" and the different reasons they offer for their claims (*Phd.* 100d and *Rep.* 474d3–475a2).

Aristotle seems to recognize the frailty of these arguments.

> An objection to what we have said, however, may be discerned in the fact that the Platonists have not been speaking about all goods, and that the goods that are pursued and loved for themselves are called good by reference to a single Form, while those which tend to produce or to preserve these somehow or to prevent their contraries are called so by reference to these, and in a different sense. Clearly, then, goods must be spoken of in two ways, and some must be good in themselves,

the others by reason of these. Let us separate, then, things good in themselves from things useful, and consider whether the former are called good by reference to a single idea. What sort of goods would one call good in themselves? Is it those that are pursued even when isolated from others, such as intelligence, sight and certain pleasures and honors? Certainly, if we pursue these also for the sake of something else, yet one would place them among things good in themselves. Or is nothing good other than the Idea of good in itself? In that case the Form will be empty. But if the things we have named are also things good in themselves, the account of the good will have to appear as something identical in them all, as that of whiteness is identical in snow and in white lead. But of honor, wisdom, and pleasure, just in respect of their goodness, the accounts are distinct and diverse. The good, therefore, is not something common answering to one Idea. (NE 1096b8–24. But for the last entry, the goods are found in Glaucon's division of goods at the beginning of *Republic* II.)

This is another argument that is liable to elicit a stare from the Platonist. Throughout the Socratic dialogues, and especially in the *Euthydemus*, Plato distinguishes so-called goods from true goods. Leaving aside precisely how to make sense of the so-called goods, the Platonist maintains that the virtues are *per se* or goods in themselves. With Glaucon's entry into the *Republic's* conversation (Rep. 357a-d2), the harmless pleasures, and, if distinct, enjoyment, are allowed to be *per se* goods. The heart of Aristotle's objection then seems to be that these pleasures, and the virtues, are not good in the same way, or good in the same sense. Granting for the moment that (harmless) pleasure and intelligence are *per se* goods, what is behind Aristotle's claim? One possibility is that because the natures of pleasure and intelligence are different, perhaps because they fall into different categories, then the same account of intrinsic goodness cannot apply – whether because the same account would be found in the essence of two categorially distinct items, or because goodness would have to be a necessary accident of two categorially distinct items. But even if we can make sense of these definitional claims in terms of Aristotle's account(s) of definitions and intrinsic accidents, the Platonist need not accept Aristotle's account. The natures of the items which bear the property of goodness may be distinct, but why should that entail a difference in the property borne?

But there are more intriguing responses. First, once we are in the realm of the *Republic*, it is an open question how we are to understand the Form of the Good and what it is for items, even items in what Aristotle would consider distinct categories, to participate in the Good. If, as seems plausible, the Good is superlatively (qualitatively) good, then nothing that partakes of it is qualitatively the same as it. Nonetheless, in virtue of their relation to the same one item, they could all be good in the same way, namely by partaking of the Good. Second, if we omit the Form of the Good, the very language Glaucon introduces and Aristotle picks up on seems to offer a single feature which all his examples exhibit, as it were: They are all welcomed as final goods; that is, they are pursued by valuing agents not as means but as ends. In Aristotelian terms, they are welcomed as parts of happiness, the practical good. Thus, nothing about the nature of the item independent of the valuations of agents makes something a *per se* good, and for that matter, the nature of things makes nothing an instrumental good. What "good" means in all cases is valued in a certain way by an agent of a certain type.

> But then in what way are things called good? They do not seem to be like the things that only chance to have the same name. Are the goods one, then, by being derived from one good or by all contributing to one good, or are they rather one by analogy? Certainly as sight is in the body, so is reason in the soul, and so on in other cases. But perhaps these subjects had better be dismissed for the present; for perfect precision about them would be more appropriate to another branch of philosophy. (NE 1096b26–31)

The presence of "rather", *mallon*, lends some credence to the belief that Aristotle's preferred position is that things are called good "by analogy". Now, how we are to reconcile this notion with his complaints about predication of a single notion across categorial barriers is, I confess, beyond my word limit, and in truth, beyond my abilities. We would have to work on a series of overlapping issues to begin to get a handle on how we are to think of the good, focality, and analogy, in Aristotle and Plato.

First, categories are attractive to the metaphysician in that they both facilitate the taking stock of the items in the ontology, and they leave open the prospect that certain categories or certain kinds of items have a more significant role to play than other items in understanding how things are structured or go together. On the other hand, since to assign items to distinct categories we need reasons to think one item goes here in virtue of certain properties that it has and that other items not of its categorial kind lack, categories serve as some kind of barrier to predicates that would try to migrate from one category to another. That there are category-crossing predicates is, of course, the very idea of the syncategorematic. Notions qualify as syncategorematic because they are so general that they apply to every item in the ontology regardless of its category. So, to be in any way is to be one; to be in any way is to be the same as one itself; different from anything else. But this does not seem true of *good*. While *good* can seem, at least to some, to feed off of the substantive or item it qualifies, it does not seem universally applicable whenever we have an item that qualifies as an item in the ontology. To be is not, simply in virtue of being (something), to be good. (A medieval might protest that being and being good do correlate through a conception of the actualization of one's nature. The more actually F something is, the "better" it is in being F. This idea, I suspect, is part and parcel of the relationship between goodness and *energeia* mentioned below. It is difficult, however, to make out how to extend this insight to items in the non-substance categories. Perhaps one might argue that every item is good in that from the cosmological perspective it is good that each item that is a part of the ontology is a part of the ontology.)

One further complication is that it is unclear when we cross a barrier or whether we even need to cross a categorial barrier to generate problems for the applicability or univocal applicability of "good". As Plato famously demonstrates in the *Republic*, there are puzzles generated when we move from meristic elements to the wholes of which the parts are parts; for instance, there are worries about how the good condition of the organs does or not does reflect on the good condition of the body. Can a body be in good condition when one of its organs is not? And there are problems generated when we move from bodies to souls, or from body and souls to individuals; from individuals to their actions; from individuals to collectives of them, for example, households or states; and from states to their activities, for example, laws.

The notion of analogy seems designed to help with understanding how predicates can be carried across boundaries. The very structure of an analogical notion with its two slots flanking the "as" – a one is to a two as a three is to a four – permits one to fill in the slots with items from different categories, or at least items that are different enough within a category: sight/body as reason/soul. One question would be whether we are to understand Aristotle here to be indicating that as sight is good for the body, so reason is good for the soul. The first part of the analogy is harder to understand. Perhaps the idea is that what is emblematic of the body is its animal aspect and that what is characteristic of animal nature is that it is locomotive and aesthetic. Thus, the well functioning of the body is encapsulated in Aristotle's favorite perceptual faculty, sight. By the same token, we can then see that well functioning of the soul is encapsulated in its rational activities.

Focality also seems suited to explain how predicates can be carried across categorial barriers. The star cases of healthy and medical point to a single notion in light of which we understand how complexions and diets and bodies and environments can all be healthy. One critical question is whether our understanding of analogy requires that we have some central notion that serves as a focal element. We saw above that Beere, while denying that there is a focal element in his account of the analogical notion of *energeia*, does allow that there is an epistemically privileged case, that of the house builder, in-virtue-of which we are to understand how the other examples all deserve the name *energeia*, though there is no definitional element in common. It is not, it seems to me, obvious whether some analogical notions admit of focal items whereas others do not. Perhaps *energeia* lacks, whereas good has a focus. But leaving aside the general analysis of analogy, the specifics of good and *energeia* deserve further study. For the final chapter of *Theta*, along with the remarks about the prime mover in *Lambda*, suggest that *energeia* and good are themselves intimately related. This will, of course, not be a surprising outcome, given the role of function (*ergon*) in the account of the good.

The provenance of functional accounts of the good is Socratic or Platonic intuitions. The *Republic* emphasizes the notion of function, beginning in Book One with the function argument (352d–354), and continuing through the first four books with its assimilation of the moral virtues under the banner of the principle of specialization: one item/one job. Without entering the debate over the unity of virtues and whether there are political/civic virtues that an individual can enjoy, the robust virtues all require knowledge of the Good. Thus in Book VI and VII Plato turns his attention to the Form of the Good, marking it first as that which all humans desire despite their unclarity as to what it is, something that offers satisfaction only when it is the genuine article one has grasped or acquired. It is then made into the special object of rational pursuit, that which our rational component by its very nature desires. Finally, it is assigned the notorious status as the item responsible for the being and truth of all that there is, canonically understood to mean in the first instance all the intelligibles, that is, Forms, and derivatively all that depends upon them.

We shall return to the global dependency in a moment. First, note that the Good is that at which reason aims, and when it is functioning best, that which it attains. The proper or best functioning of reason just is its knowing the Good, though the Good is not itself knowledge of the Good. In keeping with our effort to track the grounding or dependency relations, it is to the Good itself that priority is assigned. Now, were one able to assign a functional aspect to other creatures or their organs or parts, then one could assimilate the good for all these creatures or their parts to the well functioning of them, whatever that may be. We do not lack for terms to describe the well functioning of these aspects of creatures. So, for instance, we can think of expressions such as "being in good condition" and then distinguish this sort of second-level or generic epithet (Grice) from healthy, a first-order epithet that applies to body. Thus, a healthy body is a body in what is good condition for a body. We can then see how we might find healthy (being carried across a barrier?) to be used to speak of a mind, *mens sana, corpus sanum*, signaling at a minimum that the mind, too, is to be conceived as in a good condition, though healthy would be an analogical epithet used to describe such a mind.

Even if we can extend the notion of being in a good condition throughout all the substances, Aristotle's objection as to the predication of the good in the non-substance categories seems to hit home. What would it mean for a quality or a quantity to be in a good condition? What is it for a color to be in good condition, or the environment? There seem to be two options here.

The first is to assimilate the good and the beautiful, *kalos*, and to allow that sometimes when we predicate "good" of say a climate or a time we are predicating something like an aesthetic value. The second is to regard many, if not most, of these predications as signaling either the instrumental goodness of the subject or, perhaps equivalently at times, as having an anthropological teleological basis. That is, these items are good because they conduce to the flourishing of rational agents or at least living beings. This implies that all the goods in the non-substance categories are either roughly aesthetic goods or secondarily good or instrumentally good, finding their value in the valuations or the hypothetical valuations of agents. There is some prospect that Aristotle reckons that the division between intrinsic and instrumental goods signals the non-univocity of good.

But the lead complaint seems to be with the idea that Plato's Good is somehow transcendent and separate and thus could not account for how different non-instrumental goods could be good. Here we seem to be faced with two choices, though both will meet with objections. First, note that Plato's Good sometimes appears as an exemplar or paradigm and sometimes as an abstract property. The language of resemblance that percolates through the *Symposium* and other works plays better with the Good as exemplar that other items as diverse as sunsets and times might be said to approximate. The Good as exemplar may well be indefinable. If the indefinable is simple, then the Good is simple, and thus, one might think, only something that another can resemble or approximate. On the other hand, the idea as property seems to involve and to ground the notion of order.

It is in the Form's capacity as a property that Aristotle offers one critique. He begins EE I. 8 so:

> We must consider, therefore, what the best (*to ariston*) is, and in how many senses the term is used. The answer seems to be principally contained in three views. For it is said that the best of all things is the absolute good, and that the absolute good is that which has the attributes of being the first of goods and of being by its presence the cause to the other goods of their being good; and both of these attributes, it is said, belong to the Form of the Good (I mean both being the first of goods and being by its presence the cause to other things of their being good, since it is of that Form that goodness is most truly predicated (inasmuch as the other goods are good by participation in and resemblance to the Form of the Good) and also it is the first of goods, for the destruction of that which is participated in involves the destruction of the things participating in it, and that is the relation existing between what is primary and what is subsequent. (Loeb translation, 1217b1–16)

For Aristotle, because it is the first of goods, the Idea of Good is best among goods and in being best, it must have goodness or be goodness in a superlative or paradigmatic way. Thus, it is to be counted among the good things. In being the cause of goodness in others, it seems that it somehow transmits one and the same quality that it has to others. In short, both it and the other goods are good in the same way such that there is some one feature that all good things share. Of course, Aristotle denies that there is a separate Form of the Good. But, as Beere notes (Beere, 2009, p. 329), this does not relieve him from asking and answering two questions:

1) What is goodness? That is, what is it that all good things have in common?
2) What is the good itself? That is, what is the first of all good things, because of which all other good things are good?

Aristotle does not, I think, answer the first question directly, and perhaps not at all. (The N.E. opens with the lines: "Every sort of expert knowledge and every inquiry, and similarly every action and undertaking, seems to seek some good. Because of that, people are right to affirm that the good is 'that which all things seek'." (1094a1–3, Rowe translation) Leaving aside the issue of whether there is a fallacy here, if this remark is to serve as (the first step in an) account of goodness, much more would have to be said about how goodness applies to non-psychological activities or agents.) But he does offer an answer to the second. The good itself is the first unmoved mover of the heavens, the prime mover of *Lambda* 10. Precisely how it is responsible for the goodness of other things is obscure. But as the argument of *Theta* unfolds, with the triple priority of *energeia* over *dunamis*, and with the isolation of pure *energeia* and the denial of badness among the principles, it seems more and more that Aristotle is prepared to identify goodness itself with pure *energeia*. How the other good things are to be understood would require a proper tracing of their relation to pure *energeia* at the metaphysical level, and, at best, their goodness would have to be understood analogically and perhaps focally, in so far as these notions can be complementary. Whatever account one can provide for the relation of pure energeia to goodness – in what manner is the prime mover good? – would allow one to begin at least to see how one might build an analogical account for how other good things could be good.

The idea of the prime mover as the good and *energeia* as goodness gives credence to Aristotle's intuition that there is no single quality found in all the various good things, even supposing that all depend on the prime mover for their being good. There is pure *energeia* only in few cases (maybe one). And as we retreat, as it were, from substances, the analogy founded on *energeia* can only grow more stretched. Thus, we will likely find both differences among types of goods and, as we move away from the superlative goodness of what is the good, we will have degrees of goodness enter the picture. Plato's Form of the Good has a decided advantage in one sense over the Aristotelian assimilation of the Good itself to the Prime Mover or pure actuality. Nothing in principle precludes it from being participated in by items that cannot be *energeiai*. (But, of course, it is not without its problems as a Form. Chief among them is whether it can both be the very form that it is, namely The Good itself, and also be, as the argument requires, a good thing. If it is good in the same way as the various other good things, then it seems subject to third man arguments. (Note that only the greatest kinds will be subject to these arguments, so only they will arguably both be and have the very property each respectively is.)

Aristotelian objections to Plato's account persuade many that the variety of items across the categories that we call good cannot all be good in the same way. I have studiously avoided discussing Aristotle on meaning and signification, owing to the limits of this format. The distinction between first-order or second-order properties/universals, or between surface, shallow, or stereotypical meaning and a more robust or deeper or real meaning is available to the Platonist as well as to the contemporary realist. Indeed, an adequate discussion of these issues would have to investigate the relation between different senses and different universals, leaving open the possibilities that there is only one universal but many senses of "good", as well as that there are many universals but only one sense of the word. We considered Ackrill's attempt to explain the non-univocity of good in that our predications of goodness are grounded in different criteria that fall into distinct categories. Whether viewed as an epistemological or a metaphysical claim, we still find univocity. Victory in tennis and victory in war are the same, beating one's opponent in a competitive situation, though how it is achieved is very different. Shields, in response to the defense of the criteriological conception that relies on the categorically different ways in which a notion is realized, aptly adduces the concept of what it is to be dangerous. It is dangerous to smoke, and it is dangerous to be in the wrong place at the wrong time. But being dangerous is not therefore non-univocal. On the contrary, what it is to be dangerous will remain fixed across these applications... (Shields, 1999, p. 204)

Shield's penultimate account canvases the functional interpretation of the categorial argument. Relying on the premise that the good of a functional kind consists in that for the sake of which F's act, that is, their end, and that the ends for different functional kinds necessarily differ, the argument concludes that what goodness consists in for different functional kinds necessarily differs. The functional interpretation of the categorial argument then adds that the categories themselves are functional kinds. That categories are functional kinds is controversial. First, even if one can make out that substances have functions, what is it for the category of substance to be a functional kind, or as Shields puts it, what are the functions of substances as substances? Is one substance more functional than another such that god and mind are superlatively functional in a way that man and oak trees are not? More difficult still is to generalize this across the other categories such that qualities and locations are functional.

But leaving aside the categories themselves, what about the attractive idea that different substances have different ends and that as a result their goodness varies with the different ends that they have? There is no universal good that the different substances share in when each realizes its end. But perhaps Aristotle's idea is that each substance stands to its good in a manner analogous with other substances and their respective goods. And serving as a focus for this analogy would be the relationship of the primer mover to goodness itself. Perhaps then one could defend Schaffer and especially Fine from criticisms that have been leveled against those who seek to locate a primitive, basic Grounding relation in virtue of which the many small g grounding relations are to be understood. Grant that there is a host of grounding relations, but no common big G grounding relation that the different grounding relations share in. If Aristotle is to be a guide to modern neo-Aristotelians, perhaps the most fruitful way to understand the relations between Ground and the various grounding relations is not that of genus to species, or that of determinable to determinate realizations, but rather that they are related both focally and analogically or at least by analogy. Each of Fine's three special explanatory relations will be analogically related in virtue of the relation linking their respective metaphysical, natural, and normative explananda and explanantes, namely through a proper understanding of the essences of the normative, natural and metaphysical properties that are their concerns. If such a line is plausible, it would be a further question whether this analogical relationship admits of a focus. If so, it would be no surprise if the metaphysical relation turned out to be the focus of Grounding.

## Bibliography

Ackrill, J. 1997. "Aristotle on 'Good' and the Categories," in J. Ackrill, *Essays on Plato and Aristotle* (Oxford: Oxford University Press).

Beere, J. 2009. *Doing and Being* (Oxford: Oxford University Press).

Fine, K. Unpublished. "Guide to Ground".

Gill, M. L. 1989. *Aristotle on Substance: The Paradox of Unity* (Princeton: Princeton University Press).

Grice, H. P. 1988. "Aristotle on the Multiplicity of Being," *Pacific Philosophical Quarterly* 69: 175–200.

—— 1989. "Metaphysics, Philosophical Eschatology, and Plato's *Republic*," in H. P. Grice, *Studies in the Way of Words* (Cambridge, MA: Harvard University Press).

Rosen, G. 2010. "Metaphysical Dependence: Grounding and Reduction," in B. Hale and A. Hoffmann, (eds), *Modality: Metaphysics, Logic, and Epistemology* (New York: Oxford University Press).

Schaffer, J. 2009. "On What Grounds What," in D. J. Chalmers, D. Manley and R. Wasserman, (eds), *Metametaphysics* (Oxford: Oxford University Press).

Shields, C. 1999. *Order in Multiplicity* (Oxford: Oxford University Press).

Stewart, J. A. 1999. *Notes on the Nicomachean Ethics* (Bristol: Thoemmes Press).

# 7
# Essence, Modality, and the Master Craftsman

*Stephen Williams and David Charles*

## 1 Introduction

According to Aristotle, the notion of essence has two interrelated roles: one definitional, the other explanatory. On the one hand, it specifies what it is for something to belong to a particular natural kind of thing,[1] the specification being, of necessity, both necessary and sufficient for membership of the kind;[2] while, on the other, it explains[3] not just why members of such kinds have certain further properties, but also ultimately why they *must* have such properties.[4]

Any defense of this conception, then, will require an answer to at least the following two questions:

(A) How does explanatory role figure in the proper understanding of essence?

(B) Why should essences have both definitional and explanatory roles? (Why should they both characterize what a particular kind is and also be explanatory in the way indicated in answer to question (A)?)

As we shall see, however, it is not an immediate consequence of the answer to (A) that essences can explain why kind members *must have* certain properties (or why they have corresponding *necessary* properties). So, a full defense of Aristotle's conception should also require an answer to a third question:

(C) How can essences explain why kind members *must have* certain properties?

Beginning (§2) with question (A), we consider first a powerful and elegant way of understanding Aristotle's conception of essence that

121

seems to emerge naturally from certain passages in the *Posterior Analytics* and the *Metaphysics*. According to this interpretation, an account of the causal explanatory role of the essence of a kind enters into the very definition of the kind which constitutes its essence. Despite its power and elegance, however, we argue that such an understanding is likely to be too restrictive; moreover, in light of the fact that although the passages are consistent with the interpretation, they do not mandate it, we argue further that Aristotle is better thought of as articulating a more general account of which the model elaborated in the first interpretation is an instance. Having fixed on the general role of explanation in essence, we then turn to question (C), and it is to answering this question (§§3-6) that we devote the bulk of the chapter. This still leaves question (B). We conclude (§7) by entertaining some speculative thoughts about why it should be the case that essence has both explanatory and definitional roles.

## 2  The role of explanation in essence

Near the beginning of the *Posterior Analytics* (*Post. An. B*), Aristotle writes:

> In all these cases, it is clear that what is and why it is are the same. What is an eclipse? Privation of the light from the moon by the screening of the earth. Why is there an eclipse? Or why is the moon eclipsed? Because the light leaves it when the earth screens it. What is harmony? An arithmetical ratio of high and low. Why does the high harmonize with the low? Because there is an arithmetical ratio between them. (*Post. An.* B.10, 90a14ff)

And later, in one of the key chapters on definition, he returns to the theme with another example:

> "Why does it thunder?" Because the fire is extinguished in the clouds. But "What is thunder?" Noise of fire being extinguished in the clouds. Hence the same account is used in different ways: in one way as a continuous demonstration, in the other a definition. (*Post. An.* B.10, 94a4ff)

In this second passage, Aristotle considers two questions:

(1)  What is thunder?
(2)  Why does it thunder?

And his answer to question (1) is:

Noise in the clouds brought on by the fire being extinguished

So, a full specification of the *definiens* and *definiendum* would be:

thunder is the type of noise in the clouds that is brought on by the fire being extinguished

Aristotle reformulates question (2) to obtain the right *explanandum*, replacing "thunder" with "noise in the clouds". His question is:

(2*) Why does noise occur in the clouds?

to which his answer is:

because fire is extinguished

So a full specification of *explanandum* and *explanans* runs as follows:

a certain type of noise in the clouds occurs because fire is extinguished

where "a certain type of noise" refers to thunder, a determinate type of noise (yet to be fully defined).

Finally, in considering this structure, Aristotle explicitly identifies the cause (e.g. fire being quenched in the clouds), marked out by the middle term of the corresponding syllogism,[5] with the essence (90a1, 90a15, 93b8). Thus (at 93b8), in answer to the question "What is thunder?", he simply writes: "Extinction of fire in cloud". The cause is that which makes the phenomenon the one it is.

What emerges from these passages is a vivid picture of how the characterization of the essence of thunder might answer both the definitional (what-it-is) question and the explanatory (why-it-is) question, and how therefore it might provide an answer to our question (A).Thus, in 94aff and 93b8, Aristotle in effect identifies thunder three times over: first, with a certain type of noise in the clouds, secondly, with the extinction of fire in the clouds, and thirdly, with a certain type of noise in the clouds brought about by [its being] the extinction of fire in the clouds. He provides us, then, with three specifications, the third being the one which is complete; and it is this one that provides the full answer to the what-it-is question. But now this same specification of the essence involves combining the first two as an explanation: what is specified in the second causes, or causally explains, what is specified in the first. So, it also records the answer to the why-it-is question.

Such a picture is powerful and beautifully economical; and it is one which can evidently be extended consistently to the other examples Aristotle considers here, using the same threefold specification of the phenomenon: *being an F, a G, and an F brought on by [its being] a G*. Thus, eclipses are privations of light from the moon, screenings of the moon by the earth, and privations of light from the moon produced by [their being] screenings of the moon by the earth; and similarly harmony is a certain kind of sound, an instantiation of an arithmetical ratio of high and low, and a certain kind of sound produced by [its being] an instantiation of an arithmetical ratio of high and low. In each case, the third specification not only characterizes the essence of the kind in full, it also involves intrinsically a causal explanation of the phenomena that are instances of the kind.

Powerful though the picture is, however, the question immediately arises whether it is fully general, and in particular, whether it can be extended to other categories of being. For what is noticeable about the cases above (viz. thunderclaps, eclipses, and instances of harmony) is that they all concern objects in the category of phenomena, where we might *expect* to find causes, and especially *efficient* causes, figuring in a full understanding of the kinds in question.[6] But why should this model be appropriate to objects in other categories, particularly those in the category of substance?

It was in response to precisely this concern that David Charles, in *Aristotle on Meaning and Explanation*, tried to suggest that Aristotle was engaged in a research project of extending the model that applies to the efficient causal cases to ones governed by teleology.[7] And such an extension clearly has much going for it. For it is certainly true for artifact kinds that the notion of a final or teleological cause is well-suited to replace that of an efficient cause in an account of their essences that satisfies the tripartite structure. To use Aristotle's own example, houses are arrangements of bricks, stones, and other materials, they are shelters, and they are arrangements of bricks, stones, and other materials designed for shelter.[8] Moreover, it is possible to take Aristotle in the *Metaphysics* as applying the same model to natural kinds in the category of substance, too. In particular, it is consistent with *Metaphysics* Z.17 and H.2 to think of human beings as two-footed animals, rational souls, and two-footed animals arranged for the sake of being a rational soul.[9]

However, while teleology is ideal for the elucidation of artifact kinds, and a sort of functional explanation that is not simply *faute de mieux* might even now be appropriate in some areas of biology,[10] it would be dogmatic to insist that all natural kinds, even all biological kinds, be definable in this way. At any rate, it is unlikely that the elucidations of the essential natures of all chemical and physical natural kinds must make use of either teleological or efficient causation – witness the fact that chemical elements can effectively be defined in terms of their atomic structure. This is not to say that efficient causation (say), perhaps through essential dispositional properties, might not sometimes figure in the definition of such kinds. We simply counsel against an *a priori* insistence on its presence.[11]

Does this mean that Aristotle's project is irredeemably flawed? We think not. For his strategy may well be better understood as an attempt to carry through a research program of the type that Charles was envisaging, but not one specifically dependent on the idea that causal explanation must be built into the definitions that articulate the essences of particular kinds, that is, into the contents of the elucidations of their natures. Rather, he may be thought of as proposing a conception of essence according to which essences have the potential to explain various features of members of the kind – perhaps the features they have *by virtue of* being members of the kind – without the definitions that constitute those essences *saying* that they have such potential. An essence simply *is* a definable nature with explanatory power.[12] Of course, it might be insisted that we could cleave to the original picture by widening the concepts of causality that can figure in the content of the definition. After all, the atomic structures which characterize the various chemical elements are defined in terms of their differing material constitutions. So, we might say that in such cases their *material cause* is figuring in the content of their definitions. It is a familiar question, of course, why material causation should be thought of as a genuine species of causation at all; but what is interesting here is that, according to the more general interpretation, Aristotle has a natural answer, namely that it figures in an appropriate way in the kinds of explanations that essence provides. Remember that at no point does Aristotle claim to be able to *prove* that there are only four causes. For although in *Meta* A.7 (988b16-19), he says that it is plain that there are just the four, he also cites the failure of earlier thinkers to find any other types of cause as evidence of this claim. But this strongly suggests that he does not *rule out* the possibility of another type being uncovered; and in context there seems no better constraint on what would count as such than is provided by explanation. It is explanation that is doing all the work.

It is also worth noting that when Aristotle identifies what something *is* with what is explanatorily basic in the *Posterior Analytics* (*Post. An.* B.2, 90a14-15), he does not require that all definitions *explicitly* involve features stated to be caused by the basic features (unlike the definition of processes such as thunder or eclipses); and when he requires us to read a definition off an explanatory demonstration (*Post An. B.* 10, 94a1-4), he does not insist that the definition itself explicitly state the causal connection, even if the example in 94a5 does so: noise of fire being quenched in the clouds.[13] Moreover, the suggested definitions of substances in the *Metaphysics* do not all seem to invoke explicitly the idea of one thing being caused/explained by another. Even the definition of "man" (sketched at 1041b5-9 and 1043a5-16) does not *require* that the cause be part of the definition. At 1043b10, man is described as a two-footed animal + something else, a middle or causally explanatory term to be introduced. But again, it is not required that the fact that man's two-footedness is caused e.g. by his being a rational soul be explicitly part of the definition. According to the more general picture of Aristotle that we are endorsing here, therefore, it is not that Aristotle assumed that all natural kinds should be defined according to the eclipse model, even if processes or artifacts are defined in a way which explicitly involves causal material in the relevant definitions. Rather, we simply allow that the definitions that can be read off relevant explanatory syllogisms do not need the causal material as part of their content. Or if their content must be thought of in this way, that is only because it figures in an appropriate way as part of an explanation.

## 3   Question (C): The general structure of the argument

Our answer to Question (A), then, is that essences are, by definition, definable natures with explanatory power. But although it will follow from this that they will be able to explain why kind members have certain properties, it is not immediately apparent how they can sometimes explain why such members must have them. This was our Question (C) in §1. It is to the task of answering this question that we turn in the next four sections. We begin in the present section by indicating the general structure of how we intend to proceed.

Suppose we have a kind K with an essence G. Then according to the Aristotelian picture of essence that we wish to defend, being such as to have G *defines* K in such a way that

(Def) $\Box\forall x[Kx \leftrightarrow Gx].$[14]

But (or so we are assuming) it also *explains*, for certain properties, F, not only why it is necessary that members of K are F, i.e.

(a)  $\Box\forall x[Kx \rightarrow Fx],$

but also why it's necessary for members of K to be F, or why members of K have to be F, i.e.

(b)  $\forall x[Kx \rightarrow \Box Fx]$

Indeed, putting (a) and (b) together, it explains finally why it's *necessary* that members of K have to be F, i.e.

(c)  $\Box\forall x[Kx \rightarrow \Box Fx]$

How can it do this? Well it can explain (a) via (Def) and

(Exp) $\Box\forall x[Gx \rightarrow Fx],$

since Def and Exp entail (a).[15] And with Exp, it can also explain (c) via Def and

(Ess) $\Box\forall x[Kx \rightarrow \Box Kx],$

since Def, Exp and Ess entail (c).[16] (The explanation of (c) could also proceed via

(Ess*) $\Box\forall x[Gx \rightarrow \Box Gx],$

rather than Ess, since Ess and Ess* are necessarily equivalent given Def.)

So, the Aristotelian picture requires us to justify at least three claims: Def, Exp and Ess (or Ess*). That is to say, it has to warrant the claims that definitions of kinds are necessary; that true, explanatory, universal generalizations connecting essence and property are necessary; and that members of a kind are necessarily members of the kind. We will explore Def in §4, Exp in §5, and Ess (and Ess*) in §6. It should be emphasized here that while we will occasionally make use of resources not available to Aristotle himself, none is (in our view) materially out of sympathy with his overall metaphysics.

## 4  Definitional necessity

So, let us begin with Def – the claim that being such as to have K's essence, or being such as to have G, is necessarily equivalent to being a K. Why should a claim like this, the claim that it is necessary that something has G iff it's a K, ever be true? Here it is tempting simply to appeal to the fact that G is supposed to define K, for definitions, by definition, are surely necessary truths. However, more argument than this is needed to avoid the charge of equivocating on the notion of definition. For while some definitions will undoubtedly be necessary by virtue of the fact that the relevant *definientia* and *definienda* are synonymous, it is certainly not obvious that the kinds of definition that Aristotle has in mind here will invariably be of this sort, since some will emerge only after considerable empirical investigation. Perhaps it is necessary that someone is a bachelor iff he's an unmarried man, by virtue of the synonymy of "bachelor" and "unmarried man". It is much harder to argue that it is necessary that something is a lemon iff it has genetic structure, G, say, simply by virtue of the synonymy of "lemon" and "G". The biconditional, if true, would encapsulate an important discovery about things that fall under a concept whose verbal expression already meant something else. On the face of it, even if G did constitute a definition of "lemon", it would be a very different kind of definition from the definition of "bachelor".

Here is not the place for an exhaustive review of the ways in which such definitions might emerge as necessary. In the present context, however, one such way, one that makes use of the idea that Aristotelian essences concern the nature of kinds or what they are, has a particular claim on our attention. For it is natural to fill out this idea by supposing that being a K and being such as to have its corresponding essence, G, are identical.[17] And if so, we may then be able to appeal to the necessity of identity, as elaborated and defended in their different ways by Barcan Marcus, Kripke, and others, to conclude that this identity is necessary; whence a simple step of logic will take us finally to Def.

In more detail, then, let us suppose that K's essence is indeed G, and that the right way to fill out this idea is to say that:

Being a K = being such as to have G

By Leibniz's Law, we know that objects drawn from any ontological category are identical only if they have all their properties in common. So, if we treat being a K and being such as to have G as objects, we may deduce that

For all properties, $\Phi$, $\Phi$(being a K) iff $\Phi$(being such as to have G)

Hence, taking as a value of $\Phi$ the property which a thing has when $\square$ it is identical to being such as to have G, we may deduce that

$\square$ being such as to have G = being such as to have G iff $\square$ being a K = being such as to have G.

But trivially,

$\square$ being such as to have G = being such as to have G

Hence it follows that

$\square$ being a K = being such as to have G.

But now if being a K and being such as to have G are necessarily identical, then they are necessarily coextensive. Hence $\square\forall x[Kx \leftrightarrow Gx]$, i.e. Def.

There is a gap in the argument, however. Consider the claim that

(∗)  Being a Manchester United player in the 1968 European Cup Final = being eitherAlex Stepney or Billy Foulkes or ... or Bobby Charlton or George Best.

With the dots filled in correctly, one can quite easily hear this as true. But if it is true, it does not look on the face of it like a necessary truth. Any of the players might have broken a leg in the semi-final and been unable to play in the final. On the other hand, it is also possible to hear the claim as false: after all, *what it is* to be a Manchester United player in the 1968 European Cup Final is not to be one or other of the actual players. On the contrary, what it is to be such an individual involves what it is to be a member of the club, what it is to have been picked for the match, and so on. Either way, therefore, the identity is not necessary: it is either contingently true or actually false. But then might we not say the same thing about the claim that being a K is identical to being such as to have G? Maybe it is true insofar as it is speaking about the things that are Ks or have G, but only contingently so; and false insofar as it is a claim about what it is to be a K and what it is to be such as to have G. Either way, the identity cannot be necessary.[18]

Aristotelians, of course, can respond by pointing out that the dilemma does not apply to the claim that being K is being such as to have G. For although it is true that the extensions of K and G are identical, that's precisely because what it is to be K is identical to what it is to be such as to have G, G being an articulation of the nature of Ks. The argument could then be formulated in unambiguous terms using the rather cumbersome form of words "what it is to be X", instead of the gerundive construction ("being X").[19] Or – at the expense of being formally unfaithful to Aristotle – we could make explicit appeal to the notion of a property, to speak of the property of being a K and the property of being such as to have G. The argument would then begin with the claim that immediately by virtue of the nature of being a K, the property of being such as to have G simply is that of being a K, and, *mutatis mutandis*, it could proceed as before.

At this point, however, it might be insisted that a version of a concern that Kripke raised when considering the necessity of identity in relation to ordinary objects might equally well apply here. Using Kripke's example involving Ben Franklin,[20] the corresponding argument involving the true claim that

The first Postmaster General of the US = the inventor of bifocals

as an initial premise would be invalid. For although it would also be true that

□ The inventor of bifocals = the inventor of bifocals,

it plainly does not follow that

□ The first Postmaster General of the US = the inventor of bifocals,

since this sentence is false. And might something similar not apply in our version? Certainly, we would hope not to be able to prove the necessity of

The first property to cross Tony Blair's mind each Sunday = the property of being a sinner

from this as a premise, since even if it happens to be true, its necessitation is false. So, why should the same not be true of

The property of being a K = the property of being such as to have G?

But a Kripkean answer to the question in relation to the Ben Franklin argument applies just as well here. What makes it only contingently true that the first Postmaster General of the US = the inventor of bifocals is that at least one of the specifications of the individual Ben Franklin applies to him only contingently[21] and the specifications are not such as to co-vary necessarily. Similarly, what makes it only contingently true (if it is true) that the first property to cross Tony Blair's mind each Sunday = the property of being a sinner is the fact that the specification of the property as the first property to cross Tony Blair's mind each Sunday applies to the property of being a sinner only contingently; he could have entertained a different property. But this does not apply to the claim that the property of being a K = the property of being such as to have G, since, according to the Aristotelian picture, being a K and being such as to have G are different specifications of what it is to be a K, one tautological, the other elucidatory; they are canonical specifications of the nature of the properties in question, and hence cannot but apply to those properties.[22] It is necessary, therefore, that the properties are identical, and Def is vindicated.

## 5   Explanation and necessity

With Def vindicated, we now turn to Exp – the claim that necessarily anything with the defining essential properties of K, namely G, is F. Why, for particular properties F, should this be true? Given that in this context Aristotle is particularly interested in explanations which answer the question: what is it about Ks *as such* which accounts for their being F, we might appeal at first blush to the fact that their being F must hold in virtue of their being Ks, i.e. in virtue the essence of K. But while it is all but certain that the "in virtue of relation" involves modality in some form, it needs further argument to be sure that this modality will be straightforward necessity. After all, it may well be in virtue of his having written *The Satanic Verses* that Salman Rushdie had a *fatwa* issued against him. But there is no straightforward necessary connection between these two facts. To be sure, Aristotelians might well claim that it was not his writing the Satanic Verses *as such* that accounts for the *fatwa*. But even if this is true, it would only strengthen their case if there were independent reason for thinking that "as such" explanation, explanation in virtue of essence, involved, or at least entailed, simple necessity.

Remembering that essences are by definition causally explanatory, we might at this point appeal to the fact that there will be causal connections between the essence of the kind and the property to be explained. Here is an illustration. Notice that although it invokes causality explicitly, this does not mean that causality or causal explanation is being smuggled back into the content of the definition that constitutes the salient essence. (It could be there, but it needn't be.)[23] So, suppose, then, that it is a superficial, but universal, property of lemons that they are tart, and that this is a property of lemons *as such*, i.e. a property that lemons have in virtue of their being lemons or in virtue of their having the essence of lemons; and let us assume that this essence is their genetic structure, G. Then the tartness of lemons will be properly explained by adverting to G; and with the introduction of causality, we might expect such an explanatory connection to be articulated e.g. via the universal causal claim:

$\forall x$ [x's being such as to have G causes x's being tart]

But being universal and causal, such a claim will be necessary and entail

$\forall x$ [Gx$\rightarrow$ x is tart]

And this, in turn, will be necessary, too. Hence, the appropriate instance of Exp will be vindicated. The problem with this, however, is that it assumes that the causal connection between genetic structure and tartness is one of direct causation and is universal. For although this may be true in this case, we have no reason to suppose that all such connections between essence and property have this simple causal structure. In other cases, the structures may be much more complicated, and we have as yet no guarantee that they will bestow necessity on the corresponding instances of Exp.

What to do? Well, in using the fact that essences are explanatory, we have so far tried to appeal to the *type* of explanation involved – "as such", on the one hand, and causal, on the other. But what we have not done yet is exploit the fact that they are explanations *simpliciter*. It is this, we think, that provides the key to vindicating Exp. Remembering again that the properties that G embodies are meant, according to the Aristotelian picture, to *explain* why the things that satisfy them are F, we appeal to the limitations of Hempelian explanatory models, which we here take to be deductive-nomological and non-modal.

So, suppose first that we want to explain why a particular K is F. Then in accordance with the standard Hempelian model, we could simply advert to the fact that everything which has G is F, as in:

Everything that has G is F
This K is a G
So: This K is F

But this must be inadequate: for all that the Hempelian model tells us, the fact that everything that has G is F could simply be a massive coincidence; and a coincidence cannot explain anything. It is only if the claim that everything which has G is F embodies a stronger, modal connection that can it serve as an explanation of why particular G-things are F.[24]

What might this connection be? Whether it involved dispositions, tendencies, potentialities, or what not, anything beyond the merely accidental would avoid the coincidence. If, however, we take the non-modal, Hempelian generalization to be genuinely *exceptionless*, it seems hard to see how this could be so without the generalization's also being necessary. For if we did not insist on its being necessary as well, why should acknowledged *possible* counterexamples in fact not be actual future ones, too, thereby refuting the non-modal generalization? Unless there are specific positive grounds for thinking it could have had exceptions, even if it did not actually have any, the connection must be one of necessity: it must be necessary that everything that has G is F (i.e. Exp).[25] Of course, although Aristotle did concern himself with claims about particular individuals such as that this K is F, he is, through explanatory syllogisms, principally concerned in the cases we have been considering with general claims such as that all Ks are F.[26] But the argument here, in applying to any exceptionless, law-like explanation, is perfectly general; it does not even actually require that G be an essence. So, Exp is vindicated.[27]

## 6 Essentialism (and the master craftsman)

So far, we have provided grounds for accepting the modal claims:

(Def) $\Box\forall x[Kx \leftrightarrow Gx]$, and
(Exp) $\Box\forall x[Gx \rightarrow Fx]$,

where G embodies the essence of kind K and F is a property whose presence G explains. Our next task in explaining and defending the Aristotelian picture is to try to provide grounds for accepting

(Ess) $\Box\forall x[Kx \rightarrow \Box Kx]$, or its equivalent (via Def):
(Ess*) $\Box\forall x[Gx \rightarrow \Box Gx]$.

Now it is reasonably clear that Aristotle himself was attracted to such claims as (Ess) and (Ess)*. Throughout, he embraces an idea of objects as "this suches", individuated as the objects they are by the kinds under which they fall. Further, he insists that the cause of the object being a "such" and being one object is the same: the relevant cause accounts for the object being one persisting unity and being a K (*Meta* 1045b20ff). In effect, therefore, there is some feature sufficient for being a K whose loss entails both that the object (which suffers the loss) ceases to be a K and is no longer one persisting object. Such a feature, it seems, must be essential to being that object and to its being a K.[28] The question, then, is how to make good this conception. The feature Aristotle has in mind is clearly tantamount to the essence of the kind. What we need, therefore, is a reason for thinking that loss of essence (or, by Def, ceasing to belong to the kind) would automatically mean ceasing to exist. But this is to ask why Ess and Ess* are true.

The first thing to note is that Ess and Ess* are not entailed by Def. It's necessary that someone is a bachelor iff he is an unmarried male; but no bachelor is necessarily a bachelor, and no unmarried male is necessarily an unmarried male, since bachelors, i.e. unmarried males, can get married. So, why in this respect are natural kind terms like "lemon" or "tiger" or "helium" or "electron" not like "bachelor"? Bachelors do not have to be bachelors, but why do lemons, tigers, electrons and helium all have to be, *tout court*, lemons, tigers, electrons and helium? Indeed, outside the realm of pure logic, why does any object *have to be* anything at all? What is to prevent anything from being anything? For example, individual human beings can run, breathe, speak languages, solve quadratic equations, commit unspeakable crimes and perform acts of extraordinary kindness; they can become Lord Mayor of London and captain the Welsh rugby team. Why, then, cannot these very same things turn to stone, become a paddle-steamer, or wake up as an insect, without ceasing to exist altogether? And here it is important to remember that we are not asking why they cannot do these things *while remaining a human being*; we are asking why they cannot do them at all. What is it about such transformations that prevents them from existing any more? Perhaps it is only the limits of our imagination that keep us from thinking that they can not undergo such transformations while continuing to exist.

Given Aristotle's extensive use of teleology, one initial suggestion might be to appeal to the idea that artifacts are essentially or necessarily those artifacts: they essentially or necessarily have the functions they were originally designed and made to have; and then to reason by analogy to the natural case. (Call this "the argument from analogy".) Now, in response to this, it might be doubted initially whether particular artifacts are indeed necessarily such artifacts; or equivalently whether objects with specific defining functions necessarily have to be able to perform the functions they were originally designed to have. Why cannot a thing made to fulfill one function change into one with another function, while remaining the same thing? Consider a dual-purpose artifact like Nagel's corkscrew-bottle-opener.[29] Will this not remain the same thing even if (say) the bottle-opener end becomes too rusty to function as a bottle-opener, that is, even if it will not any longer have its dual-function? Or consider a cricket bat put to use for some purpose other than that for which it was originally intended. Will this not remain the same thing even if it is put to a different use (e.g. as a tent prop or even an offensive weapon)?

However, if there is a problem with the argument from analogy, it is probably not with the premise, i.e. with the proposition that artifacts are necessarily those artifacts. At any rate, with suitable adjustments to the gloss we put on it, there is reason to think that at least *these* problems can be overcome. Thus, it may well be that dual-purpose arti-facts can remain the same thing even if their ability to perform one of their original functions falters. We might, for example, think that the identity of such an artifact is preserved if it can still perform one of its functions properly, provided it retains the superficial form of some-thing that can perform the other – if it remains genuinely a corkscrew (say), while being a bottle-opener only homonymously.[30] (Of course, if it loses the ability to perform *all* its original functions, it will not be the same thing and will accordingly cease to exist, again except homony-mously.) As to the cricket bat, we might argue that just because it is being used for other purposes, it does not *automatically* lose its ability to function as a cricket bat, and thereby cease to be one (and hence to exist). Thus, in the envisaged circumstances, perhaps it remains the same thing throughout: it is still a cricket bat, but now put to use as a tent prop or weapon. Indeed, it might even remain the same thing if it was buried, cricket died out, and it was discovered centuries later and put to some different use by people who did not know what cricket was. (But what if the bat were *modified* so as to serve some different purpose? Would it then no longer be the same thing? Much will depend on whether it would be able to *function* as a cricket bat: if so, it will still be one, and otherwise, not.)[31]

No, the real problem with the argument is how to sustain the analogy with the natural. If the natural world were the product of a Cosmic Designer, then the analogy might well be sustainable. But how would a secular alternative work? As we have already noted,[32] even if some contemporary functional analogue of Aristotle's species-specific tele-ology can be made to work in certain areas of biology, it is not at all obvious that it can be extended to cover all physical, chemical and biological kinds. As before, we counsel against any *a priori* insistence on such extensions.

Let us return to the question, "Why can't anything be anything?". One way of addressing it would be to think of how in practice we apply Leibniz's Law. Despite what the law says, when confronted by a change in property, ordinarily conceived, we do not automatically conclude that we have a different object. On the contrary, often convinced that we have the same object, we search for a feature that would render the change consistent with the law. Thus, in familiar ways, we might rela-tivize either the changing properties of the thing, or its possession of them, to a time. Nevertheless, given the law, the *default* position is surely always that if a thing changes any of its properties, ordinarily conceived, it must be thought of as a different thing, *unless there is a good reason for thinking otherwise*. What we need, therefore, are grounds for thinking that when an object loses its essence (or its membership of the corre-sponding kind) all such reasons are lost as well.

Now, the essence of an artifact is its function or purpose, suitably qualified, no doubt, to accommodate dual-function artifacts, etc. in the manner indicated above. And should it cease to possess this function or stop being able to fulfill its purpose, it is plausible to suppose that we would have no good reason for supposing it to continue to exist. At best, such artifacts would continue to be such (and hence exist) only homon-ymously. But, again, what are we to say about members of natural kinds? It is here that we may find the quintessentially Aristotelian notion of the master craftsman, or artisan, to be a useful stepping stone. For although there may be no direct analogy with artifacts themselves (because of the pervasive lack of teleology in the natural world), it may well be that what artisans uncover about the materials and objects they work with in making such artifacts will perform a similar role to the artifact's func-tion or purpose. What is important here is that in order to know how to fashion functional objects out of natural materials and objects, artisans must have knowledge of how these natural materials and objects work. Otherwise, they will not be able to guarantee that the artifacts can do what they are supposed to do. They need not have complete knowl-edge, of course, only what is required to be able to make the things in question. But as experts in their field, they must have what might be thought of as a *good working knowledge* of the materials and objects, and this will typically involve knowledge of what can and cannot be done with particular objects or stuffs in virtue of their being the objects or stuffs they are. They will sometimes need to know what such objects or stuffs allow, or rule out, in virtue of being the very objects or stuffs they are and to separate these from those features which can be altered in different conditions or with better implements.

But, it may be said, what is to *guarantee* that the kinds of objects and stuffs that the artisans find useful or important in their work, even with good working knowledge, will always be genuinely *natural* kinds? After all, their concern is principally with *what works*, and the truth about the underlying nature of the constituent objects and materials is only secondary or instrumental. Thus, perhaps a chair is designed to be made of wood in the early years of its existence, but to petrify in calculated manner later in its existence. It is of no concern to the carpenter who makes this chair whether it's the same stuff or not after petrification. Or again, consider igloo-builders or ice-sculptors. It will typically be no consolation to them to be told that the water their masterpieces have turned into is still the same stuff as ice, just in a different form. It is irrelevant to them whether the sum of ice is the same aggregation of stuff as the resulting bucket of water, or a different material altogether. As far as they are concerned, what is important for the production of igloos and ice-sculptures is that *they remain solid*. This may involve awareness at some level of the circumstances in which ice melts, and, conceivably, whether melting is reversible. But such knowledge need not require knowing whether it is the same stuff.

To some extent, such worries can be assuaged, by observing that artisans will be working within a wider community: They will have colleagues who use materials differently or apprentices who use different types of object altogether. And who knows whether such individuals will, at some stage, use processes that depend on a conscious awareness of the common features of water and ice in virtue of which they are the same stuff; certainly, many carpenters will have a vested interest in producing pieces of wooden furniture that do not petrify. Even more important, there are certain practical experts, such as master gardeners, artisans typically interested in objects rather than stuffs, who are not necessarily concerned with what can be done to this object *qua* member of a kind (like *oak*) for which we happen to have an existing sortal term. Rather, the sortals they will often find useful will be based on the groupings they use to track inevitabilities in nature (what such objects can or cannot do). As a result, their kind (sortal) terms will not always be circumscribed merely by the conventions of their practice, that is, even if they select them because of their interests in plant breeding or cultivation. Moreover, they are interested at some level in grasping what it is about these objects so grouped which accounts for their distinctive abilities or inabilities; they are looking for something which answers both the explanatory question "Why do these things behave as they do?" and the definitional question "What is it to be such an object?"

Nevertheless, the fact remains that the activities of such experts will remain subordinate to what works, and there is no reason in principle why the sortals they fix on, even in their most successful activity, should have to match the natural world exactly. Even plant breeders may want flowers that smell or look or grow a certain way – such may be what the market demands – and the kinds they uncover in achieving these goals need not cut nature at its joints. That said, however, in a close neighboring category to such artisans lie individuals who are not so subordinate, people we may call *scientific experimentalists*.[33] For although they are similarly concerned with practical matters, such as how to make their equipment work properly, their investigations are not, as such, designed to resolve such matters, to see e.g. whether their equipment does indeed work. Their overriding aim is not practical; rather, what they are concerned with is finding out how things *are*, by testing theories about this or that kind, or this or that material. And they can only properly be said to be successful if the kinds they uncover are scientifically correct.

With this in mind, we can now see why essences are necessary. For there will be nothing in science – i.e. no good reason in the proper articulation of the kinds whose existence experimentalists will verify when they are successful – to insist that objects that lose their essence continue to exist. A tree that has petrified has nothing at the level of biological, chemical or physical theory to warrant the supposition that it continues to exist. It may look a lot like a tree, but it will only continue to exist as such homonymously.

But there is still a question: Why should the interaction of the master craftsman or at least his successor, the experimentalist, have this type of authority? Why give so much weight to their dealings with the stuffs or objects in question? Given our discussion so far, however, we may legitimately respond that what makes their classifications important is that they are devised in the context of a search for what it is about these objects or stuffs as such that explains their characteristic behavior as manifested by what can and cannot be done to them in the workshop or the laboratory. The craftsman and the experimentalist invoke standards of assessment that appeal to real-world natures, inevitabilities and possibilities. Other classificatory strategies are of course conceivable. Someone might simply try to follow objects (such as the cricket bat that gradually loses its ability to function as such, or an oak tree that petrifies) along their spatio-temporal routes, no matter what transformations they undergo along their route; he or she might even insist that they are the very same objects which persist through all such possible changes. But the challenge for an advocate of such a strategy would to explain why it should be preferred. What would be the point? And if a good reason were to be found, would that not simply mean that there were further objects in addition to the artifacts and natural things already present?

How far is this from Aristotle's own picture, particularly in regard to the master craftsman's being superseded by the experimentalist? Maybe it is not clear what Aristotle would say at this point. On the one hand, we are interested in understanding the objects and stuffs we encounter in craft interaction; on the other, the drive for explanation-based classification supports the introduction of the new kinds. It may be that Aristotle himself did not consider the possibility that such cases could arise, perhaps thinking that craft engagement with the world would, in the long run, latch on to the kinds that there are.[34] However, if we are right to see the experimentalist as the natural successor to the master craftsman, one with access to better instruments to grasp the natures of the things and stuffs encountered, contemporary Aristotelians may reasonably prefer the experimentalist picture, seeing experiment as the natural extension of craft activity. This is not to say, of course, that they should accept a similar sort of classification revision in the case of kinds postulated on the basis of abstract, mathematical, models or reasoning alone, unsupported by craft or experimentalist involvement with the objects in question. As in Aristotle's original craft-based picture, the experimentalist sets limits to the kinds to be studied in order to guard against the excesses of unconfined "pure" theory that he saw in Platonism.

## 7 Question (B): What is essence?

In developing the Aristotelian picture, we have tried to argue for the view that essences are definable natures with explanatory power. With this in mind, we then tried to isolate and defend the theses Aristotle needed in order to ensure that such explanatory power ranged over necessary properties, too – namely, Def, Exp, and Ess (or Ess*). It was this discussion that yielded our answer to Questions (A) and (C) of §1. However, this still leaves Question (B): what is it about essences that ensures that they have the twin definitional and explanatory roles? We conclude our partial defense of Aristotelian essentialism with a cautious proposal.

One strategy would be to start with the definitional role of essence, and draw out the explanatory role of essence from it. And it is clear that the conditions of unity and priority that Aristotle places on defini- tion would allow him to do this, since for him such conditions actually require the introduction of explanatory role.[35] However, our emphasis in this chapter on the importance of explanation suggests an alterna- tive, possibly complementary approach, which begins instead with explanatory role.[36] For in light of the fact that essences, for Aristotle, are *basic* causes, the possibility emerges that we could simply define the essence of a natural kind as its *explanatorily basic* properties. And then, it might be thought, it would be entirely straightforward why essences should have a definitional role as well. After all, to be given a definition, broadly speaking, is to be given non-redundant information that allows one to understand the *definiendum* properly. This may consist, in part, in being given enough information to deduce the analytic properties of the *definiendum* (as, e.g., with various abstract concepts); such informa- tion might constitute a dictionary definition. But to be given explana- tory basic information about a kind, non-redundant information which can explain (say) a wide range of other features, and in particular other non-logical necessary properties, of its members, would seem enough to gain a proper understanding of the kind too. So, it would fulfill the definitional role as well.

Clearly, this needs filling out and defending in detail. We content ourselves here with a brief formal statement of the proposal, while noting one or two of its ramifications. According to the proposal, the *essence of a kind* consists of those non-logical properties

(a) in terms of which we may explain a wide range of other features, including other non-logical necessary features, of members of the kind; and

(b) the possession of which by members of the kind is *not* explicable in terms of other properties of members of the kind.

(The reference to non-logical properties is to prevent properties grounded in logical truths, such as being self-identical, from being part of the essence of a kind, even if they figure in particular explanations.)

Now plainly it is clause (a) that ensures that the properties that essences consist of are explanatory, and clause (b) that ensures that such properties are explanatorily *basic*; and it is through this notion of basicness that we can highlight a striking advantage of the proposal. For it has remained a serious puzzle amongst philosophers of essence how to distinguish essential properties from other necessary properties.[37] But the above proposal suggests a natural criterion: the essential properties of a kind are its basic explanatory properties, while its remaining necessary properties, including those derivable from its essence, are its non-essential ones.[38]

This is not to say that there are no difficulties. For example, there is nothing in the proposal to stop there being two equally good, *competing* candidates to be regarded as the essence of a given kind, both empirically adequate because of the underdetermination of theory by all possible data. Faced with this, we could go down the epistemicist route and insist that there is one genuine essence; remember that it is a requirement of a genuine explanation that it be *true*. Alternatively, despite its opening the door to the possibility of a limited conventionalism, we could accept that there is a measure of objective indeterminacy. (It would be limited, since the objective features of explanation massively constrain what can go into an essence.) However, perhaps we could adopt an eirenic approach here. If there is a single set of explanatory properties in any given case, then they would constitute the essence; if not, and there is objective indeterminacy, then a modest conventionalism remains possible: either would do. Doubtless, Aristotle the realist would have found the epistemicist route the more congenial. But should there be no fact of the matter in any particular case, his lack of dogmatism would surely have allowed him to make room for the alternative.[39]

## Notes

Thanks to Sabina Lovibond, Michael Peramatzis, Greg Salmieri, Josh Schechter, and the editor for very helpful comments on earlier drafts.

1. Aristotle's general picture, of course, applies just as much to artificial kinds as it does to natural kinds. However, although we discuss the former, we do so principally insofar as they cast light on the latter.
2. It is to be emphasized that such modal necessary and sufficient conditions do not exhaust even the definitional role. As Kit Fine has made clear (see Fine 1994), the essence of a kind for Aristotle articulates its nature; but the mere presence of conditions which, of necessity, are necessary and sufficient for kind membership may involve elements partly or wholly divorced from the nature of the kind. For example, if the essence of physical kind K is G, then one could obtain appropriately modal necessary and sufficient conditions

for membership of K by conjoining G with Fermat's Last Theorem. But this theorem would have nothing to do with the nature of K. Fine himself offers some suggestions for filtering out such cases.

3. And not merely in the trivial sense of being a formal cause by virtue of its definitional role.

4. Indeed, the resources Aristotle has available may also allow him to explain why in certain circumstances they are *apt* to have such properties, or why they are *disposed* to have such properties, even if they don't always; see fn. 27, below. We confine ourselves here to the exceptionless cases.

5. The syllogism being: Noise belongs to all fire-quenchings; fire-quenching belongs to the clouds; so noise belongs to the clouds.

6. It is interesting to note that for a long time, Donald Davidson (see Davidson 2001a) thought that causes and effects individuated events at a category level. As is familiar, however, he finally came to acknowledge it as unlikely that this view can withstand the charge of circularity; (see Davidson 2001b). But there is nothing to prevent someone from adopting a *piecemeal* approach, involving specific kinds of event, which appeals to causality; there is nothing necessarily circular in that. Indeed, it would be in the spirit of Aristotle to reject Davidson's project of providing category-wide individuation conditions for events, in just the way that philosophers like David Wiggins, following Aristotle, have rejected category-wide individuation conditions for objects in the category of substance; see Wiggins (2001, ch.3).

7. See Charles (2000, pp. 274–76, 336).

8. See *Metaphysics* Z.17, 1041a26-29, 1041b5ff, and *Metaphysics* H.2, 1043a13ff. For exposition and commentary, see Charles (2000, pp. 283–94), and Charles (2010, §2); see also Peramatzis (forthcoming), §1.

9. See *Metaphysics* Z.17, 1041b5-9 and *Metaphysics* H.2, 1043b10-11. Again, for exposition and commentary, see Charles (2010) and Peramatzis (forthcoming).

10. See, e.g., Godfrey-Smith (1993).

11. It is worth noting that the effects that Aristotle typically notes in specifying the causal role of a kind exhibit a direct link to observable features of the kind. And this provides a natural connection with the practice of science – or perhaps more importantly for Aristotle, with the proto-science practised by the master craftsman; see later, §6. But it is equally important to recognize that such direct links need not always be available. Indeed, the existence of some, doubtless highly theoretical, kinds may only follow from the observable existence of other kinds plus the general theory that governs them.

12. See *Meta* A.3, 983a24ff, and especially the bracketed sentence at 983a28-9. Here the essence, or the primary *logos*, is a first principle and a cause; it has explanatory power, but without incorporating any specific kind of causation. (Thanks to Michael Peramatzis here for highlighting the importance of this passage, and later in the paragraph in the discussion of the four causes.)

13. And even this assumes that the genitive absolute, "fire being quenched", indicates a causal connection.

14. Here "Kx" means "x is a K" or "x is a member of kind K", and "Gx" means "x is such as to have G"; "Fx" in the next sentence means "x is F" or "x has the property of being F". For detailed discussion of Aristotle's views on the varying types of predication involved, see Grice (1988) and Code (1983).

15. The sequent underpinning this entailment, namely, $\Box\forall x[Ax\leftrightarrow Bx], \Box\forall x[Bx\rightarrow Cx]$ $\vdash\Box\forall x[Ax\rightarrow Cx]$, is valid in any sensible logic of metaphysical necessity.
16. $\Box\forall x[Ax\leftrightarrow Bx], \Box\forall x[Bx\rightarrow Cx], \Box\forall x[Ax\rightarrow\Box Ax] \vdash\Box\forall x[Ax\rightarrow\Box Cx]$ is valid in K4, and hence in both S4 and S5.
17. As we shall see presently, this will need a little modification – and for reasons that Aristotle might well have had sympathy for; but for the moment, let us assume that this is indeed the best way to fill out the idea.
18. The gap in the argument is one that Aristotle himself would doubtless have appreciated, given that he thought that certain identities, such as "Socrates is what is seated", were at most only contingently true. It is perhaps also worth noting that Aristotle thought that some identity statements were not merely necessarily true, but essentially true; see. fn. 2 and §7. For details, see *Topics*, 103a27ff.
19. An alternative suggestion would be to appeal in English to the infinitive construction ("to be X"), in formulating the necessity of identity. We might say that to be a K just *is* to be such as to have G. Unfortunately, it is still possible to hear the following as true, though contingent (again with dots filled in correctly): to be a Manchester United player in the 1968 etc. just is to be Alex Stepney or … or George Best.
20. See Kripke (1993, pp. 166–67).
21. The corresponding definite descriptions are of course what Kripke refers to as "non-rigid designators".
22. Indeed, it seems true quite generally that any correct specification of a property in the form "the property of being X" will be similarly canonical; whence any true identity of the form "the property of being X = the property of being Y" will be necessary.
23. Cf. §2.
24. For a detailed elaboration of this type of argument, see Foster (1982–83, pp. 87–102). Notice that contemporary Humeans might argue that Hempelian generalizations could achieve explanatory power by virtue of their location within a sizeable theoretical network of similar claims. But again it is hard to see how this could come about. Without the introduction of modality, each such generalization will still be a matter of coincidence, and multiplying generalizations that are genuinely a matter of coincidence will not make them any the less of a coincidence. (Such a network might, of course, be evidence that they are *not* a coincidence; but the network would then qualify as evidence of a modal connection as well.)
25. It is to be emphasized that so far as the argument as stated goes, the necessity here is simply metaphysical necessity; it is not, for example, a weaker causal necessity. This follows from the assumption that there are no positive grounds for supposing there to be possible exceptions to the law. For without such grounds, there will be no reason to divide the space of possible worlds into the salient (the causally possible, say) and the others. Should such grounds be found, however, and should it prove plausible, therefore, to divide the space of possible worlds in this way, then the necessity which attaches both to the laws and then to any derived properties will be correspondingly weaker.
26. Though perhaps not always completely general: at any rate, his claims about the moon being eclipsed at least *look like* claims about the one and only one moon.

27. It is perhaps worth noting that although we have focused here on exceptionless universal claims here, Aristotle did also take an interest in explanatory generalizations that fall short of universality; see e.g. his discussion of "general claims" at *Post. An.* 87b22ff and *Pr. An.* 43b30ff. Given that he sometimes describes such generalizations as "holding by nature", it may well be that the above considerations can be extended to cover them, but using less strong modalities than outright necessities.
28. This is, no doubt, why he regards dead objects, ones that no longer belong to their individuating kinds, only as members of those kinds homonymously. They may be better described as other objects or as heaps, collections of bits.
29. See Nagel (1972, p. 255).
30. Cf. fn. 28.
31. There will also undoubtedly be borderline cases. Perhaps it is just metaphysically vague whether a certain gradually deteriorating object can still function as a cricket bat. But if so, then it will equally be vague whether the cricket bat exists at all. And that generates no inconsistency with Ess or Ess*. For what Ess* tells us is that if a has G, then in any world in which a exists, a has G. The worlds in which it's metaphysically vague whether a exists are irrelevant.
32. See §2.
33. In fact, we may see Aristotelian artisans, particularly those like the master gardener, as being a kind of *proto*-scientific experimentalist – perhaps even seeing their activity as typically a model for the explanatory-based classification that is being sought.
34. After all, in order to accommodate possible future developments in their craft, really *canny* craftsmen may well try to uncover the nature of stuffs and things in full; they would be acting as if they were experimentalists, seeking to discover, for example, where their activities are constrained by the nature of the stuffs and things they encounter.
35. See Charles (2010; cf.) also Koslicki (2012, pp. 187–206).
36. For the suggestion that these two approaches are, in fact, complementary, see Charles (2000, pp. 213–17).
37. See Fine (1994) for some suggestive first steps, and Koslicki (2012, pp. 189–95), for critical discussion of Fine.
38. So, like Koslicki (2012, pp. 195ff), we think that the distinction between essential and non-essential necessary properties cannot be properly drawn without the introduction of explanatory considerations in something like the way indicated.
39. Cf. here his open-mindedness about the four causes discussed earlier; see in particular the text surrounding fn. 12.

# References

Charles, David. 2000. *Aristotle on Meaning and Essence* (Oxford: Oxford University Press).

——— 2010. "Definition and Explanation in the *Posterior Analytics* and *Metaphysics*," in David Charles, (ed.) *Definition in Greek Philosophy* (Oxford: Oxford University Press).

Code, Alan. 1983. "Aristotle: Essence and Accident," in R. Grandy and R. Warner, (eds), *Philosophical Grounds of Rationality: Intentions, Categories, Ends* (Oxford: Oxford University Press).

Davidson, Donald. 2001a. "The Individuation of Events," in Donald Davidson, *Essays on Actions and Events* (Oxford: Oxford University Press).

_____ 2001b. "Reply to Quine on Events," in Donald Davidson, *Essays on Actions and Events* (Oxford: Oxford University Press).

Fine, Kit. 1994. "Essence and Modality," *Philosophical Perspectives* 8: 1–16.

Foster, John. 1982–3. "Induction, Explanation, and Natural Necessity," *Proceedings of the Aristotelian Society* 83.

Godfrey-Smith, Peter. 1993. "Functions: Consensus without Unity," *Pacific Philosophical Quarterly* 74: 196–208.

Grice, H. P. 1988. "Aristotle on the Multiplicity of Being," *Pacific Philosophical Quarterly* 69: 175–200.

Koslicki, Kathrin. 2012. "Essence, Necessity, and Explanation," in Tuomas E. Tahko, (ed.) *Contemporary Aristotelian Metaphysics* (Cambridge: Cambridge University Press).

Kripke, Saul. 1993. "Identity and Necessity," in A. W. Moore, (ed.) *Meaning and Reference* (Oxford: Oxford University Press).

Nagel, Thomas. 1972. "Aristotle on *Eudaimonia*," *Phronesis* 17 (3).

Peramatzis, Michael. forthcoming. "Science and Metaphysics in Aristotle's Philosophy," *Metascience*.

Wiggins, David. 2001. *Sameness and Substance Renewed* (Cambridge: Cambridge University Press).

# 8
# Being, Unity, and Identity in the Fregean and Aristotelian Traditions

*Gyula Klima*

## 1 Post-Fregean Common Wisdom about Being, Unity and Identity

These are some of the things we nowadays learn about the notions of being or existence,[1] identity and unity, through being exposed to any standard system of post-Fregean predicate logic and the related philosophical literature. Existence is a second-order concept, meaning that it is a logical connective, what in the Aristotelian tradition used to be called a syncategorematic concept.[2] A concept of this sort does not have the function of representing or characterizing some extramental objects, as categorematic or first-order concepts do, such as the concepts of "man" or "horse"; rather, they have the function of operating on these concepts, forming more complex concepts with them. The resulting complex concepts or thoughts, then, will have different functions, determined by the functions of their components. For example, by Fregean lights, if the function of the concept of "horse" is to represent horses in a universal fashion (as opposed to the concept of "Bucephalus" that represents a single horse in a singular fashion), and the function of the concept of existence is to state that the first-order concept with which it is construed has a non-empty extension, then the thought expressed by the sentence "Horses exist" or "There are horses" has the function of denoting the True, just in case the extension of the predicate denoting the concept of horses is not empty. Or, equivalently, but sticking closer to Frege's original ideas, the concept denoted by the predicate "horse" is nothing but a function from individuals to truth-values (the True and the False), and the thought resulting from the application of the concept of existence to this concept denotes the True, just in case this function yields the True as its value for some individual.

In general, if C(P) is the first-order concept expressed by the predicate P, then C(P) is a function from individuals to truth-values, that is to say, $C(P)(u) \in \{T, F\}$, where $u \in U$, where U is the universe of discourse and T and F are the truth values, namely the True and the False. Thus, the Fregean concept of existence, the concept expressed by the existential quantifier of predicate logic, $C(\exists)$, is a function from such functions to truth values, such that $C(\exists)(C(P)) \in \{T, F\}$, and $C(\exists)(C(P)) = T$, if for some u, $C(P)(u) = T$, otherwise $C(\exists)(C(P)) = F$. So, the concept of existence is just this function, namely, $C(\exists)$, on this conception.[3]

Thus, on this conception, the notion of existence (whatever is expressed by the "existential uses" of "is" and "exists" and their cognates in English and their equivalents in other languages, i.e., whatever is formalized by means of the existential quantifier) is a logical connective, expressed by a primitive, undefinable term, although the concept itself is very precisely characterized as the semantic function just described.

The notion of identity is likewise treated in standard predicate logic as expressed by a primitive logical connective, although actually it might as well be treated as being expressed by a distinguished binary relation with a fixed interpretation, namely, as one whose denotation is the set of ordered pairs of the elements of the universe of discourse paired with themselves (i.e., R(=), the denotation or extension of the identity-sign is just the set {<u,u>: u ∈ U} in all models of our language). Again, sticking closely to the Fregean conception above, we might say that the Fregean concept of identity, C(=), is a function from individuals to truth-values, such that $C(=)(u,v) = T$, just in case u is the same individual as v, otherwise $C(=)(u,v) = F$.[4]

But then, once we have these two logical primitives on hand in our logic, the expression expressing the notion of a unit, the third crucial metaphysical notion we should deal with here, does not have to be treated as primitive, as it is explicitly definable by means of the well-known quantificational formula stating that there is exactly one thing that satisfies a certain predicate: $(\exists!x)(Px) \leftrightarrow (\exists y)[(Py \ \& \ (\forall x)(Px \rightarrow x = y)]$.

## 2 Buridan on being, unity, and identity

In stark contrast to this picture, for medieval authors in general, the concept of identity is derivative with regard to the more fundamental, transcendental concept of unity, which in turn is convertible with the even more primitive notion of being, insofar as it signifies the same as the notion of being, except that it also connotes indivision, i.e., the lack of division, based on the formulaic Aristotelian description of the notion of a unit as an undivided being (*unum est ens indivisum*). The 14th-century nominalist author John Buridan is very explicit about this "derivation" of the notion of identity from the notion of unity in the following passage:

> The name "one" is taken from indivision, as is clear in Metaphysics V, for which reason it is also stated there that whatever has no division, insofar as it has no division, as such, is said to be "one". Therefore, the name "one" is a privative name, privatively opposed to the name "many", as is clear from Metaphysics X. However, a privative name includes in its definition the name of the opposite habit with negation; thus in a certain way it signifies or connotes that which the name of the habit signifies, and that is extrinsic to that of which the privative name is verified. [...] But about the term "same" I say that it is even more connotative than the term "one" is, and thus "same" is said to be an attribute of "one" and "one" is said to be its subject and foundation. For the signification of "same" presupposes the signification of "one" and connotes besides a relation, namely, that [the thing that is said to be one thing] is the same as something, and that is but the thing with which it is the same.[5]

On this approach, therefore, identity is but the unity of whatever is referred to by the terms flanking an identity claim, that is to say, the terms flanking such a claim both refer to *one* thing and not two distinct things. However, given that what is said to be *one* thing is an undivided being by the lights of the Aristotelian formula, the notion expressed by the predicate "one" connotes negatively the division of the thing that is said to be one; that is to say, it connotes the lack of division of the thing in question.[6] But then, since division comes in degrees, and so its lack comes in degrees, too, it is no wonder that on this conception, unity and the derivative notion of identity come in degrees as well.

Accordingly, it should come as no surprise that Buridan distinguishes three main types of identity, namely, what we may call *total*, *partial*, and *successive* identity.

> We usually say in three ways that something is numerically identical with something. In the first way, totally, namely, that this is that and there is nothing belonging to the integrity of this that would not belong to the integrity of that, and conversely; and this is to be numerically identical in the strictest sense. And in this sense we have

to say that I am not the same as I was yesterday, for yesterday something belonged to my integrity that by now is dissolved, and something did not belong to my integrity yesterday that after eating has become part of my substance. In the second way something is said to be identical with something partially, because this is a part of that, and this is said to be especially the case when it is a greater or more principal part, or even because this and that overlap in something that is a greater or more principal part of both. For it is in this sense that Aristotle claims in the Ethics that man is primarily his intellect, just as a city or any aggregate primarily is its most principal part, as we have noted in the previous question, and it is from this that the denominations of the wholes derive from the denominations of their parts. And this is also how a man remains the same throughout his whole life, because his soul remains the same, which is his more principal part. This is not, however, how a horse remains the same, indeed, nor even the human body. But yet in a third way, something is said to be numerically identical with regard to the consideration of its diverse part in their succession, one after the other, and this is how the Seine is said to be the same river after a thousand years, even if strictly speaking now there is no part of the Seine that is the same as what was a part of the Seine ten years ago. For this is how the sea is said to be the same, and how this sublunary world is said to be perpetual, and how a horse is said to be the same throughout its whole life, and how the human body is said to be the same likewise. And this kind of identity is sufficient for calling a name a discrete or singular term in accordance with the commonly accepted way of speaking, which, however, is not strictly speaking true. For it is not true, strictly speaking that the Seine that I see now is the same thing that I saw ten years ago. But the proposition is conceded in the sense that the body of water that we now see and call Seine, and the body of water that I saw then, which was also called Seine, and also the bodies of water that were there in the intervening times, each were called Seine, and they were continuous in succeeding one after the other. It is with regard to this sense of identity, which is said to obtain because of this sort of continuity, that we call the name "Seine" a discrete and singular term, although it is not as strictly discrete as it would be if the thing were remained totally the same before and afterwards.[7]

When we are wondering about identity over time, as when we are wondering whether the thing that was Brunellus yesterday is the same as the thing that is Brunellus today, the question is whether the referents of the terms of such an identity claim are one and the same thing. In terms of Buridan's distinctions, those referents of the terms of such claims can be said to be *totally* identical that have no parts not in common (i.e., that have all parts in common, if they have any parts at all), those are *partially* identical that have only some parts (especially the greater and/ or principal parts) in common, and those are *successively* identical that have no parts in common but are related to each other by a continuous succession of parts.

But then, the question inevitably emerges: How can the last type of identity even be called identity at all, if the extremes of the corresponding identity claim refer to two totally distinct things, such as two totally distinct bodies of water, one of which is the body of water that was the Seine ten years ago, and the other is the body of water that is the Seine now?

Actually, a similar question can be raised about partial identity. How can it be taken to be some sort of "identity", if it is not even transitive? For, clearly, even if A is a whole having three parts, such as <1,2,3>, partially identical with B, namely, <2,3,4>, on account of sharing a greater part, and B is partially identical with C, namely, <3,4,5>, for the same reason, A will not be partially identical with C, for they do not share a greater part. Clearly, this is Buridan's point of saying that partial identity and successive identity are not identity in the strict sense, except somewhat loosely speaking, on account of the lack of perfect and total unity of whatever is referred to by the terms of the, nevertheless true, identity claims formed with them. Indeed, if we take part 3 to be their "principal part", A and B and C will still turn out to be partially identical in a stricter, transitive sense, on account of the strict, absolute identity of part 3. On the other hand, if we continue the series with D, namely, <4,5,6>, then now we have a whole that has no part in common with A; so, one would think it is totally distinct from A. Nevertheless, Buridan still claims that in an even less strict sense, A is at least successively identical with D. Well, how can that be?

Buridan's answer lies in the *continuity* of succession. Suppose A and D are two distinct bodies of water; say, A is the body of water Buridan saw in Paris and pointing to it truly claimed, "This is the Seine", and D is the body water I see today and pointing to it I truly claim, "This is the Seine". In this scenario, I can truly claim that this is the same river that Buridan saw, namely, the Seine, even if the body of water he saw is totally distinct from the body of water I see now. For even if those two bodies of water are completely distinct, so that no part of A is a part of D and *vice versa*, there is *a continuous succession of partially identical bodies of water* connecting A and D. So, even if A and D, considered synchronically, are discontinuous, the same bodies of water are *diachronically continuous* in the sense that between the time of A and the time of D there were times (quantifying over time intervals and not time-points, true to the spirit of Buridan's temporal logic) at which there were bodies of water at each time such that each was partially identical with bodies of water at an earlier and at a later time, and the first of these was partially identical with A and the last of these is partially identical with D.

In this way, just as the notion of partial identity was reduced to the notion of absolute identity (as the absolute identity of a principal or greater part), so the notion of successive identity is reduced to the notion of a continuous succession of partial identities, and so, whoever is prepared to accept true predications of partial identity, should also be prepared to accept true predications of successive identity. To be sure, there is still an important difference between successive and partial identity as distinguished by Buridan: for successive identity is diachronic continuity *without the permanence of any single part*, whereas partial identity, as Buridan described it, is synchronic or diachronic continuity *with the permanence of the greater or some principal part*. Furthermore, we should note that the successive identity grounded by the unity of successively permanent things, such as a river, is still different from the unity of successive entities, such as processes, movements or events. For in the case of the river, all its integral, quantitative parts co-exist at any given time, even if those parts do not remain the same at any later time, whereas in the case of a movement or a process, no two integral parts of it coexist at any given time.

But even without going into further details, all this just goes to show that the three main types of identity distinguished by Buridan may admit even finer distinctions, as is testified by his use of comparatives all over the relevant passages, as for instance in his claim that *in the successive identity sense* we are able to say *even more* that Brunellus is numerically the same horse from his birth to his death than that the Seine has been the same river for a 1,000 years. What is still generally important in all these considerations is that the conditions of identity of a given kind of thing are dependent on the kind of unity this sort of entity is required to have in order to remain in existence as one and the same entity.

Consequently, I believe that it should make perfectly good sense for Buridan to claim that corresponding to, or rather grounding, these identity claims of different strengths, there are different degrees of unity exhibited by things of different natures: there is the absolutely absolute unity of God incompatible with any real division whatsoever, followed by the unity of angels, in which there is the division of substance and accident, as is testified by their mutable will (see the fall of the Devil), followed by the unity of humans, having an immortal, permanent part, followed by living things that have at least the permanence of their organic structure, while their quantitative parts are in constant exchange with their environment, followed by merely synchronically continuous bodies, which, however, can have diachronically distinct stages, connected only through diachronically continuous parts, followed by processes (*res successivae*) which have *only* diachronically continuous parts so that no two parts of them coexists at the same time, followed, finally, by synchronically discontinuous and possibly even diachronically disconnected bodies, which are properly speaking not numerically one, but many, which can still be considered as forming a unit on account of their order, contiguity, or position (say, as an army, or a heap), or just on account of the mere consideration of the intellect, lumping these things together under some nominal conjunction or on a mere list.

Now, given this conception of "the gradation of unity" (to give it a catchy name), it will make perfectly good sense to claim that even if Brunellus is not as strongly numerically one as a human being is, Brunellus is still more numerically one than is a river, and both are more numerically one than is a heap, which is not numerically one at all, except maybe equivocally. To be sure, Buridan does not go into these finer details, and he might not even approve these further speculations about "the gradation of unity". But there was another medieval philosopher of at least equal stature, who, I think, would definitely endorse these considerations, namely, Thomas Aquinas.

## 3  Aquinas on being, unity and identity[8]

For Aquinas, the notion of unity, being an analogical, transcendental notion, convertible with the notion of being, must come precisely in those finer degrees as does the notion of being determined by the nature of each entity. In fact, the degree of perfection of a being is sometimes best indicated by the degree of unity or indivision, that is, the metaphysical simplicity of the thing. This should be clear if we consider the following passage:

> We have to say that God is maximally and most truly one. For just as something is related to being undivided, so it is related to unity; since, according to the Philosopher, a being is said to be one insofar as it is

not divided. Thus, those things which are undivided *per se* are more truly one than those things that are undivided *per accidens*, as Socrates and a white thing, which are one *per accidens*. But among the things that are one *per se*, those which are undivided absolutely speaking are more truly one than those which are undivided in respect of a genus, or species, or some analogy [*proportio*]. Hence they are not even said to be one absolutely speaking [*simpliciter*], but one in genus, or in species, or by analogy; but what is absolutely undivided is said to be absolutely one, and that is numerically one. But even among such things there are degrees. For there is something which is such that even though it is actually undivided, still it is potentially divisible, either by a division of quantity, or by an essential division, or by both: by the division of quantity, as something which is one by continuity; by an essential division, as those things which are composed of matter and form or from the act of being and that which is; or by both divisions as the natural bodies. And that some of these are not actually divided derives in them from something outside of the nature of composition or division, as is obvious in the case of the body of the heavens and the like, which are such that although they are not actually divisible, they are nevertheless divisible by the intellect. But there are things which are indivisible both actually and potentially, and such are of various kinds. For some involve something else in their concept besides the concept of indivisibility, as a point, which besides being undivided involves also position. But there is something which involves nothing else, but is its own indivisibility, as is the unity which is the principle of number; yet this inheres in something which is not this unity itself, namely, in its subject. Whence it is clear that that in which there is no composition of parts, no continuity of dimension, no variety of accidents, and which inheres in nothing, is maximally and most truly one, as Boethius concludes. And hence follows that His unity is the principle of all unity and the measure of all things; for that which is the maximal is the principle in every genus, just as that which is maximally hot is the principle of all hot things, as is said in bk. 2 of the Metaphysics, and that which is the simplest is the measure in any genus, as is said in bk. 10 of the Metaphysics.[9]

Since we are interested here in the unity of individual substances, concerning which Buridan established three degrees of unity corresponding to the three types of identity distinguished by him, we may disregard here the issue of *per accidens* unity, or the unity of accidents themselves, or the unity of reason of species and genera mentioned here by Aquinas. What is clear even from this passage concerning these substances is that for him, there are degrees of unity even among these substances, corresponding to their various sorts of composition determined by their nature.

However, if there are degrees of unity among primary substances, then, given the convertibility of being and unity, there also have to be *degrees of being* among them. But how can this be? How can we interpret such "degrees of being"? Should we say that God exists more than an angel does, or that a human being exists more than a dog does? What can it even mean to say that something is or exists more than another thing?

To respond to these questions, we should briefly consider how Aquinas can interpret different degrees of being in terms of his conception of the analogical predication of the term "being" *simpliciter*, i.e., absolutely speaking, without any qualification, and *secundum quid*, that is, with some qualification. Now, we should note here in the first place that, in general, whenever we have to distinguish the predication of some common term *simpliciter* and *secundum quid*, that is, without and with some qualification, then this is a sure sign that the term is being predicated analogically of its inferiors, as far as Aquinas is concerned. He makes this quite clear in the following passage:

> ...There are two ways in which something common can be divided into those that are under it, just as there are two ways in which something is common. There is the division of a univocal [term] into its species by differences by which the nature of the genus is equally participated in the species, as animal is divided into man and horse, and the like. Another division is that of something common by analogy, which is predicated according to its perfect concept [*ratio*] of one of those that divide it, and of the other[s] imperfectly and with qualification [*secundum quid*], as being is divided into substance and accident, and into being in actuality and in potentiality...[10]

This general feature of analogical predication (regardless of the details of how an analogical concept is formed, and consequently what sorts of analogy may or need be distinguished)[11] betrays a common feature of analogical concept-formation. This common feature is that our analogical notions presuppose a primary, primitive, univocal concept; it is this primary concept which is then further modified somehow in the process of some analogical concept-formation, yielding those further, qualified senses of the term subordinated to this concept which allow the term to be extended in a less strict sense, and analogically applied to things to which in its primary, strict sense it could not apply without qualification.

The primary, unqualified sense of being is that on account of which any primary substance can be said to be a being without qualification insofar as it exists. But for Aquinas, for a primary substance to be is for it to have its essence in actuality, that is, for a primary substance to be, absolutely speaking, is at the same time for it to be with respect to its essence. So even the primary, unqualified predication of being implies a certain implicit qualification, namely, the determination of a thing's substantial being by its own essence.[12] Clearly, for a cat to be is for it to live a feline life, whereas for a dog to be is for it to live a canine life, which is different precisely because of the essential differences between cats and dogs. But is this not equally true in the case of God? Is for God to be not for Him to live a divine life? Could we not say that even for God to be is for Him to be with respect to the divine essence, and so also in this case there is a certain implicit qualification, namely, the determination of divine being by divine essence?

To answer this question, we should consider it in the general context of Aquinas's analysis of the difference between predication *secundum quid* and *simpliciter*, distinguishing between diminishing and non-diminishing determinations.[13] To use the common medieval example, if I say: "This shield is white with respect to its one half", this obviously does not entail that the shield is white, absolutely speaking, for its other half may be black. So, in this case the qualification is diminishing [*determinatio diminuens*], in the sense that it "diminishes", that is, takes away from, the conditions of the absolute, strict, unqualified applicability of the predicate, and this is why the predicate so qualified can apply to something which is not absolutely white, but only in its half. So, precisely because the qualification is intensionally diminishing, it is extensionally enlarging. By contrast, if I say: "This shield is white with respect to its whole surface", then the qualification added to the predicate is not diminishing, for this qualification states that the shield is white all over, which is precisely what the absolute, unqualified predicate would say, namely, that the shield is white, so this qualification does not take away anything from the conditions of the strict applicability of the unqualified predicate and hence it applies only to what is white all over, without qualification.

But, further, if I say: "This shield is white with respect to its whiteness", then, again, the qualification added to the predicate does not take away anything from the conditions of its strict, unqualified applicability, whence it applies only to something that is absolutely white, without any limitation. The reason for this clearly is that when the qualification refers to what is signified by the predicate, then the qualification is not diminishing; on the contrary, since the predicate can apply to the subject only in respect of what it signifies anyway, the predicate so qualified can apply only to that to which it applies also in itself, absolutely, without any qualification.[14] So, a diminishing qualification has to refer to something which is distinct from what is signified by the predicate, but when there is no such a distinction, then the qualification is not diminishing. But this is precisely the case in the predication: "God exists with respect to His divinity", for God's existence being the same as His essence, the qualification refers to what the predicate signifies, namely, divine existence, which is divinity, the divine essence. On the other hand, according to Aquinas, in everything else, i.e., in every created thing, the nature of the thing is not the same as the existence of the thing, and this is why the created nature imposes a certain diminishing, limiting qualification and determination upon the existence of the thing. As Aquinas says:

> A created spiritual substance has to contain two principles one of which is related to the other as potency to act. And this is clear from the following. It is obvious that the first being, which is God, is infinite act, namely, having in Himself the whole plenitude of being not contracted to the nature of some genus or species. Therefore it is necessary that His being itself should not be an act of being that is, as it were, put into a nature which is not its own being, for in this way it would be confined to that nature. Hence we say that God is His own being. But this cannot be said about anything else; just as it is impossible to think that there should be several separate whitenesses, but if a whiteness were separate from any subject and recipient, then it would be only one, so it is impossible that there should be a subsistent act of being, except only one. Therefore, everything else after the first being, since it is not its own being, has being received in something, by which its being is contracted; and thus in any created being the nature of the thing that participates being is other than the act of being itself that is participated.[15]

So, although all created substances are beings in the primary, unqualified sense, this unqualified sense of being is still not, indeed, cannot be, the absolutely unlimited sense of being according to which only God can be said TO BE. The reason for this is that everything is said to exist with respect to its essence, for the substantial existence of each and every thing is precisely the actuality of its essence. But it is only God whose essence is His own existence, so everything else's essence, being distinct from its existence, imposes some diminishing qualification, some limitation upon the sense of being in which only God can be said to exist. So the substantial being of created substances, on account of which the predicate "is" or "exists" applies to them without qualification, for it is the act of being by which they exist *simpliciter*, is at the same time an act of being which can be signified by the predicate "is" or "exists" only in a sense which can be derived by some diminishing qualification of the sense of the same predicate in which it applies only to God.

Therefore, what accounts for the difference between the senses of "exists" in which a creature and God can be said to exist is precisely God's absolutely undivided unity, that is, God's absolute simplicity, as opposed to the necessary intrinsic multiplicity of the constitutive parts of any creature, in particular, the distinction between their essence and existence. Indeed, it is precisely this intrinsic multiplicity that distinguishes creatures from God as well as from one another, thereby causing the extrinsic multiplicity of the number of creatures, for created substances differ from one another in their essence insofar as their essences are different determinations of their acts of being. Furthermore, when their essence itself is composite, because it comprises both matter and form, the determination it imposes upon the substantial act of being of material substances also allows the numerical multiplicity of individuals within the same species, divided from one another by their designated matter, that is, their matter informed by their dimensions.[16]

However, it is individuals of this kind that are the most familiar to us, and so it is the unity and being of these individuals that provides *for us* the primary, unqualified notions of being and unity. So first it is relative to these individuals that we have to recognize that their integral parts (whether quantitative parts, other accidental parts or even essential parts), their collections, and their species and genera also exhibit some sort of unity and being which is analogous to the unity and being of these primary substances.[17]

But once we recognize the analogical character of the applicability of these notions in the realm of created substances, their parts, species, genera, and collections, and we also recognize how the created order of these primary beings is determined by their metaphysical unity on account of which they approach more or less the absolute unity of divine simplicity, we also have to admit that even the being of these is subject to certain qualification and limitation in comparison to the being of He who IS, without any limitation.

And this is why, when he discusses whether "He who is" [*qui est*] is the most appropriate name of God, St. Thomas says the following:

> All other names say something determinate and particularized, as "[to be] wise" says [to be] something.[18] But the name "He who is" says being absolutely, not determined by something added [to it] and this is why Damascene says that it does not signify what God is, but it signifies a certain infinite ocean of substance, as it were, something not determinate. Therefore, when we move toward God in the way of removal, first we deny of Him corporeal attributes, and secondly even intellectual ones, in the way they are found in creatures, such as goodness and wisdom; and then it remains in our understanding only that He is, and nothing more, whence He is there in a sort of confusion. And finally we remove even this being itself, according to the way it is in the creatures; and then He remains there in a sort of shadow of ignorance, and by this ignorance, as it pertains to our present state, we are most appropriately tied to God, as Dionysius asserts, and this is a sort of haze, in which God is said to dwell.[19]

So, if we try to capture this absolute being in its simplicity, the notion of absolute being we arrive at leaves us in some confusion, because of a lack of determinate understanding. On the other hand, as soon as we try to reach a more determinate understanding of divine nature, it is precisely the determinate character of our concepts, and their resulting multiplicity, which will be incompatible with the absolutely unlimited nature and simplicity of divine being. Indeed, even when a determinate concept represents some absolute perfection which in its absolute, unlimited form is nothing but the plenitude of divine being, but which we can find in the creatures only in a limited and determinate manner, the very determinacy of the concept matches the determinacy, and so also the limited character, of the perfection in question as it is found in the creatures. For even though the perfection represented by the concept in itself is absolute, insofar as by its own nature it does not demand any determination, *the way* in which it is represented by the concept, as being a perfection which is distinct from other creaturely perfections, involves a multiplicity that is not compatible with the absolute, divine simplicity.

But this is precisely the reason why St. Thomas has to claim that although those names which signify such absolute perfections apply primarily to God *quantum ad rem significatam*, still, *quantum ad modum significandi* they apply primarily to creatures. As he says:

We should consider, therefore, that because the names we apply to God are imposed by us, and we do not know God except from the creatures, these names are always defective in their representation with respect to their mode of signifying [*quantum ad modum significandi*], for they signify divine perfections in the way in which they are participated by the creatures. But if we consider the thing signified [*res significata*] by the name, which is that which the name is imposed to signify, we find that some names are imposed to signify primarily the perfection itself exemplified by God absolutely, not implying some [determinate] mode in their signification, while others are imposed to signify a perfection in accordance with such a mode of participation. For example, every cognition is [primarily] exemplified by divine cognition, and every knowledge by divine knowledge. The name "sense", however, is imposed to signify cognition in the manner in which it is received materially by a power of an organ. But the name "cognition" does not signify a mode of participation in its principal signification. Therefore, we have to say that all those names which are imposed to signify some perfection absolutely are properly said of God, and they apply to Him primarily as far as the thing signified is concerned, although not as far as the mode of signifying is concerned, such as "wisdom", "goodness", "essence", and the like.[20]

So, divine simplicity necessarily defies any adequate characterization by us. The only name that could most appropriately express this absolute simplicity by its indeterminacy, the name *qui est*, leaves us in confusion precisely because of its indeterminacy. On the other hand, any other name that gives us a more determinate concept is inappropriate in its mode of signifying to express divine simplicity precisely because of the determinacy of the concept in question.

Therefore, since the names signifying some absolute perfection apply primarily and absolutely to God *only* with respect to *what they signify*, but none of them can properly apply to Him with respect to their *mode of signifying*, these names can also absolutely be denied of Him:

Since a name has both a mode of signifying and the thing signified itself, it can always be denied of God either on account of one of these or on account of both; but it cannot be said of God except on account of only of one them. And since the truth and appropriateness of an affirmation requires that all be affirmed, whereas for the appropriateness of a negation it is sufficient if only one of them is lacking, this is why Dionysius says that negations are absolutely true, but affirmations only in some respect [*secundum quid*]: for only with respect to what is signified, but not with respect to the mode of signifying.[21]

Thus, on the basis of these considerations, we have to recognize the following paradox: These names *could* be predicated *only* of God in an absolutely unqualified sense (for the perfection they signify can be found only in God in an absolutely unqualified manner), and not of the creatures (for they apply to creatures in an unqualified sense only because it is from them that we abstracted the primary concepts of the perfections these names signify); still, because of the inherent multiplicity in their mode of signifying, reflecting their origin from the multiplicity of creaturely perfections, we can more appropriately deny them than affirm them of God. But it is precisely the recognition of this paradox that helps us gain some insight into the incomprehensible divine unity reflected in created multiplicity.[22]

## 4   The "Fusion of Our Horizons"

At this point, given the obvious, far-reaching differences among the conceptions sketched out so far, one is obviously tempted to raise the question: Who is right? – Aquinas, Buridan, or Frege and his modern ilk? Clearly, we cannot say that they are "just different", because their differences imply enormously different and apparently incompatible consequences, based on what they take to be self-evidently true in accordance with their respective conceptions. For instance, if we try to apply the Fregean conception in interpreting Aquinas' claim that God is the same as his own existence, we either find the claim hopelessly obscure (how can we even talk about "God's own existence"?) or, if we interpret the term "existence" as referring to what we very clearly understand by it (namely, our C($\exists$) as described earlier), then we should find the claim trivially false: Why would anyone in their right mind claim that God is identical with a second-order concept? So, differences in the interpretation of these primary concepts clearly have far-reaching consequences concerning our interpretation and evaluation of various metaphysical claims and arguments made in their respective conceptual frameworks.[23]

But then, since in metaphysics we want to find out *the truth* about "ultimate reality", it seems we *have to* decide which one of these (and other) competing conceptions is "the right one". Now, clearly, we cannot complacently settle in the Fregean conception on the grounds that it is more modern, whence it is more "advanced". After all, one of the main complaints about metaphysics has been, since at least early modern times, that "it is not making any progress" in the way the sciences do; so "more modern" in this field certainly does not equal "more advanced". And we can no longer afford the safety of common modern mantras either, such as "existence is not a predicate", as if their frequent repetition made them any more relevant or true. After all, we know that there is nothing impossible in *defining* an existence-predicate, in terms of the Fregean existential quantifier and identity: Ex ↔ (∃y)(x = y). Furthermore, the post-Kantian slogan, in the sense in which it is trivially true, is not relevant, and in the sense in which it *is* relevant, it is just not true. For if it means that the Fregean second-order concept of existence is not a Fregean first-order concept expressed by a predicate, then it is trivially true, but then it has nothing to do with Aquinas's or other medieval Aristotelians' concept. On the other hand, if it means that medieval Aristotelians could not have expressed by "est", "existit" and their cognates in their Medieval Latin a different concept, then the slogan is just false, because, as we have seen, they just did. And the same goes, *mutatis mutandis*, for the other related metaphysical concepts we have considered here, namely, the concepts of unity and identity.

But then, what else remains? Who is right? After all, either Frege and his ilk are right, and the concepts of existence and identity are primitive, syncategorematic concepts defining a precise, unambiguous, mathematical concept of unity, or Buridan and Aquinas are right (now disregarding *their* differences), and the primary, transcendental, categorematic notion of being grounds the equally transcendental, but derivative notion of unity, which in turn grounds the systematically ambiguous notion of identity.

My suggestion in conclusion is that we do not have to choose among these alternatives. The question is not whether "existence is a predicate" or whether *the* notion of unity is primitive or whether *the* notion of identity must be unambiguous. In fact, posed in this way, these questions are pseudo-questions, without properly specifying what they are about. Clearly, as the foregoing analyzes have shown, different thinkers have different concepts corresponding to the words in their languages that are supposed to express what one might justifiably identify as Frege's concept of existence or unity or identity, or as Buridan's or Aquinas' respective concepts they use in their metaphysical considerations. Indeed, their differences in their understanding of these basic concepts determine different self-evident truths formed with these concepts, just as differences in the understanding of the notion of parallel lines determines different axioms or postulates for Euclidean and non-Euclidean geometries. But then, just as after the realization of the possibility of non-Euclidean geometries we cannot raise the question whether a triangle has three angles equal to two right angles without further specifying whether we are talking about a Euclidean, Bolyai, or Riemann triangle, so we cannot raise the issue whether essence and existence are distinct in creatures, for instance, without specifying whether it is the Fregean, Buridanian, or Thomistic (or, for that matter, Scotistic or Ockhamist) notion of existence we should apply in answering the question.

Does this mean, then, that we cannot have the absolute, ultimate answers to our ultimate questions, except relative to the thought of this or that major thinker? Where would that leave us with the truth about these ultimate questions? In response, I would say that we, the posterity of these major thinkers, can raise these questions, only because we are capable of forming the concepts required for forming these questions, relying on their thought and the thought of other countless and "nameless" thinkers whose basic concepts have been handed down to us encoded in the languages we acquire, shaping our own conceptual idioms, in a mostly unreflected process. But once in the process of philosophical reflection, we realize the variety of ways such concepts can be formed to serve as the basis of large, (mostly) consistent systems of thought, we have to build them all into our reflected, consciously constructed conceptual idiom, thereby achieving a "fusion of our horizons" (to use Gadamer's catchy phrase), yielding a deeper and more precise understanding of our questions themselves. It is only with this sort of understanding that we can legitimately raise and answer these questions. However, based on this deeper and more precise understanding, we *can* have our answers, even if they may not be the simple or even simple-minded answers we originally hoped for, just as it happens in the development of mathematics. But then, what else can count as "progress" in the development of an *a priori* science?

## Notes

1. In this chapter, I will ignore the somewhat contrived verbal distinction between "being" and "existence" supposed to distinguish "eternalist" and "presentist" conceptions of these notions or some other such subtly different interpretations of them, even if some authors do want to use these terms in this way. By equal rights, I will not, and I will use these terms interchangeably.
2. Thus, the Fregean distinction between first- and second-order concepts must not be conflated with scholastics' distinction between first and

second intentions: Fregean second-order concepts are concepts operating on first order concepts, just as the scholastics claimed about syncategore-matic concepts, whereas scholastic second intentions are concepts of first intentions, i.e., they are not operating on first intentions; rather, they are representations of first intentions. For the traditional syncategorematic/cate-gorematic distinction, see Klima (2005).

3. Here and above, the symbol "∃" is used in a meta-language of standard predicate logic, in this case English plus the language of set theory, autonymously, to refer to the corresponding symbol in the language of predicate logic. The same goes, *mutatis mutandis* for meta-linguistic references to the identity sign of predicate logic below, as opposed to the use of that sign in the Russellian formula at the end of this section or its use in our meta-language as part of the language of set theory in the foregoing and below. But no confusion should arise from this trivial ambiguity of this sign in these passages.

4. Instead of treating $C(=)$ as a two-place function, we might as well treat it as a one-place compound function, such that $C'(=)(u)(v) = T$ if u is the same as v, otherwise $C'(=)(u)(v) = F$.

5. Hoc nomen "unum" ab indivisione sumitur, ut patet quinto Metaphysicae, propter quod ibidem dicitur, quod quaecumque non habent divisionem in quantum non habent divisionem, ut sic, "unum" dicuntur. Ideo hoc nomen "unum" est nomen privativum privative oppositum huic nomini "multa", ut apparet decimo Metaphysicae. Modo nomen privativum claudit in sua ratione nomen habitus sibi oppositum, cum negatione; ideo: aliquo modo significat vel connotat illud quod nomen habitus significat, et illud est extraneum ei de quo verificatur nomen privativum.' [...] Sed de isto termino "idem" ego dico, quod adhuc est magis connotativus quam iste terminus „unum"; et ideo "idem" dicitur passio „unius" et „unum" dicitur tamquam subiectum et funda-mentum ipsius. Nam significatio huius termini "idem" praesupponit significa-tionem „unius" et connotat ultra illam respectum, scilicet quod aliquid sit ad quod sit idem, et hoc est illudmet quod est idem... QiPI, q. 11, pp. 171–72.

6. By "connoting a privation" in the context of Buridan's semantics, we should not understand anything like connoting a "negative entity" a privation; rather, it is simply the connotation of a positive entity, namely, the corre-sponding habit, only negatively, with the additional signification of another positive entity, the mental act of negation, a syncategorematic concept, which is a positive quality of the mind of anyone using the privative term with understanding. For more on this issue, and how it is related to the nominalist program of "ontological reduction", see Klima (2012a); cf. Klima (2008).

7. "Tripliciter enim consuevimus dicere aliquid alicui esse idem in numero. Primo modo totaliter, scilicet quod hoc est illud et nihil est de integritate huius, quod non sit de integritate illius, et e converso; et hoc propriissime esse idem in numero. Et secundum illum modum dicendum est, quod ego non sum idem, quod ego eram heri, nam aliquid heri erat de integritate mea, quod iam resolutum est, et aliquid etiam heri non erat de integri-tate mea, quod post per nutritionem factum est de substantia mea. Sed secundo modo aliquid dicitur alicui idem partialiter, scilicet quia hoc est pars illius, et maxime hoc dicitur, si sit maior pars vel principalior vel etiam, quia hoc et illud participant in aliquo, quod est pars maior vel prin-cipalior utriusque. Sic enim dicit Aristoteles nono Ethicorum, quod homo

maxime est intellectus, sicut civitas et omnis congregatio maxime est prin-
cipalissimum prout allegatum est in quaestione praecedente, et exinde
etiam proveniunt denominations totorum a denominationibus partium.
Et ita manet homo idem per totam vitam, quia manet anima totaliter
eadem, quae est pars principalior. Sic autem non manet equus idem immo
nec corpus humanum. Sed adhuc tertio modo et minus proprie dicitur
aliquid alicui idem numero secundum considerationem partium diver-
sarum in succedendo alteram alteri, et sic Secana dicitur idem fluvius a
mille annis citra, licet proprie loquendo nihil modo sit pars Secanae, quod
a decem annis citra fuit pars Secanae. Sic enim mare dicitur perpetuum,
et ille mundus inferior perpetuus, et equus idem per totam vitam, et
similiter corpus humanum idem. Et iste modus identitatis sufficit ad hoc,
quod nomen significativum dicatur discretum vel singulare secundum
communem et consuetum modum loquendi, qui non est verum proprie.
Non enim est verum proprie, quod Secana, quem ego video, est ille, quem
ego vidi a decem annis citra. Sed propositio conceditur ad illum sensum,
quod aqua, quam videmus, quae vocatur Secana, et aqua, quam tunc vidi,
quae etiam vocabatur Secana, et aquae etiam, quae intermediis temporibus
fuerunt, vocabantur quaelibet in tempore suo Secana et continuate fuerunt
ad invicem in succedendo. Et ex identitate etiam dicta secundum huius-
modi continuationem dicimus hoc nomen "Secana" esse nomen discretum
et singulare, quamvis non ita proprie sit discretum sicut esset, si maneret
idem totaliter ante et post." QP I, q. 10.

8. This section uses material from Klima (2000). For a more detailed discussion,
   please consult that paper.

9. "...dicendum, quod deus summe et verissime unus est. Secundum enim
   quod aliquid se habet ad indivisionem, ita se habet ad unitatem; quia,
   secundum philosophum, ens dicitur unum in eo quod non dividitur. Et ideo
   illa quae sunt indivisa per se, verius sunt unum quam illa quae sunt indivisa
   per accidens, sicut albus et socrates quae sunt unum per accidens; et inter
   illa quae sunt unum per se, verius sunt unum quae sunt indivisa simpliciter quam quae sunt indivisa respectu alicujus vel generis vel speciei vel
   proportionis. Unde etiam non dicuntur simpliciter unum, sed unum vel in
   genere vel in specie vel in proportione; et quod est simpliciter indivisum,
   dicitur simpliciter unum, quod est unum numero. Sed in istis etiam inven-
   itur aliquis gradus. Aliquid enim est quod quamvis sit indivisum in actu,
   est tamen divisibile potentia, vel divisione quantitatis, vel divisione essentiali, vel secundum utrumque. Divisione quantitatis, sicut quod est unum
   continuitate; divisione essentiali, sicut in compositis ex forma et materia,
   vel ex esse et quod est; divisione secundum utrumque, sicut in naturalibus
   corporibus. Et quod aliqua horum non dividantur in actu, est ex aliquo in
   eis praeter naturam compositionis vel divisionis, sicut patet in corpore caeli
   et hujusmodi; quae quamvis non sint divisibilia actu, sunt tamen divisibilia intellectu. Aliquid vero est quod est indivisibile actu et potentia; et hoc
   multiplex est. Quoddam enim habet in sui ratione aliquid praeter rationem
   indivisibilitatis, ut punctum, quod praeter indivisionem importat situm:
   aliquid vero est quod nihil aliud importat, sed est ipsa sua indivisibilitas,
   ut unitas quae est principium numeri; et tamen inhaeret alicui quod non
   est ipsamet unitas, scilicet subjecto suo. Unde patet quod illud in quo nulla

est compositio partium, nulla dimensionis continuitas, nulla accidentium varietas, nulli inhaerens, summe et vere unum est, ut concludit boetius. Et inde est quod sua unitas est principium omnis unitatis et mensura omnis rei. Quia illud quod est maximum, est principium in quolibet genere, sicut maxime calidum omnis calidi, ut dicitur 2 metaphysic., Et illud quod est simplicissimum, est mensura in quolibet genere, ut 10 metaphysic. dicitur." 1SN d. 24, q. 1, a. 1.

10. "Respondeo dicendum, quod est duplex modus dividendi commune in ea quae sub ipso sunt, sicut est duplex communitatis modus. Est enim quaedam divisio univoci in species per differentias quibus aequaliter natura generis in speciebus participatur, sicut animal dividitur in hominem et equum, et hujusmodi; alia vero divisio est ejus quod est commune per analogiam, quod quidem secundum perfectam rationem praedicatur de uno dividentium, et de altero imperfecte et secundum quid, sicut ens dividitur in substantiam et accidens, et in ens actu et in ens potentia: et haec divisio est quasi media inter aequivocum et univocum." 2SN d. 42, q. 1, a. 3, in corp. Cf.: "Unum enim eodem modo dicitur aliquid sicut et ens; unde sicut ipsum non ens, non quidem simpliciter, sed secundum quid, idest secundum rationem, ut patet in 4o Metaphysicae, ita etiam negatio est unum secundum quid, scilicet secundum rationem." in Peri lb. 2, lc. 2, n. 3.

11. Since here we need not consider in detail exactly how an analogical concept is formed, we need not consider what the different modes of analogy are, which is in the focus of the debates concerning Aquinas's theory of analogy. See McInerny (1961) and McInerny (1996). Cf. also Ashworth (1992a, p. 399); Ashworth (1992b, p. 94); and Hochschild (2010).

12. For this point, see (Wippel 1987); cf. Te Velde (1995).

13. For a more comprehensive discussion of the logical doctrine behind Aquinas's analysis of this difference (in connection with St. Thomas's use of the related theoretical apparatus in his theology of the Incarnation) see the criticism of Allan Bäck's argument against Aquinas's theory of the Incarnation in Klima (1984). Bäck still did not manage to get this right in his later work on the subject.

14. According to the medieval logical literature concerning the fallacy secundum quid et simpliciter, the general rule for distinguishing diminishing vs. non-diminishing qualifications is that a qualification is non-diminishing if and only if it refers to a part of the subject which is such that the predicate would apply to the whole subject without qualification only in respect of that part anyway. For references, see my paper referred to in the previous note. For a detailed discussion of how this distinction fits into Aquinas' semantic doctrine in general, see Klima (1996), Klima (2002), Klima (2012b) and Klima (2012c).

15. "Oportet enim in substantia spirituali creata esse duo, quorum unum comparatur ad alterum ut potentia ad actum. Quod sic patet. Manifestum est enim quod primum ens, quod Deus est, est actus infinitus, utpote habens in se totam essendi plenitudinem non contractam ad aliquam naturam generis vel speciei. Unde oportet quod ipsum esse eius non sit esse quasi inditum alicui naturae quae non sit suum esse; quia sic finiretur ad illam naturam. Unde dicimus, quod Deus est ipsum suum esse. Hoc autem non potest dici de aliquo alio: sicut impossibile est intelligere quod sint plures albedines separatae; sed si esset albedo separata ab omni subiecto et recipiente, esset una

tantum; ita impossibile est quod sit ipsum esse subsistens nisi unum tantum. Omne igitur quod est post primum ens, cum non sit suum esse, habet esse in aliquo receptum, per quod ipsum esse contrahitur; et sic in quolibet creato aliud est natura rei quae participat esse, et aliud ipsum esse participatum." *De spir. creat.* q. un., a. 1.

16. Cf. Wippel (1985).
17. See again the text quoted in n. 9.
18. Cf. In Boethii De Hebdomadibus, lc. 2. nn. 20–35.
19. "Ad quartum dicendum, quod alia omnia nomina dicunt esse determinatum et particulatum; sicut sapiens dicit aliquid esse; sed hoc nomen qui est dicit esse absolutum et indeterminatum per aliquid additum; et ideo dicit Damascenus quod non significat quid est deus, sed significat quoddam pelagus substantiae infinitum, quasi non determinatum. Unde quando in deum procedimus per viam remotionis, primo negamus ab eo corporalia; et secundo etiam intellectualia, secundum quod inveniuntur in creaturis, ut bonitas et sapientia; et tunc remanet tantum in intellectu nostro, quia est, et nihil amplius: unde est sicut in quadam confusione. Ad ultimum autem etiam hoc ipsum esse, secundum quod est in creaturis, ab ipso removemus; et tunc remanet in quadam tenebra ignorantiae, secundum quam ignorantiam, quantum ad statum viae pertinet, optime deo conjungimur, ut dicit Dionysius, et haec est quaedam caligo, in qua deus habitare dicitur." 1SN d. 8, q.1, a. 1, resp. 4.
20. "Considerandum est igitur, quod cum nomina sint imposita a nobis, qui deum non nisi ex creaturis cognoscimus, semper deficiunt a divina repraesentatione quantum ad modum significandi: quia significant divinas perfectiones per modum quo participantur in creaturis. Si autem consideremus rem significatam in nomine, quae est id ad quod significandum imponitur nomen, invenimus, quaedam nomina esse imposita ad significandum principaliter ipsam perfectionem exemplatam a deo simpliciter, non concernendo aliquem modum in sua significatione; et quaedam ad significandum perfectionem receptam secundum talem modum participandi; verbi gratia, omnis cognitio est exemplata a divina cognitione, et omnis scientia a divina scientia. Hoc igitur nomen sensus est impositum ad significandum cognitionem per modum illum quo recipitur materialiter secundum virtutem conjunctam organo. Sed hoc nomen cognitio non significat aliquem modum participandi in principali sua significatione. Unde dicendum est, quod omnia illa nomina quae imponuntur ad significandum perfectionem aliquam absolute, proprie dicuntur de deo, et per prius sunt in ipso quantum ad rem significatam, licet non quantum ad modum significandi, ut sapientia, bonitas, essentia et omnia hujusmodi; et haec sunt de quibus dicit Anselmus, quod simpliciter et omnino melius est esse quam non esse. Illa autem quae imponuntur ad significandum perfectionem aliquam exemplatam a deo, ita quod includant in sua significatione imperfectum modum participandi, nullo modo dicuntur de deo proprie; sed tamen ratione illius perfectionis possunt dici de deo metaphorice, sicut sentire, videre et hujusmodi. Et similiter est de omnibus aliis formis corporalibus, ut lapis, leo et hujusmodi: omnia enim imponuntur ad significandum formas corporales secundum modum determinatum participandi esse vel vivere vel aliquam divinarum perfectionum." 1SN d. 22, q. 1, a. 2 co.

21. "Ad primum igitur dicendum, quod cum in nomine duo sint, modus signifi-
    candi, et res ipsa significata, semper secundum alterum potest removeri a Deo
    vel secundum utrumque; sed non potest dici de Deo nisi secundum alterum
    tantum. Et quia ad veritatem et proprietatem affirmationis requiritur quod
    totum affirmetur, ad proprietatem autem negationis sufficit si alterum tantum
    desit, ideo dicit Dionysius, quod negationes sunt absolute verae, sed affirma-
    tiones non nisi secundum quid: quia quantum ad significatum tantum, et
    non quantum ad modum significandi." 1SN d. 22, q. 1, a. 2, ad 1-um
22. So, from this point of view, I do not find the contrast between "Neoplatonic
    henology", as opposed to "Thomistic ontology", so sharp as some Thomistic
    scholars, most notably Gilson, would. But this would deserve a separate
    study. The issue receives intriguing discussion in Taylor (1998).
23. For more on this particular issue, see Klima (2012d).

# References

Ashworth, E. J. 1992a. "Analogical Concepts: The Fourteenth-Century Background
to Cajetan," *Dialogue* 31.
____ 1992b. "Analogy and Equivocation in Thirteenth-Century Logic: Aquinas in
Context," *Mediaeval Studies* 54.
Hochschild, Joshua P. 2010. *The Semantics of Analogy: Rereading Cajetan's De
Nominum Analogia* (Notre Dame, IN: University of Notre Dame Press).
Klima, G. 1984. "Libellus pro Sapiente: A Criticism of Allan Bäck's Argument
against St. Thomas Aquinas' Theory of the Incarnation," *The New Scholasticism*
58: 207–19.
____ 1996. "The Semantic Principles Underlying Saint Thomas Aquinas's Metaphysics of Being," *Medieval Philosophy and Theology* 5: 87–141.
____ 2000. "Aquinas on One and Many," *Documenti e Studi sulla Tradizione Filosofica
Medievale* 11: 195–215.
____ 2002. "Aquinas' Theory of the Copula and the Analogy of Being," *Logical
Analysis and History of Philosophy* 5: 159–76.
____ 2005. "Syncategoremata," in Keith Brown, (ed.) *Encyclopedia of Language and
Linguistics*, 2nd Ed. vol. 12 (Elsevier: Oxford).
____ 2008. "The Nominalist Semantics of Ockham and Buridan: A Rational
Reconstruction," in D. Gabbay and J. Woods, (eds), *Handbook of the History of
Logic* (North Holland: Amsterdam).
____ 2012a. "Ontological Reduction by Logical Analysis and the Primitive Vocabulary
of Mentalese," *American Catholic Philosophical Quarterly*, 86: 303–414.
____ 2012b. "Being," in J. Marenbon, J., (ed.) *The Oxford Handbook of Medieval
Philosophy* (Oxford: Oxford University Press).
____ 2012c. "Theory of Language," in B. Davies and E. Stump, (eds), *The Oxford
Handbook to Aquinas* (Oxford: Oxford University Press).
____ 2012d. "Aquinas vs. Buridan on Essence and Existence, and the
Commensurability of Paradigms," in L. Novák, D. Novotný, P. Sousedík, and
D. Svoboda, (eds), *Metaphysics: Aristotelian, Scholastic, Analytic* (Ontos Verlag:
Heusenstamm).
McInerny, R. 1961. *The Logic of Analogy* (Martinus Nijhoff: The Hague).

—— 1996. *Aquinas and Analogy* (Washington, D.C.: Catholic University of America Press).

Taylor, R. C. 1998. "Aquinas, the Plotiniana Arabica, and the Metaphysics of Being and Actuality," *Journal of the History of Ideas* 59: 217–39.

Te Velde, R. A. 1995. *Participation and Substantiality in Thomas Aquinas* (Brill: Leiden-New York-Köln).

Wippel, J. F. 1985. "Thomas Aquinas on the Distinction and the Derivation of the Many from the One: a Dialectic between Being and Nonbeing," *The Review of Metaphysics* 38: 563–90.

—— 1987. "Thomas Aquinas and Participation," in J. F. Wippel, (ed.) *Studies in Medieval Philosophy* (Washington, D.C.: The Catholic University of America Press).

# 9
# Substance, Independence, and Unity

*Kathrin Koslicki*

## 1 Introduction

Hylomorphism is the position popular among neo-Aristotelian metaphysicians according to which unified wholes (such as presumably organisms) are in some sense compounds of matter (hylē) and form (morphē). Neo-Aristotelians also often find themselves drawn to an account of substancehood which centers on the idea that the substances are just those entities which are ontologically independent, according to some preferred notion of ontological independence. But what this preferred notion of ontological independence is in terms of which a successful criterion of substancehood can be formulated has been a difficult and controversial question.[1]

Aristotle, in the *Categories*, seems to have been the first to propose explicitly an independence criterion for substances.[2] Those entities which are classified as primary substances in the *Categories* (e.g., individual organisms and artifacts) are, in Aristotle's view, ontologically independent, since they are neither "said of" nor "in" anything else as a subject. Entities belonging to other categories, on the other hand, are ontologically dependent on the primary substances, since in his view they are either "said of" the primary substances as subjects or are "in" them as subjects. The first class of entities, those dependent on the primary substances by being said of them, comprises the so-called secondary substances, i.e., universals in the category of substance (e.g., the species, human being, and the genus, animal); these entities correspond to classifications of the primary substances into more general taxonomic categories. The second class of entities, which are dependent on the primary substances by being in them, comprises individuals and universals in categories other than substance (e.g., quantities, qualities, relations, times, places, actions, passions); these entities correspond either to individual accidental features (e.g., a particular instance of red), which directly inhere in primary substances, or to more general taxonomic categories into which these individual accidental features fall (e.g., color, quality).

When we attempt to combine hylomorphism with an independence criterion of substancehood, an apparent conflict emerges. Consider, for example, organisms, which are widely regarded by neo-Aristotelians as paradigmatic examples of substances. If these alleged substance candidates are also to be construed along hylomorphic lines as compounds of matter and form, one wonders whether they will not then turn out to be ontologically dependent on entities numerically distinct from themselves (viz., their form and possibly their matter as well) and thereby jeopardize their status as substances.[3] My main focus in this chapter will be to examine the apparent tension between these two prominent strands within neo-Aristotelian metaphysics, hylomorphism and independence criteria of substancehood, and explore some possible resolutions to this apparent conflict.

## 2  Lowe's account[4]

E. J. Lowe has proposed the following criterion of substancehood:[5]

> (ICS1) *Independence Criterion for Substances* (Lowe): x is a substance $\equiv_{\text{def}}$ (i) x is a particular; and (ii) there is no particular y such that (a) y is not identical with x and (b) x is essentially identity dependent on y.[6]

Clause (ii.b) of (ICS1) makes use of Lowe's notion of essential identity dependence, defined as follows:

> (EID) *Essential Identity Dependence* (Lowe): x is essentially identity dependent on y $\equiv_{\text{def}}$ There is some function $\varphi$ such that it is part of the essence of x that $x = \varphi(y)$.

We are to construe "function", as it occurs in (EID), with the notion of a *criterion of identity* in mind.[7] Lowe (1989) offers the following general schema for a criterion of identity, where "$\Phi$" stands for a sortal term of some kind (e.g., "set") and "R" stands for a relation in terms of which the criterion of identity in question is formulated (e.g., the relation of having the same members):

(CI)   $(\forall x)(\forall y) ((\Phi x \ \& \ \Phi y) \rightarrow (x = y \leftrightarrow Rxy))$

An instance of (CI), in Lowe's view, is given for example by the Axiom of Extensionality for sets: if x and y are sets, then x and y are the same set just in case x and y have the same members; or, as Lowe would put it, *which* set a certain set is is fixed by *which* members the set in question has. For entities that exist in time, we are to construe (CI) for present purposes as yielding a *synchronic* criterion of identity or what is also known as a "principle of individuation", i.e., a criterion that specifies what it takes for an entity to be the very entity that it is *at* a time, rather than a *diachronic* criterion of identity, i.e., a criterion that specifies what it takes for an entity to persist *over* time. If it is to be part of the essence of the entity, x, in question that a certain function specifies a criterion of identity for x in terms of a certain relation x bears to y, then what is at issue in (EID) is a transworld principle of individuation, not one which applies merely within a given world.[8]

(EID) also speaks of a function as being part of the essence of an entity. We can understand this locution in the following way. Suppose real definitions are propositions (or collections of propositions) which state the essence, or what it is to be, a certain thing. Suppose further that propositions can have constituents. Then, for an entity to be part of the essence of another entity is for the first entity to be a constituent in the real definition of the second, i.e., for the first to be a constituent of the proposition (or of one of the propositions that belongs to the collection of propositions) that states the essence of the second entity.[9]

With this in mind, we may now approach (EID) as follows: an entity, x, is essentially identity dependent on an entity, y, when *which* entity x is is fixed by x's relationship to y. If a substance candidate, such as Socrates, is to count as an ontologically independent entity in the sense of (EID), then it must be the case that *which* entity Socrates is is not fixed by his relationship to any other entities. For Lowe, this means that no synchronic criterion of identity or principle of individuation that appeals to numerically distinct entities can be given at all for substance candidates such as Socrates: that they are the very entities they are at each time at which they exist is simply to be taken as a non-derivative fact about these entities. Thus, if Socrates is in fact to qualify as a substance, then it must be the case that he does not owe his individuation or synchronic identity, i.e., his being the very entity that he is at each time at which he exists, to his relationship to any other entity numerically distinct from himself.

Lowe's conception of the ontological independence of substances is presumably incompatible with the essentiality of origins, which he finds in any case implausible. For if it were part of Socrates' essence, for example, to have originated from a particular zygote, then it might seem that a criterion of individuation or synchronic identity could be found for a substance-candidate such as Socrates, viz., one which appeals to Socrates' origins.[10] Morever, Lowe's conception of the ontological independence of substances also conflicts with a certain natural interpretation of the neo-Aristotelian conception of unified wholes as compounds of matter and form. For if it were part of the essence of a substance candidate, such as Socrates, to be a compound of some matter and some form, then it might appear again that Socrates could be individuated by appeal to his form or matter. Since Lowe is sympathetic to the neo-Aristotelian conception of unified wholes as compounds of matter and form, he cannot avoid the conflict just raised by denying the premises that generate it. Instead, he adopts a different escape route, which itself carries with it considerable costs: in Lowe's (1999), he argues that hylomorphic compounds should be *identified* with their form and therefore are not strictly speaking *compounds* of matter and form at all.

## 3   Gorman's modifications of Lowe's account

Michael Gorman has recently argued that Lowe's independence criterion for substances should be modified in the following way:[11]

> (ICS2) *Independence Criterion for Substances* (Gorman): x is a substance $\equiv_{def}$ (i) x is a particular; (ii) there is no particular y such that (a) y is not identical with x, (b) x is essentially identity dependent on y, and (c) y is not one of x's proper parts; and (iii) x is unified in the right way.

(ICS2) is just like (ICS1) with the exception that Gorman adds two clauses to Lowe's criterion, viz., (ii.c) and (iii). The first of these, (ii.c), allows an entity to qualify as a substance even if it is essentially identity dependent on entities numerically distinct from itself, as long as these entities are among its own proper parts. The second added clause, (iii), requires substances to be unified "in the right way".

These additional clauses are intended to exclude the following types of cases which Gorman considers to be counterexamples to Lowe's independence criterion, as stated in (ICS1). First, to motivate the unity-clause in (iii), Gorman asks us to consider the Berlin Philharmonic Orchestra. Assuming that orchestras are particulars, it might seem that (ICS1), as it stands, classifies such entities as substances, which Gorman takes to be an unwelcome result. Since its inception in 1882, the Berlin Philharmonic Orchestra has managed to survive all sorts of changes, e.g., with respect to its conductor or the musicians that are its members at each time at which the orchestra exists. In this way, orchestras are more similar to putative substance candidates such as organisms, which can also persist through changes with respect to their parts, than they are to alleged non-substances such as sets and mereological sums, which are not capable of surviving changes with respect to their members or parts. Since the synchronic identity of the Berlin Philharmonic Orchestra at each time at which it exists is apparently not fixed by its essential relations to any other particulars numerically distinct from itself, such as its conductor or the musicians that are members of it, (ICS1) therefore seems to have the consequence that the Berlin Philharmonic Orchestra is classified as a substance. To avoid this result, Gorman introduces the unity requirement in (iii), since he believes that what accounts for the difference between putative substance candidates such as organisms and alleged non-substances such as orchestras, sets, mereological sums, and the like is that entities which belong to the former categories are more unified than entities which belong to the latter categories. Since he does not spell out further in what way putative substance candidates are more unified than alleged non-substances, however, the exact content of the unity requirement in (iii) at this point remains to be determined.

Secondly, Gorman's exclusion of proper parts in (ii.c) rests on the idea that even entities which he regards as plausible substance candidates can have essential proper parts.[12] To illustrate, Gorman takes it to be part of the essence of $H_2O$ molecules (which, in his view, are likely substance candidates) to be composed of the very hydrogen and oxygen atoms of which they are, in fact, composed. In that case, it appears that $H_2O$ molecules would be classified by (EID) as essentially identity dependent on particulars numerically distinct from themselves, since there would be some function, $\varphi$, e.g., the "molecule composition" function, such that it is part of the essence of an $H_2O$ molecule that it is the result of applying $\varphi$ to the oxygen and hydrogen atoms that are its essential proper parts. The molecule's synchronic identity at each time at which it exists, in that case, would be fixed by appeal to these atoms which are its essential proper parts, much like a set's identity is fixed by appeal to its members. Unless the essential identity dependence of an entity on its own proper parts is explicitly excluded as irrelevant to its status as a substance, as is done by clause (ii.c) of (ICS2), an $H_2O$ molecule would therefore be classified as a non-substance by (ICS1). Such alleged non-substances as mereological sums, which are apparently also essentially identity dependent only on their own proper parts, in Gorman's view, are to be ruled out by way of the unity requirement in (iii).

## 4   The stipulative exclusion of non-particulars

Both Lowe's original criterion in (ICS1) and Gorman's modified criterion in (ICS2) contain clauses which explicitly exclude non-particulars from the range of entities which might qualify as substances. But the stipulative exclusion of non-particulars from an independence criterion of substancehood is problematic, because it renders apparently substantive ontological disputes over questions of fundamentality non-substantive.[13]

Consider for example two philosophers who agree that both universals and particulars exist, but disagree over which taxonomic category of entities deserves to be granted substance status: one philosopher, let us say, regards universals as occupying the ontologically fundamental role of substances, while the other takes the substances to be particulars. Given (ICS1) and (ICS2), the first philosopher's thesis, "The substances are universals", is classified as contradictory (assuming that nothing is both particular and universal), since the criteria require that by definition something is a substance only if it is a particular. The second philosopher's thesis, "The substances are particulars", in contrast, is classified by (ICS1) and (ICS2) as trivial, since it simply follows from clause (i) of the definition that the substances are particulars. If we now attempt to remedy this situation by interpreting the two philosophers engaged in this dispute as subscribing to distinct criteria of substancehood, then we reach the equally unfortunate result that these two philosophers, instead of being engaged in what appears to be a substantive disagreement over questions of ontological fundamentality, are now simply talking past each other, with each of them subscribing to a different criterion of substancehood.

Given these considerations, I take it that clause (i) should be regarded as an unattractive addition to an independence criterion of substancehood: it should turn out to be a philosophically interesting and meaningful question which taxonomic category or categories of entities (if any) satisfy a given criterion of substancehood and whether these entities are particulars or universals. We thereby arrive at the following first revision of Gorman's independence criterion in (ICS2), with the restriction to particulars deleted:

(ICS3) *Independence Criterion for Substances* (First Revision): x is a substance $\equiv_{def}$ (i) there is no y such that (a) y is not identical with x, (b) x is essentially identity dependent on y, and (c) y is not one of x's proper parts; and (ii) x is unified in the right way.[14]

## 5   The stipulative exclusion of proper parts

As we have seen above, one of the two ways in which Gorman's modified criterion in (ICS2) differs from Lowe's original criterion in (ICS1) is in its addition of clause (ii.c), which eliminates part-dependence as a possible threat to an entity's status as a substance. I now want to consider the question of whether such a stipulative exclusion-clause governing proper parts should be regarded as an admissible element in an independence criterion of substances.[15] In principle, considerations analogous to those I adduced in connection with the stipulative exclusion of non-particulars appear to be relevant in this context as well: for it ought not simply to be settled by fiat whether entities which are ontologically dependent only on their own proper parts can be classified as occupying the ontologically fundamental role of substances. But instead of pursuing this line of argument, I will bring other issues to bear on the question of whether a clause excluding part-dependence should be considered an admissible component of an independence criterion of substancehood.

### 5.1   The possibility of simple substances

In a recent discussion of this issue, Patrick Toner has objected to the stipulative exclusion of proper parts from an independence criterion of substancehood on the following grounds (Toner 2010). In Toner's view, we should at least in principle allow for the possibility of simple substances, i.e., substances which have no proper parts at all and which therefore, *a fortiori*, cannot ontologically depend on their essential proper parts. Possible examples of such simple substances might include God, if God exists; minds, souls, or persons, according to certain conceptions of these entities; or physical simples, i.e., incomposite concrete material objects which may be included in the inventory of fundamental physics. Toner asks:

> Why accept that simple substances, which are self-sufficient in one way (a way that doesn't except dependence on their parts) are the same kind of things as 'substances' that are self-sufficient in a very

different kind of way (a way that does except dependence on their parts)? (Toner (2010), p.40)

If there are any simple entities which are not ontologically dependent on anything numerically distinct from themselves, then (ICS2), in Toner's mind, turns the category of substances into a heterogeneous collection. For one thing, this category would then comprise these simple entities which are completely ontologically independent from everything else. These entities are admitted into the category of substances by (ICS1)-(ICS3) without requiring any special exemption. But, in addition to these simple entities, the category of substances according to (ICS2) and (ICS3) would also include composite entities which may be ontologically dependent on their own essential proper parts, as long as these entities are not ontologically dependent on anything numerically distinct from them besides their own essential proper parts. These composite entities are admitted into the category of substances by (ICS2) and (ICS3) only by way of the special exception clause governing proper parts. But why believe, Toner asks, that we have thereby arrived at a unified category? This stipulative exclusion strategy, so Toner argues, is analogous to allowing into the class of all flying things not only things that have the ability to propel themselves through the air by their own power, but also things that can be carried along by something else. This way of allegedly delineating the class of flying things does not yield a unified category; nor, in Toner's view, do we arrive at a unified category of substances by allowing entities which ontologically depend on their essential proper parts to count as substances, along with entities which have no proper parts and hence cannot ontologically depend on their essential proper parts.

## 5.2   The threat of heterogeneity

As Toner's observations bring out, as far as simple substances are concerned (if there are such entities), Lowe's original criterion in (ICS1), stated here with the restriction to particulars deleted and a restriction to simple entities added, would do just as well as the modified criteria in (ICS2) or (ICS3):

> (ICSS) *Independence Criterion for Simple Substances*: x is a simple substance $\equiv_{def}$ (i) x is simple and (ii) there is no y such that (a) y is not identical with x and (b) x is essentially identity dependent on y.

According to (ICSS), the simple substances are those entities which are simple and completely ontologically independent from everything else numerically distinct from them. Since these entities are simple, the question of whether they are appropriately unified presumably does not arise for them; nor is there any danger that such entities might depend ontologically on their essential proper parts, given their simplicity. There is therefore no need for the addition of Gorman's unity requirement in an independence criterion for simple substances, just as there is no need for a clause exempting part-dependence.

The question now arises as to whether there are any composite substances and, if so, whether a revised version of Gorman's independence criterion might be appropriate for composite substances:

(ICCS1) *Independence Criterion for Composite Substances*:
x is a composite substance $\equiv_{def}$ (i) x is composite and (ii) there is no y such that (a) y is not identical with x, (b) x is essentially identity dependent on y, and (c) y is not one of x's proper parts; and (iii) x is unified in the right way.

According to (ICCS1), composite entities may qualify as substances, as long as they are not ontologically dependent on anything besides their own essential proper parts and as long as they are appropriately unified.

Even if (ICCS1) carries promise as an independence criterion for composite substances, Toner would no doubt object to the resulting bifurcation of the notion of substance into simple substances, on the one hand, and composite substances, on the other, with each kind being governed by its own independence criterion. Toner's challenge to a proponent of an independence criterion for substances who endorses a bifurcated account in the style of (ICSS) and (ICCS1) is to indicate wherein the alleged unity of the category of substances lies. What, so he might ask, gives us the right to think of both (ICSS) and (ICCS1) as criteria allegedly delineating a single ontological category, rather than two separate categories, viz., the simple entities which are completely ontologically independent, on the one hand, and the appropriately unified composite entities which are ontologically independent only in a modified way?

In response to Toner's worry concerning the apparent heterogeneity or disjunctiveness in the notion of substance to which the bifurcated account indicated above seems to lead, a proponent of such an account may at least point to the fact that there is after all a *non-ad-hoc* and metaphysically significant distinction between simple entities and composite entities. Assuming that a criterion of substancehood serves as an indicator of ontological fundamentality, it is perhaps no surprise that there might be distinct roads towards ontological fundamentality, among them one for simple entities and another for composite entities. For the time being, then, although I do feel the force of Toner's worry, I want to set it aside and examine instead the question of whether (ICCS1) might be appropriate as an independence criterion for composite substances. In what follows, I want to focus on a different challenge which arises for (ICCS1) as an independence criterion for composite substances: this challenge centers on the selective emphasis on proper parts, as opposed to constituents more generally.[16]

## 5.3 Proper parts vs. constituents

Something can be a constituent of a composite entity without being a proper part of it. For example, the members of sets are constituents of the sets of which they are members (where "constituency" is here construed in the set-theoretic sense of "membership"), but the members of sets should not be regarded as proper parts of the sets of which they are members.[17] Among other things, proper parthood is plausibly taken to be a transitive relation, but set-membership is not a transitive relation. (In what follows, I use the term "constituent" in such a way that proper parts are to be included among an entity's constituents; but the reverse cannot always be assumed to be true, since not all constituents are also proper parts, as the set-theoretic example just cited illustrates.)

Why should the stipulative exclusion of proper parts from an independence criterion of substance not also extend to constituents more generally? Insofar as any justification for this exclusion is given by those who endorse the stipulative exclusion of proper parts, the reasons stated would seem to carry over to non-mereological constituents as well. Gorman, for example, adduces the following considerations in favor of the exemption in question:

> To say this [i.e., that composite entities may qualify as substances even if they are ontologically dependent on their own essential proper parts] is, of course, only to follow up on Fine's own suggestion when he says that a substance does not depend on anything 'or, at least, upon anything other than its parts'. Nor is there any reason to fear that the move is *ad hoc*, as it is a development of the pre-philosophical intuition that the theory of substance is intended to make sense of. Putting the point a bit vaguely, as

pre-philosophical intuitions must be put, the things that philosophers come to call substances are not dependent on others but are
instead self-sufficient in some way. Now a thing with an essential
part is (of course) distinct from that part, but it does not follow
that the thing is not self-sufficient, because this is not a way for
the thing to be related to something *outside itself*. Expressed differently, the kind of independence here sought is not compromised by
dependence that, so to speak, stays within the thing in question.
(Gorman (2006b), p.151)[18]

In a similar vein, Peter Simons remarks as follows:

An object A is *strongly dependent* on an object B if necessarily, if A
exists, so does B, and B is neither A nor part of A. [...] An object is
independent in the corresponding sense when it depends on nothing
apart from itself and perhaps parts of itself, giving a sense to the
idea of something depending on nothing 'outside of itself'. (Simons
(1998), p.236)

Both Simons and Gorman point to the idea that an entity's ontological
dependence on its own essential proper parts should be rated differently from an entity's ontological dependence on entities numerically
distinct from itself which do not number among the entity's own essential proper parts for the following reason. In the second case (non-part
dependence), the entity in question is ontologically dependent on
numerically distinct entities that lie "outside" of it, while in the first case
(part-dependence) the entity in question is ontologically dependent on
numerically distinct entities (viz., its own essential proper parts) which
do not lie "outside" of it. But whatever exactly is meant by "outside" in
this context, surely if an entity's proper parts do not lie "outside" of it,
then neither do an entity's non-mereological constituents.

Supposing then that entities which are ontologically dependent only
on their own essential constituents more generally may also qualify as
substances, as long as they are appropriately unified, we arrive at the
following revision of (ICCS1):

(ICCS2) *Independence Criterion for Composite Substances* (First Revision):
x is a composite substance $\equiv_{def}$ (i) x is composite and (ii)
there is no y such that (a) y is not identical with x, (b) x is
essentially identity dependent on y, and (c) y is not one of x's
constituents; and (iii) x is unified in the right way.

Clause (ii.c) of (ICCS2) now allows back in some alleged non-substances, e.g., sets, which were previously excluded from the reaches of (ICCS1) by virtue of the restriction to proper parts. In addition to sets, we might also cite as possible further examples of alleged non-substances which are arguably ontologically dependent only on their own essential constituents such entities as quantities, collections, propositions, sentences, events, facts, and states of affairs. All of these categories of entities, if they are to be classified as non-substances, would now have to be ruled out by way of the unity requirement in clause (iii). This not only creates serious pressure for the as-of-yet unspecified unity requirement, it also makes us wonder whether clause (ii), i.e., the ontological independence requirement, is really doing any work at all in the so-called independence criterion for composite substances. Given the long list of alleged non-substances which are arguably ontologically dependent only on their own essential constituents, it seems that a *unity* criterion for composite substances might hold more promise than an *independence* criterion, assuming, of course, that we can make good on the promise of spelling out in more detail in what respects putative substance candidates, such as organisms, are more unified than alleged non-substances such as sets, orchestras, committees, quantities, collections, mereological sums, propositions, sentences, events, facts, and states of affairs. This line of reasoning seems to suggest the following significant change of direction in our attempt to provide a criterion of substancehood for composite entities:

> (UCCS) *Unity Criterion for Composite Substances*: x is a composite substance $\equiv_{def}$ (i) x is composite and (ii) x is unified in the right way.[19,20]

I will return to the role of unity in a criterion of substancehood for composite entities briefly below. For the time being, I want to turn instead to a loose thread which arose in connection with the revised independence criterion for composite substances in (ICCS2).

## 5.4   Intrinsicness

In the passages cited above, we saw that Gorman and Simons make at least an informal attempt to justify the exemption for part-dependence by appeal to a distinction they allude to between what lies "inside" and what lies "outside" the boundaries of a given entity. According to Gorman, an entity's ontological dependence on its own essential proper parts does not take away from the sort of "self-sufficiency" he takes to be required for substance status, since in that case the entity in question ontologically depends only on what lies "inside" its boundaries. But non-part dependence, in his view, does disqualify an entity from substance status, since an entity's ontological dependence on what lies "outside" of its boundaries diminishes the "self-sufficiency" he takes to be required for substance status. On the basis of these considerations, we might therefore propose the following revision of (ICCS2), which makes the justification offered for the exclusion of proper parts explicit in clause (ii.c):

> (ICCS3) *Independence Criterion for Composite Substances* (Second Revision):x is a composite substance $\equiv_{def}$ (i) x is composite and (ii) there is no y such that (a) y is not identical with x, (b) x is essentially identity dependent on y, and (c) y lies "outside" of x's boundaries; and (iii) x is unified in the right way.

Since, for the proponent of an independence criterion for substancehood, "self-sufficiency" is presumably merely another name for whatever is captured by the criterion of substancehood in question, the notion of "self-sufficiency" that is appealed to informally by Gorman does not provide us with any additional information besides what is brought to the table by all the components of the independence criterion taken together. The question that is most relevant for present purposes, then, is what sense can be attached to the distinction between what lies "inside" the boundaries of a given entity and what lies "outside" of its boundaries.

The first thing to note in this connection is that we ought to separate ourselves right away from the spatial overtones that the distinction between what lies "inside" and what lies "outside" a given entity tends to evoke. (Hence the quotation marks around "inside" and "outside".) In Section IV, I argued that the stipulative exclusion of non-particulars from an independence criterion of substancehood ought to be regarded as inadmissible, since it has the unwelcome consequence that apparently substantive disputes in ontology are classified as either trivially answerable or as based on a contradiction. For similar reasons, an independence criterion of substancehood should not be formulated in terms that can meaningfully apply only to material entities, i.e., entities which occupy regions of space-time. For then the thesis "Only material entities are composite substances" would again trivially follow from the criterion of substancehood in question, while the opposing thesis, "Some non-material entities are composite substances", could not be coherently maintained by a reasonable philosopher who subscribes to (ICCS3). Hence, a dispute between two philosophers who find themselves drawn to these two opposing theses respectively would be mistakenly classified as non-substantive. But I suspect that Gorman himself would wish to allow that the question of whether some composite substances are non-material is substantive and can be a legitimate subject of dispute between two reasonably-minded metaphysicians. If sets and other abstract entities, for example, are to be classified as non-substances by (ICCS3), then it would seem that this criterion must at least be formulated in such a way that we can sensibly ask whether the entities in question satisfy or fail to satisfy the requirements stated by each of its clauses. It would be disturbing if sets and other abstract entities were denied substance status only because the "outside"/"inside" distinction does not meaningfully apply to them.

One natural approach to the "outside"/"inside" distinction appealed to in (ICCS3) which does not require the stipulative restriction to material entities just cited is to understand it in terms of the distinction between what is *intrinsic* and what is *extrinsic* to a given entity.[21] Presumably, in whatever way exactly we construe the distinction between what is intrinsic and what is extrinsic to a given entity, any plausible account of this distinction should allow that we can just as sensibly speak of the non-mereological constituents of a non-empty set (i.e., its members) as being intrinsic to the set as we can speak of the mereological constituents of a material entity (i.e., its parts) as being intrinsic to the whole they compose. We thus arrive at the following reformulation of clause (ii.c) of (ICCS3):

> (ICCS4) *Independence Criterion for Composite Substances* (Third Revision): x is a composite substance $\equiv_{def}$ (i) x is composite and (ii) there is no y such that (a) y is not identical with x, (b) x is essentially identity dependent on y, and (c) y is extrinsic to x; and (iii) x is unified in the right way.

If (ICCS4) strikes the proponent of an independence criterion of substancehood as attractive, he would now face the non-trivial task of having to link his criterion for composite substances to a suitable account of the intrinsic/extrinsic distinction. This requirement, for example, immediately rules out any appeals to the notion of substancehood in an account of the intrinsic/extrinsic distinction, since such an appeal would then render the overall theory in question circular. Even if we grant the proponent of an independence criterion for substances that the content of clause (ii.c) can be specified in a suitable fashion, however, we should note that (ICCS4) has some interesting consequences which may or may not be found to be objectionable by those in favor of an independence criterion for composite substances. For reasons of space, I will here only point to one such consequence to which (ICCS4) may lead, depending on the additional metaphysical assumptions with which (ICCS4) is combined.

Consider artworks and artifacts more generally. Suppose Michelangelo's *David*, for example, is essentially identity dependent on the artist, Michelangelo, who created the artwork in question with the intention of achieving a certain artistic representational goal. Given Lowe's notion of essential identity dependence, in order for the sculpture in question to be essentially identity dependent on the artist who created it with a certain artistic intention in mind, there must be some function, $\varphi$, e.g., the "is the sculpture which was artistically created with a certain representational intention" function, such that it is part of the essence of the sculpture in question that it is the result of applying $\varphi$ to Michelangelo. In other words, if the condition just stated in fact holds, then which sculpture the artwork in question is is at least in part fixed by reference to the artist who created it with the intention to achieve a certain representational goal. But the artist, Michelangelo, is of course under any reasonable conception of the intrinsic/extrinsic distinction, extrinsic to the sculpture he has created. Thus, regardless of whether artworks are appropriately unified, such entities could not be awarded substance status by (ICCS4), since their ontological dependence on a numerically distinct entity that is extrinsic to them constitutes a violation of clause (ii.c). If artifacts in general are essentially identity dependent on the artisans who create them, perhaps with a certain functional intention in mind, then the same result follows more broadly for the entire category of artificially created objects. Those proponents of independence criteria of substancehood who take it to be a desideratum of their account that art works or artifacts more generally are classified as substances would thus have to weigh their options in the face of the possibility that these entities might be excluded from the category of substances, due to the extrinsicness of their individuation conditions.[22]

## 6 Hylomorphic compounds

In the foregoing sections, we have focused on two recent and promising attempts at providing an independence criterion of substancehood in the neo-Aristotelian tradition, viz., E.J. Lowe's criterion, in (ICS1), and a modified version of it, in (ICS2), proposed by Michael Gorman. I objected above to the stipulative exclusion of non-particulars contained in both (ICS1) and (ICS2) on the grounds that this restriction makes it difficult to account for the apparently substantive nature of certain ontological disputes over questions of fundamentality. Moreover, our discussion of Gorman's stipulative exclusion-clause governing part-dependence seemed to indicate that unity might have an important role to play, instead of or at least in addition to independence, in drawing a substance/non-substance distinction for composite, rather than simple, entities.

I now want to bring these considerations to bear on the question raised at the very beginning of this chapter, namely whether and how it might be possible to preserve the alleged substance status of hylomorphic compounds. As I pointed out there, an apparent conflict emerges when we combine two central tenets popular among neo-Aristotelian metaphysicians: hylomorphism (the doctrine according to which unified wholes are best analyzed as compounds of matter and form) and independence accounts of substancehood, such as those investigated above. For if alleged substance candidates, such as organisms, are analyzed in the hylomorphic fashion, as compounds of matter and form, one wonders whether they will not then turn out to be ontologically dependent on entities numerically distinct from themselves (viz., their form and possibly their matter as well), thereby jeopardizing their inclusion in the category of substances. This question should certainly be of concern to neo-Aristotelians who find themselves attracted to both the hylomorphic analysis of unified wholes and an account of substancehood in terms ontological independence.

## 6.1   Lowe's strategy

When we attempt to apply Lowe's criterion in (ICS1) to the case of hylomorphic compounds, we seem to run into the following problem. Suppose that a hylomorphic compound is numerically distinct from its form and matter. If, following Lowe's definition in (EID), a hylomorphic compound turns out to be essentially identity dependent on its form or its matter (assuming that the form or matter associated with a hylomorphic compound are particulars), then (ICS1) will exclude such compounds from the category of substances. To prevent the outcome that hylomorphic compounds are disqualified from substance status, Lowe therefore must deny one (or more) of the following claims:

(1) A hylomorphic compound is numerically distinct from its form.
(2) A hylomorphic compound is numerically distinct from its matter.
(3) A hylomorphic compound is essentially identity dependent on its form.
(4) A hylomorphic compound is essentially identity dependent on its matter.
(5) The form which partially composes a hylomorphic compound is a particular.
(6) The matter which partially composes a hylomorphic compound is a particular.

As noted earlier, Lowe opts for the denial of (1), among other things, and endorses an interpretation of hylomorphism according to which unified wholes are to be *identified* with their forms (see Lowe (1999)). On this conception, (so-called) hylomorphic "compounds" are not strictly speaking compounds at all; rather, the form with which a (so-called) hylomorphic compound is identified, so to speak, only "resides" in the matter which embodies it and possibly does so only temporarily.[23]

Following Lowe's strategy, then, (so-called) hylomorphic "compounds" turn out to be numerically identical with their forms. If forms are non-material, and presumably essentially so, then of course the same applies to (so-called) hylomorphic "compounds", which, according to Lowe's account, are to be identified with their forms: these (so-called) hylomorphic "compounds" then turn out to be essentially non-material entities as well, which at most (and possibly only temporarily) "reside" in their material embodiments. For someone who is already for independent reasons committed to a Cartesian conception of the mind (as Lowe is), the identification of a (so-called) hylomorphic "compound" with its form may perhaps carry some measure of plausibility for specific cases, e.g., human beings, persons or conscious beings in general. But when we apply Lowe's strategy to unified wholes across the board, strange consequences follow. For example, if $H_2O$ molecules are unified wholes (and thus are included within the range of cases to which the hylomorphic analysis of unified wholes can be expected to apply), then Lowe's strategy would lead us to identify $H_2O$ molecules with their forms as well. But, assuming that forms are essentially non-material, $H_2O$ molecules will then also (surprisingly, I take it) turn out to be essentially non-material entities which only "reside" in their material embodiments and possibly do so only temporarily. It would thus be preferable from the point of view of the neo-Aristotelian to investigate whether alternative interpretations of hylomorphism are available which do not commit us to a radical expansion of Cartesian dualism to unified wholes in general, even those which lack any kind of mental life.

## 6.2 Gorman's exemption for part-dependence

If an independence criterion for substances is formulated in such a way that it contains an exemption for part-dependence, constituent-dependence, dependence on what lies "inside" the boundaries of an entity, or dependence on what is intrinsic to the entity in question, along the lines of Gorman's modified criterion in (ICS2) and the series of revisions we have considered in (ICS3) and (ICCS1)-(ICCS4), then further possibilities are opened up for the neo-Aristotelian who is attempting to resolve the apparent conflict identified above between his commitment to hylomorphism and his sympathy for accounts of substancehood that are based on ontological independence. For given the modified criterion and its subsequent revisions, a hylomorphic compound, assuming that it is appropriately unified, would be able to qualify as a substance as long as those numerically distinct entities (if any) on which it is essentially identity dependent are either among its proper parts (in accordance with (ICS2), (ICS3) and (ICCS1)); or among its constituents (in accordance with (ICCS2)); or "inside" of the boundaries of the hylomorphic compound in question (in accordance with (ICCS3)); or intrinsic to the hylomorphic compound in question (in accordance with (ICCS4)). But I take it that, on any reasonable formulation of the hylomorphic position, the form and/or matter of which a hylomorphic compound consists would satisfy at least one, and possibly all, of these conditions. According to the mereological reading of the hylomorphic position, compounds of matter and form strictly and literally speaking contain their form and matter as proper parts, thus qualifying as substances under any of the versions of Gorman's criterion.[24] A modified version of this position is also available according to which the form and/or matter of which a hylomorphic compound consists are at least regarded as constituents, if not proper parts, of the entity in question. Even those who find neither of these interpretations of the hylomorphic position palatable may avoid the extreme measure taken by Lowe by endorsing one of the revised versions of Gorman's modified criterion I offered for composite substances in (ICCS3)-(ICCS4). Hence, even if hylomorphic compounds turn out to be essentially identity dependent on their form and/or their matter, they would not thereby be excluded from substance status given either Gorman's exemption for part-dependence or any of the revised formulations I offered subsequently.[25]

## 6.3   Form as principle of unity

But there is a further and, in my view, preferable option available to the neo-Aristotelian who already accepts hylomorphism for independent reasons and who wishes to support the inclusion of hylomorphic compounds in the category of substances. After all, in the view of the neo-Aristotelian, what distinguishes hylomorphic compounds from other, less unified, composite entities (e.g., sets, mereological sums, committees, and the like) is precisely that hylomorphic compounds contain within themselves a principle of unity which these other, less unified, composite entities lack, namely their forms. Traditionally, forms are assigned the special role of acting as the principle of unity within the hylomorphic compound, i.e., as that active power within the hylomorphic compound which somehow ties together its material components into a single unified whole, as opposed to, for example, a mere heap, aggregate or plurality. The neo-Aristotelian thus would seem to be missing out on an important advantage he gains through his commitment to hylomorphism if he did not also capitalize on the special role of form as the principle of unity within the compound in his quest to formulate an adequate criterion for substancehood.

If we are to take this option seriously, as providing us with a credible route towards a unity criterion for composite substances, we would, of course, need to know more about what it means to designate form as that active principle which plays the role of the unifying the hylomorphic compound. Different answers to this question are available to the neo-Aristotelian, depending on the particular version of hylomorphism he embraces. Given the interpretation of the hylomorphic position I defend in Koslicki (2008), a hylomorphic compound counts as unified, due to the presence of form within it, in the following sense. Since wholes, on my view, are by definition mereologically complex objects, i.e., objects which have parts, the unity of a whole cannot very well consist in its being completely indivisible into parts. Rather, for a whole to be unified is just for its material components to satisfy the structural constraints posed by the formal components associated with the kind to which it belongs. To illustrate, with respect to the kind, $H_2O$ molecule, a successful case of composition requires two hydrogen atoms and one oxygen atom to enter into the configuration of chemical bonding that is required to form a particular specimen of the kind in question. The degree of unity had by wholes of this kind is just the degree of unity that is conferred on hydrogen and oxygen atoms when they are configured in the particular arrangement of chemical bonding that is characteristic of $H_2O$ molecules. The material components composing

$H_2O$ molecules are of course not completely inseparable from each other by means of the application of physical forces; nor do their spatiotemporal boundaries even have to touch in order for these hydrogen and oxygen atoms together to compose a unified whole, i.e., *one* exemplar of the kind, $H_2O$ molecule. If we expected the material components of a unified whole to hang together in a different way, e.g., in a way that makes them physically inseparable or at least requires their spatiotemporal boundaries to touch, then I would argue that, in following these expectations, we would have set ourselves up for failure in our search for a reasonable account of how the formal components of a hylomorphic compound contribute to its unity.[26] But much more, no doubt, remains to be said about the role of form as a principle of unity in the hylomorphic compound, and I intend to return to this important and interesting topic in future discussions.

## 7   Conclusion

In this chapter, I considered particular attempts by E. J. Lowe and Michael Gorman at providing an independence criterion of substancehood and argued that the stipulative exclusion of non-particulars and proper parts (or constituents) from such accounts raises difficult issues for their proponents. The results of the present discussion seem to indicate that, at least for the case of composite entities, a unity criterion of substancehood might have at least as much, and perhaps more, to offer than an independence criterion and therefore ought to be explored further by neo-Aristotelians in search of a defensible notion of substancehood. I indicated briefly how such a unity criterion might be used by neo-Aristotelians to support the inclusion of hylomorphic compounds in the category of substance, given the traditional role of form as the principle of unity within the compound.

### Notes

1. Many different definitions of ontological dependence have been offered in the literature. For example, some formulations are given in terms of necessity and existence; others in terms of the explanatory connective "because"; and yet others in terms of a non-modal conception of essence. Some of these formulations concern relations among particulars; others are generic concepts which concern entities of a certain kind in general. In this chapter, I will consider only formulations of ontological dependence which (in my view) carry promise from the point of view of the neo-Aristotelian, who is interested in using ontological independence for the purposes of demarcating the

substances from the non-substances. For a discussion of alternative conceptions, see Koslicki (2013).

2. He remarks there as follows: "Thus all the other things are either said of the primary substances as subjects or in them as subjects. So if the primary substances [were] not it would be impossible for any of the other things to [be]" (*Cat.*, Ch.5, 2b3–6; translation by J. L. Ackrill (cf. Barnes (1984)). Since I do not read Aristotle's independence criterion in an exclusively existential way, I have substituted occurrences of the verb "to be" in place of occurrences of the verb "to exist" in the passage just cited; for more discussion, see Koslicki (2013).

3. In what follows, I intend to use the term, "substance candidate", in such a way that it applies to entities (such as organisms) which neo-Aristotelians are tempted to include in the category of substances. However, for the time being, since we are currently engaged in a discussion of what sort of criterion of substancehood neo-Aristotelians should adopt, I take it to be an open question which of the kinds of entities that are designated as "substance candidates" really, at the end of the day, make it into the category of substances.

4. In what follows, I will refer to Lowe's and Gorman's criterion as an "independence criterion of substancehood", even though ontological independence is not the only component of their respective accounts.

5. For Lowe's most up-to-date views concerning ontological dependence, see Lowe (2006), (2005) (last revised in 2009), (2008), (2012), (2013). For discussions of ontological dependence in his earlier work, see Lowe (1994), (1998). Also relevant are his views concerning criteria of identity; see for example Lowe (1989), (1997), (2009).

6. (ICS1) is a slightly reformulated version of what is called "(SUB-4)" in Lowe (2005).

7. I provide a more detailed discussion of Lowe's notion of essential identity dependence in Koslicki (2013).

8. Expressions like "is fixed by" or "is determined by" of course themselves indicate a certain explanatory asymmetry which is not explicitly stated in (EID) or (CI). For example, according to Lowe, a trope, x, is essentially identity dependent on a concrete particular object, y, that is x's bearer; that is, the individuation of x is parasitic on the identity of y. But if we stated this relation between x and y merely by means of a material biconditional, we would not have fully exhausted the asymmetric dependence that obtains between them.

9. Lowe is operating with a *non-modal* conception of essence which contrasts with the more mainstream *modal* conception of essence in the following way. An essential truth, according to a modal conception of essence, is just a modal truth of a certain kind (viz., one that is both necessary and *de re*, i.e., about a certain object); and an essential property is just a feature an object has necessarily, if it is to exist. The essential truths, according to this approach, are thus just a subset of the necessary truths; and the essential properties of objects are just a special kind of necessary property. (For some representatives of the modal tradition, see, for example, Plantinga (1974), Forbes (1985), Mackie (2006).) In contrast, according to a non-modal conception of essence, such as that developed by Aristotle and Kit Fine, the necessary truths are distinct and derivative from the essential truths; and the necessary features of objects, traditionally known as the "propria" or "necessary accidents", are distinct and

derivative from, the essential features of objects. (See for example Aristotle's *Posterior Analytics*; Fine (1994), (1995a), (1995b), (1995c); I discuss Aristotle's and Fine's non-modal conception of essence in Koslicki (2012).)

10. Though whether concrete particular objects can in fact be individuated across worlds by means of their origins is a controversial question, as the voluminous literature on this topic indicates. See, for example, Forbes (1985), (1986), (1997), (2002); Mackie (2002), (2006); and the references to be found therein.

11. Gorman (2006a), p.116. (ICS2) is a slightly reformulated version of what Gorman calls "RLS*".

12. Only essential, rather than accidental, parts are relevant to the question of whether an entity should be disqualified from its status as a substance due to the fact that it is ontologically dependent on entities numerically distinct from itself (namely, in this case, its own proper parts). For clause (i.b) in (ICS2) narrows down the range of entities which might pose a threat to x's status as a substance to those entities, y, on which x is essentially identity dependent. But no entity, x, would count as essentially identity dependent on its accidental parts, since it would not be the case that there is a function, $\varphi$, (e.g., the "is mereologically composed of" function) such that it is part of x's essence that x is the result of applying $\varphi$ to any of its accidental parts. Since x can survive through changes with respect to its accidental parts, x's identity at any time or world at which it exists cannot be fixed by which entities, y, z, w, ..., are its accidental parts at that time or world. In what follows, when I consider the question of whether the exclusion of proper parts from the criterion of substancehood is admissible, I will therefore limit myself to the discussion of essential, rather than accidental, parts.

13. The restriction to particulars is also present in an independence criterion of substancehood proposed in Schnieder (2006), according to which x is a substance just in case x is a particular and there is no y such that x rigidly and permanently existentially depends on y. "Rigid and permanent existential dependence" is defined as follows: x rigidly and permanently existentially depends upon y just in case there is a property, F, such that necessarily for any time, t, at which x exists, x exists at t because y is F at that time" (Schnieder 2006, p. 412). Correia's notion of "basing" (Correia 2005, pp.66 ff) and his definition of "simple dependence" in terms of "basing" is similar to Schnieder's "rigid and permanent existential dependence"; see also Correia (2008). For discussion of this approach to ontological dependence, see Koslicki (2013).

14. Both Lowe's criterion in (ICS1) and Gorman's criterion in (ICS2) contain an additional restriction to particulars in clause (ii), which I have also removed in this revision of Gorman's criterion in (ICS3). According to this additional restriction, given that both Lowe and Gorman take it to be a settled question that only particulars may qualify as substances, the only entities, y, which could pose a threat to an entity, x's, status as a substance are other particulars numerically distinct from x on which x is essentially identity dependent. But again we may wonder whether the exclusive focus on particulars is legitimate. If an entity, x, is essentially identity dependent on an entity, y, that is numerically distinct from it, then should x's status as a substance not thereby be jeopardized, even if y is a non-particular (e.g., a universal)? As far as I can see, this kind of possibility is already ruled out by other considerations

and the second restriction to particulars in clause (ii) may therefore be safely removed. For suppose that it is part of Socrates' essence to be human and that Socrates' humanity is here construed as a universal. Still, the universal, humanity, could not have a role in fixing Socrates' identity at every time and world at which he exists, since it is also part of the essence of many other particulars (e.g., Plato, Aristotle) that they exemplify the same universal. Thus, in order to determine which exemplar of the universal, humanity, Socrates is at every time and world at which he exists presupposes that Socrates' identity is already settled.

15. Gorman is again not alone in opting for the stipulative exclusion of proper parts from an independence criterion of substancehood. Kit Fine for example states that " ... a substance may be taken to be anything that does not depend upon anything else or, at least, upon anything *other than its parts*" (Fine (1995a), pp. 269–70; my emphasis). Similarly, Peter Simons offers an independence criterion of substancehood in terms of what he calls "strong independence", which also explicitly excludes proper parts from its range: an entity x is strongly dependent on an entity y just in case necessarily, x exists only if y exists and y is neither identical to x *nor a proper part of x* (Simons (1998), p. 236; my emphasis).

16. Gorman replies to Toner's heterogeneity worry in Gorman (2011) and argues that his account does, in fact, provide a unified criterion of substancehood: the substances are all and only those entities which are ontologically independent from all numerically distinct entities "outside" of themselves; this, according to Gorman, applies to both simple and composite entities. When we focus on what goes on "inside" the boundaries of an alleged substance, however, we can still discern a difference between simple and composite entities. The "inside"/"outside" distinction which is invoked by Gorman and others in an attempt to give at least an informal justification of the stipulative exclusion of proper parts from an independence criterion of substancehood itself raises interesting questions to which we will turn shortly below.

17. Though see Fine (2010) for a more generalized notion of parthood which allows for members to be parts of sets and which is closer to what I am calling here "constituency".

18. See also Gorman (2006a), p. 116, for a similar comment.

19. Given that ontological independence has completely dropped out of the picture in (UCCS), Toner's earlier heterogeneity worry of course arises again with a vengeance: if simple entities (if there are any) qualify as substances for one reason (their ontological independence) and composite entities qualify as substances for a completely different reason (their unity), why should we believe that (ICSS) and (UCCS) point to a single ontological category, rather than two distinct ontological categories which have been misleadingly called by the same name? As noted earlier, the proponent of such a bifurcated account can at least draw on the non-ad hoc and metaphysically significant distinction between simplicity and complexity. Moreover, we may point out as well that simple entities are presumably also unified in the right way, due to their simplicity; in that sense, a unity account applies both to simple and composite substances, but perhaps only trivially so in the case of simple substances.

20. One interesting case to consider in connection with (ICSS) and (UCCS) is that of tropes. Lowe and Gorman take tropes to be entities which are both simple

and essentially identity dependent on their "bearers", viz., the substances in which they inhere. They would therefore be classified (correctly, in their view) as non-substances by (ICSS). Being simple, tropes are presumably also unified by default; but their unity is irrelevant to their alleged status as non-substances, since they are subsumed under (ICSS), the criterion governing simple entities, rather than under (UCCS), the criterion governing complex entities.

21. The question of how best to draw the intrinsic/extrinsic distinction has generated an enormous literature and I will not at present try to enter into this debate; but see for example Humberstone (1996), Lewis & Langton (1998), Sider (1996) and Yablo (1999) for discussion.

22. Those who find (ICCS4) attractive might, of course, respond to the consideration just raised by rejecting the central assumption used in generating it, viz., that artworks in particular, and perhaps artifacts more generally, are in fact essentially identity dependent on their creators, in Lowe's sense. Since a proper discussion of this question would carry us too far into the special metaphysical issues raised by art works and artifacts more generally, I will not pursue this issue further here. For present purposes, I am content to note that, given apparently plausible assumptions which at least cannot be dismissed out of hand, (ICCS4) will exclude these objects from substance status as well as any other objects (if there are any) whose synchronic identity is fixed by appeal to numerically distinct entities extrinsic to them. The same result would have followed from any of the previous formulations of Gorman's independence criterion as well. Thus, it is not the addition of the extrinsicness clause in particular which generates the result that artworks and/ or artifacts in general are excluded from substance status; the most recent revision merely attempts to make explicit the motivation which presumably lies behind the exemption for proper parts in the first place. Alternatively, those in favor of (ICCS4) might also consider it to be an advantage that this criterion excludes art works and artifacts from the category of composite substances due to the extrinsicness of their individuation conditions.

23. Lowe would, no doubt, be happy to deny (4) as well: since hylomorphic compounds can apparently survive changes with respect to their material parts, it cannot be the case, given (EID), that the synchronic numerical identity of a hylomorphic compound is fixed by the matter which composes it at any time or world at which it exists. But the denial of (4) alone is not enough to escape our current quandary: for, as long as (1) and (3) still hold, a hylomorphic compound nevertheless threatens to be essentially identity dependent on an entity that is apparently numerically distinct from itself (namely its form) and its (alleged) substance status would thus still be in jeopardy, even if (4) is rejected.

24. This is the version of hylomorphism for which I argue in Koslicki (2008) and which is also endorsed in Fine (1982) and (1999).

25. For alternative ways of spelling out the hylomorphic position, see, for example, Harte (2002); Johnston (2002), (2006); Rea (2012).

26. This is by no means the only direction available to neo-Aristotelians who wish to account for the role of form as the principle of unity within the hylomorphic compound. For a very different conception of unity, see, for example, Hoffman & Rosenkrantz (1999).

# References

Barnes, Jonathan (ed.) 1984. *The Complete Works of Aristotle: The Revised Oxford Translation*, Volume One and Two, Bollingen Series LXXI.2 (Princeton, NJ: Princeton University Press).

Bottani, Andrea, Carrara, Massimiliano and Giaretta, Pierdaniele (eds) 2002. *Individuals, Essence and Identity* (Dordrecht, The Netherlands: Kluwer Academic Publishers).

Correia, Fabrice. 2005. *Existential Dependence and Cognate Notions* (München, Germany: Philosophia Verlag).

_____ 2008 "Ontological Dependence," *Philosophy Compass* 3: 1–20.

Correia, Fabrice, and Schnieder, Benjamin (ed.) 2012. *Metaphysical Grounding: Understanding the Structure of Reality* (Cambridge, UK: Cambridge University Press).

Fine, Kit. 1982. "Acts, Events and Things," in *Language and Ontology: Proceedings of the Sixth International Wittgenstein Symposium*, pp. 97–105.

_____ 1994. "Essence and Modality," *Philosophical Perspectives* 8 (Logic and Language): 1–16.

_____ 1995a. "Ontological Dependence," *Proceedings of the Aristotelian Society* 95: 269–90.

_____ 1995b. "Senses of Essence," in Sinnott-Armstrong et al. (eds), pp. 53–73.

_____ 1995c. "The Logic of Essence," *Journal of Philosophical Logic* 24: 241–73.

_____ 1999. "Things and Their Parts," *Midwest Studies in Philosophy* 23: 61–74.

_____ 2010. "Towards a Theory of Part," *Journal of Philosophy* CVII (11) (November 2010): 559–89.

Forbes, Graeme. 1985. *The Metaphysics of Modality*, Clarendon Library of Logic and Philosophy series (Oxford, UK: Oxford University Press).

_____ 1986. "In Defense of Absolute Essentialism," *Midwest Studies in Philosophy*, Vol. XI (*Studies in Essentialism*) (ed.) by P.A. French, T.E. Uehling and H.K. Wettstein (Minneapolis, Minnesota: University of Minnesota Press), pp. 3–31.

_____ 1997. "Essentialism," in Hale and Wright (eds), pp. 515–33.

_____ 2002. "Origins and Identities," in Bottani et al. (eds), pp. 319–40.

Frege, Gottlob. 1953. *The Foundations of Arithmetic: A Logico-Mathematical Enquiry into the Concept of Number*, translated by J. L. Austin, 2nd Edition (Oxford, UK: Blackwell).

Gorman, Michael. 2006a. "Substance and Identity-Dependence," *Philosophical Papers* 35 (1): 103–18.

_____ 2006b. "Independence and Substance," *International Philosophical Quarterly* 46 (2), Issue 182 (June 2006): 147–59.

_____ 2011. "On Substantial Independence: A Reply to Patrick Toner," *Philosophical Studies*, published online February 4, 2011.

Hale, Bob, and Wright, Crispin (eds.) 1997. *Companion to the Philosophy of Language* (Malden, MA: Blackwell).

Harte, Verity. 2002. *Plato on Parts and Wholes: The Metaphysics of Structure* (Oxford, UK: Clarendon Press).

Hoffman, Joshua, and Rosenkrantz, Gary. 1999. "On the Unity of Compound Things," in Oderberg (ed.), pp. 76–102.

Humberstone, I. Lloyd. 1996. "Intrinsic/Extrinsic," *Synthese* 108: 205–67.

Johnston, Mark. 2002. "Parts and Principles: False Axioms in Mereology," *Philosophical Topics* 30(1): 129–66.

—— 2006. "Hylomorphism," *Journal of Philosophy* 103 (12): 652–98.

Koslicki, Kathrin. 2008. *The Structure of Objects* (Oxford: Oxford University Press).

Koslicki, Kathrin. 2012. "Essence, Necessity and Explanation," in Tahko (ed.), pp. 187–206.

—— 2013. "Ontological Dependence: An Opinionated Survey," in Schnieder et al. (eds).

Le Poidevin, Robin (ed.) 2008. *Being: Developments in Contemporary Metaphysics* (Cambridge, UK: Cambridge University Press).

Lewis, David, and Langton, Rae. 1998. "Defining Intrinsic," *Philosophy and Phenomenological Research* 58: 333–45.

Lowe, E. J. 1989. "What Is a Criterion of Identity?," *The Philosophical Quarterly* 39 (154): 1–21.

—— 1994. "Ontological Dependency," *Philosophical Papers* XXIII (1): 31–48.

—— 1997. "Objects and Criteria of Identity," in Hale & Wright (eds), pp. 613–33.

—— 1998. *The Possibility of Metaphysics: Substance, Identity, and Time* (Oxford, UK: Oxford University Press).

—— 1999. "Form Without Matter," in Oderberg (ed.) (1999), pp. 1–21.

—— 2005. "Ontological Dependence", *Stanford Encyclodedia of Philosophy*, <http://plato.stanford.edu/entries/dependence-ontological/>; last revised in 2009.

—— 2006. *The Four-Category Ontology: A Metaphysical Foundation for Natural Science* (Oxford, UK: Clarendon Press).

—— 2008. "Two Notions of Being: Entity and Essence," in Le Poidevin (ed.), pp. 23–48.

—— 2009. *More Kinds of Being: A Further Study of Individuation, Identity, and the Logic of Sortal Terms* (Malden, MA and Oxford, UK: Wiley-Blackwell).

—— 2012. "Asymmetrical Dependence in Inviduation," in Correia and Schnieder (eds), pp. 214–33.

—— 2013. "Some Varieties of Metaphysical Dependence," forthcoming in Schnieder, Hoeltje and Steinberg (eds).

Mackie, Penelope. 2002. "Forbes on Origins and Identities," in Bottani et al. (eds), pp. 341–52.

—— 2006. *How Things Might Have Been: Individuals, Kinds and Essential Properties* (NY: Clarendon, Oxford University Press).

Oderberg, David (ed.) 1999. *Form and Matter: Themes in Contemporary Metaphysics* (Oxford, UK: Blackwell).

Plantinga, Alvin. 1974. *The Nature of Necessity* (Oxford, UK: Clarendon Press).

Rea, Michael. 2012. "Hylomorphism Reconditioned," *Philosophical Perspectives* 25 (1): 341–58.

Schnieder, Benjamin. 2006. "A Certain Kind of Trinity: Dependence, Substance, Explanation," *Philosophical Studies* 129: 393–419.

Schnieder, Benjamin, Hoeltje, Miguel, and Steinberg, Alexander (eds) (2013. *Varieties of Dependence (Basic Philosophical Concepts)* (München, Germany: Philosophia Verlag).

Sider, Theodore 1996. "Intrinsic Properties," *Philosophical Studies* 83: 1–27.

Simons, Peter. 1998. "Farewell to Substance: A Differentiated Leave-Taking," *Ratio (New Series)*, 11 (3): 235–52.

Sinnott-Armstrong, Walter, Raffman, Diana, and Asher, Nicholas (eds) 1995. *Modality, Morality, and Belief,* Essays in Honor of Ruth Barcan Marcus, (New York, NY : Cambridge University Press).

Tahko, Tuomas (ed.) 2012. *Contemporary Aristotelian Metaphysics* (Cambridge, UK : Cambridge University Press).

Toner, Patrick. 2010. "Independence Accounts of Substance and Substantial Parts," *Philosophical Studies*, published online May 13, 2010.

Yablo, Stephen. 1999. "Intrinsicness," *Philosophical Topics* 26: 479–505.

# 10
# Neo-Aristotelian Metaphysics: A Brief Exposition and Defense

*E. J. Lowe*

The aim of this chapter is to show how, by combining a neo-Aristotelian account of essence with a neo-Aristotelian four-category ontology (of individual substances, modes, substantial universals, and property universals), a thoroughgoing metaphysical foundation for modal truths can be provided – one which avoids any appeal to "possible worlds" and which renders modal truths objective, mind-independent, and yet also humanly knowable. If successful, this combination of a system of fundamental ontology with a theory of essence and metaphysical modality promises to vindicate the Aristotelian vision of metaphysics as "first philosophy", a discipline that is conceptually and epistemologically prior to any of the empirical sciences and an intellectual prerequisite of their pursuit of truth concerning the natural world and the human mind.

## 1 Ontology

In Aristotle's mature ontological system, as presented in the *Metaphysics*, individual substances are taken to be combinations of *matter* and *form*, with each such substance being constituted by a particular parcel of matter embodying, or organized by, a certain form. For example, an individual house has as its immediate matter some bricks, mortar and timber, which are organized in a certain distinctive way fit to serve the functions of a human dwelling. Similarly, an individual horse has as its immediate matter some flesh, blood and bones, which are organized in a certain distinctive way fit to sustain a certain kind of life, that of a herbivorous quadruped. In each case, the "matter" in question is not, or not purely, "prime" matter, but is already "informed" in certain distinctive ways which makes it suitable to receive the form of a house or a horse. Thus, bricks, mortar and timber would not be matter suitable to receive the form of a horse, but at

196

best that of something like a *statue* of a horse. According to this view, the matter and form of an individual substance are both "incomplete" entities, completed *by each other* in their union in that substance. But its form is *essential* to the substance, unlike its matter, in the following sense: an individual house, say, cannot lose the form of a house without thereby ceasing to be, whereas – while it must always *have* matter of an appropriate kind so long as it continues to be – it need not always have the *same* matter of that kind. Individual bricks and timbers in a house may be replaced without destroying the house – indeed, this may be the only way to *preserve* a certain house – but once its bricks and timbers cease to be organized in the form of a house, the house necessarily ceases to be.

So far, I have spoken about *forms*, but not about *features*, and how they might be accommodated by the approach now under discussion. Very roughly, I think that the answer should run somewhat as follows. The *form* of a substance constitutes its *essence* – *what it is*, its "quiddity" – whereas its features, or "qualities", are *how it is*. A *horse* is *what* Dobbin is, for example. If Dobbin is *white*, however, that is partly *how* he is – a *way* that he is. But how, then, are a substance's features related to its form? Some of its features, it seems, are *necessitated* by its form – such as warm-bloodedness in the case of Dobbin – and these may be called, in the strictest sense of the term, the substance's *properties*. Other of its features, however, are "accidental", such as Dobbin's whiteness, which may therefore be denominated one of his *accidents*. Even so, although Dobbin's whiteness is accidental, that Dobbin has *some* color is necessitated by his form and is thus essential to him. So, we arrive at the following picture: an individual substance possesses a certain *form*, which constitutes its *essence*, from which "flow" by necessity certain features of the substance, which are its *properties* in the strictest sense of the term. Some of these properties are "determinables" rather than "determinates", such as *color* in the case of Dobbin, and then it is necessary that the substance should possess *some* determinate feature falling under the relevant determinable, but contingent which feature this is. Such contingent determinate features are the substance's *accidents*, which can obviously change over time compatibly with the continued existence of the substance. The overall picture, even in this relatively simplified version of it, is quite complex, with an individual substance portrayed as having a rich and in some respects temporally inconstant constituent structure of *form*, *matter*, *properties* and *accidents*, with form and properties remaining constant while matter and accidents are subject to change.

Hylemorphism certainly has many attractive aspects. But its core difficulty lies in its central doctrine – that every concrete individual substance is a "combination" of matter and form. For what, really, are we to *understand* by "combination" in this sense? Clearly, we are not supposed to think that combination in this sense just is, or is the result of, a "putting together" of two mutually independent things, since matter and form are supposed to be "incomplete" items which *complete each other* in the substance that combines them. Now, certainly, when some concrete things – such as some bricks, timbers and quantities of mortar – are put together to make a new concrete object, such as a house, those things have to put together *in the right sort of way*, not just haphazardly. But does this entitle us to suppose that the completed house is some sort of "combination" of *the things that have been put together* and *the way in which they have been put together*? The challenge that the hylemorphist presents us with is to explain why, if we do not say something like this, we are entitled to suppose that a *new* individual substance is brought into being. One presumption behind that challenge would seem to be that a substance cannot simply be a so-called *mereological sum* of other substances – and with this I can agree, at least if by a "mereological sum" we mean an entity whose identity is determined solely by the identities of its "summands", rather as the identity of a set is determined solely by the identities of its members. I agree that only when other substances have been put together *in the right sort of way* does a new substance of a certain kind come into being, the *way* in question depending on the *kind* in question. Moreover, I have no objection to the "reification" of "ways", understood as features or forms, provided that we do not treat ways as *substances* – so, here, too, I am in agreement with the hylemorphist. Reification is not the same as *hypostatization*, but is merely the acknowledgement of some putative entity's *real existence*. What I *do not* understand is what it means to say that the completed house's *form* – the way in which its "matter" is organized – is an "incomplete" constituent of the house which "combines" together with that equally "incomplete" matter to constitute the house, a complete substance. The words that particularly mystify me in this sort of account are "incomplete", "combine" and "constitute". It is not that I do not understand these words perfectly well as they are commonly used in other contexts, just that I do not understand their technical use in the hylemorphic theory and, equally importantly, why any *need* should be felt for this use of such terms.

The hylemorphist ontology described above is inspired by Aristotle, as modified perhaps by later thinkers such as Aquinas. But the basis of another kind of ontology can also be traced to Aristotle, this time to the Aristotle of his presumed early work, the *Categories*. The kind of ontology that I now have in mind is one whose key notions are briefly sketched in the opening passages of that work, before the classificatory divisions commonly known as the Aristotelian "categories" are set out later in the treatise. In those opening passages, Aristotle articulates a fourfold ontological scheme in terms of the two technical notions of "being *said of* a subject" and "being *in* a subject". *Primary* substances – what we have hitherto been calling "individual" substances – are described as being *neither said of* a subject *nor in* a subject. *Secondary* substances – the *species* and *genera* to which primary substances belong – are described as being *said of* a subject but *not in* a subject. That leaves two other classes of items: those that are *both said of* a subject *and in* a subject, and those that are *not said of* a subject but are *in* a subject. Since these two classes receive no official names and have been variously denominated over the centuries, I propose to call them, respectively, *attributes* and *modes*. It seems that secondary substances and attributes are conceived to be different types of *universal*, while primary substances and modes are conceived to be different types of *particular*. Since the Aristotelian terminology of "being said of" and "being in" is perhaps less than fully perspicuous, with the former suggesting a linguistic relation and the latter seemingly having only a metaphorical sense, I prefer to use a different terminology: that of *instantiation* and *characterization*. Thus, I say that attributes and modes are *characterizing* entities, whereas primary and secondary substances are *characterizable* entities. And I say that secondary substances and attributes are *instantiable* entities, whereas primary substances and modes are *instantiating* entities. These terminological niceties, which though necessary are apt to prove confusing, are most conveniently laid out in diagrammatic form, using the familiar device known as *the Ontological Square*. I present it below.

In my own version of the Ontological Square, I prefer to use the terms "object" and "kind" in place of the more cumbersome "primary substance" and "secondary substance". I also include a "diagonal" relationship between objects and attributes, which is distinct from both instantiation and characterization, calling this, as seems appropriate, *exemplification*. Here is my version:

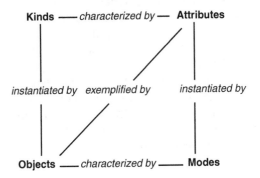

Kinds —— *characterized by* —— **Attributes**

*instantiated by*    *exemplified by*    *instantiated by*

**Objects** —— *characterized by* —— **Modes**

I call the four classes of entities depicted here *ontological categories*, albeit with a cautionary note that these are not to be confused with, even though they are not unrelated to, Aristotle's own list of "categories" later in his treatise. More precisely, I regard these four as the *fundamental* ontological categories, allowing that within each there may be various *sub*-categories, *sub-sub*-categories, and so on.

How exactly are the two "Aristotelian" systems of ontology related to one another? Unsurprisingly, they overlap in many respects, but one key respect in which they obviously differ is that the *four-category ontology*, as I call it (Lowe 2006), unlike the hylemorphic ontology, does not include the category of *matter*. It might be thought that it also lacks the category of *form*, but that is not in fact so. For I believe that form, conceived as a type of universal, and more perspicuously termed *substantial* form, is really nothing other than *secondary substance* or substantial *kind*. We may refer to such universal forms either by using certain *abstract* nouns, such as "humanity" and "equinity", or else by using certain *substantival* nouns – what Locke called "sortal" terms – such as "man" and "horse". I believe that this is a grammatical distinction which fails to reflect any real ontological difference. However, if that is so, then there is a very important ontological consequence. This is that primary substances, or individual concrete objects, "have" forms only and precisely in the sense that they are particular *instances* of forms. Thus, Dobbin is a particular instance of the substantial kind or form *horse*, whereas Dobbin's *whiteness* is a particular instance of the color universal or attribute *whiteness*. By this account, it makes no sense at all to say that Dobbin is a "combination" of the form *horse* and some "matter". He is, to repeat, just a particular *instance* of that form, other such instances being the various other particular horses that exist or have existed. Being an instance of this form, Dobbin must certainly have *material parts*, such as a head and limbs, but in no sense is he a "combination" of anything material and the universal form in question. What I am saying, then, is that individual objects or primary substances are nothing other than *particular forms*, or *form-particulars* – particular instances of universal forms, in precisely the same sense in which modes (or "tropes", as they are now often called) are particular instances of attributes.

It cannot have escaped notice that, in discussing questions of fundamental ontology, I have frequently used *modal* notions, such as those of necessity and possibility, and also the notion of *essence*. In the remainder of this chapter, therefore, I shall try to explain and defend my usage, which is once more inspired by the work of Aristotle.

## 2 Essence

Currently dominant accounts of the traditional metaphysical distinction between *essence* and *accident* attempt to explain it in modal terms, and more specifically in terms of the notions of metaphysical necessity and possibility. These, in turn, are commonly explicated in terms of the language of "possible worlds". Thus, a property $F$ is said to be an *essential* property of an object $a$ just in case, in every possible world in which $a$ exists, $a$ is $F$. And $a$'s *essence* is then said to consist in the set or sum of $a$'s essential properties. One difficulty of this approach, brought to our notice by the work of Kit Fine (1994), is that it seems grossly to over-generate essential properties. For instance, by this account, one of Socrates's essential properties is his property of *being either a man or a mouse*, and another is his property of *being such that 2 + 2 = 4*. It might be objected that these are not genuine properties anyway and so *a fortiori* not essential properties of Socrates. But there are other examples which cannot be objected to on these grounds, such as Socrates's property of being the sole member of the set *singleton Socrates*, that is, the set {Socrates} whose sole member is Socrates. Fine urges, plausibly, that it is not part of Socrates's essence that he belongs to this set, although it is plausibly the case that it is part of the essence of singleton Socrates that Socrates is its sole member. The modal account of essence cannot, it seems, accommodate this asymmetry. These points are too well-known for it to be necessary for me to dwell on them further. Suffice it to say that I am persuaded by Fine's objections to the modal account of essence and accept the lesson that he draws: that it is preferable to try to explicate the notions of metaphysical necessity and possibility in terms of the notion of essence, rather than *vice versa*. This may also enable us to dispense with the language of possible worlds as a means of explicating modal statements. That would be a good thing, in my view, since I regard this language as being fraught with ontological difficulties, even if it can sometimes have a heuristic value.

However, if we are to take this alternative line of approach, we need, of course, to provide a perspicuous account of the notion of essence which does not seek to explicate it in modal terms. Fortunately, we do have at our disposal some resources wherewith to accomplish this, drawing on the Aristotelian and Scholastic traditions in metaphysics. One key notion here, pointed out and exploited by Fine himself, is that of a *real definition*, understood as being a definition of a *thing* (a *res*, or entity), in contradistinction to a *verbal definition*, which is a definition of a word or phrase. A real definition of an entity, $E$, is to be understood as a proposition which tells us, in the most perspicuous fashion, *what E is* – or, more broadly, since we do not want to restrict ourselves solely to the essences of actually existing things, *what E is or would be*. This is perfectly in line with the original Aristotelian understanding of the notion of essence, for the Latin-based word "essence" is just the standard translation of a phrase of Aristotle's which is more literally translated into English as "the what it is to be" or "the what it would be to be". We find a similar turn of phrase in Locke's *Essay Concerning Human Understanding*, where he tells us that the word "essence", in what he calls its "proper original signification", just means "the very being of any thing, whereby it is, what it is" (III, III, 15).

As I intimated earlier, the view of essence and real definition that I have just been articulating is one with a lengthy philosophical pedigree. We find it, for instance, in Spinoza's *On the Improvement of the Understanding*. Now, any *essential* truth is *ipso facto* a *metaphysically necessary* truth, although not *vice versa*: there can be metaphysically necessary truths that aren't essential truths – understanding an essential truth to be a truth concerning the essence of some entity. If we can truly affirm that it is part of the essence of some entity, *E*, that *p* is the case, then *p* is an essential truth and so a metaphysically necessary truth. Thus, for example, it is part of the essence of a certain ellipse, *E*, that its foci are a certain distance apart, whence it follows that it is metaphysically necessary that *E*'s foci are that distance apart. By something's being a "part of the essence" of a certain entity, I just mean that it either is the *whole* essence of that entity or else is *properly included* in its essence. Consider now a metaphysically necessary truth such as the fact that *an ellipse is the closed curve of intersection between a cone and a plane cutting it at an oblique angle to its axis greater than that of the cone's side*. It is not part of the essence of any *ellipse* that this condition holds, nor is it part of the essence of any *cone* that it does. What it is very plausible to contend, however, is that this metaphysically necessary truth holds *in virtue of* the essences of an ellipse and a cone, respectively. It is because of *what an ellipse is*, and *what a cone is*, that this relationship necessarily holds between ellipses and cones. But it is not *part of anything's essence* that it holds. For ellipses and cones, which are the only things whose essences have a role to play in explaining why this necessary truth holds, are quite *different* things. Our proposal concerning metaphysically necessary truths is, then, this: a metaphysically necessary truth is a truth which is either an *essential* truth or else a truth that obtains *in virtue of* the essences of two or more distinct things. On this account, all metaphysical necessity (and by the same token, all metaphysical possibility) is *grounded* in essence (Lowe 2008).

It will be recalled that, according to the currently prevailing modal account of essence, an entity's essence consists in the set or sum of its essential properties, these being the properties that it possesses in every possible world in which it exists. Hence, according to this view, an entity's essence is *a further entity*, namely, a set or sum of certain properties. According to my version of the neo-Aristotelian account of essence, however, an entity's essence is *not* some further entity (Lowe 2008). Rather, an entity's essence is just *what that entity is*, as revealed by its real definition. But *what E is* is not some entity distinct from *E*. It is either *identical* with *E* (and some scholars think that this was Aristotle's view) or else it is *no entity at all*: and the latter is my own view. On my view, we can quite properly say that it is *part of the essence* of a certain entity, *E*, that it possesses a certain property, *P*. But this does not entitle us to say that *P* is a part of the essence of *E*. The latter would imply that *E*'s essence is a further entity, with *P* as a part, which accords with the orthodox view that *E*'s essence is a set or sum of certain properties. But I have rejected that view. We should not, in my opinion, *reify* essences. And although I speak of essences as having "parts", I have already explained what I mean by this, in a way that does not require us to reify essences. Note that there is a particularly objectionable feature of the view that an entity's essence is some further entity. This is that, since it seems proper to say that *every* entity has an essence, the view generates an infinite regress of essences. Neither the view that an entity is identical with its own essence, nor my preferred view that an entity's essence is not an entity at all, has this defect. And my view, as we shall shortly see, has an additional advantage when we come to consider the *epistemology* of essence, that is, the proper account of our *knowledge* of essence.

Given that all metaphysical modality is grounded in essence, we can have knowledge of metaphysical modality if we can have knowledge of essence. Can we? Most assuredly we can. We have already seen this in the case of geometrical figures, such as an ellipse. Knowing an entity's essence is simply knowing *what that entity is*. And at least in the case of *some* entities, we must be able to know *what they are*, because otherwise it would be hard to see how we could know anything at all about them. How, for example, could I know that a certain ellipse had a certain eccentricity, if I did not know what an ellipse *is*? In order to *think* comprehendingly about something, I surely need to know *what it is* that I am thinking about. And sometimes, at least, we surely succeed in thinking comprehendingly about something – for if we do not, then we surely never succeed in thinking at all, which is absurd.

I mentioned earlier that, according to my account of essence, essences are *not entities*. This means that grasping an essence – knowing what something is – is not, by my account, a kind of *knowledge by acquaintance* of a special kind of entity, the thing in question's *essence*. All that grasping an essence amounts to, on my view, is *understanding a real definition*, that is, understanding a special kind of *proposition*. To know *what a circle is*, for instance, I need to understand that *a circle is the locus of a point moving in a plane at a fixed distance from a given point*. Provided that I understand what a *point* and a *plane* are, and what *motion* and *distance* are, I can understand what a circle is, by grasping this real definition. And bear in mind that I do not insist that we need *fully* grasp the *whole* essence of a thing in order to be able to think about it to some degree adequately, so that even if I do not *fully* grasp what *motion*, say, is, I can still achieve at least a *partial* grasp of what a circle is by means of the foregoing real definition. If, by contrast, knowledge of essence were knowledge by acquaintance of a special kind of entity, then indeed we would have cause to be doubtful about our ability ever to grasp the essences of things. For what mental faculty of ours could possibly be involved in this special kind of acquaintance? Surely not our faculty of *sense perception*. Sense perception may provide us with knowledge by acquaintance of concrete, physical things, existing in space and time, but hardly with knowledge of their *essences*, conceived as further entities somehow grounding modal truths about those concrete things. If appeal is instead made to some special intellectual faculty of "insight" or "intuition", with essences as its special objects, then one is open to the charge of anti-naturalistic obscurantism. My own account of what it is to grasp an essence appeals only to an intellectual ability that, by any account, we must already be acknowledged to possess: the ability to understand at least some propositions, including those that express real definitions.

We now have in place the basic ingredients for a thoroughgoing epistemology of metaphysical modality. Put simply, the theory is this. Metaphysical modalities are grounded in essence. That is, all truths about what is metaphysically necessary or possible are either straightforwardly essential truths or else obtain in virtue of the essences of things. An essence is what is expressed by a real definition. And it is part of *our* essence as rational, thinking beings that we can at least sometimes understand a real definition – which is just a special kind of proposition – and thereby grasp the essences of at least some things. Hence, we can know at least sometimes that something is metaphysically necessary or possible: *we can have some knowledge of metaphysical modality*. This *itself* is a modal truth, of course, and one that obtains in virtue of our essence as rational, thinking beings. And since we can, it seems clear, grasp our own essence – at least sufficiently well to know the foregoing modal truth about ourselves – *we know* that we can have some knowledge of metaphysical modality.

## References

Fine, Kit 1994. "Essence and Modality," in James E. Tomberlin (ed.) *Philosophical Perspectives, 8: Logic and Language* (Atascadero, CA: Ridgeview), pp. 1–16.

Lowe, E. J. 2006. *The Four-Category Ontology: A Metaphysical Foundation for Natural Science* (Oxford: Oxford University Press).

_____ 2008. "Two Notions of Being: Entity and Essence," in Robin Le Poidevin (ed.) *Being: Developments in Contemporary Metaphysics* (Cambridge: Cambridge University Press), pp. 23–48.

# 11

# Synthetic Life and the Bruteness of Immanent Causation

*David S. Oderberg*

## 1 Introduction

When Craig Venter announced, in 2010, the production of a bacterium with a synthetic genome, the reaction in the media was typically hyperbolic. Headlines screamed that scientists at the J. Craig Venter Institute had created "synthetic life",[1] a "synthetic life form",[2] "artificial life",[3] with the use of the word "creation" sprinkled liberally across the front pages. The prize for compacting as much hyperbole as possible into the shortest space went, as so often, to the *Daily Mail*: "Scientist accused of playing God after creating artificial life by making designer microbe from scratch – but could it wipe out humanity?"

Some of these headlines used scare quotes for their preferred frightening catchphrases, and they did so advisedly. For, in reply to Frequently Asked Questions about its achievement, specifically question 1, "Is your work in creating a synthetic bacterial cell 'creating life from scratch'?", the Institute stated: "No we do not consider this to be 'creating life from scratch' but rather we are creating new life out of already existing life using synthetic DNA to reprogram the cells to form new cells that are specified by the synthetic DNA".[4] This somewhat more modest explanation of what Venter and his team achieved is the same as that given by virtually all the biologists and biotechnologists who have been quoted on the subject, a typical response being that of Nobel laureate Sir Paul Nurse: "Venter's work is a major advance. But it's not a creation of synthetic life... Creation of synthetic life would be to make an entire bacterial cell through chemicals."[5]

Interestingly – and perhaps not so surprisingly – some philosophers have been less cautious in the way they have expressed themselves. Bioethicist Arthur Caplan exclaimed:[6]

Venter and his colleagues have shown that the material world can be manipulated to produce what we recognize as life. In doing so they bring to an end a debate about the nature of life that has lasted thousands of years. Their achievement undermines a fundamental belief about the nature of life that is likely to prove as momentous to our view of ourselves and our place in the Universe as the discoveries of Galileo, Copernicus, Darwin and Einstein.

And again:[7]

Scientists, theologians and philosophers have been wrangling over this issue for eons. For many, the wondrous nature of what permits something to be alive has been a mystery that science never, ever could penetrate. Life is sacred, special, ineffable and beyond human understanding. Except it isn't.

More importantly, leading philosopher of "artificial life" Mark Bedau incautiously elaborated on Venter's achievement thus:[8]

There are a couple of reasons why this achievement should not be called the creation of "new" life. First, the form of life that was created was not new. What was essentially done was the re-creation of an existing bacterial form of life, except that it was given a prosthetic genome (synthesized in the laboratory), and except that the genome was put into the cytoplasm of a slightly different species.

The impression he gives here is that the Venter Institute did not create *new* life but that it did create life. To be fair, he goes on to acknowledge the objection that life was not created at all, if creation implies the synthesis of a organism other than by modifying an existing one, more precisely if it implies the synthesis of a *whole organism*. But this, for him, is a mere technical obstacle: "A handful of research teams around the globe are working on trying to create fully synthetic cells (sometimes called "protocells") using materials obtained solely from a chemical supply company. Even a living protocell would still not qualify as creation from nothing, of course, since it would be created from pre-existing materials."[9]

Needless to say, no one is suggesting that the big question here is whether life can literally be created *ex nihilo*, so the last sentence is a red herring. The heart of the matter – what really shocks and excites in equal measure – is whether the synthesis of a whole organism from a non-organism merely awaits further technological progress. The Venter achievement does not prove this. What his team did was as follows.[10] First, they began with the computerized genome of the naturally-occurring bacterium *Mycoplasma mycoides*. Then, they synthesized this genome in yeast by the method of oligonucleotide synthesis, well known for decades as a way of producing short fragments of DNA, RNA, and other organic molecules. These fragments were assembled in yeast to form the complete genome of *M. mycoides*. The team inserted some artificial sequences into the genome, representing encoded watermarks: instead of an amino acid being associated with a codon (a nucleotide triple), the team produced codons associated with letters of the alphabet, resulting in a cipher encoding a quotation from James Joyce,[11] a copyright statement, an email address, names of team members, and so on.[12] This synthetic genome was isolated from the yeast and transplanted into a cell of *Mycoplasma capricolum*, a naturally-occurring goat parasite, that had had its defenses against foreign DNA removed. The *M. capricolum* genome was destroyed by the new genome or otherwise lost during cell replication. After two days, the team detected viable *M. mycoides* cells with no trace of the *M. capricolum* DNA in them, only the synthesized DNA, watermarks and all.[13]

## 2   An unreasonable appeal to cosmology

Despite the breathy headlines and typical over-reaction in the media and even among some in the academy, the Venter Institute did not produce life from non-life, nor did they claim to. Their technical achievement of synthesizing a bacterial genome from a computerized sequence is without doubt a marvel of modern biotechnology. As a feat of pure bio-engineering, the world was right to stand in amazement. Venter did not, however, violate the traditional maxims *omne vivum e vivo* and, more specifically, *omnis cellula e cellula*. The first – all life comes from life – is commonly attributed to the celebrated physician William Harvey, but in fact originates with the German naturalist Lorenz Oken.[14] The second – every cell comes from a cell – is usually attributed to the German physician and biologist Rudolf Virchow (1821–1902), who in fact popularized an epigram originating with the French chemist and physiologist François-Vincent Raspail (1794–1878).[15] Venter, in full conformity with these doctrines (which in my view better describes them than "maxims"), transformed an existing cell into a new one (perhaps of a new species) using a synthetic genome. The achievement does, however, reanimate the debate over biogenesis versus abiogenesis – whether life can only come from life or can also come from non-life – since proponents of the latter assume it is only a matter of time before an organism will be synthesized *in toto* from pre-existing materials none of which will itself be an organism.

What is it to be alive? The answer to this question is key to resolving the biogenesis/abiogenesis debate. It will not tell us whether abiogenesis is a practical possibility, but it should help us to determine whether there are reasons of *principle* that stand in its way. Before addressing the question of what life is, I want to put aside a consideration that merely forestalls discussion. One might think – as do many scientists – that what we know of the origin of the universe is simply inconsistent with biogenesis. Our best cosmology tells us there was a Big Bang around fourteen billion years ago and that the only things that began to exist at that time were inorganic. The earliest life forms found on earth are said to have existed about 3.5 billion years ago.[16] Since they did not originate with the universe, they must have come into existence from something non-living. Therefore, abiogenesis must not only be possible in principle but must have actually occurred.

It is not hard to see the force of this objection, but I do not find it decisive, primarily for dialectical reasons. It reminds me of something a former lecturer told me she had said in her undergraduate philosophy class on Kant. When her lecturer proclaimed that Kant's big question in epistemology was "how is knowledge possible?", she quickly interjected that it was obviously possible because it was actual. Just as her teacher was not impressed, so I do not think anyone who considers the biogenesis debate seriously ought to be much taken by the proposal that life simply *must* have arisen from non-life because cosmology implies it. What we want is an intellectually satisfying account of how this could have happened. Physicists generally agree on a satisfying account of how light chemical elements formed in the first few minutes after the Big Bang. It would be bizarre, at least in the current state of knowledge, to object that cosmology unreasonably forestalls debate about whether, say, deuterium could have formed from protons and neutrons.

Life seems to be a different sort of case. On one side, we have had the demonstrable failure of numerous attempts to synthesize an organism from a non-organism in the laboratory. It is not that the experimenters typically intended to do this and failed by their own lights, though no doubt any of them who did produce such an organism would understandably have taken the credit and the prizes. Most have been interested in producing organic molecules such as amino acids and carbohydrates from conditions similar to those thought to have existed on earth at the time life appeared. In this, there have been notable successes. Still, these are far from demonstrating how life itself could have been produced by non-life, something openly and honestly admitted by the biochemists themselves working in this field.[17]

The current smorgasbord of theories on offer, each with its adherents and detractors, is ample testimony to the state of the discipline. There is the famous "primordial soup" theory in its many versions such as deep sea vents and radioactive beaches responsible for the formation of organic molecules. When it comes to the transition from organic molecules to primitive life forms, we have for example: the RNA-first hypothesis; the metabolism-first hypothesis with its variations such as an iron-sulfur world, ocean bubbles, pumice rafts, and others; the lipid world; the clay hypothesis; and of course either primitive life, or essential chemicals for organic processes, from stars, meteorites, comets, and/or interstellar dust.[18]

On the other side, we have the famous experiments of Pasteur and his predecessors Francesco Redi (C17th), Lazzaro Spallanzani (C18th), and others, which demonstrated the absence of spontaneous generation of life from non-life at least in the relatively simple laboratory conditions they were able to set up. In effect, current theories are merely a more sophisticated continuation of these kinds of experiment, yielding no positive result so far to refute what Pasteur seemed at the time to have established. I lay all this out not to ridicule the supporters of abiogenesis, which is the vast bulk of the scientific community with any knowledge of the topic, but simply to loosen the dialectical hold of the thought that it must be true because cosmology says so and all we need to do is find out how it happened. Suppose that the First Law of Thermodynamics is not a law after all, maybe only a generalization with near-universal application: that would be consistent both with current cosmology and biogenesis if life came into existence from absolutely nothing. I do not think this is the case, but that is not the point: rather, for those proponents of abiogenesis who do not regard the First Law as a logical truth or a metaphysical necessity (perhaps because, like Hume, they do not think any laws are metaphysically necessary), the scenario should weaken the appeal to cosmology as a way of closing down debate on whether abiogenesis is true. I will return to this when considering another alternative, namely that life is the product of some kind of non-naturalistic activity.

## 3   The essence of life: preliminaries

There is plenty of skepticism about whether life has an essence, that is, whether it can be captured in a definition. There is the perennial worry about borderline cases (e.g., viruses).[19] There is the thought that life has certain hallmarks but cannot be encapsulated by one or more character- istics shared by all living things or at least those things we intuitively grasp as alive.[20] And, of course, there is a more general anti-essentialism according to which nothing, not even life, has an essence.[21]

I am going to assume a modest variety of essentialism here, more precisely that at least *some* things have essences and that nothing precludes the possibility of life's being among those things. Indeed, life is as good a thing as any for having an essence, given its being a proper object of a special science and its perennial fascination for philosophers and scientists: there just *seems* to be something special about living things, moreover their existence appears to be something of a miracle even in the metaphorical, naturalistic sense. Further, the massive, on-going disagreement at the purely empirical level as to how life came from non-life, if it did so at all, at least suggests that we are dealing with a unique phenomenon within the natural world, baffling and resisting all attempts at explanation in inorganic terms.

There are well-known lists of hallmarks, notes, criteria, signs, or however one wishes to call them – even essential characteristics – associated with living things. For example, there is homeostasis, that is, an organism's regulation of its functions and processes so as to maintain stability despite changes in its environment, particularly those that tend to undermine stability. Another is the storage and copying of informa- tion, via DNA, RNA and other chemicals and processes, so as to cause and maintain right functioning.[22] There is what Mark Bedau calls "supple adaptation", meaning the "unending capacity [of evolution by natural selection] to produce novel solutions to unanticipated changes in the problems of surviving, reproducing, or, more generally, flourishing."[23] Indeed, evolution by natural selection and a history of common descent themselves are sometimes taken to be among the defining features of life.[24] Metabolism also features on most lists, that is to say, the ability of an organism to take in material from its environment (primarily through nutrition, but also respiration and other processes) and convert it into its own organic matter so as to sustain its life, growth, development, reproduction, and other functions and operations.[25]

This is but a sample of the major characteristics of life that are regu- larly noted in both the scientific and philosophical literature, but they are sufficient to enable the making of a general point. The features to which theorists of life commonly appeal tend to be either irrelevant to life's essence or else are best thought of as evidences, signs, or even causes of organic functions that are of the essence, rather than being of the essence *themselves*. Historical descent, for example, is irrelevant even if it is non-accidentally true of every organism that has ever lived or will live on this earth.[26] It is metaphysically possible that there should be life, even an historical sequence of kinds of living thing, with no lines of descent. Suppose the first organism of each kind appears by some relatively common natural process, the kind persists for a short period and is then extinguished by a meteorite, whereupon a new kind arises by the same process and is extinguished.[27] Mayr might respond that these organisms have at least to be *capable* of possessing lines of descent (whether via evolution by natural selection or something similar). It is not clear why this should be so, but even if true it merely points in the direction of what we should say about more relevant features such as supple adaptation, information storage (and related processes), also hereditary variation and evolution itself. Note first that some of these features are true only of populations rather than individuals: if anything evolves, it is a species or population, not a single organism.[28] So, whilst such a feature – also *evolvability* rather than actual evolution itself, and Bedau's supple adaptation – might essentially characterize a living population, it does not characterize the individual member itself qua living thing. If it is claimed that the feature does characterize the individual insofar as it is a member of such a population, it would make the organism's essence qua organism objectionably relational: if any essence should be considered intrinsic to a thing, it is being alive. Being alive is about what a living thing *does*, not whether it belongs to a certain kind of population.[29]

Secondly, commonly indicated features that are relevant to grasping the essence of life – including features that are implausible candidate essences because relational – are usually only signs, evidences, or causes of essential organic functions. For an organism to be capable of having an historical lineage, more particularly to be a result of hereditary variation, or to be able to produce later variation (through mutated offspring, for example), it has to contain the material – such as DNA – that makes this possible. But that material is involved in far more processes than those concerning reproduction, heredity, and variation. It is these other processes that get us closer to the essence of life.[30]

# 4  The essence of life: immanent causation

That essence, I claim, is what Aristotelians and Thomists sometimes call *immanent causation.*[31] This is causation that originates with an agent and terminates in that agent for the sake of its self-perfection. It is a kind of teleology, but metaphysically distinctive in what it involves. Immanent causation is not just action for a purpose, but for the agent's *own* purpose, where "own purpose" means not merely that the agent acts for a purpose it possesses, but that it acts for a purpose it possesses such that fulfillment of the purpose contributes to the agent's self-perfection. Hence, in immanent causation, the agent is both the cause and the effect of the action, and the cause itself is directed at the effect as perfective of the agent.

The following points clarify and elaborate the concept of immanent causation. (i) It is to be distinguished from the other broad category of causation, usually called *transient.*[32] In transient causation, the activity terminates in something distinct from the agent.[33] If A does F to B transiently, then A does F to B, and A is not the same K as B (for some kind K). (ii) For a sufficient condition, we need something stronger, since if A does F to a part of itself, this does not entail transience even though the part is not the same K as A, for any K. As long as the self-perfective condition is met, A's doing F to a part of itself is immanent, since by doing something to a part of itself (say, repairing a damaged limb or destroying a piece of wrongly copied DNA), A does something to itself, so we need to say: If A does F to B, and A is not the same K as B (for some K), and B is not a part of A, then A does F to B transiently.

(iii) The self-perfective condition – that the agent act for the sake of its self-perfection – rules out cases where the effect merely happens to terminate in the agent, that is, does so accidentally. Note that the effect might be neutral, harmful, or even perfective, but it still will not be part of immanent causal activity. In growing towards natural light, a plant might activate a motion-sensitive spotlight that shines on it with no beneficial or harmful effect: the shining of the spotlight is neutral, and it is even a consequence of other immanent activity, but is not itself part of any immanent causal chain since activating the spotlight was not something the plant did for the sake of its self-perfection. A tree sends out roots in search of water, thereby undermining a wall which topples onto the tree and damages it. The damage is a harmful effect but not part of any immanent activity (albeit a side effect of it). An animal escaping a predator may stumble fortuitously upon a source of food for itself, but it is the achievement of safety that is the proper effect of immanent activity, not the animal's finding itself presented by a source of nutrition. Needless to say, a human being might quite deliberately do something that terminates in himself, but if what he does is for the sake of harm rather than self-perfection, his activity is not immanent. Hence, transient and immanent causation do not exhaust all the possibilities: a more detailed taxonomy of agent causation is not possible here, but we could for example call activity that terminates accidentally in the agent *reflexive* rather than immanent, and activity that deliberately terminates in the agent but is neither neutral nor self-perfective *anti-immanent*, for want of a better term.[34]

(iv) It should be emphasized that the self-perfective condition does not entail the consciousness, let alone self-consciousness, of any agent engaging in immanent activity. It is not just that plants lack consciousness but still act immanently, true though this be, but that nothing in the very idea of self-perfection implies any level of awareness. One of the advantages of immanence as the essence of life is that it is neutral as to what state or condition the organism has to be in to engage in such activity (other than being alive, of course). It is neutral as well with respect to *how* the organism acts immanently. Immanence is compatible with living things' being in some sense "programmed" to act this way, or designed – whether by Mother Nature, God, or some other source – to do so, or organized in a certain way. A more specific definition, say, in terms of a certain kind or level or organizational complexity, or a certain very particular power such as information storage and usage, or replicability, makes ontological commitments that are a hostage to empirical fortune. Not so immanence.

(v) Following on from this point, immanent causation has the advantage of generality inasmuch as it picks out just the sorts of features commonly appealed to in proposed definitions of life, whether the features are taken singly or in combination. Homeostasis clearly exemplifies immanence: organisms work to regulate themselves and preserve their stability both internally and with regard to changes in the environment. Metabolism is probably the paradigmatic example of immanence: the organism takes in matter/energy, uses it for its sustenance, growth, and development, and expels what is noxious or surplus to requirement. Hence, with only a little more work we have an answer to the question of why fire is not alive.[35] A fire takes in and releases energy, increases in size, and reduces when fuel is not available; we even speak of it "dying away" or "dying out". But it cannot metabolize because it is not even a substance in the first place. A flame is a modification of one or more substances, but itself it has no ontologically independent reality. In fact, it is no more than an aggregation of molecules in various states of oxidation, with growth by accretion (the further oxidation of molecules) rather than by a suite of internal powers belonging to a substance that acts on its environment. Because a fire is not a substance, it is not an agent, and so it cannot act at all, let alone for itself, any more than a nuclear chain reaction acts (as opposed to its substantial constituents, which do act albeit not for themselves; similarly with fire).[36] Adaptive flexibility is clearly an example of immanence: the organism flexibly adapts to its environment and changes internal condition for the sake of its growth, development, and proper functioning.

Next to last, I have argued that population-features such as supple adaptation and evolvability (or evolution itself) are objectionably relational and so cannot be part of the essence of life. But even if we waive this objection, we can see that they are yet more examples of immanence. For no population can flourish, proliferate, or adapt unless its members all engage in immanent activity. It is the living members of the population that do what results in that population's success. Hence, the appeal to membership in a population with a certain feature is the appeal to something that is wholly explained by a more fundamental characteristic of individual members. It would be a misdirection for the critic to suggest that by this reasoning we might as well say that uranium atoms are alive since radiation proliferates and this proliferation is wholly explained by characteristics of its atomic (and sub-atomic) constituents. For both sides are supposed to have *agreed* on what populations we had in mind *before* worrying about whether life is a population-based feature of living things. I assume that neither side had radiation in mind, or gases, or some chemical. What is at issue are populations that do have living members, and that do proliferate and adapt in ways that distinguish them from non-living populations. Assuming agreement on that, the question is whether the being alive of their members is wholly a matter of their belonging to such populations. Waiving any potential circularity in an affirmative answer, my claim is that it is what the individual members of such populations do, and do for themselves, that explains the success of the populations. I would add, as a further and more general point, that we cannot even understand *how* an individual organism contributes to the success of a population without first grasping what it does for itself. Nor *can* it contribute to the success of a population without first (in the order of explanation) doing a great many things for itself, that is, for *its* survival, its health, its stability, its development.

A survey of all the other plausible hallmarks or criteria of life would take us too far afield, but the above examples indicate the strong likelihood that they will all be revealed as yet more cases of immanent causation. I want lastly, however, to mention information as the possible essence of life. Since the unraveling of the many mysteries of DNA and genetics generally, it has become commonplace to think of information (storage, retrieval, usage, replication) as *the* essence of life.[37] Let us leave aside the important questions of what information is exactly, whether there is a sharp line between information and non-information, whether there really *is* information in DNA – at least in an important sense in which there isn't information in the non-living world (in particular, encoded information). Assuming that organisms uniquely contain information (via their parts), or at least information of a unique kind, this cannot be the essence of life, because such information and the mechanisms employing it are of no interest except insofar as they subserve the imma- nent functions of the organism.[38] Venter's artificial DNA watermarks are instructive here. They are of interest for a number of reasons, of course, but not because they contribute to the functioning of the synthesized bacterium. Indeed, as I understand it, they were engineered precisely not to be expressed phenotypically. Suppose all DNA were like that in every organism: would anyone be so interested in it? The answer is clear enough: It is what the information *does* that makes it interesting for a biologist or philosopher of biology. And what it does is precisely, and exclusively, cause and enable the organism to act immanently, that is, for its self-perfection.

(vi) Finally, some clarification of "self-perfection" is in order. No organism can be perfect in an absolute sense. The self-perfection condi- tion is that living things act for the sake of their own proper function; so self-perfection should be understood more in its Latin etymological sense of completion or accomplishment. There is, put simply, a good way for an organism to be, and a bad way. That organisms act for the sake of their self-perfection has to be understood as a *ceteris paribus* law, where the exceptions can be spelled out in a principled way, the main – perhaps only ones – being: (a) damage to the organism may prevent its doing so; (b) hostile environmental conditions may prevent its doing so.

## 5    Can immanence come from transience?

The central claim that a defender of biogenesis ought to make is that immanent causation can never arise, in any way, from transient causation. I mean "arise" in the diachronic sense: no amount of transient causation can ever, over time, give rise to immanent causation. The abiogenetic idea is as follows. Start with some transient causation of the simplest kind: A doing F to B. Add to it: A doing G to B; A doing F, G, H...to C; C acting on A and B; all of these acting jointly on D, E, F.... At some point, if the right transient causal chains are in operation, there will come into being a substance consisting wholly, exclusively, of parts engaged in transient causal relations, but which itself engages in immanent causation – doing F, G, H...to itself for itself.[39] At what point? No one knows, of course; but my claim is that no one *could* know. For immanent causation just is causation of a *wholly different kind* from transient causation. As an early twentieth-century follower of Aquinas puts it, there is in living things a "positive addition" to the properties of non-living things, so that "the living thing possesses the properties of non-living ones, and in addition, certain active characteristics which are entirely its own."[40] To illustrate this idea, consider the by-now almost hackneyed comparison to the liquidity of water. Galen Strawson fairly represents the standard view when he claims that just as liquidity is a property that is wholly explicable without remainder in terms of physics and chemistry, so life too can be so explained. Both are "emergent properties" of underlying physico-chemical phenomena in the sense that although there is a time at which the former are not present but the latter are, there is a later time at which the latter, organized in a way that they earlier were not, have now taken on the characteristics of liquidity or life. In other words, once we have *identified* the right things in the physico-chemical category, we have ipso facto *identified* liquidity or life.[41] Now, Strawson's motive is to repel the objection to his anti-emergence concerning consciousness, to the effect that since it is plausible to count life as emergent from physics and chemistry, so the same should be said about consciousness. His reply is that whilst this is true of life, it is not true of consciousness. Quite why he thinks so is difficult to discern, there being more here in the way of insistence rather than argument. My concern, however, is with his nonchalant waving aside of the problem of life. For if we look at the comparison with liquidity more closely, we can see how the analogy breaks down.

First, a simple dialectical point. We *know* that liquidity emerges from physico-chemical phenomena from which liquidity is absent, since we have seen it happen – typically, by condensation of water molecules. We have seen no such thing in the case of life: at best, the putative emergence is inferred from other things we know. Hence, we cannot take the comparison as an epistemic given.

Secondly, although – perhaps surprisingly – there is no agreement among scientists as to the exact molecular structure that uniquely instantiates liquid water, there is broad agreement that it involves the rapid breaking and re-forming of hydrogen bonds (rapid relative to ice).[42] The full picture is not well understood even now, but that the liquidity of water just *is* a certain kind of molecular structure is beyond dispute.[43] It is, however, the metaphysics behind the contrast with life that is key. In the case of water, a certain structure of molecules, at some level of concentration, is identical to the structure of a liquid. When you identify liquidity, you identify a property of a physical structure of molecules in motion, as you do when you identify ice or gaseous properties. There is nothing *metaphysically* salient about liquidity: if there were, we would have to say the same about ice and steam as well. Yet, to do so would be bizarre, and no scientist would think of wondering about it.

Why, then, can we not say the same about life? If we could, we would be bound to say that immanent causation – the essence of life, on my view – was to be identified with some kind of structure of *transient* causal relations. Yet, what could that be? There is no single transient causal chain, whether linear, cyclical, with multiple causes and/or effects, or of some other complexity, with which any kind of immanent causation could be identified, since no causal chain can be immanent and transient at the same time. By definition, they are two essentially different kinds of causation: transience and immanence are *mutually exclusive*. For instance, when a person eats they act immanently. They do not act transiently, although a multitude of transient causal relations subserve the immanent action, in particular the chemical reactions that take place from the time food enters the mouth to the time it is fully absorbed into the body. The same is true for any immanent activity of any organism. Just as the chemical reactions and physical interactions are not immanent, so the immanent action is not transient.

One objection to this line of thought is that immanent causation should be thought of simply as a kind of transient causation plus something extra. Suppose an organism O does F to itself for itself. Suppose, in addition, that there is a single transient causal chain C, however complex, that obtains when O does F: with typical philosopher's simplisticness, let's say that C begins with two proteins' doing P and ends with two enzymes' doing E. The transience-plus account holds that the definition of O's doing F immanently is C's obtaining with the addition of some other element. What element could that be? It cannot be another transient causal relation, because then we would be back with identifying immanence – this time not the whole action, but the peculiarly immanent quality of it – with just another transient relation, and the question arises again in a slightly different but equally potent form: What is it about this *additional* transient relation that makes *it* immanent as well? If the same answer as before is given, then it has to be that there is yet *another* extra ingredient which makes this additional transient relation immanent in quality; and so on without end. So, the extra ingredient cannot be yet more transience. Nor would it suffice to say that the extra ingredient simply *is* the fact that C occurs within an organism, for this is merely to recognize immanence, not to explain it non-immanently; if offered as an explanation, it would be patently circular. I confess to lacking the imagination to conceive of what the extra ingredient could be that would make the transience-plus model plausible.

A second objection takes its inspiration from neutral monism and/or dual aspect theory. Why not say that both immanent and transient causation are but manifestations of, or reducible to, or even just ways of looking at, one fundamental kind of causation that is in itself neutral between the two? Clearly there are a number of shades in which such a general position might come, so I offer only some equally general remarks. Whatever one may think about the intelligibility of neutral stuff in the philosophy of mind – not essentially mental, not essentially physical – it is very hard to grasp the idea of neutral causation – neither essentially transient nor essentially immanent, unless perhaps one defines it precisely in terms of its neutral relata. In which case, the relata have to be neither essentially organic nor essentially inorganic. But the sort of causation I have been discussing is all of the general form *A does F to B*. Now, even if A and B are not essentially organic and not essentially inorganic, for them to be neutral relata we have to say they are essentially *non*-organic. That is, we would have to take the properties of being organic and inorganic to be mere contraries, not also contradictories (as I hold). To be essentially non-organic, then – on the neutralist view I am sketching – is to be neither essentially organic nor essentially inorganic. The problem for the neutralist is that transience is not defined in terms of inorganic relata. Immanent causation is defined in terms of organic relata, to be sure, since I am not leaving conceptual space for immanent causation involving non-living things; as I have defined life, it is essentially marked by immanent causation and nothing else. Transient causation, by contrast, I have defined only negatively, giving causation between inorganic relata as the paradigmatic (and, on my view, only known or knowable) examples of where transient causation is to be found. Transient causation is thus defined operationally as the causation that obtains between non-living things, but in itself it is simply any causation that occurs when A does F to B but B is not identical to A nor is B part of A. Given this definition, even causation between neutral entities as just defined must be transient as long as the transience conditions are met. It will not matter that the relata are neutral. Hence, the position will not really be neutralist after all; rather, it will be taking a partisan position on which kind of causation is fundamental.[44]

To take immanence and transience as mere ways of looking at the same thing – or, perhaps more plausibly for many, to take immanence as a mere way of looking at transience – is effectively to deny the reality of immanence, about which more shortly; but even if not, it is to fail to take it seriously in an ontological sense. Rather than argue against this lack of seriousness here, for which there is no space, I will note that the reduction of immanence to appearance, or perspective, or aspect, is in my view effectively an acknowledgement that ontologically serious immanence *cannot* be explained in terms of transience. If this is unfair, it is fair to see such a reduction as an easy stopping point for someone who does not want to confront the seriousness of the problem as I have posed it.

A third objection to my argument is that although immanence cannot, by definition, be identified with any transient causal relation, it can be identified with a network or system of such relations. This is what self-organization and related theories of abiogenesis amount to, since life is hypothesized to emerge once a certain kind and level of system complexity is reached, where the components of the system are causal relata engaged in transient activity, such as the catalysis of chemical reactions. Once there are enough components of the right kind, and enough catalytic reactions of the right kind, a system becomes self-sustaining (autocatalytic), able to maintain and reproduce itself.[45]

Lack of empirical evidence aside as far as a self-organizational theory of abiogenesis is concerned, the conceptual problem remains: if no transient causal relation can be identified with an immanent one, how can a network or system of such relations? Superficially, this looks like the absurd question as to how, if no single $H_2O$ molecule is liquid, any number of them could be. But the similarity is only on the surface. The simple answer to the liquidity question is that if enough $H_2O$ molecules engage in enough of the movements and chemical reactions in which they already engage or are capable of engaging in non-liquid states, they will be in the liquid state. One parallel claim about self-organizing systems is that if enough elements engage in enough of the transient causal interactions in which they already engage or are capable of engaging when they are in a non-immanent state, they will be in the state of immanent activity. But all they are engaged in in the non-immanent state is, precisely, transient activity. So, all the claim amounts to is the bare assertion that immanence can arise from transience, which is where we started. In the case of liquidity, the phase just is more of the same that the molecules engage in when in other phases – motion and bonding. In the case of life, it is not that the inorganic elements just do more of the same when they are – so the hypothesis goes – elements of an organism. It is not that these elements merely take on new characteristics, though they do. It is, rather, that these characteristics now all, without exception, define activity that, also without exception, subserves an entirely different way in which the system[46] operates, distinct from anything transient either in the parts taken alone or collectively. The system is now operating *for itself*. Perhaps there is something of the well-known philosophical objection called "the incredulous stare" in this way of arguing, but there are stares and there are stares. One might be incredulous that such astonishing complexity as we find in even the simplest life form could ever emerge from non-living material. Such is the incredulity of the Paleyan design theorists and, arguably, their contemporary representatives in the intelligent design movement. Or one might be *metaphysically* incredulous that one essential kind of causation could ever emerge from another, where by "essential kind of causation" I mean a kind that either defines (if only partially) the essence of an entity that engages in it or else is so closely connected to its essence that it is rightly deemed to be "of the essence" of the entity. I take transient causation to be, largely, in the latter category. Immanent causation I take to be in the former. If you take immanent causation metaphysically seriously, you ought to be at least incredulous in the way I suggest.

This way of thinking seems to me to be what is right about Paul Davies's criticism of Kauffman-style self-organization theories.[47] Referring first to the absence of experimental evidence, he goes on to raise the conceptual problem that life is not, in fact, an example of self-organization at all, but of *"specified, i.e. genetically directed, organization"*.[48] Whereas all inorganic examples of self-organization, such as convection cells, are also examples of *spontaneous* organization determined at least in part by environmental conditions, the organization of living beings is determined *internally*, "by the genetic software encoded in their DNA (or RNA)".[49] On the face of it, this looks like a recapitulation of the intelligent design argument that life is defined by its "specified complexity" (albeit Davies is not a supporter of intelligent design). Stephen C. Meyer, for example, takes "specified complexity" to mean "information content", which he distinguished from "mere complexity". Information content specifies a particular function; mere complexity specifies none, though it has information-carrying capacity inasmuch as its elements are arranged in some way or other, possibly randomly, thereby excluding all other arrangements and carrying a certain probability of occurring given all the possible ways of occurring.[50] Davies goes on, however, to refer to "the very concept of software control" and to the fact that " [t]his [the emergence of software control] is not merely a matter of adding an extra layer of complexity, it is about a fundamental transformation in the very nature of the system."[51]

Now, it might still seem as though there is not much to separate Davies from Meyer (whom I take, perhaps a little unfairly, as my representative of ID theory) as far as what puzzles them is concerned. In fact, Meyer even speaks, albeit rarely, of specified complexity at the genetic level as being "determined 'top-down' by the larger system-wide informational and organismal context – by the needs of the organism as a whole."[52] It is the last part that shows a passing concern with immanent causation, and I suggest that this is, albeit perhaps indirectly, Davies's concern as well when he speaks of control. What separates Davies from standard ID theory, though, is his emphasis on *fundamental transformation*. An ID theorist such as Meyer sees life as originating in the work of an artificer with sufficient power to produce the requisite level of complexity for specified functions to appear. In which case, even the "needs of the organism" are in principle the product of the right kind of assembly by the right kind of intelligence. Davies, by contrast, concludes that the information in the organism originates in the information in the environment, which he then glosses, quite importantly, as follows: "This begs [sic] the question of how the information got into the environment in the first place. *It is surely not waiting, like fragments of a pre-existing blueprint, for nature to assemble it.* The environment is not an intelligent designer" (my emphasis).[53] Not only does Davies here correctly represent the standard position of ID theorists, but he denies that information ever was composed of elements waiting to be assembled; his conclusion being that information has been in the universe from the Big Bang, its transformation into the stuff of living things being an outcome of natural laws and initial conditions, probably of a global nature and as yet unknown to scientists.[54]

The point of this exegetical digression, for my purpose, is to stress the distinction between treating immanence as just a matter of enough complexity, and treating it as fundamentally different in kind from what goes on at the physical and chemical levels. To be sure, Davies's position does allow the logical possibility of information's having been assembled from prior, non-informational elements, by a sufficiently intelligent designer. And, of course, his emphasis is on information, not immanence, which, as I noted earlier, is not what ought to be the primary focus in the debate over abiogenesis. Still, his recognition of a fundamental gap between physico-chemical behavior and that of living things, coupled with his insistence that information is, at least in fact, a brute fact about the universe, shows some affinities with the position I am defending.

## 6 A clarification on supervenience

By denying that life could ever have emerged from non-living matter – by, to put it somewhat rhetorically, preferring the empirical discoveries of Pasteur and his corroborators to the speculations of contemporary scientists – I am not compelled to deny, nor do I deny, that an organism can be *completely metaphysically dependent* on the matter that composes it. In common with materialists, I hold this to be a fact about the overwhelming majority of earthly organisms.[55] Hence, I hold the following supervenience thesis about organisms: the totality of an organism's characteristics, functions, and behavior are determined by the matter composing it, whether with or without the inclusion of environmental matter (as in epigenetic causation). Materially identical organisms (with perhaps materially identical environmental conditions) will of metaphysical necessity be identical in their characteristics, functions, and behavior. The correlative explanatory thesis is that there is nothing about an organism that cannot be given a wholly material explanation. These theses are neutral as to whether an organism's characteristics, functions, and behavior are determined exhaustively by physics and/ or chemistry. They are consistent with any of the following scenarios: (i) an organism's total state (shorthand for characteristics, function, and behavior) is caused by its total physico-chemical state with or without the total physico-chemical state of (some part of) its environment. The most likely account of this would embrace so-called "trans-ordinal laws" of the kind defended by emergentists such as C.D. Broad.[56] (ii) An organism's total state is not caused by, but is necessarily correlated with, its total physico-chemical state with or without the total physico-chemical state of (some part of) its environment. This correlation, being non-causal, would not be of any kind amenable either to empirical or metaphysical classification; it would simply be a brute correlation, one which because of its necessity we could call lawlike. (iii) An organism's total state is caused by its total physico-chemical state with or without the total physico-chemical state of (some part of) its environment, along with the state (partial or total) of at least one other organism. In this case there would be no metaphysical room for a world in which only a single organism existed: there could only be more than one, and each of their states would causally depend at least in part on the state of the other.

This does not exhaust all the possibilities, but what is more important is that which is excluded by the kind of materialism I am defending: the total state of an organism can never be *identified* with any physico-chemical state. In this sense, the materialism involved here is non-reductive (though it would be reductive relative to an out-and-out vitalist of the old school). But how is abiogenesis excluded if causal superveni-ence is allowed, as on the first scenario? The exclusion is achieved partly by the fact that *synchronic* causal dependence does not entail *diachronic* causal dependence. So, the diachronic appearance of life from inorganic matter is not entailed by scenario (i). The establishment of the *negation* of this possibility is the weight borne by all of the preceding argument, and this makes out the full exclusion of abiogenesis. The non-entailment of diachronic by synchronic supervenience is just the notion that even if life is wholly causally dependent on physico-chemical factors, it does not follow that it ever could have emerged from them over time. The term "emergence" is one of the most obfuscatory in philosophy, whatever the merits of any theory that goes by the name. For my part, conceptual hygiene mandates that the term be reserved wholly for a process that is supposed to occur over time; the very connotation and etymology of the term require it. Maybe, though, synchronic causal dependence makes no sense without the possibility of diachronic dependence? It would if we could make sense of the possibility of simultaneous causa-tion, where the cause (here, the physico-chemical state) acts as a kind of *sustaining* or *maintaining* cause, a causal substrate of the organism. This causation would imply nothing about whether such a substrate or one of its precursors could ever *give rise* to an organism over time. Yet, I am happy to leave simultaneous causation as the vexed issue it is, noting that if it does not make sense then scenario (i) is a non-starter – again implying nothing about the possibility of life's emergence over time from the non-living.

## 7   Two objections

First, an objector might simply deny the existence of immanent causa-tion altogether as an illusion or vitalist fantasy. I have said a little already about not taking such causation seriously, but I will add here that the hallmarks of life most commonly noted in the literature do certainly appear to have something in common. They are not a random list, nor are they taken from a small sample of organisms: every single indisputable organism ever examined displays them. I have noted that some of what passes for hallmarks are in fact irrelevant, so it cannot be that every feature called a hallmark of life, even by a majority of scientists, really is such. There is, however, widespread agreement on a core set of features such as metabolism, growth, homeostasis, and self-repair, all of which have immanence in common. And there is widespread agreement that non-living things do *not* display such features. If you take biology seriously (whether or not you regard it as an autonomous special science), then you should take immanence seriously. Moreover, it is hard to see why you would not unless you had a prior commitment to physicalism, or perhaps physico-chemicalism. But this seems to put the cart before the horse, since such a commitment could only be justified once you had *already* given a physicalist, or physico-chemicalist, account of life. To do this on the basis of a flat denial of the reality of immanence would be to argue in a circle: Immanence is not real because physicalism/physico-chemicalism is true; life is no exception because whilst it seems to involve a special kind of causation, it really does not. Physicalists/physico-chemicalists, fortunately for them, do not have to argue like this. It is only if they deny the reality of immanence on the basis of their prior commitment that they end up doing so whether they recognize it or not.

A second objection concerns vagueness. Suppose there are metaphysically borderline cases between the living and the non-living, viruses being the most common example.[57] If there is one there could be many, and they could form a relative continuum over time such that there was no conceptual worry about a step from one member to the next; life would simply be the endpoint of the spectrum. What looked problematic when compared to the extreme at the other end would not look so when compared to its immediate predecessor.

I share the position of McCall that there are no borderline cases between life and non-life, though not for his reason, which is the sharp distinction "between DNA molecules and the coded information they carry".[58] He does not say where a virus would fit into the picture, but the point I made earlier is the crucial one: It is what the organism *does* that matters, not *how* it does it. And it is hard to see how immanence can come in degrees. Either an organism does something to itself for its self-perfection or it does not. To clarify scope issues: "partly" might qualify the organism – it does something partly to itself and partly to something else. Eating is an obvious case in point, since the organism absorbs the food and maintains its health at the same time. Again, "partly" might qualify the self-perfection: a lactating mammal might eat a certain food partly for its own health and partly to produce the right kind of milk for its offspring.[59] What "partly" cannot qualify is the whole act of doing something to itself for itself: either it does or it does not. Similarly, there are no borderline cases of transient causation: either the effect is distinct from the cause or it is not (modulo much broader questions of onto-logical vagueness that infect most metaphysics). So, by taking imma-nence as the essence of life, borderline cases are eliminated. This helps us to avoid another pitfall involved in defining life simply in terms of its more specific hallmarks like metabolism and homeostasis. For if life were defined by such a list, one could then ask worrying questions about the borderline: viruses replicate but they do not have homeostasis; they do not metabolize, but they do evolve and adapt to their environ-ment in a remarkably plastic way. If it were a numbers game, even a weighted numbers game as in weighted phenetics,[60] there would obvi-ously be borderline cases. The question that should be asked, however, is simply whether the entity in question does anything to itself for its self-perfection. Even if it performs only one such activity, it will count as alive. Since the idea of a single activity, at least in this context, borders on impossibility, since every activity an organism performs has multiple effects of diverse aspects of its life cycle, there will almost certainly always be more than one thing that an organism does immanently, obviating the pseudo-concern of basing a judgment as to whether something is alive on a lone fact. What needs to be distinguished are two classificatory practices that are superficially similar: counting off the members on a list of hallmarks on the one hand, and making a judgment as to whether enough hallmarks are present – even if they are on a canonical list – to enable a confident, if fallible, classification of something as being alive because, and only because, it acts towards itself for its self-perfection. It is this latter criterion which is either met or not met.

## 8   Conclusion

On the present analysis, the existence of life comes out as a brute fact about the universe, relative at least to any abiogenetic naturalistic expla-nation.[61] This will seem less palatable to many than the brute existence of information defended by Davies, but unpalatability in both cases is irrelevant to truth. The question then becomes one of whether life had an origin at all. If the universe is eternal, life also had no temporal beginning. If the universe had a beginning, then life came into existence at that beginning, and since the Big Bang model seems to exclude this, then some other cosmogony is needed. For most theists, at least those who consider God to be a literal creator, both of these possibilities leave room for, and arguably mandate, the existence of an ultimate cause of the universe and all that is in it, life included. If the universe began in time, but life appeared sometime after that origin, but not through abiogenesis, then a theistic explanation looks like the only option. This latter is what most theists have believed throughout history, and I am content to count myself among them. To demonstrate that they have not all been victims of collective delusion, however, is another matter for another time.

# Notes

1. http://www.wired.com/wiredscience/2010/05/scientists-create-first-self-replicating-synthetic-life/ [last accessed 14.5.12].
2. http://www.guardian.co.uk/science/2010/may/20/craig-venter-synthetic-life-form [last accessed 14.5.12]
3. http://www.bbc.co.uk/news/10132762; http://www.dailymail.co.uk/sciencetech/article-1279988/Artificial-life-created-Craig-Venter – wipe-humanity.html [last accessed 14.5.12].
4. http://www.jcvi.org/cms/research/projects/first-self-replicating-synthetic-bacterial-cell/faq#q1 [last accessed 14.5.12]. Venter has repeated the assertion elsewhere: "We've created the first synthetic cell...We definitely have not created life from scratch because we used a recipient cell to boot up the synthetic chromosome" (http://www.newscientist.com/article/dn18942-immaculate-creation-birth-of-the-first-synthetic-cell.html; last accessed 14.5.12).
5. As reported by the BBC and quoted by *The Times of India*: http://articles.timesofindia.indiatimes.com/2010–05–24/science/28301741_1_genome-synthetic-life-j-craig-venter [last accessed 14.5.12].
6. http://www.nature.com/news/2010/100520/full/news.2010.255.html [last accessed 15.5.12].
7. http://blogs.scientificamerican.com/guest-blog/2010/05/20/now-aint-that-special-the-implications-of-creating-the-first-synthetic-bacteria/ [last accessed 15.5.12].
8. http://news.sciencemag.org/sciencenow/2010/05/synthetic-biology-answers.html [last accessed 15.5.12].
9. Ibid.
10. For a lay exposition, see http://www.jcvi.org/cms/press/press-releases/full-text/article/first-self-replicating-synthetic-bacterial-cell-constructed-by-j-craig-venter-institute-researcher/. For the published paper, see Gibson, Glass, et al. (2010).

11. Somewhat ironically, from my point of view, the following from *A Portrait of the Artist as a Young Man*: "To live, to err, to fall, to triumph, to recreate life out of life!"

12. For more on the watermarks, see http://www.arcfn.com/2010/06/using-arc-to-decode-venters-secret-dna.html [last accessed 15.5.12].

13. Is the bacterium with synthetic genome a new species? The JCVI sometimes speaks of the bacterium with genome *M. mycoides* JCVI-syn1.0, and sometimes of the bacterium itself as having this name. In my view, it would be a member of a new species if the altered fragments of DNA showed up as differences in the characteristic behavior and function of the new bacterium. The Venter team state in their paper that three of the four watermarks contained restriction sites – involved in recognition as foreign DNA – that do not occur in the natural bacterium. This indicates an important morphological difference counting in favor of treating the synthesized bacterium as a member of a new species.

14. What Harvey (1578–1657) did imply in his writings, as Oken points out – though Harvey never said it explicitly – is *omne vivum ex ovo*, all life comes from an egg. What Harvey meant by "egg", however, is not altogether clear. Oken (1779–1851), at the end of his book *Die Zeugung* (On Generation, 1805), exclaims boldly: "*Nullum vivum ex ovo! Omne vivum e vivo!*" See further Harris (1995): 3.

15. Well, it is supposed to have originated with Raspail in 1825, according to numerous sources. A strenuous search I conducted of the *Annales des Sciences Naturelles*, where the maxim is supposed to have appeared in one of Raspail's papers, failed to reveal it.

16. For example, prokaryotic microbes living in extreme environments: Brasier, McLoughlin, et al. (2006).

17. For a technical survey, see Herdewijn and Kisakürek (eds.) (2008). For a useful and accessible review of this book, see Kaufmann (2009).

18. The very useful Wikipedia entry on abiogenesis lists and surveys most of the theories, with ample references to the primary sources: http://en.wikipedia.org/wiki/Abiogenesis [last accessed 18.5.12].

19. Cairns-Smith (1985).

20. Farmer and Belin (1992). See also Taylor (1992).

21. I defend essentialism at length, and respond to some well-known anti-essentialism objections, in Oderberg (2007).

22. What the medium of information storage is should be considered irrelevant, at least for our purposes. I doubt there is anything special about DNA as such, and we should expect life's essence, if it does involve information, to allow for possible worlds in which living things use some other medium for information storage (retrieval, copying, processing).

23. Bedau (1996): 338.

24. Mayr (1982): 56–7, where (p.53ff.) he lists a number of other defining characteristics.

25. Strictly, by defining metabolism in this way, I am speaking synecdochically, since I am referring only to anabolism – an organism's intake of material in order to build itself up and maintain its proper functioning. Metabolism also includes catabolism, the breaking down and explusion of matter from the organism into the environment as waste or by-products of its proper functioning. Both

kinds of process are aspects of the same overall activity, which is the organism's employment of environmental material for its own benefit.

26. For completeness, historical descent would have to include the descent of the first organism from some particular inorganic entity (such as a crystal or some other pre-biotic macromolecule). If the first life appeared more than once from distinct inorganic entities, each organism would have its own lineage. Mayr is not saying anything here about whether monogenesis or polygenesis about life is correct, only that members of each class of organism have a common history.

27. These assertions of possibility are qualified, of course: *if* abiogenesis is metaphysically possible, then the sort of scenario I describe is metaphysically possible.

28. Leave aside the theory of David Hull and Michael Ghiselin that populations are themselves individuals: Ghiselin (1974), Hull (1978).

29. Bedau responds to the objection that his definition of life applies primarily to populations by saying that what he is really trying to explain is "the diversity of living phenomena", adding: "Supple adaptation could provide this explanation even though an individual living organism is itself only a small and transitory part of the whole adapting population" (Bedau 1996: 340). Apart from this being a major departure from what he seems initially to set out to achieve, the response is not particularly helpful. Even if the population is the primary living entity, and the organism a transitory member, he still has not explained what it is for that transitory entity to be alive. If he is implying that *all there is* to being alive is being a member of a supply adaptive population, then he is offering yet another objectionably relational essence of living things.

30. For an interesting discussion of the "signs" of life and their relation to life ("vitality") itself, see Lange (1996). Lange argues, using examples from the history of science, that something's being alive can have an explanatory function over and above reference merely to the signs of life. Indeed, being alive might (i) constitute an explanation of why the thing concerned does display some or many of the signs of life, as well as (ii) constitute a unifying account of why all the things that are alive display signs of life; and (iii) enable a principled determination as to whether a purported example of "artificial life", such as a piece of software or a combination of software and hardware, really is alive: does it display the signs of life for the same reason that paradigmatic living things do? Lange's appeal to the methodological value of the concept of life does not presuppose an essentialist account of life, let alone a non-reductive definition, so his position is much weaker than what I defend here. But his account offers considerations that an essentialist could happily take on board.

31. See, for example: Mercier (1916): 169–71; Phillips (1934): 179ff.; Maher (1923): 551. Aquinas speaks of self-movement rather than immanent causation, but he means the same thing: organisms change themselves (*motus* meaning "change" for Aquinas); see *Summa Theologica* I.q18.aa1 and 2 (Aquinas 1911: 246–50). Aristotle tends to use the phrase "moves itself" (*heauto kinei*) in the sense of local movement only: see *Physics* VIII.4, 254b18 (Ross (ed.) 1930). But it is also clear from *De Anima* II.1 and 2 that the essential features of life are for him what Aquinas means by self-movement and what the Scholastics mean by immanent causation.

32. I wish to distinguish between the terms "immanent" and "transient" as used here and as used in Chisholm (2001). There, Chisholm – accepting the deviation from older usage – employs the term "immanent causation" simply for what we now call "agent causation", where the agent is a human or other rational creature, as contrasted with "transeunt [rather than transient] causation" which he uses for event or state of affairs causation. The following is either explicit or implicit in my more traditional use of the terms. (a) Not all immanent (agent) causation in Chisholm's sense is immanent in my sense. If I hit another person to defend myself against attack, I am doing something transient in my sense (making violent contact with another thing) as well as something immanent in my sense (defending myself). I do the latter by doing the former. Although all immanent (in my sense) causation plausibly entails some transient (in my sense) causation, since transient activity subserves immanent activity, not everything an agent (in Chisholm's sense) does is immanent (in my sense). Furthermore, even if "agent" is broadened (as I do) to include non-rational living things, they do things immanently (Chisholm) that they do not do immanently (me): when a bacterium eats something it acts immanently (Chisholm) but acts both immanently and transiently (me), viz. sustaining itself and digesting food material respectively. Nevertheless, all cases of immanent causation (in my sense) will be immanent in Chisholm's sense. (b) Not all transient (in my sense) causation is transeunt causation (in Chisholm's sense), since transient agent causation, whether the agent be Chisholmian or (in my broader sense) any substance living or even non-living, will not be event (or state of affairs) causation since one of the relata will not be an event or state of affairs. Nevertheless, all cases of Chisholm's transeunt causation will be transient in my sense.

33. I use the term "agent" neutrally, i.e. without presupposing anything about the nature of the agent. For present purposes, an agent is any object (as opposed to event) that is the source (even if not the ultimate source) of some causal activity. (Similarly, "terminate" does not entail that the patient is the ultimate terminus of the causal activity. As long as there is a discrete piece of the causal nexus that can reasonably be identified as an agent's acting on a patient, we have causation.)

34. Although I have reserved the term "reflexive" for causal activity that accidentally terminates in the agent, giving certain organic behavior as an example, there is the further question of whether there is any lawlike reflexive causation; if there were, this might be thought to be the important intermediate stage between transient and immanent causation. I cannot examine this question in detail here, and so confine myself to two points. First, there do not seem to be any clear examples of such causation in nature, i.e., leaving aside artifacts such as computers and robots – which require a wholly separate treatment because of their artefactual nature. There are plenty of examples of structures, materials, and particles that maintain stability in the face of forces acting on them; indeed most kinds of inorganic substance tend to some degree of stability in the face of perturbations in the environment. Many inorganic substances have a tendency to resume a given shape or configuration following some disturbance (think elastic, certain crystals, various kinds of steel, and newer materials exploited in engineering for precisely this tendency).

These phenomena do not amount to reflexive causation in the sense of a substance's doing something to itself as opposed to its undergoing certain processes. The difference concerns whether a substance can be correctly described as exerting a force upon itself or manipulating or configuring itself, and this requires some kind of control mechanism. Secondly, even if such a description could be applied to an inorganic substance, so that it was an example of lawlike reflexive causation, the case would be far closer to pure transient causation than to immanent causation. Even terms like "control" and "manipulation" are not really the right way to characterize reflexive causation without immanence, redolent as they are of self-perfective notions. Once we separate "to itself" from "for itself", what is left is a substance whose action upon itself is exactly like its action on some other thing in terms of the processes involved: only the terminus is different (itself rather than another). There is no reason to posit any "addition of being", any radically new kind of causation, in such behavior, and there should be no metaphysical puzzle about how a thing could act on itself in this non-immanent way. Admittedly, we are in highly speculative waters about what such substances could be and how we can explain their behavior. Perhaps, as has been suggested to me by James Barham, quantum field theory has something to say about this kind of behavior in non-living systems. But the behavior is still so far from the self-perfective activity of living things that it cannot be considered a viable halfway house between the transient and the immanent.

35. A question posed by Bedau (2008: 458), who thinks a candle flame has "something like a metabolism", citing in support Maynard Smith (1986). I have not been able to find this phrase in Maynard Smith, nor any suggestion to that effect.

36. Needless to say, claiming that it is for example a burning candle that is alive rather than its flame achieves nothing, since the candle is merely fuel for the fire, not a thing that takes in fuel – a condition of metabolism – itself.

37. Paul Davies is a popular exponent of a view held by many biologists and philosophers of biology: Davies (2003). It has recently been endorsed by McCall (2012).

38. Unless one has a narrow interest in information for information's sake, e.g., its mathematical properties or complexity; but that is irrelevant here.

39. Note that F, G, H...are all variables ranging over things done. I am not building into the abiogenesis idea the claim that the organism does or does not do to itself, immanently, anything of the same kind as parts of it do to each other transiently.

40. Phillips (1934): 325.

41. Strawson (2008): 60–7.

42. For the classic survey, see Eisenberg and Kauzmann (1969).

43. Hence, the mistake of John Searle (1983) in claiming that the liquidity of water is both realized *and caused by* its molecular structure. See Thompson (1986).

44. Compare this to the common objection leveled against neutral monism itself, namely that it is not really neutral as between the essentially mental or physical character of the fundamental stuff, but tends towards idealism or some kind of phenomenalism. See, e.g., Strawson (2010): 97, n.6 contra Russell.

45. The classic proponent of the autocatalytic theory of life's origin is Stuart Kauffman (1993).
46. In fact substance, though I do not intend to hang anything on the fact alone that a new substance comes into existence. What matters is how the substance behaves.
47. Davies (2003): ch.6, locations 2223–2297 of 5959 in the Kindle edition.
48. Ibid.: loc. 2266.
49. Ibid:. loc. 2266.
50. What Meyer (2009) calls Shannon information after the celebrated information theorist C.E. Shannon.
51. Davies (2003): loc. 2279.
52. Meyer (2009): 473, loc. 7920 of 12530 in the Kindle edition.
53. Davies (2003): loc. 991–1004.
54. Ibid.: locs. 1028, 1115.
55. They hold it true of all earthly organisms; I take human beings to be an exception.
56. Broad (1925).
57. Cairns-Smith (1985): 11, loc. 202 of 1711 in the Kindle edition; Dennett (1995):156.
58. McCall (2012): 175, invoking Davies (2003) in support, but I can find no such view in Davies. Indeed, Davies says the exact opposite: "It is a mistake to seek a sharp dividing line between living and non-living systems" (loc. 606–18). McCall also claims that the anti-vagueness position contradicts that of Aristotle, citing *The History of Animals* 588b4–6 where he speaks of nature's proceeding "little by little from things lifeless to animal life in such a way that it is impossible to determine the exact line of demarcation, nor on which side thereof an intermediate form should lie." (*"Outō d'ek tōn apsychōn eis ta zōia metabainei kata mikron hē physis, hōste tēi synexeiai lanthanein to methorion autōn kai to meson poterōn estin."*) Compare also *The Parts of Animals* 681a12–14 where Aristotle speaks in almost identical terms. I do not, however, think one can read off a belief by him in metaphysical vagueness as easily as McCall. In *History* Aristotle uses the epistemic term *"lanthanein"* = "escape notice, be unseen"; in *Parts* he uses the epistemic term *"dokein"*="seem". (See Smith and Ross 1910 for the passage from *History*, and Smith and Ross 1912 for the passage from *Parts*.)
59. Needless to say, one organism's doing something for the perfection of another organism often also, of itself, does something for the former – making it happy or content, helping it to protect itself, and the like.
60. Farris (1966).
61. I have presented this defense of biogenesis as being in the Aristotelian-Thomistic tradition, but it will be objected that both Aristotle and Aquinas themselves believed in abiogenesis. In *Metaphysics* 1032a31, Aristotle says that in nature "the same things sometimes are produced without seed [*sperma*] as well as from seed" (Ross (ed.) 1928). In his *Commentary on Aristotle's Metaphysics*, secs. 1398–1401, Aquinas glosses this by saying that "imperfect animals, which are akin to plants" [*animalia vero imperfecta quae sunt vicina plantis*] can sometimes be generated without seed, e.g. by the action of the sun on a suitably disposed earth [*bene disposita*] (Aquinas 1995: 467). He clarifies this point in the *Summa Theologica* as follows [my paraphrase of a view scattered across several places].

Yes, some living things (including animals) are produced naturally by seed, and others by decay under the influence of the heavenly bodies (as was, pre-Pasteur, the common scientific opinion) and hence without seed. At the origin of life, it was God working on "material elements" [*ex materia elementari*] who produced living things. That some kinds of living thing are now capable of coming into existence without seed is due to the power given to the elements by God, at the origin, of so producing life; the same for living things that do come from seed. (I.q71.a1 ad 1. See also I.q72 ad 5, I.q105.a1 ad 1; Aquinas (1922a): 250–1, 255–6; (1922b): 31.) I think the simplest way of understanding their position is by appreciating that both philosophers, as good empiricists in the true sense of the term, and like every other observer of the world around them for thousands of years, had to confront the apparently obvious fact that some plants and animals (generally the hardest to detect with the naked eye) appeared from earth, water, and decaying matter, without the evident intervention of any prior living thing.

A caricature of Aristotle and Aquinas would have them denying the evidence of their senses and pronouncing the fact impossible given an aprioristic conception of the essence of life, something ripe for a Molière comedy. The caricature of Aquinas would continue by having him, finally prostrate before empirical fact, pronouncing it proof of God's continuing miraculous intervention in the world. Needless to say, neither thinker did anything like this. Aristotle simply took on board what he regarded as a fact, the implication being that he did not see anything special in immanent causation as such to preclude its emergence from the inorganic. Aquinas believes in direct divine intervention at the origin but makes no suggestion that this intervention involved the assembly/miraculous coming together of bits of inorganic material to compose a living thing. Rather, he sees it in terms of the simultaneous corruption of inorganic material and generation of life (I.q72 ad 5), all under divine influence. The continuing occurrence of spontaneous generation he attributes to God's having initially imparted to inorganic matter the power to produce life, a property it continues to possess and to manifest under the right conditions.

For Aquinas, then, a purely naturalistic explanation, whether of the origin of life or of its subsequent emergence from the inorganic on another occasions, is out of the question. We cannot say to what extent his view was shaped by prior religious principles or by purely metaphysical considerations concerning the nature of life. What I think we can say with some confidence (if I may indulge in a little counterfactual speculation) is that, had Aristotle and Aquinas been alive to witness the work of Pasteur and others both before and after him, they would have quickly shed the thought that spontaneous generation was an empirical given. That would have left greater room for purely metaphysical considerations to shape their thinking.

# References

Aquinas, St T. 1995. *Commentary on Aristotle's* Metaphysics, trans. J. P. Rowan (Notre Dame, IN: Dumb Ox Books) [orig. pub. 1961].
—— 1922a. *The 'Summa Theologica' of St Thomas Aquinas*, trans. Fathers of the English Dominican Province, vol. 3 (London: Burns Oates & Washbourne Ltd).

_____ 1922b. *The 'Summa Theologica' of St Thomas Aquinas*, trans. Fathers of the English Dominican Province, vol. 5 (London: Burns Oates & Washbourne Ltd).

_____ 1911. *The 'Summa Theologica' of St Thomas Aquinas*, trans. Fathers of the English Dominican Province, vol. 1 (London: R. and T. Washbourne, Ltd).

Bedau, M. A. 2008. "What is Life," in S. Sarkar and A. Plutynski (eds) *A Companion to the Philosophy of Biology* (Oxford: Blackwell): 455–71.

_____ 1996. "The Nature of Life," in M. Boden (ed.) *The Philosophy of Artificial Life* (Oxford: Oxford University Press), 332–57.

Brasier, M., McLoughlin, N., et al. 2006. "A fresh look at the fossil evidence for early Archaean cellular life," *Philos Trans R Soc Lond B Biol Sci*. 361: 887–902. Available at http://www.ncbi.nlm.nih.gov/pmc/articles/PMC1578727/?tool = pubmed [last accessed 16.5.12].

Broad, C. D. 1925. *The Mind and its Place in Nature* (London: Kegan Paul, Trench, Trubner and Co., Ltd.).

Cairns-Smith, A. G. 1985. *Seven Clues to the Origin of Life* (Cambridge: Cambridge University Press).

Chisholm, R. 2001. "Human Freedom and the Self," in R. Kane (ed.) *Free Will* (Oxford: Blackwell, 2001), 47–58 [orig. pub. 1964].

Davies, P. 2003. *The Origin of Life* (London: Penguin; orig. pub. 1998 as *The Fifth Miracle*).

Dennett, D. 1995. *Darwin's Dangerous Idea* (London: Penguin).

Eisenberg, D. and Kauzmann, W. 1969. *The Structure and Properties of Water* (New York: Oxford University Press; repr. 2005).

Farmer, D. and Belin, A. (1992) "Artificial Life: The Coming Evolution," in C. Langton, C. Taylor, J. D. Farmer, and S. Rasmussen (eds) *Artificial Life II* (Redwood City, CA: Addison-Wesley), 815–40.

Farris, J. S. (1966) "Estimation of conservatism of characters by constancy within biological populations", *Evolution* 20: 587–91.

Ghiselin, M. (1974) "A Radical Solution to the Species Problem," *Systematic Zoology* 23: 536–44.

Gibson, D. G., Glass, J. I., et al. 2010, "Creation of a Bacterial Cell Controlled by a Chemically Synthesized Genome", *Science* 329: 52–6, available at http://www.sciencemag.org/content/329/5987/52.full [last accessed 15.5.12].

Harris, H. 1995, *The Cells of the Body: A History of Somatic Cell Genetics* (Plainview, NY: Cold Spring Harbor Laboratory Press).

Herdewijn, P. and Kisakürek, M. Volkan (eds) 2008. *Origin of Life: Chemical Approach* (Zürich: Wiley-VCH).

Hull, D. 1978. "A Matter of Individuality," *Philosophy of Science* 45: 335–60.

Kauffman, S. 1993. *The Origins of Order: Self-Organization and Selection in Evolution* (New York: Oxford University Press).

Kaufmann, G. B. 2009. Review of Herdewijn, P. and Kisakürek, M. Volkan (eds) (2008), *HYLE – International Journal for Philosophy of Chemistry* 15: 53–6.

Lange, M. 1996. "Life, 'Artificial Life,' and Scientific Explanation," *Philosophy of Science* 63: 225–44.

Maher, M. 1923. *Psychology: Empirical and Rational*, 9th edn. (London: Longmans, Green and Co.).

Maynard Smith, J. 1986. *The Problems of Biology* (Oxford: Oxford University Press).

Mayr, E. 1982. *The Growth of Biological Thought* (Cambridge, MA: Harvard University Press).

McCall, S. 2012. "The Origin of Life and the Definition of Life," in T. E. Tahko (ed.) *Contemporary Aristotelian Metaphysics* (Cambridge: Cambridge University Press), pp. 174–86.

Mercier, D. 1916. *A Manual of Modern Scholastic Philosophy*, vol. 1, ed. and trans. T. L. Parker and S. A. Parker (London: Kegan Paul, Trench, Trubner, and Co. Ltd).

Meyer, S. C. 2009. *Signature in the Cell: DNA and the Evidence for Intelligent Design* (New York: HarperCollins).

Oderberg, D. S. 2007. *Real Essentialism* (London: Routledge).

Phillips, R. P. 1934. *Modern Thomistic Philosophy*, vol. 1 (Westminster, MD: The Newman Bookshop).

Ross, W.D. (ed.) 1930. *The Works of Aristotle*, vol. 2 (Oxford: Clarendon Press).

____ 1928. *The Works of Aristotle*, vol. 8, 2nd edn. (Oxford: Clarendon Press).

Searle, J.R. 1983. *Intentionality* (Cambridge: Cambridge University Press).

Smith, J.A. and Ross, W.D. (eds) 1910. *The Works of Aristotle*, vol. 4 (Oxford: Clarendon Press).

____ 1912. *The Works of Aristotle*, vol. 5 (Oxford: Clarendon Press).

Strawson, G. 2008. "Realistic Monism: Why Physicalism Entails Panpsychism," in his *Real Materialism and Other Essays* (Oxford: Clarendon Press), pp. 53–74 [orig. pub. 2006].

____ 2010. *Mental Reality*, 2nd edn. (Cambridge, MA: MIT Press).

Taylor, C. 1992. "'Fleshing Out' Artificial Life II," in C. Langton, C. Taylor, J. D. Farmer, and S. Rasmussen (eds) *Artificial Life II* (Redwood City, CA: Addison-Wesley), pp. 25–38.

Thompson, D.L. 1986. "Intentionality and Causality in John Searle," *Canadian Journal of Philosophy* 16: 83–97.

# 12
# Motion in Aristotle, Newton, and Einstein

*Edward Feser*

## 1 The purported contradiction

In Book VII of the *Physics*, Aristotle famously maintains that "everything that is in motion must be moved by something."[1] This serves as a crucial premise in his argument for an Unmoved Mover. Aquinas's related First Way of arguing for the existence of God rests on a variation of the premise, to the effect that "whatever is in motion is moved by another."[2] Let us call this the "principle of motion."[3] Newton's First Law states that "every body continues in its state of rest or of uniform motion in a straight line, unless it is compelled to change that state by forces impressed upon it."[4] Call this the "principle of inertia."

It is widely thought that the principle of motion is in conflict with the principle of inertia and that modern physics has therefore put paid to Aristotelian natural theology. The assumption is that Aristotle, followed by Aquinas and other Scholastics, held that an object cannot keep moving unless something is continuously moving it, but that Newton showed that it is simply a law of physics that, once set in motion, an object will remain in motion without any such mover.[5] Hence, Anthony Kenny judges that "it seems that Newton's law wrecks the argument of the First Way" (1969, p. 28).

Common though this view is, it is not only mistaken, but also unfounded. To think otherwise requires reading into each of the principles in question claims they do not make. When we consider what Aristotelian philosophers have actually said about the principle of motion and what modern physicists have actually said about the principle of inertia, we will see that they do not contradict one another. Indeed, when we consider the philosophical issues raised by motion, by the idea of a law of nature, and so forth, we will find that there is a sense in which the principle of inertia *presupposes* the principle of motion.[6]

## 2 Why the conflict is illusory

There are at least five reasons to think that any appearance of conflict between the two principles is illusory:

*1. No formal contradiction*: Suppose that "motion" is being used in the two principles in the same sense. Even given this assumption, there is no *formal* contradiction between them. Newton's law tells us that a body *will* in fact continue its uniform rectilinear motion if it is moving at all, as long as external forces do not prevent this. It does not tell us *why* it will do so. In particular, it does not tell us one way or the other whether there is a "mover" of *some* sort which ensures that an object obeys the First Law, and which is, in that sense, responsible for its motion. As G. H. Joyce writes:

> Newton, indeed, says that a body in motion will continue to move uniformly in a straight line, unless acted upon by external forces. But we need not understand him to deny that the uniform movement itself is due to an agency acting *ab extra*; but merely [to deny] that it is produced by an agency belonging to that category of agents which he denominates "external forces"...forces whose action in each case is of necessity confined to a particular direction and velocity. (1924, p. 100)

Of course, one might ask what sort of "mover" an object obeying the principle of inertia could have if it is not an "external force" of the sort Newton intended to rule out. One might also ask whether such a mover, whatever it might be, really serves any explanatory purpose, and thus whether we ought to bother with it, given Ockham's razor. Those are good questions, and we will return to them. But they are beside the present point, which is that the principle of motion and the principle of inertia do not actually contradict one another, *even if* we assume that they are talking about the same thing when they talk about motion.

*2. Equivocation*: In any event, we should not make that assumption, because they are *not* talking about the same thing, or at least not exactly the same thing. "As usually happens when science appears to contradict philosophy," notes Henry Koren, "there is here an ambiguity of terms" (1962, p. 95). Newton's principle of inertia is concerned solely with *local* motion, change with respect to place or location. When Aristotelians speak of "motion," they mean change of *any* kind. This would include local motion but also includes change with respect to quantity, change with respect to quality, and change from one substance to another.[7] More to the point, for the Aristotelian, all such change involves the actualization of a potency or potential. Hence, what the principle of motion is saying is that *any potency that is being actualized is being actualized by something else (and, in particular, by something that is already actual).*

So understood, the principle of motion is, so the Aristotelian would say, something we can hardly deny. For a potency or potential, being merely potential, can hardly actualize itself or anything else. In any event, the principle is, we see once again, not in formal contradiction with the principle of inertia, because they are not talking about the same thing. When the Newtonian principle states that a body in motion will tend to stay in motion, it is not saying that a potency that is being actualized will tend to continue being actualized. Even if it were suggested that the principle *entails* this claim, the point is that that is not what the principle of inertia itself, as understood in modern physics, is *saying*. Indeed, modern physics has defined itself in part in terms of its eschewal, for purposes of physics, of such metaphysical notions as act and potency and final causality. So, it is not that modern physics has falsified the principle of motion so much as that it simply makes no use of it.

Now, one might ask whether modern physics has not, for that very reason, made the principle of motion otiose and of nothing more than historical interest. We will return to this question as well, but it is also beside the present point, which is that there is no *necessary* conflict between the principle of motion and the principle of inertia.

3. *The "state" of motion*: Having said all that, we must immediately emphasize that there is a sense in which the Newtonian principle implicitly *affirms* at least an aspect of the Aristotelian principle it is usually taken to have displaced. To see how, consider first that modern physics characterizes uniform motion as a "state." Now this has the flavor of paradox. Reginald Garrigou-Lagrange objects:

> Motion, being essentially a change, is the opposite of a state, which implies stability. There is no less change in the transition from one position to another in the course of movement, than in the transition from repose to motion itself; if, therefore, this first change demands another cause, the following changes demand it for the same reason. (1939, p. 273)[8]

Yet, the modern physicist would respond to this objection precisely by collapsing the distinction between repose and motion. As Lee Smolin writes:

Being at rest becomes merely a special case of uniform motion – it is just motion at zero speed.

How can it be that there is no distinction between motion and rest? The key is to realize that whether a body is moving or not has no absolute meaning. Motion is defined only with respect to an observer, who can be moving or not. If you are moving past me at a steady rate, then the cup of coffee I perceive to be at rest on my table is moving with respect to you.

But can't an observer tell whether he is moving or not? To Aristotle, the answer was obviously yes. Galileo and Newton were forced to reply no. If the earth is moving and we do not feel it, then it must be that observers moving at a constant speed do not feel any effect of their motion. Hence we cannot tell whether we are at rest or not, and motion must be defined purely as a relative quantity. (2007, pp. 21–2)

Now, this sort of move raises philosophical questions of its own. As Smolin goes on to note:

This is a powerful strategy that was repeated in later theories. One way to unify things that appear different is to show that the apparent difference is due to the difference in the perspective of the observers. A distinction that was previously considered absolute becomes relative....

Proposals that two apparently very different things are the same often require a lot of explaining. Only sometimes can you get away with explaining the apparent difference as a consequence of different perspectives. Other times, the two things you choose to unify are just different. The need to then explain how things that seem different are really in some way the same can land a theorist in a lot of trouble. (2007, pp. 22–3)[9]

Indeed, I will suggest later on that the attempt to explain away what Aristotelians mean by "motion" by means of such relativizing moves faces limits in principle.

But the point to emphasize for the moment is that, precisely because the principle of inertia treats uniform local motion as a "state," it treats it thereby as the *absence* of change. Moreover, it holds that external forces *are* required to move a thing out of this "state" and thus to bring about a change. One more quote from Smolin:

There is an important caveat here: We are talking about uniform motion – motion in a straight line.... When we change the speed or direction of our motion, we do feel it. Such changes are what we call *acceleration*, and acceleration *can* have an absolute meaning. (2007, p. 22)

But then the Newtonian principle of inertia hardly conflicts with the Aristotelian principle that "motion" – that is, change – requires something to cause the change. The disagreement is at most over whether a particular phenomenon *counts* as a true change or "motion" in the relevant sense, *not* over whether it would require a mover or changer if it *did* so count.

4. *Natural motion:* If Newton is closer to the Aristotelians than is often supposed, so too are the Aristotelians (or at least Aristotle and Aquinas) closer to Newton than is often supposed. As James A. Weisheipl (1985) has shown, the idea that Aristotle and Aquinas held that no object can continue its local motion unless some mover is continuously conjoined to it is something of an urban legend. To be sure, this was the view of Averroes and of some Scholastics, but not of Aristotle himself or of St. Thomas. On the contrary, their view was that a body will of itself tend to move toward its natural place by virtue of its form. That which generates the object and thus imparts its form to it can be said thereby to impart motion to it, but neither this generator nor anything else need remain conjoined to the object as a mover after this generation occurs. Aquinas comments:

> [Aristotle] says, therefore, that what has been said is manifested by the fact that natural bodies are not borne upward and downward as though moved by some external agent.
> By this is to be understood that he rejects an external mover which would move these bodies *per se* after they obtained their specific form. For light things are indeed moved upward, and heavy bodies downward, by the generator inasmuch as it gives them the form upon which such motion follows…. However, some have claimed that after bodies of this kind have received their form, they need to be moved per se by something extrinsic. It is this claim that the Philosopher rejects here.[10]

Even Aquinas's understanding of projectile motion is more complicated than modern readers often suppose:

> An instrument is understood to be moved by the principal agent so long as it retains the power communicated to it by the principal agent; thus the arrow is moved by the archer as long as it retains the force wherewith it was shot by him. Thus in heavy and light things

that which is generated is moved by the generator as long as it retains the form transmitted thereby … And the mover and the thing moved must be together at the commencement of but not throughout the whole movement, as is evident in the case of projectiles.[11]

To be sure, even though that which initiated a projectile's motion need not remain conjoined to it for the motion to continue, Aquinas still thought projectiles required other, conjoined movers, given that a projectile's motion is not motion toward its *natural* place but is rather imposed on it contrary to its natural tendency. But, as Thomas McLaughlin points out, the motions of projectiles require such conjoined movers in Aquinas's view

> because of the *kinds* of motions that they are and *not* because of a general conception of the nature of motion itself. In this respect, projectile … motions resemble accelerated motions in Newtonian physics, for accelerated motions require a force to act on a body throughout the time that it is accelerating. (2004, p. 243. Emphasis added.)

And insofar as *natural* motions require no such conjoined mover, the Aristotelian-Thomistic view sounds to that extent quite Newtonian indeed: "Thus, the Law of Inertia in the sense of absence of forces is similar to Aristotle's concept of natural gravitation, which is very remarkable" (Moreno 1974, p. 323).

Obviously, the Aristotelian notion of an object having some specific place toward which it tends naturally to move is obsolete, as is Aquinas's view that projectile motions require a continuously conjoined mover.[12] There are also questions to be raised about Aquinas's view that the generator of a natural object moves that object instrumentally by virtue of having imparted to it its form. For how can the generator move the object as an instrument if by Aquinas's own admission it is no longer conjoined to it?

We will return to this question. The point for now is just to emphasize yet again that when one examines the principles of motion and inertia more carefully, the assumption that they are *necessarily* in conflict can readily be seen to be unfounded.

5. *Natural science versus philosophy of nature*: That certain key aspects of Aristotelian physics have been falsified is not in dispute. However, as contemporary Aristotelians often complain, the moderns have been too quick to throw the Aristotelian metaphysical baby out with the physical

bathwater. Though Aristotle and pre-modern Aristotelians did not clearly distinguish the metaphysical aspects of their analysis of nature from the physical ones (in the modern sense of "physical"), these aspects *can*, in fact, be clearly distinguished. In particular, questions about what the natural world *must* be like in order for any natural science at all to be possible must be distinguished from questions about what, as a matter of *contingent* fact, are the laws that govern that world. The latter questions are the proper study of physics, chemistry, biology, and the like. The former are the proper study of that branch of metaphysics known as the philosophy of nature.[13] Geocentrism, the ancient theory of the elements, and the notion that objects have specific places to which they naturally move, are examples of Aristotelian ideas in physics that have been decisively superseded. But the theory of act and potency, the doctrine of the four causes, and the hylemorphic analysis of material objects as composites of form and matter are examples of notions that have (so the contemporary Aristotelian argues) abiding value as elements of a sound philosophy of nature.

Now the principle of motion is, the Aristotelian will insist, another thesis whose import is *metaphysical*, a corollary of the distinction between act and potency, which is the foundation of the Aristotelian philosophy of nature. The principle of inertia, by contrast, is a claim of natural science. Since the domains they are addressing are different, there can be no question of any conflict between them, certainly no direct or obvious conflict.

Physics, as that discipline is understood in modern times, abstracts from concrete material reality and describes the natural world exclusively in terms of its mathematical structure. Though philosophers and scientists beholden to scientism suppose that it thereby gives us an exhaustive picture of reality, in fact what it gives us is very nearly the opposite. As Bertrand Russell once wrote:

> It is not always realized how exceedingly abstract is the information that theoretical physics has to give. It lays down certain fundamental equations which enable it to deal with the logical structure of events, while leaving it completely unknown what is the intrinsic character of the events that have the structure. We only know the intrinsic character of events when they happen to us. Nothing whatever in theoretical physics enables us to say anything about the intrinsic character of events elsewhere. They may be just like the events that happen to us, or they may be totally different in strictly unimaginable ways. All that physics gives us is certain equations

giving abstract properties of their changes. But as to what it is that changes, and what it changes from and to—as to this, physics is silent. (1985, p. 13)

Newton's laws of motion reflect this tendency, insofar as they provide a mathematical description of motion suitable for predictive purposes without bothering about the origins of motion or the intrinsic nature of that which moves. Indeed, that is arguably the whole point of the principle of inertia. As Weisheipl writes:

> Rather than proving the principle, the mechanical and mathematical science of nature *assumes* it ... [and] the mathematical sciences must assume it, if they are to remain mathematical ....
>
> The basis for the principle of inertia lies ... in the nature of mathematical abstraction. The mathematician must equate: a single quantity is of no use to him. In order to equate quantities he must assume the basic irrelevance or nullity of other factors, otherwise there can be no certainty in his equation. The factors which the mathematician considers irrelevant are ... motion, rest, constancy, and unaltered directivity; it is only the *change* of these factors which has quantitative value. Thus for the physicist it is not motion and its continuation which need to be explained but change and cessation of motion – for only these have equational value ....
>
> In the early part of the seventeenth century physicists tried to find a physical cause to explain the movement [of the heavenly bodies]; Newton merely disregarded the question and looked for two quantities which could be equated. In Newtonian physics there is no question of a cause, but only of differential equations which are consistent and useful in describing phenomena ....
>
> [T]he nature of mathematical abstraction ... must leave out of consideration the qualitative and causal content of nature. ... [S]ince mathematical physics abstracts from all these factors, it can say nothing about them; it can neither affirm nor deny their reality .... (1985, pp. 42 and 47–8)[14]

The philosophy of nature, however, and in particular the principle of motion and the other components of the Aristotelian metaphysical apparatus, are concerned precisely to give an account of the intrinsic nature of material phenomena and their causes, of which modern physics gives us only the abstract mathematical structure.

### 3   Is inertia real?

Now, some Aristotelians have gone so far as to insinuate that the principle of inertia really has only an instrumental import, with the Aristotelian philosophy of nature alone providing a description of the reality of motion. Hence, Joyce writes that "the mathematician may for practical purposes regard motion as a *state*. Philosophically the concepts of movement and of a state are mutually exclusive" (1924, p. 95). And Garrigou-Lagrange claims: "[T]hat the motion once imparted to a body continues indefinitely, is a *convenient* fiction for *representing* certain mathematical or mechanical relations of the astronomical order" (1939, p. 275, note 24; emphasis in the original).

Certainly, a realist construal of inertia is at least open to challenge, not least because the principle is not directly susceptible of experimental test. As William Wallace writes:

> It is never found in ordinary experience that a body in uniform motion continues in such motion indefinitely. All the bodies met with in ordinary experience encounter resistive forces in their travel, and sooner or later come to rest. Nor does refined experimentation and research supply any instances where such resistive forces are absent. (1956, p. 178)

And as N.R. Hanson emphasizes, the problem is not merely that we *have* not observed bodies that are force-free and thus operate in accordance with the principle of inertia, but that we *could* not observe them, given Newton's own Law of Universal Gravitation. The law of inertia thus "refers to entities which are unobservable as a matter of physical principle" (Hanson 1963, p. 112; cf. Hanson 1965a).

To be sure (and as Wallace and Hanson acknowledge), the principle can be argued for by extrapolating from observational data to the limiting case, and Galileo and Newton argued in precisely that way. But no such argument can provide a true demonstration. Wallace's remarks are worth quoting at length:

> The observational data are certainly true, but the only way in which it may be maintained that the limiting case is also true would be by maintaining that what is verified in the approach to a limit is also verified at the limit itself. The latter statement, however, cannot be maintained, because it is not universally true. There are many instances in mathematics where it is known to be violated. One illustration is

the approach of polygon to circle as the number of sides is increased indefinitely. All through the approach to the limit, assuming the simple case where all figures are inscribed in the limiting circle, every figure constructed that has a finite number of sides is a polygon. The limiting case is a figure of a different species, it is no longer a polygon, but a circle. It is not true to say that a polygon is a circle; the difference is as basic and irreducible as that between the discrete and the continuous. In this case, what is verified in the approach to the limit (polygon), is not verified at the limit itself (circle).

Now if it is not *always* true that what is verified during the approach is necessarily verified at the limit...then the fact that the observational base for the principle of inertia is true cannot be used to prove, or demonstrate, that the limiting case stated in the principle is also true. (1956, pp. 179–80)[15]

Nor need one be an Aristotelian to wonder about the epistemic credentials of Newton's principle. Einstein wrote:

The weakness of the principle of inertia lies in this, that it involves an argument in a circle: a mass moves without acceleration if it is sufficiently far from other bodies; we know that it is sufficiently far from other bodies only by the fact that it moves without acceleration. (1988, p. 58)

Eddington is even more pithy, and sarcastic to boot: "Every body continues in its state of rest or uniform motion in a straight line, except in so far as it doesn't" (1963, p. 124). Isaac Asimov makes the same point and at least insinuates an instrumentalist conclusion:

The Newtonian principle of inertia...holds exactly only in an imaginary ideal world in which no interfering forces exist: no friction, no air resistance....

It would therefore seem that the principle of inertia depends upon a circular argument. We begin by stating that a body will behave in a certain way unless a force is acting on it. Then, whenever it turns out that a body does not behave in that way, we invent a force to account for it.

Such circular argumentation would be bad indeed if we set about trying to prove Newton's first law, but we do not do this. Newton's laws of motion represent assumptions and definitions and are not subject to proof....The principle of inertia has proved extremely useful in the study of physics for nearly three centuries now and has involved physicists in no contradictions. For this reason (and not out of any considerations of "truth") physicists hold on to the laws of motion and will continue to do so. (1993, pp. 25–6)[16]

Yet, while the difficulty of proving the principle of inertia should certainly give further pause to anyone who claims that modern physics has refuted the Aristotelian principle of motion, that difficulty hardly *forces* a non-realist interpretation on us. Still, it might seem that the Aristotelian's commitment to natural teleology, and in particular to the idea that a potency or potential is always a potential *for* some definite actuality or range of actualities, would require a non-realist construal of inertia. Andrew van Melsen writes:

> If the law of inertia, that a local motion never stops of its own account, is true, then the conclusion seems obvious that a motion does not have an "end" in the Aristotelian sense of this term. ... [I]t seems that the analysis of motion in terms of potency and act assumes the existence of a definite end of each motion as the natural achievement or perfection of that motion. ... [But in] such [inertial] motions there seem to be eternal potency but no act. (1954, p. 174)

And as van Melsen indicates, this might lead some Aristotelians to argue that

> such motions as the law of inertia describes do not exist. The law of inertia is not supposed to speak of real motions, for it assumes the absence of physical forces, which, as a matter of fact, are never absent in reality. Since Aristotle's analysis deals with real motions, the difficulty [of reconciling Aristotle with Newton] does not exist. (Ibid.)

But van Melsen immediately goes on to reject such a non-realist interpretation of inertia, as have other Aristotelians. In van Melsen's view, it is an error to assume in the first place that the Aristotelian's commitment to teleology must lead him to conclude that what moves must come to rest:

> Aristotle himself ... would have referred to the eternal circular movement of heavenly bodies as an instance of ceaseless motion. So it must be possible to apply analysis in terms of potency and act to motions which are endless ...

There may be…no *final* act which gives the motion its unity, but such a final act is not necessary for motion to possess unity. The process of gradual actualization in a definite direction is sufficient. (1954, p. 175)[17]

To be sure, there are other questions that an Aristotelian might raise about the idea of ceaseless motion, as we shall see presently. But in any event, an alternative position is suggested by John Keck, who, while like van Melsen affirming a realist interpretation of inertia, also argues that all natural motion does, in fact, tend toward a definite state of rest, namely the unity of the thing moving with the larger material world. (2011; cf. Keck 2007). That there is no conflict between these claims can, in his view, be seen when we recognize that inertia is a *passive* and *incomplete* aspect of an object's motion, which cannot by itself account for the object's actual determinate movement but needs completion by an external agent. (Compare the Aristotelian conception of matter as something which, though a real constituent of things, is essentially passive and incomplete until actualized by form.)

So, an Aristotelian need not deny the reality of inertia, and I think most Aristotelians would not. A mathematical description of nature is not an exhaustive description, but it can capture real features of the world. And that the principle of inertia has been especially fruitful in physics is reason to think that that it does capture them. As Thomas McLaughlin writes:

Because inertia is common to so many different kinds of bodies, the proper principles of many different natures can be neglected for various purposes and nature can be analyzed at a minimal level. That a given inertial body is a pumpkin is irrelevant for some purposes, and this is not only a consequence of the mathematization of nature. Inertia is undoubtedly a thin treatment of nature, but that is not the same as treating a body as if it had no nature nor need it exclude a fuller treatment of a body's nature. Failure to recognize this point may mislead a thinker into maintaining that the principle of inertia denies inherent principles of nature. (2008, p. 259)

In short, just as acceptance of the Newtonian principle of inertia does not entail rejection of the Aristotelian principle of motion, neither need the Aristotelian take an instrumentalist or otherwise anti-realist approach to the Newtonian principle. They can be regarded as describing nature at different but equally real levels.[18]

## 4   How the principles are in fact related

But what, specifically, does this claim amount to? If the principle of motion and the principle of inertia are not at odds, how exactly are they related?

Whatever else we say in answer to these questions, the Aristotelian will insist that real change of any sort is possible only if the things that change are composites of act and potency. And since no potency can actualize itself, whatever changes is changed by another. In this way, the principle of motion, as a basic thesis of the philosophy of nature, is necessarily more fundamental than the principle of inertia – at least if we allow that the latter principle does, indeed, apply to a world of real change. (More on this caveat presently.) Determining how the principle of motion and the principle of inertia are related, then, has less to do with how we interpret the former principle than with how we interpret the latter. And here there are several possibilities:

*1. Inertial motion as change*: We have noted that writers like Garrigou-Lagrange object to the idea that inertial motion is a kind of "state." Suppose, then, that we were to take that to be merely a loose way of speaking and regard inertial motion as involving real change, the actualization of potency. As van Melsen describes it:

> The moving body goes continuously from one place to another, say from A towards B, from B towards C, etc. If this body is actually in place A, then it is *not* in place B, but is moving towards B. Therefore, there is a definite potency of being at B. The arrival at B means the actualization of that potency…However, the arrival at B includes the potency of going on to C, etc. In other words, each moment of the motion has a definite tendency towards some further actualization, and it is this which gives the motion its unity. (1954, p. 175)

The question, then, is what actualizes these potencies. Now, the very point of the principle of inertia is to deny that the continued uniform rectilinear local motion of an object requires a continuously operative external force of the sort that first accelerated the object; so, such forces cannot be what actualize the potencies in question. But could we say that the force that first accelerated the object is itself what actualizes these potencies? For example, suppose a thrown baseball were not acted upon by gravitational or other forces and thus were to continue its uniform rectilinear motion indefinitely, with the actualization of its potency for being at place B, followed by the actualization of its potency for being at place C, followed by the actualization of its potency for being at place D, and so on *ad infinitum*. Could we say that the thrower of the baseball is, in effect, himself the actualizer of all of these potencies?

It might seem that Aquinas could sympathize with such a view, since, as we have seen, he regarded the motion of an object to its natural place as having been caused by whatever generated the object. The notion of a natural place is obsolete, but if we substitute for it the notion of *inertial* motion as what is natural to an object, then – again, so it might seem – we could simply reformulate Aquinas's basic idea in terms of inertia. That is, we could say that the inertial motion of an object, which involves an infinite series of actualized potencies with respect to location, is caused by whatever force first accelerated the object (or, to preserve a greater parallelism with Aquinas's view, perhaps by whatever generated the object *together with* whatever accelerated it).

But there is a potential problem with this proposal. Natural motions, as Aquinas understood them, are finite; they end when an object reaches its natural place. Inertial motion is not finite. And while there is no essential difficulty in the notion of a finite cause imparting a finite motion to an object, there does seem to be something fishy about the idea of a finite cause (such as the thrower of a baseball) imparting an *infinite* motion to an object.[19] Furthermore, as noted above, Aquinas also regarded the motion of an object toward its natural place as being caused *instrumentally* by the generator of the object, even though the generator does not remain conjoined to the object. And this seems problematic even when modified in light of the principle of inertia. For how could the inertial motion of the baseball in our example be regarded as caused *instrumentally* by the thrower of the baseball, especially if the ball's motion continues long after the thrower is dead?[20]

So, it is difficult to see how inertial motion, when interpreted as involving real change, could have a *physical* cause. But as we implied above, even if it lacks a physical cause, there is nothing in the principle of inertia that rules out a *metaphysical* cause. Indeed, if inertial motion involves real change, then given the principle of motion together with the absence of a physical cause, such a metaphysical cause is necessary.

Of course, that raises the question of what exactly this metaphysical cause is. One suggestion would be that it is something *internal* to the object – an "impetus" imparted to it by whatever initiated its inertial motion, and which continuously actualizes its potencies with respect to spatial location.[21] But, as Joyce notes, there are serious problems with the impetus theory (1924, pp. 98–9). For one thing, a finite object (such as the baseball of our example) can only have finite qualities. And yet, an impetus, in order to have local motion *ad infinitum* as its effect, would at least in that respect be an infinite quality. In other respects, it would be finite (it would, for example, be limited in its efficacy to the object of which it is a quality), but that leads us to a second problem. For an impetus would continually be bringing about new effects and thus (as a finite cause) itself be undergoing change; and in that case, we have only pushed the problem back a stage, for we now need to ask what causes these changes in the impetus itself.

*If* inertial motion involves real change, then, only a metaphysical cause *external* to the moving object could be the ultimate source. Now, we already have a model for such a cause in the Aristotelian tradition. For the motions of celestial bodies were in that tradition regarded as unending, just as inertial motion is (barring interference from outside forces) unending; and while this view was associated with a mistaken astronomy, a metaphysical kernel can arguably be extracted from the obsolete scientific husk. The causes of celestial motion in this earlier Aristotelian tradition were, of course, intelligent or angelic substances. Such substances are regarded as *necessary* beings of a sort, even if their necessity is ultimately derived from God.[22] What makes them necessary is that they have no natural tendency toward corruption the way material things do (even if God could annihilate them if He so willed). Given this necessity, such substances have an unending existence proportioned to the unending character of the celestial motions they were taken to explain. And while it turns out that celestial objects do not, as such, move in an unending way, *inertial* motion (including that of celestial bodies, but that of all other objects as well) *is* unending. Hence, the only possible cause of inertial motion – again, at least *if* it is considered to involve real change – might seem to be a necessarily existing intelligent substance or substances, of the sort the earlier Aristotelian tradition thought moved celestial objects. (Unless it is simply God Himself causing it *directly* as Unmoved Mover.)[23]

*2. Inertial motion as stasis*: Needless to say, that would seem for most contemporary readers a pretty exotic metaphysics. But alternatively, of course, we could take seriously the idea that inertial motion is a state, involving no real change and thus no actualization of potency. In this case, the question of how the principle of motion and the principle of inertia relate to one another does not even arise, for there just *is* no motion (in the relevant, Aristotelian sense) going on in the first place when all an object is doing is "moving" inertially in the Newtonian sense. To be sure, *acceleration* would in this case involve motion in the Aristotelian sense, but as we have seen, since Newtonian physics itself requires a cause for accelerated motion, there is not even a prima facie conflict with the Aristotelian principle of motion.

Now some defenders of the Aristotelian argument from motion for the existence of God as Unmoved Mover of the world have suggested that precisely for this reason, the principle of inertia really poses no challenge at all to that argument. As long as the Newtonian admits that acceleration involves real change, that will suffice for an argument which, given the principle of motion, leads inexorably to an Unmoved Mover. The other three kinds of change (qualitative, quantitative, and substantial) will also serve well enough for the argument. Newton will have eliminated real change in one area (inertial motion) but not in the others.

But things are a bit more complicated than that. For the tendency of the mechanical picture of the world, of which Newtonian physics is a chief component, has been to try to reduce the other kinds of change to local motion. Qualitative, quantitative, and substantial changes are all, on this view, "really" just a matter of (say) the local motions of basic particles, and any appearance to the contrary is just that – mere appearance, a feature of our subjective, conscious representation of the external world but not of that world as it exists objectively, apart from us. Local motion, in turn, is on this picture then taken to be eternal and thus in no need of any explanation in terms of a first mover – or at least it is so taken by the atheistic successors of Newton (who did not himself go in this atheistic direction)[24].

The details of this kind of story have gotten increasingly complicated since the Greek atomists first introduced it, but the basic idea is clear enough. Yet, the story is insufficient to eliminate *all* possible starting points for an Aristotelian argument from motion to an Unmoved Mover, as long as local motion is admitted in *some* respect or other to involve real change. As serious students of the argument know, what matters in reasoning to an Unmoved Mover is not whether motion had a beginning in time, but what *keeps motion going* (even if it has been going on perpetually).[25] But that brings us at last to another view of motion, inertial and otherwise, associated with modern science.

3. *The world as stasis*: To some, bothering with the question of how the Aristotelian principle of motion relates to the Newtonian principle of inertia might seem quaint. For it might be thought that the controversy

has, for the Newtonian no less than for the Aristotelian, been made moot by Einstein, or at least the construction Hermann Minkowski famously put on relativity theory. As Michael Lockwood sums up a common view:

> To take the space-time view seriously is indeed to regard everything that ever exists, or ever happens, at any time or place, as being just as real as the contents of the here and now. And this rules out any conception of free will that pictures human agents, through their choices, as selectively conferring actuality on what are initially only potentialities. Contrary to this common-sense conception, the world according to Minkowski is, at all times and places, actuality through and through: a four-dimensional *block universe*. (2005, pp. 68–9)

Leave aside the question of free will, with which we are not concerned here. What is relevant is Lockwood's point that on the Minkowskian interpretation of relativity, there is in the natural order no real actualization of potency or potentiality; everything in the world, whether "past," "present," or "future," is all "already" actual, as it were. Thus, there is no genuine *change* in the world – not even the sort Newtonian physics would allow occurs with the acceleration of an object. As Hermann Weyl put it:

> The objective world simply *is*, it does not *happen*. Only to the gaze of my consciousness... does a section of this world come to life as a fleeting image in space which continuously changes in time. (1949, p. 116)

Thus, as Karl Popper (1998) noted, does Einstein recapitulate Parmenides.

Now, I do not myself believe for a moment that modern physics really *has* shown that there is no genuine change in the physical world. But supposing for the sake of argument that it has, even that would not show that the Aristotelian principle of motion has no application, for two reasons. First, what we have in this case is another instance of the strategy we saw Smolin describe earlier, wherein science attempts to unify phenomena by relativizing the apparent differences between them to the observer. But the observer himself – the "the gaze of [his] consciousness," as Weyl would put it – remains. And as Popper pointed out, there is no getting around the fact that change really occurs *at least within consciousness itself.* Nor could we appeal to the Minkowskian view to justify an eliminativist line on consciousness, since it is conscious experience which provides the empirical evidential basis of the theory in whose name we would be denying it![26]

Hence, if Einstein is Parmenides *redevivus*, his position faces the same incoherence the Eleatic philosopher's did, at least *if* the Minkowskian interpretation is correct and *if* we want to say that the conscious subject is a *part* of a natural world that is purportedly free of change. Alternatively, we could adopt a dualist view according to which the conscious subject is *not* a part of that world. That will save the Minkowskian view from incoherence, but at the cost of merely relocating change rather than eliminating it. (And also, of course, at the cost of leaving us with the problem of explaining how the conscious subject *is* related to the natural world if it is not part of it.)

A second point is that, unlike Parmenides' own block universe, the block universe of Minkowski is supposed to be governed by laws that are *contingent*.[27] And if they are contingent, then, the Aristotelian will argue, they are merely potential until actualized. That means that even if there were no real change or actualization of potency *within* an Einsteinian four-dimensional block universe, the sheer existence of that universe as a whole *would* involve the actualization of potency and thus (given the principle of motion) an actualizer or "mover" distinct from the world itself.

## 5 The mythology of inertia

It seems, then, that we simply cannot avoid the existence of change, and thus the actualization of potency, and thus the principle of motion. The most we can do is move them around like the pea in a shell game, producing thereby the *illusion* that we have eliminated them. The notion that they have been largely or completely abolished by modern physics is therefore a myth – part of what we might call "the mythology of inertia," to borrow a phrase from David Braine (1988, p. 14).[28]

That the world is inherently "inert" or changeless is only part of the myth, however. The other part of the myth is the idea that "physical laws," such as the law of inertia, suffice all by themselves to explain what philosophers traditionally took to be in need of a *metaphysical* explanation. Braine cites some remarks from Wittgenstein in the *Tractatus*:

> The whole modern conception of the world is founded on the illusion that the so-called laws of nature are the explanations of natural phenomena.
>
> Thus people today stop at the laws of nature, treating them as something inviolable, just as God and Fate were treated in past ages. (Wittgenstein 1961, sec. 6.371 and 6.372)

The supposition that "the so-called laws of nature are the explanations of natural phenomena" is, for the Aristotelian, an "illusion" for two reasons (which do not necessarily correspond to Wittgenstein's reasons). First, "laws of nature" are mere abstractions and thus cannot by themselves explain anything. What exist in the natural order are concrete material substances with certain essences, and talk of "laws of nature" is merely shorthand for the patterns of behavior they tend to exhibit given those essences. As David Oderberg puts it, *"the laws of nature are the laws of natures,"* i.e., of the natures or essences of the things that behave in accordance with the laws (2007, p. 144).[29] This is as true of the law of inertia as it is of any other law.[30]

Second, that some fundamental material substances (basic particles, say) exist and behave in accordance with such laws can also never be the ultimate explanation of anything, because we need to know not only how such substances came into existence but also what keeps them in existence. For as compounds of act and potency, they cannot possibly account for themselves, but require something outside them to actualize them at every moment. Or so the Thomist will argue.[31]

So, neither the Newtonian principle of inertia, nor the existence of material substances which behave in accordance with that principle, nor the Minkowskian interpretation of Einstein either undermine the Aristotelian principle of motion or obviate the need to explain the existence and operation of material substances in accordance with the latter principle. Physics provides genuine explanations, but not complete or ultimate explanations. Only metaphysics can do that.[32]

## Notes

1. *Physics* 241b34, as translated by R. P. Hardie and R. K. Gaye in Aristotle (1930).
2. *Summa Theologiae* I.2.3, as rendered by the Fathers of the English Dominican Province in their original 1911 edition of the *Summa Theologica*. The revised 1920 edition instead reads, "whatever is in motion is put in motion by another." The change was no doubt motivated by considerations about inertia of the sort we will be discussing.
3. Here, I follow Wippel (2000, p. 453). The premise is labeled the "motor causality principle" by Wallace (1983). It is called the "mover causality principle" by McLaughlin (2004).
4. This is a common rendering of Newton's statement in Latin of his First Law in *Philosophiae Naturalis Principia Mathematica* (London, 1687).
5. DeWitt (2004) contrasts Newton's principle of inertia with what he calls the "Pre-1600s Principle of Motion," according to which "an object in motion will come to a halt, unless something keeps it moving" (p. 109).

6. For a useful survey of some earlier treatments of the relationship between Aristotle's principle and Newton's, see Augros (2007, pp. 68–78).

7. To be sure, there is in Aristotle and Aquinas a narrow sense of "motion" in which substantial change does not count as motion, though there is also a broader sense in which it does. For discussion of these senses and of whether substantial change is included in the scope of what Aquinas's First Way is meant to explain, see Wippel (2000, pp. 445–7).

8. Cf. Joyce (1924, p. 95).

9. For an illuminating discussion of the explanatory strategy in question and its application to motion, see Simon (2001), chapters II and III.

10. *Sententia de caelo et mundo* I.175, as translated in Aquinas (1964).

11. *Quaestiones disputatae de potentia Dei* 3.11 ad 5, as translated in Aquinas (1952).

12. Though modern writers should not be too quick to ridicule the latter notion. As Ashley (2006) comments: "Aristotle...suppos[ed] that when the ball is struck some force is communicated to the medium through which it moves, which then keeps it moving after it has left the bat that put it in motion. This seems to us absurd, but we should recall that today science still relies on the notion of 'field,' that is, a medium, to explain the motion of bodies through that field" (p. 99). Cf. Sachs (1995, p. 230).

13. The term "philosophy of nature" is perhaps not widely used these days outside the circles of Thomists and other modern Scholastics. But that it is not completely unknown to contemporary analytic philosophers, or at least to those with neo-Aristotelian sympathies, is indicated by the title of Ellis (2002).

14. Cf. Wallace (1956, pp. 163–4).

15. Cf. Weisheipl (1985, pp. 36–7).

16. Cf. Ellis (1965) and Hanson (1965b).

17. While Aquinas thought the ceaseless motion of the heavenly bodies was due to something external to them, other medieval philosophers regarded it as the result of a natural inclination. See Weisheipl (1985, pp. 43–4).

18. For a debate over realism about inertia and related matters conducted from a non-Aristotelian point of view, see Earman and Friedman (1973) and the response in Sklar (1985).

19. Cf. Garrigou-Lagrange (1939, p. 274).

20. Cf. Joyce (1924, p. 98): "What is no longer existing cannot be actually operative."

21. The impetus theory is associated historically with Buridan. Garrigou-Lagrange is one recent advocate.

22. For the reasons why, see Aquinas's Third Way, which I discuss and defend at pp. 90–9 of Feser (2009).

23. Cf. Wallace (1956, p. 184). Though it might be objected that to regard God as the immediate cause of inertial motion goes too far in the direction of occasionalism.

24. Indeed, Newton did not so much reject the argument from motion to the existence of God as transform it in light of his new conception of motion. For a comparison of Aristotelian, Newtonian, and other conceptions of the relationship between motion and God, see Buckley (1971).

25. I discuss and defend the argument from motion for God's existence at pp. 65–81 of Feser (2009).

26. As Erwin Schrödinger emphasized, there is a paradoxical tendency in modern science in general to leave out of its picture of the world the very sense perceptions that led to that picture. See Schrödinger (1956) and chapter 6 of Schrödinger (1992). This removal of sensory qualities from the material world and relocation of them into the mind – which was a key part of the anti-Aristotelian revolution inaugurated by Galileo, Descartes, Newton, and Co. – is the origin of the "qualia problem" that has so bedeviled contemporary materialists, who generally seem unaware that the problem derives, not from some irrational urge to resist materialist reductionism and the advances of science, but rather from the very conception of matter and of scientific method to which they are committed.
27. But see the qualification in note 29.
28. Alfred North Whitehead attributes to the principle of inertia a quasi-religious status, characterizing it as "the first article of the creed of science; and like the Church's creeds it is more than a mere statement of belief: it is a paean of triumph over defeated heretics. It should be set to music and chanted in the halls of Universities" (1948, p. 171).
29. For this reason, laws of nature are, as Oderberg explains, *not* contingent – they describe the ways things *necessarily* behave or at least tend to behave, given their natures – but they can be said to be contingent in a loose sense insofar as the *existence* of the things that behave in accordance with the laws is contingent.
30. See McLaughlin (2008) for a useful analysis of the law of inertia as a description of how material bodies will tend to behave, given their natures, in the Aristotelian sense of "natures."
31. For a defense of this claim, and of the further claim that what actualizes them can only be God, see Feser (2011).
32. For comments on an earlier version of this paper, I thank Michael Rota and audience members at the Society for Medieval Logic and Metaphysics session at the 2011 American Catholic Philosophical Association meeting in St. Louis, Missouri.

# References

Aristotle. 1930. *Physics*, trans. R. P. Hardie and R. K. Gaye. (Oxford: Clarendon Press).

Aquinas, Thomas. 1952. *On the Power of God*, trans. English Dominican Fathers (Westminster, MD: The Newman Press).

—— 1964. *Exposition of Aristotle's Treatise On the Heavens*, trans. Fabian R. Larcher and Pierre H. Conway (Columbus: College of St. Mary of the Springs).

Ashley, Benedict. 2006. *The Way toward Wisdom* (Notre Dame, IN: University of Notre Dame Press).

Asimov, Isaac. 1993. *Understanding Physics: 3 Volumes in 1* (New York: Barnes and Noble Books).

Augros, Michael. 2007. "Ten Objections to the *Prima Via*," *Peripatetikos* 6: 59–101.

Braine, David. 1988. *The Reality of Time and the Existence of God* (Oxford: Clarendon Press).

Buckley,   Michael J. 1971. *Motion and Motion's God* (Princeton: Princeton University Press).

DeWitt, Richard. 2004. *Worldviews: An Introduction to the History and Philosophy of Science* (Oxford: Blackwell).

Earman, J. and M. Friedman. 1973. "The Meaning and Status of Newton's Law of Inertia and the Nature of Gravitational Forces," *Philosophy of Science* 40: 329–59.

Eddington, Arthur. 1963. *The Nature of the Physical World* (Ann Arbor: The University of Michigan Press).

Einstein, Albert. 1988. *The Meaning of Relativity*, Fifth edition (Princeton, NJ: Princeton University Press).

Ellis, Brian. 1965. "The Origin and Nature of Newton's Laws of Motion." In Robert G. Colodny, (ed.) *Beyond the Edge of Certainty: Essays in Contemporary Science and Philosophy* (Englewood Cliffs, NJ: Prentice-Hall).

____ 2002. *The Philosophy of Nature: A Guide to the New Essentialism* (Chesham: Acumen).

Feser, Edward. 2009. *Aquinas* (Oxford: Oneworld Publications).

____ 2011. "Existential Inertia and the Five Ways," *American Catholic Philosophical Quarterly*, Vol. 85, No. 2.

Garrigou-Lagrange, Reginald. 1939. *God: His Existence and His Nature*, Volume I (London: B. Herder).

Hanson, Norwood Russell. 1963. "The Law of Inertia: A Philosophers' Touchstone," *Philosophy of Science* 30: 107–21.

____ 1965a. "Newton's First Law: A Philosopher's Door into Natural Philosophy," in Robert G. Colodny, (ed.) *Beyond the Edge of Certainty: Essays in Contemporary Science and Philosophy* (Englewood Cliffs, NJ: Prentice-Hall).

____ 1965b. "A Response to Ellis's Conception of Newton's First Law," in Robert G. Colodny, (ed.) *Beyond the Edge of Certainty: Essays in Contemporary Science and Philosophy* (Englewood Cliffs, NJ: Prentice-Hall).

Joyce, George Hayward. 1924. *Principles of Natural Theology*, Second edition (London: Longmans, Green and Co.).

Keck, John W. 2007. "The Natural Motion of Matter in Newtonian and Post-Newtonian Physics," *The Thomist* 71: 529–54.

____ 2011. "The Messiness of Matter and the Problem of Inertia." Paper presented at the Society for Aristotelian Studies Meeting, June 17, 2011, Santa Paula, California.

Kenny, Anthony. 1969. *The Five Ways: St. Thomas Aquinas' Proofs of God's Existence* (London: Routledge and Kegan Paul).

Koren, Henry J. 1962. *An Introduction to the Philosophy of Nature* (Pittsburgh: Duquesne University Press).

Lockwood, Michael. 2005. *The Labyrinth of Time* (Oxford: Oxford University Press).

McLaughlin, Thomas. 2004. "Local Motion and the Principle of Inertia: Aquinas, Newtonian Physics, and Relativity," *International Philosophical Quarterly*, Vol. 44, No. 1.

McLaughlin, Thomas J. 2008. "Nature and Inertia," *Review of Metaphysics*, Vol. 62, No. 2.

Moreno, Antonio. 1974. "The Law of Inertia and the Principle '*Quidquid movetur ab alio movetur*,'" *The Thomist*, Vol. 38.

Oderberg, David S. 2007. *Real Essentialism* (London: Routledge).

Popper, Karl. 1998. "Beyond the Search for Invariants," in Karl Popper, *The World of Parmenides* (London: Routledge).

Russell, Bertrand. 1985. *My Philosophical Development* (London: Unwin Paperbacks).

Sachs, Joe. 1995. *Aristotle's* Physics: *A Guided Study* (New Brunswick: Rutgers University Press).

Schrödinger, Erwin. 1956. "On the Peculiarity of the Scientific World-View." In Erwin Schrödinger, *What is Life? and Other Scientific Essays* (New York: Doubleday).

—— 1992. "Mind and Matter," in Erwin Schrödinger, *What is Life? with Mind and Matter and Autobiographical Sketches* (Cambridge: Cambridge University Press).

Simon, Yves R. 2001. *The Great Dialogue of Nature and Space* (South Bend, Indiana: St. Augustine's Press).

Sklar, Lawrence. 1985. "Inertia, Gravitation, and Metaphysics," in Lawrence Sklar, *Philosophy and Spacetime Physics* (Berkeley and Los Angeles: University of California Press).

Smolin, Lee. 2007. *The Trouble with Physics* (New York: Mariner Books).

Van Melsen, Andrew G. 1954. *The Philosophy of Nature*, Second edition (Pittsburgh: Duquesne University).

Wallace, W. A. 1956. "Newtonian Antinomies Against the *Prima Via*," *The Thomist* 19: 151–92.

Wallace, William A. 1983. "Cosmological Arguments and Scientific Concepts." In William A. Wallace, *From a Realist Point of View: Essays on the Philosophy of Science*, Second edition (Lanham, MD: University Press of America).

Weisheipl, James A. 1985. *Nature and Motion in the Middle Ages*, (ed.) William E. Carroll (Washington, D.C.: Catholic University of America Press).

Weyl, Hermann. 1949. *Philosophy of Mathematics and Natural Science* (Princeton: Princeton University Press).

Whitehead, Alfred North. 1948. *Essays in Science and Philosophy* (New York: Philosophical Library).

Wippel, John F. 2000. *The Metaphysical Thought of Thomas Aquinas* (Washington, D.C.: Catholic University of America Press).

Wittgenstein, Ludwig. 1961. *Tractatus Logico-Philosophicus*, trans. D. F. Pears and B. F. McGuinness (London: Routledge and Kegan Paul).

# 13
# Incomposite Being

*Lloyd P. Gerson*

## 1.

In Book *Lambda* of his *Metaphysics,* Aristotle presents an argument for the uniqueness of the universe.[1] He derives the conclusion from the fact that the Prime Mover must be one both in formula (λογῷ) and in number (ἀριθμῷ). This is so because the primary essence (τὸ πρῶτον τὸ τί ἦν εἶναι) has no matter; it has no matter because it is actuality (ἐντελέχεια). So, since the Prime Mover is the cause of the single ever-lasting motion that explains the motion of everything that moves, there can be only one universe. If there were more than one universe, then there would need to be more than one Prime Mover. The reason that this is impossible is that if there were more than one Prime Mover, then these would somehow have to differ from each other. If this were the case, then there would have to be a principle of difference, either matter or something that functions like matter. So, on this scenario, these putative Prime Movers *could* be the same insofar as they had the same nature, but they would have to differ insofar as the "matter" of each differed (if only numerically) from the other. But the Prime Mover can be nothing but actuality. For, if it were actuality "plus" some matter, then it would have a potency for change of some sort. But if it could change, this change would either be locomotion, or it would depend on locomotion of some sort, since locomotion is the basis for all change.[2]

The argument has puzzled scholars, since it appears in a chapter of *Book Lambda* in which Aristotle also argues that there must be an Unmoved Mover for each of the numerous spheres comprising the universe.[3] How can there be more than one Unmoved Mover if there is only one universe requiring only one Unmoved Mover? Would not the argument for the claim that the Unmoved Mover is one in number and

259

in formula eliminate the very possibility of there being more than one? One traditional solution has been to hold that *each* of the multitude of Unmoved Movers is, in its own sphere, one in number and in formula. After all, the immateriality of an Unmoved Mover only precludes there being a multiplicity with a single formula. This is a possible interpretation, but it requires that we ignore the fact that the argument specifically pertains only to the "first" (τὸ πρῶτον) Unmoved Mover. It is this alone that is identified with actuality. One might reply that there could be, after all, different kinds of actuality, one for each Unmoved Mover of each sphere. But this interpretation, as I will argue below, requires that the prime Unmoved Mover *have* an οὐσία, differing in kind from that of every other Unmoved Mover.[4] These οὐσίαι would have only a generic unity. But if this is the case, then the prime Unmoved Mover is not *identical* with οὐσία; it is not *per se* πρώτη οὐσία.

Although this, too, is a possibility, and is part of the motivation for trying to separate Aristotle's science of being from his theology, it does not cohere well with the argument in the rest of *Lambda* for the incompositeness of the prime Unmoved Mover. We might follow those scholars who have argued that the Prime Mover is not intended to explain the being of everything else. Theology, on this interpretation, is not identical with a science of being, despite Aristotle's explicit remark to the contrary.[5] Here, I am just going to assume the traditional interpretation according to which the establishment of the existence of the Prime Mover is a first step in the confirmation of the hypothesis that the science of being is the science of οὐσία and that this science is πρὸς ἕν. The next and final step would be to show that the focus of this science explains the being of everything else. So, we shall need to ask why the Prime Mover or primary οὐσία could only perform this role by being nothing but οὐσία.

When Aristotle turns to the analysis of the nature of this unique actuality, he argues that the object of desire and the intelligible object move in this way.[6] The *primary* objects of desire and intellect are identical. The argument for this claim appears to be this. Good is a property of being, that is, being as desirable.[7] The primary intelligible object will be that which is unqualifiedly being. Since we all desire the real good, what we desire is identical with that which is primarily intelligible. It is, therefore, on the basis of the proof of the existence of that which is pure actuality and is at the same time the primary object of desire and of intellect that Aristotle concludes the actuality (ἐνέργεια) of the Prime Mover is life (ζωή), indeed, that it has the best possible life. It has a life because its actuality is thinking, and life is the actuality of the intellect, that is, thinking.[8] The only reason given for claiming that the actuality of the Prime Mover is thinking is that this is the best possible activity. And since the best thinking is of the highest object, the Prime Mover must be supposed to be thinking of himself.[9] As it turns out, the identification of the Prime Mover as the actuality of thinking and the claim that it can have no matter produces an odd result: The Prime Mover must not be a thinker thinking of himself, but thinking itself thinking of itself.[10] A distinction between thinker and thinking would import an illicit potency into the being that the Prime Mover is.[11] Thus, an activity of any οὐσία is an actualization or realization of it. If thinking is an actualization of the οὐσία that is the prime Unmoved Mover, then the subject of that activity is in potency to that actualization.

That the commitment to eliminating potency from the being of the Prime Mover means eliminating from it any complexity whatsoever is clear when Aristotle concludes the chapter by considering the objection that the objects of the Prime Mover's thinking must be complex or composite (σύνθετον).[12] Aristotle responds that the Prime Mover must think what it thinks undividedly (ἀδιαίρετον), because the object of his thinking is without matter, and what is without matter is undivided or perhaps, more strongly, indivisible.[13]

This familiar, yet elusive, series of arguments of course raises many problems, not the least of which is how, if at all, the discovery of the existence and nature of the Prime Mover is supposed to contribute to the confirmation of the hypothesis that the science of being is just the science of οὐσία and that being is a πρὸς ἕν equivocal with a primary referent and derivative referents.[14] Is the self-thinking Prime Mover the focus of this science such that the being of absolutely everything else is somehow causally derived from the primary referent? How is thinking primary being? And if thinking *is* primary being, must everything that has being in any way somehow think? Finally, the broader question is how theology is supposed to be related to the science of being.

In this paper, I am not primarily concerned with answering these questions. Rather, I want to focus on the issue raised by later Platonists when they come to reflect on the Prime Mover. For remarkably, they follow Aristotle without hesitation when he argues for a primary intellect, eternally engaged in self-thinking. They even concur with Aristotle in holding that primary thinking is primary being, so long as we understand being appropriately. They also agree with Aristotle in his claim that the first principle of all must be unqualifiedly incomposite. Where they disagree is with Aristotle's claim that that which is thinking could be thus incomposite. Even if it is granted that there can be no distinction between thinker and thinking which would imply a potency in the former for the latter, still the very activity of thinking belies incompositeness. Thinking—to use the contemporary terminology—is an intentional activity and an intentional activity is irreducibly composite. Hence, Platonists wish to "demote" the Prime Mover to the status of Plato's Demiurge, that is, an intellect eternally thinking all that is thinkable but definitely subordinate to the absolutely simple first principle of all. That principle they identify with the Idea of the Good in *Republic* and the One, which Aristotle himself says Plato identified with the Good, presumably because the Good is posited as the first principle of all and so is the One.[15]

I am concerned here with the question of whether the primary referent of being must be incomposite, and if so, whether it makes any sense to say that if it is incomposite, then it is thinking. For all Platonists and for Aristotle, too, the first question has a straightforward answer in the affirmative. The real problem arises regarding the nature of incomposite being and whether it could be identified with an activity of thinking. Aristotle evidently says yes; later Platonists say no.[16] In the next section of the chapter, I will set out the later Platonists' understanding of incompositeness according to which a first principle of all must be incomposite. I will here emphasize what they took to be the Platonic provenance for this view. In the following section, I will turn to Aristotle's analysis of composition, of parts and of whole, in order to see if what must evidently be a looser sense of "incomposite" can apply to that which is absolutely first.

## 2.

I begin with some rapid tilling of what may appear to be unpromising ground: the second part of Plato's *Parmenides*. Actually, apart from the highly contentious large interpretative issue of the meaning of the "hypotheses" examined by Parmenides, it is fairly clear that the second part of this dialogue provides a wealth of arguments and distinctions that find their echo in Aristotle's works.[17] Here I shall only focus on what the first and second hypotheses tell us about being and compositeness. In the first hypothesis, we are asked to consider what follows if "one exists". The first immediate inference is that this one cannot be a many (πολλά).[18] If it is not many, it cannot have parts or be a whole. Thus, if the one exists, it must be absolutely one (= not many). We do not as yet have any light thrown on what sort of parts or whole are meant; it appears that the claim is completely general. From the fact that that which is one must be absolutely one and not many, a number of radical conclusions are shown to follow: the one has no limits, extension or shape, is nowhere, is neither at motion nor at rest, is neither identical with itself nor different from itself, nor is it the same as or not the same as itself, is neither older nor younger than itself nor the same age as itself, is not in time, and is neither nameable nor cognizable in any way.[19]

This bewildering array of deductions ends with the young Aristotle agreeing with Parmenides that these things cannot possibly be true of that which is one.[20] Yet, the bewilderment ends abruptly when, in the second hypothesis, we learn precisely what sort of complexity must minimally occur for all of these apparently contradictory consequences not to follow.

> Look at it from the beginning: if it is one, is it therefore possible for it to be and yet not partake of (οὐσίας)[21]?—It is not possible—Then, the essence of that which is one would not be identical with that which is one. For otherwise, that essence would not be its essence, nor would that one partake of that essence; rather, it would be the same thing to say "one is" and "one is one". But now the hypothesis is not intended to show what must follow if "one is one" but if "one is". Is that not so?—It is indeed.—Then the "is" and the "one" mean different things?—Necessarily—So, when someone makes the compact statement "one is" what is meant is that "one partakes of essence?"—Indeed.[22]

From this passage, it is clear that the prior hypothesis was assuming that "one is" should be taken as "one is one", that is, the elimination of parts or of a whole includes the elimination of the minimal composition of the subject and the οὐσία that that subject partakes of. In short, "one is one" is taken to be a purely formal identity statement. Now, "one is" is taken to imply just that compositeness absent in "one is one".[23] Whatever "one" refers to, its οὐσία must be somehow distinct from it. And as the subsequent deductions show, the contraries that were in the previous hypothesis denied of the one, are, accordingly, here both affirmed of it.[24]

The question of the compositeness of a subject and its οὐσία is a critical one for both Plato and Aristotle. For Plato, the question arises in the discussion of the "greatest kinds" (μέγιστα γένη) in *Sophist* 254Cff. The five kinds—"Existence" (ὄν), "Motion" (κίνησις), "Rest" (στάσις), "Identity" (ταὐτόν), and "Difference" (θάτερον)—are each shown to be the subjects of numerous true statements. For example, "motion exists", "existence is different from motion", and "rest is (self)-identical". Yet, if we take the kinds as five different subjects, we immediately run into difficulties. For the argument goes on to claim that every kind is different from every other, not because of its own nature, but because it partakes of difference.[25] Excluding difference itself from this general rule is entirely arbitrary and has no textual warrant. So, we want to explain how difference can be different from the other kinds by partaking of difference, not "because of its own nature" (διὰ τὴν αὐτοῦ φύσιν).

The above *Parmenides* passage seems to give us at least a partial solution to the problem. Within the "one" that a Form is, there is a distinction between it and its οὐσία. In the present case the Form of Difference partakes of the οὐσία of difference and is thereby different from the other kinds. Clearly, this is only a partial solution because it leaves unexplained what the Form of Difference's "own nature" is if it is not the οὐσία of difference. If the nature of the Form of Difference is not identical with the οὐσία of difference and, say, the nature of the Form of Rest is not identical with the οὐσία of rest, then, among other questions, we might well wonder how these Forms can be different from each other. That is, given that the Form of Different is different from the Form of Rest because it partakes of the οὐσία of difference, wherein lies the difference within the nature of the Form owing to the οὐσία in which it partakes?

Let me put this problem aside for the moment and briefly mention the other central passage in the dialogues relevant to this discussion. At *Republic* 509B6–10 we read,

> For things knowable, not only is their knowability to be said to be present to them owing to the Good, but their existence (εἶναι) and their οὐσία are provided to them by the Good, while the Good itself is not οὐσία, but even beyond essence, exceeding it in seniority and in power.

In this most contentious and portentous passage, I only wish here to focus on the implicit compositeness of each Form (τὸ εἶναι τε καὶ τὴν οὐσίαν) and the deduction that the Good, as first principle of all, must be incomposite in the relevant sense.[26] It cannot have οὐσία and therefore it cannot have the existence that is distinct from οὐσία, although apparently as first principle of all it must have existence in some way. We need not here pause to attempt to explore the so-called Neoplatonic interpretation of Plato according to which the Good in *Republic* is identical with the "one" in the first hypothesis of *Parmenides*. The distinction between a "one" and its οὐσία stands apart from this hermeneutical question.

Aristotle in *Metaphysics Zeta* 6 raises the Platonic question of whether each thing and its essence (τὸ τί ἦν εἶναι) are identical or different.[27] Aristotle's answer to this question, though not entirely lucid, is that in the case of sensible οὐσίαι, they are distinct from their essences. Socrates and the essence of Socrates cannot be identical; if they were, then no one else could have that essence. But as for "things that are primary and stated by themselves, then, it is clear that each of them and its essence are identical or one".[28] As the chapter emphasizes, Aristotle is speaking primarily about Forms. So, Aristotle seems to reject the distinction that is explicitly found in *Parmenides* and *Republic* and is implicit in *Sophist*. But there is an interesting ambiguity in the passage in which Aristotle makes this point:

> As for things which are stated in themselves, is it necessary for them to be identical with their essences? For example, this would be the case if some οὐσίαι exist, to which there are not other prior οὐσίαι or natures, as some thinkers say the Ideas are.[29]

Aristotle here speaks broadly about those who believe in the existence of Ideas. But there seem to be two groups distinguished: (1) those who hold that Ideas are ultimate, that is, there is nothing prior to them, and (2) those who hold that there are οὐσίαι or natures that are prior to them. It is clear from Aristotle's own testimony that Plato is among those who think that there are principles prior to Forms.[30] As he says in *Metaphysics Alpha*,

> Since the Forms are the causes of other things, [Plato] thought that the elements of Forms are the elements of all things. As matter, the Great and the Small are the principles; as οὐσία, it is the One. For from the Great and the Small and by participation in the One come the Forms and these are Numbers.[31]

The implication of the previous passage is that if Plato, unlike presumably other members of the Academy, believes there are principles prior to Forms, then he will not be forced to say that a Form and its essence are identical.[32] Only those for whom Forms are ultimate is the identification necessary. Of course, if for other reasons Aristotle rejects the existence of independent Forms, then he does not have to either agree with or refute the notion that there can be a distinction between a thing and its essence, at least at the level of immaterial being. He could continue to maintain that such a distinction cannot be foisted upon his absolute first principle, the Prime Mover. And indeed, his reason for holding that this Prime Mover cannot be thinking a multiplicity of objects becomes clearer in this light. Aristotle in fact agrees that that which is primary and stated by itself is identical with its essence.[33]

The dispute between Aristotle and Plato now seems to come down to this. Given that the absolutely first principle of all cannot have an essence (οὐσία) distinct from it, can this principle be said in any sense to have an essence? For Plato, the Good or the One, owing to its absolute simplicity, is beyond essence; that which has an essence must be composite. For Aristotle, the Prime Mover, although absolutely simple, must have an essence, namely, the essence of the activity of thinking.[34] Why should the Platonist suppose that this Prime Mover cannot have an essence unless it is a composite of essence and something else? Why must thinking be irreducibly complex?

One reason for supposing that Aristotle cannot avoid complexity or compositeness in the Prime Mover is his claim that "intellect thinks itself according to participation in the intelligible".[35] This participation does not preclude the Prime Mover from being one, though participation does seem to require complexity of some sort.[36] Aristotle's position seems to be that the uniqueness of the Prime Mover follows from its being perfectly actual, and perfect actuality precludes complexity. The only way of importing complexity is by importing potency or matter, the possibility of which has already been eliminated. Potency is other than and a function of actuality. If the Prime Mover had any potency, not only might it not actualize that, but more critically, its compositeness would threaten its primacy as the focus of the science of being. The primary οὐσία must be nothing but οὐσία; otherwise, it could not explain the being of everything, including its own.[37]

If the Prime Mover had an οὐσία instead of just being οὐσία, there would be two distinct but related things we could say about it: (1) the Prime Mover exists, and (2) it has such-and-such a nature or essence or οὐσία. Aristotle himself seems to treat these facts about the Prime Mover as distinct in *Lambda*, first proving that a Prime Mover must exist and then going on to infer the nature it must possess. But if we grant this distinction, then the existence of the Prime Mover is not self-explaining even if it exists necessarily. Necessary existence does not mean self-explaining existence, for the simple reason that a necessary existent could have dependent existence, dependent upon another necessary existent.[38] But the οὐσία of the Prime Mover cannot explain the existence of the Prime Mover so long as that existence is distinct from that οὐσία. Indeed, Aristotle nowhere infers the existence of a Prime Mover from the idea or concept of a Prime Mover or of an incomposite thinker. The inference for him is always the other way, supporting the contention that the existence of his first principle and its οὐσία must be distinct in some way.

## 3.

Porphyry in his *Life of Plotinus* (14.4ff) says that "his *Enneads* are full of concealed (λανθάνοντα) Stoic and Peripatetic doctrines. In particular, Aristotle's *Metaphysics* is concentrated (καταπεπύκνωται) in them". Nowhere is this revealing observation more evident than in Plotinus' treatment of the first principle of all and in his rejection of the Prime Mover as that first principle. The Prime Mover is acknowledged along with its noetic essence, and the absolute simplicity of the first principle is affirmed, but the identification of the two is denied.

One of Plotinus' principal arguments against the claim that the first principle of all could be the essence of thinking is found in *Ennead* 5.4.1, where he argues for two conclusions: (1) every composite must be accounted for by that which is incomposite or absolutely simple, and (2) there can be only one absolutely simple thing. Both of these conclusions are, no doubt, parts of the *Metaphysics* "concealed" in the *Enneads*. As Plotinus argues, a minimally composite thing has an οὐσία that is really distinct from its existence. If the οὐσία and the existence were not really distinct, then that thing would be absolutely incomposite. But there can only be one absolutely incomposite thing or principle. Assume that there is more than one absolutely incomposite thing. Then, there would have to be something that each one had that made it at least numerically different from the other, say, for example, a unique position. But that which made it different would have to be really (not merely conceptually) distinct from that which made it to be the one thing it is. That which had the position would be really distinct from the position itself. But then something which had a position and so was distinct from it would not be absolutely incomposite. So, that which is absolutely incomposite must be absolutely unique.

The necessity of recognizing a real distinction within entities is evident for the Platonist. For the central idea of Platonism is that two or more things can be the same, though they be numerically different. So, that which accounts for their sameness must be really distinct from that which account for their difference. Only the nominalist need not assent to "internal" real distinctiveness. But Aristotle, too, must acknowledge internal real distinctions, for the unique putative incompositeness of the Prime Mover implies that everything else is internally composite. For Aristotle, the internal compositeness is principally hylomorphic, but nowhere does Aristotle actually argue that hylomorphic composition is the only possible type.

Only the first principle of all is, according to Plotinus' argument, unqualifiedly self-identical; the self-identity had by anything else, that is, any composite, is necessarily qualified. A composite is anything that is distinct from any property it has. What we might call a "minimally composite individual" is one with one and only one property from which it is itself distinct. Compositeness is then equivalent to qualified self-identity. Unqualified self-identity is uniquely instantiable.

It is owing to the compositeness of everything other than the One that potency is introduced into the intelligible world.[39] To be the principle that Plotinus calls "Intellect" and that he identifies with Aristotle's Prime Mover, is then to be in potency, a potency that Intellect's cause, the One, does not possess. The One is not just the cause of the οὐσία in which Intellect partakes, but the cause of Intellect's being itself. Intellect is limited by the οὐσία in which it partakes, even though it partakes of all possible οὐσία.[40]

So, now the question is: Why should any composite need the unique, absolutely first principle of all to account for it? Plotinus' concise answer is: "All beings (ὄντα) are beings by the One (i.e., the first principle of all)".[41] Here, the divide between Plotinus and Aristotle is clear: the Prime Mover, having the οὐσία of thinking, does not seem to be a cause of the being of anything.[42] Indeed, if the Prime Mover is a composite and it were the cause of the being of any composite, it would either be the cause of itself, or there would need to be another composite to be the cause of its being. We have already seen why it cannot be the cause of itself, which, for Plotinus, is precisely why it cannot be the cause of the being of anything else.

Plotinus introduces into the discussion, apparently for the first time in history, the claim that the One is self-caused (αἴτιον ἑαυτοῦ).[43] Only that which is self-caused or self-explicable could be the cause of the being of anything else. But only that which is absolutely incomposite could be self-caused.

The One is needed to explain any composite being because no composite being is self-explicable. The One explains as an efficient cause of the being of any composite whatsoever.[44] Composites are necessarily heteroexplicable. Heteroexplicability follows from the fact that the οὐσία in which something partakes could not uniquely constitute the being's identity. If it could, then that being would be unqualifiedly identical with its οὐσία, a possibility which has already been excluded by the argument for the uniqueness of that which is absolutely self-identical. Something gets to be what it is by partaking in some οὐσία, which means, minimally, that the οὐσία is what that thing is. The One is, however, as Plato said, "above οὐσία". It cannot be the οὐσία that explains the being of anything with οὐσία. Instead, the One is "virtually all things" (δύναμις τῶν παντῶν),[45] roughly in the way that "white" light is virtually all the colors of the spectrum or in the way that a function is virtually its domain and range. As such, it is absolutely self-explicable or self-caused.[46]

Since the One is virtually all things, and its existence is identical with its activity, and since it is beyond οὐσία, we have to say that οὐσία operates as a principle of limitation, not as a principle of being.[47] It could not operate as a principle of being if it is really distinct from being in the putative first principle of all. If it is not really distinct from its being, then indeed οὐσία does not limit and absolute incompositeness follows, but what is the justification for continuing to call this principle οὐσία? The justification obviously cannot be the question-begging one that in doing so we thereby confirm the hypothesis that the nature of being is just the primary referent of οὐσία.

## 4.

The dispute, as characterized here, has evolved into whether οὐσία can ever be other than a principle of limitation, that is, whether a first principle could be incomposite and be οὐσία, not limiting the being of that whose οὐσία it is. The self-thinking of the Prime Mover is supposed to be this incomposite οὐσία. Although as we have seen, Aristotle does both call the Prime Mover οὐσία and say that in its activity it is identical with οὐσία, one might speculate that the emphasis should be placed on its being incomposite ἐνέργεια so that in saying that "the actuality of the Prime Mover consists in having the intelligible object or οὐσία", we do not need to see this as a limitation. Proceeding in this way, we might suppose that the presence of an intelligible object in an intellect is a sort of limitation or definition only for a being already determined to be composite. Thus, when I have intellection of some intelligible object, or intellection simultaneously of all intelligible objects should this be possible, I am, accordingly, limited, but only because the object is present in an intellect that is already limited by embodiment. Intellection in this case is an actualization, but the actualization is necessarily limited.

By contrast, Aristotle insists that, "if the manner of god's existence is as good as ours sometimes is, but eternally, then this is marvelous, but if it is better, then it is even more marvellous".[48] If the activity of thinking that identifies the Prime Mover is more marvellous than is ours, then perhaps this is because that activity does not entail any limitation. In effect, the Prime Mover is, like the One or the Idea of the Good, "beyond οὐσία", but only in the sense that its οὐσία is supposedly uniquely unlimiting.[49]

On this interpretation, the "life" (ζωή) of the Prime Mover should really be said to be a "sort of" (οἷον) life, as Plotinus would put it, because life is no longer a property of it, but rather attributable to it only in the sense that it is the ultimate cause or explanation for the life of anything else. Thus conceived, the Prime Mover is, like the One, virtually all of the things of which it is the cause, which means, all of the things there are. But the problem with this interpretation is, on reflection, evident. If the Prime Mover is "promoted" to the level of the One, then it is no longer fit for doing the job that Plotinus assigns exclusively to the second principle, Intellect. That job requires us to acknowledge Intellect not as an absolutely incomposite one, but as a "one-many" as Plotinus puts it.[50] For Intellect really is engaged in thinking eternally all that is thinkable. It is, therefore, really distinct from the contents of its thoughts, which are themselves really distinct from each other.

According to Plotinus, the One is the cause of the being of everything, but Intellect is an instrument of the One's causal activity.[51] Since Intellect is eminently all things, that is, the locus of the paradigms of all intelligibile entities, it performs a role that is irreducible to that of the One, which is only virtually all things. If, *per impossibile*, the One's activity were bereft of the instrumental activity of the Intellect, the One could only be the cause of being as such, not the cause of beings of any kind. But there is no one within the tradition who suggests even for a moment that A can cause B to be without B being some sort of thing or other. To be is *always* to be some kind of thing or other. The One cannot cause the variety of beings merely by being virtually all things. Virtuality is prior to eminence because virtuality does not imply compositeness, whereas eminence does. But without eminence, the many cannot arise from the incomposite One.

On the above interpretation of Aristotle's Prime Mover, the putative unlimited activity of thinking is either absolutely incomposite, in which case it cannot be eminently all things or it has sufficient compositeness to be eminently all things, but it is then no longer fit to fulfill the role of first principle. Of course, the Prime Mover so conceived could function merely as final cause. But in that case, it could no longer be the focus of the science of being qua being. For the being of those things for which the Prime Mover is the final cause must already be present, that is, existing, for final causality to operate. That being would remain unexplained, at least by the Prime Mover. The πρὸς ἕν science of being qua being could get no further than the results of *Book Zeta* of *Metaphysics*, namely that, among sensible οὐσίαι form has more being than the composite. Aristotle states in *Book Epsilon*, if there were no οὐσία other than that which is treated in physics, then physics would be first philosophy.[52] It is only by transposing the discussion of form into a discussion of ἐνέργεια in *Book Theta* that Aristotle opens the way for separate form, that is, being that is immaterial and nothing but ἐνέργεια, to be a possible candidate for the primary referent of the science of being. Unfortunately, the requisite incompositeness does not comport with an ἐνέργεια that is nothing but thinking.

There is a further problem. At the end of chapter 7, Aristotle claims that he has shown that the Unmoved Mover cannot possess any magnitude, or parts; it is completely indivisible (ἀδιαίρετος).[53] Whether this is a reference to the previous discussion or to his *Physics* is not clear, but on the basis of these claims, he goes on to assert that the Unmoved Mover must be partless and indivisible because (γάρ) it causes motion for an unlimited time (ἄπειρον χρόνον) and nothing that was limited, that is, divisible or with parts, could have the unlimited power (δύναμιν ἄπειρον) necessary to do this. As we saw above, the proof for the uniqueness of the universe depends on the uniqueness of the Unmoved Mover. Because it is perfect actuality, it could not be multiple. In the present passage, Aristotle is implying that the Unmoved Mover has unlimited potency, no doubt in the sense of an active, not a passive, potency.[54] Nevertheless, either its active potency for causing motion is identical with its actuality or not. If not, then Aristotle can hardly continue to insist on the incompositeness of the Unmoved Mover. If this potency, or perhaps power, is just its actuality, then incompositeness is not in this regard threatened. But then the manner in which this unlimited power is exercised is quite obscure. For the Unmoved Mover has been identified as an οὐσία separated (κεχωρισμένη) from sensibles. It would seem that it must exercise its unlimited power exclusively by causing motion. Yet, to have such an unlimited power is to be nevertheless limited in the sense that it does not have any other power but this. The contrast between the unlimited power of the Unmoved Mover and Plotinus' One could not be more striking. The unlimited power of the latter is unqualifiedly unlimited, since there is nothing outside of or apart from it to provide a limit.[55]

The problem I have identified with Aristotle's Prime Mover, admittedly a problem that arises solely within the framework of the larger Platonic tradition, is perhaps at least part of the reason why his *Metaphysics* had minimal impact among later Peripatetics. Plotinus was the first philosopher we know of to absorb the lessons of the *Metaphysics* and to try to make good on the hypothesis that the science of being qua being is a πρὸς ἕν science, acknowledging the status of thinking as a principle, without accepting the claim that it is the first principle of all. Plotinus' basic response to Aristotle is that the starting hypothesis of his *Metaphysics*, namely, that being (τὸ ὄν) is οὐσία, is false.

## Notes

1. See *Meta.* 12.8.1074a31–8: ὅτι δὲ εἷς οὐρανός, φανερόν. εἰ γὰρ πλείους οὐρανοὶ ὥσπερ ἄνθρωποι, ἔσται εἴδει μία ἡ περὶ ἕκαστον ἀρχή, ἀριθμῷ δέ γε πολλαί. ἀλλ' ὅσα ἀριθμῷ πολλά, ὕλην ἔχει (εἷς γὰρ λόγος καὶ ὁ αὐτὸς πολλῶν, οἷον ἀνθρώπου, Σωκράτης δὲ εἷς)· τὸ δὲ τί ἦν εἶναι οὐκ ἔχει ὕλην τὸ πρῶτον· ἐντελέχεια γάρ. ἐν ἄρα καὶ λόγῳ καὶ ἀριθμῷ τὸ πρῶτον κινοῦν ἀκίνητον ὄν· καὶ τὸ κινούμενον ἄρα ἀεὶ καὶ συνεχῶς· εἷς ἄρα οὐρανὸς μόνος ("It is clear that there is only one heaven. For if there were more than one as there are more than one human being, the principle for each will be one in form but many in number. But such things as are many in number have matter, for the formula is one or identical for the many, for example, that of human being, while Socrates is just one. But the primary essence does not have matter, for it is actuality. Therefore, the first mover, being immovable, is one in formula and in number. And, therefore, that which is always and continuously moved [is one]. Therefore, the heaven is one").

2. On the primacy of locomotion, see *Phys.* 8.7. See *Meta.* 12.7.1072b4–13 where Aristotle shows why the Unmoved Mover exists as actuality. He has already shown in chapter 6 that there must be an Unmoved Mover. In this chapter, he also gives another argument (1071b17–19) for the identification of the Prime Mover as actuality: If it had potency, then it might not be actualizing it. But it is impossible that truly everlasting motion could be caused by that which might not cause it.

3. The number is either 47 or 55, depending on whether we consider the planets to have their own spheres. See 12.8.1074a1–14. The actual number is left by Aristotle to the expertise of astronomers. See Lloyd (2000, pp. 266–7), for the problems raised by this passage.

4. I am going to leave the word οὐσία untranslated for now.

5. See *Meta.* 6.2.1026a23–32 where Aristotle says that if an immovable οὐσία exists, it would be the role of a science of this immovable οὐσία (i.e., theology) to study being qua being (τοῦ ὄντος ᾗ ὄν) and what belongs to being qua being.

6. *Meta.* 12.7.1072a26.

7. See *NE* 1.4.1096a23–4: τἀγαθὸν ἰσαχῶς λέγεται τῷ ὄντι... It is true that the present passage has τὸ καλόν and not τὸ ἀγαθόν as the object of desire. At 13.3.1078a31 Aristotle distinguishes τὸ καλόν and τὸ ἀγαθόν, for the good is always in action, though the beautiful may also be in that which is immovable. But the primary object of desire, as Aristotle goes on to argue, is a final cause, that is, a good as end. So, the Unmoved Mover attracts us because it is beautiful, and we desire it as an end, specifically, as an ideal to be imitated.

8. *Meta.* 12.7.1072b26–7: καὶ ζωὴ δέ γε ὑπάρχει· ἡ γὰρ νοῦ ἐνέργεια ζωή, ἐκεῖνος δὲ ἡ ἐνέργεια·

9. *Meta.* 12.7.1072b18–20. Aristotle is perhaps assuming, on the basis of argument in *De Anima* 3.430a2–3, that that which is unqualifiedly intelligible is identical with an intellect: ἐπὶ μὲν γὰρ τῶν ἄνευ ὕλης τὸ αὐτό ἐστι τὸ νοοῦν καὶ τὸ νοούμενον. ("For in the case of objects without matter, that which thinks and that which is being thought are identical").

10. *Meta.* 12.9.1074b28–35 concluding in the famous phrase καῖ ἔστιν ἡ νόησις νοήσεως νόησις.

11. *Meta.* 12.9.1074b35–1075a5 which poses the problem of the putative complexity of the divine ἐνέργεια and answers that when the νόησις is of a pure intelligible: οὐχ ἑτέρου οὖν ὄντος τοῦ νοουμένου καὶ τοῦ νοῦ, ὅσα μὴ ὕλην ἔχει, τὸ αὐτὸ ἔσται, καὶ ἡ νόησις τῷ νοουμένῳ μία. Cf. *De An.* 3.4.430a3–4: ἐπὶ μὲν γὰρ τῶν ἄνευ ὕλης τὸ αὐτό ἐστι τὸ νοοῦν καὶ τὸ νοούμενον· But this identity has been previously described as a "touching" (θιγγάνων). See 12.7.1072b21, a metaphor which scarcely makes sense without presuming some sort of duality.

12. *Meta.* 12.9.1075a5–10.

13. Cf. *Meta.* 14.2.1088b26–8: οὐδεμία ἐστὶν ἀΐδιος οὐσία ἐὰν μὴ ᾖ ἐνέργεια, τὰ δὲ στοιχεῖα ὕλη τῆς οὐσίας, οὐδεμιᾶς ἂν εἴη ἀϊδίου οὐσίας στοιχεῖα ἐξ ὧν ἐστιν ἐνυπαρχόντων ("no substance is eternal unless it is actuality, whereas if the elements of substance are matter, there can be no eternal substance that consists of elements").

14. See *Meta.* 4.2.1003a33ff.

15. See *Meta.* 13.4.1091b30–5; *EE* 1.8.1218a15–32

16. One must here add a tantalizing qualification for Aristotle, namely, the fragment in Simplicius' commentary on *De caelo*, 485.19–23 where he says: ὅτι γὰρ ἐννοεῖ τι καὶ ὑπὲρ τὸν νοῦν καὶ τὴν οὐσίαν ὁ Ἀριστοτέλης, δῆλός ἐστι πρὸς τοῖς πέρασι τοῦ *Περὶ εὐχῆς* βιβλίου σαφῶς εἰπών, ὅτι ὁ θεὸς ἢ νοῦς ἐστιν ἢ καὶ ἐπέκεινά τι τοῦ νοῦ. ("that Aristotle thought that there is something above intellect or οὐσία is clear from the end of his book *On Prayer* where he says clearly that god is either intellect or something beyond intellect"). If the fragment is genuine, then Aristotle did at least at one point in his career admit the possibility that the first principle must be "above" intellect or intellection. But the fragment is offered without context, and we should not take it to express an "unwritten teaching" lurking behind Book *Lambda* of *Metaphysics*. See Menn (1992). At p. 552, n.13 Menn mentions the importance of this fragment, though he takes the words "god is either intellect or something beyond intellect" as referring to two views of different philosophers (Aristotle and Plato) rather than to two alternatives

over which Aristotle is himself unsure. This seems to me to be a rather implausible reading of the phrase. Usually when Aristotle is expressing the views of different thinkers, he will oppose the different groups in a way like this: οἱ μὲν λέγουσιν ... οἱ δὲ λέγουσιν vel sim. He does not use a simple ἤ.

17. See especially Allen (1983), whose analysis of the argument of the second part of the dialogue is rich in references, especially from *Metaphysics* and *Physics*, to Aristotle's debt to this dialogue.

18. *Parm.* 137C4–5.

19. The deductions follow in rapid succession at 137D5–142A8.

20. *Parm.* 142A7–8.

21. I shall leave this term untranslated in order to avoid begging any questions. Suffice to say it is a Platonic term, taken over by Aristotle and perhaps best translated by the barbarism "beingness", that is, whatever may turn out to be that which justifies us in saying that anything has being.

22. *Parm.* 142B5-C7.

23. Cf. *Soph.* 244B-245E where the Eleatic Stranger argues against Parmenides that his "one" must be a whole if it is to exist. Aristotle, *Meta.* 4.2.1003b22–4 says: εἰ δὴ τὸ ὂν καὶ τὸ ἓν ταὐτὸν καὶ μία φύσις τῷ ἀκολουθεῖν ἀλλήλοις ὥσπερ ἀρχὴ καὶ αἴτιον, ἀλλ᾽ οὐχ ὡς ἑνὶ λόγῳ... This claim seems to allude to the *Parmenides* passage in its denial of the real distinction between being and unity.

24. *Parm.* 142C7–155E3.

25. *Soph.* 255E4–6.

26. On the Good as unhypothetical first principle of all, see 511B6–7.

27. *Meta.* 7.6.1031a14–15. In the context of the argument in *Zeta* we may assume that Aristotle is using τὸ τί ἦν εἶναι to indicate what Plato uses οὐσία to indicate in the above passages.

28. *Meta.* 7.6.1032a4–6. Cf. 7.11.1037b3; 8.3.1043b2.

29. *Meta.* 7.6.1031a28–31. Presumably, what Aristotle thinks is false for Ideas is true for at least one separate entity, namely, the Unmoved Mover. See *Meta.* 5.5.1015b11–12 where Aristotle identifies necessity in existence with "simples" whether these be immediate premises in syllogisms or simple entities. Cf. 12.7.1072a33; 1072b10.

30. Aristotle may here be alluding to *Tim.* 48C2–6, where Timaeus is about to talk about the principles of Form, copy, and space or the receptacle, he declines to talk on this occasion about the principle or principles of all things (τὴν ἀρχὴν εἴτε ἀρχὰς ἁπάντων) owing to difficulty of explaining them by the present method of exposition. Cf. 53D4–7.

31. *Meta.* 1.6.987b18–22.

32. Admittedly, Aristotle says that the One is the οὐσία of the Forms, which seems to contradict the passage from *Republic* in which the Good (= the One) is "above οὐσία". But I take it that when Aristotle says this he means οὐσία as he, Aristotle, uses the term. Accordingly, for Aristotle, the primary referent of "being" could be οὐσία.

33. See *Meta.* 12.10.1075a12–13 where the good of the universe is said to be both in that which is separate (κεχωρισμένον) and by itself (αὐτὸ καθ᾽ αὐτό) or in the order (τάξιν) of the universe; Aristotle says it is in both.

34. See *Meta.* 12.7.1072b22: "For that which is capable of receiving the intelligible object or the essence is the intellect, and the latter is in actuality by

having that". So, the Prime Mover is the actuality of the essence of that which it thinks.

35. *Meta.* 12.7.1072b19–20: αὐτὸν δὲ νοεῖ ὁ νοῦς κατὰ μετάληψιν τοῦ νοητοῦ·

36. *Meta.* 12.9.1075a4–5.

37. See *Meta.* 12.8.1073a30.

38. Aristotle seems to treat at least the outermost sphere of the heavens as a necessary existent because its motion necessarily exists given that it exists now. But he does not infer primacy from this necessity; on the contrary, the necessary existence of the outermost sphere is dependent existence.

39. See 5.9.6.9–10 where Intellect is said to be in relation to particular intellects like a genus to species or a whole to parts.

40. See 5.1.7; 6.7.17.14–16. The term οὐσία, in its original non-philosophical usage, refers to one's property, as opposed to another's. Specifically, if refers to all that which is contained within the perimeter of a defined piece of property. So, it is quite natural to conclude that if Intellect is cognitively identical with all the Forms, it is defined or limited by them.

41. See 6.9.1.1.

42. There is a puzzling passage in *Alpha Elatton* (1.993b23–31) in which Aristotle argues that "the principles of eternal things" (τὰς τῶν ἀεὶ ὄντων ἀρχὰς) are the cause of the being (εἶναι) of other things, whereas nothing is the cause of them. There are basically two problems here: (1) why is there a plurality of principles, and (2) how do they cause the being of other things? The example Aristotle gives, namely, that fire is the cause of hotness in hot things, hardly seems applicable to the Prime Mover.

43. See 6.8.14.41–2: "it is cause of itself or from itself or because of itself; for it is primarily itself, a self beyond being (ὑπερόντως)". The One is "beyond being" only in the sense that it does not have the being that follows from and requires participation in οὐσία.

44. See 5.3.15.12–13; 5.3.15.28; 5.3.17.10–14; 6.4.10; 6.7.23.22–4.

45. See 5.4.1.23–6; cf. 5.4.2.38, 6.7.32.31, 6.9.5.36. I would resist the dominant scholarly opinion that the δύναμις of the One is a "power" or "active potency". Active potencies are still potencies of some sort and they therefore require compositeness, i.e., the entity plus its potency, even if this potency is actualized in another. In addition, an active potency actualized in *another* necessarily implies a real relation between that entity and the entity in which the potency is actualized. But the One is not really related to anything. See 6.8.8.12–13:ιΔεῖ δὲ ὅλως πρὸς οὐδὲν αὐτὸν λέγειν ("we should say that it [the One] is altogether related to nothing").

46. 6.8.14.41. Cf. 6.8.7.46 and 6.8.20.9ff where the One is also said to be "activity" (ἐνέργεια), but activity "without οὐσία". In contrast to Aristotle, Plotinus does not identify primary activity with primary οὐσία. He identifies it with existence (ὑπόστασις).

47. 5.1.7.26–7: "stability in the intelligible world is definition and shape" (ὁρισμὸς καὶ μορφή).

48. *Meta.* 12.7.1072b24–5.

49. Such an interpretation of Aristotle's Prime Mover would put him in line with the so-called Middle Platonists, who tended to the view that the distinct functions of Demiurge, Forms, and Good in Plato's dialogues should be

"collapsed" into one. It is a view that even found some favor after Plotinus, in particular, in his student Porphyry, though not much after that among pagan Platonists. It was left to Christian and Muslim Platonists to try to revive the Middle Platonic position by the application of an overlay of Scripture-based theology.

50. See 5.1.8.26; 5.3.15.10, 22; 6.2.15.14.
51. 6.7.42.22: "all things depend on [the One] through intermediaries (διὰ μέσων)". Cf. 6.9.1.20ff.
52. *Meta.* 6.1.1026a27–9. This claim does not mean that if immaterial being did not exist, then there could be a science of being qua being purely of physical being. Such is the view of, e.g., Kirwan (1980, p. 189) and Irwin (1988, p. 544, n.42). For as Books *Beta* and *Gamma* show, "being" is not univocal; that is, if there is to be a science of being, that science must be πρὸς ἕν. And as the central books of *Metaphysics* show, the primary referent of the science of being cannot be identified with the composite being that is found in nature. If immaterial, that is, incomposite being, did not exist, then first philosophy would be physics, not a metaphysics of the physical world.
53. *Meta.* 12.7.1073a5–14. Here, indivisibility must be more than the undividedness of a line as such, which is nevertheless potentially divisible. See 7.13.1039a6–7.
54. See *Meta.* 5.12; 9.6.
55. The problem of whether the Unmoved Mover is an efficient cause as well as a final cause was recognized at least as early as Ammonius, the teacher of Simplicius. See Simplicius, *In Phys.* 1361.11–1363.24. Among contemporary scholars, Sarah Broadie and Enrico Berti, among others, have argued that efficient causality is not excluded from the causal nature of the Unmoved Mover. As I interpret the relevant texts, the ambivalence over the Unmoved Mover's causality springs from Aristotle trying to maintain the incompositeness and primacy of the Unmoved Mover while insisting that it must be the activity of thinking.

# References

Allen, R. E. 1983. *Plato's Parmenides* (Minneapolis: University of Minnesota Press).

Irwin, T. 1988. *Aristotle's First Principles* (Oxford: Clarendon Press).

Kirwan, C. 1980. *Aristotle's Metaphysics* (Oxford: Clarendon Press).

Lloyd, G. E. R. 2000. "*Metaphysics* ⊠ 8," in M. Frede and D. Charles, (eds), *Aristotle's Metaphysics Lambda* (Oxford: Oxford University Press).

Menn, S. 1992. "Aristotle and Plato on God as *Nous*," *Review of Metaphysics* 43: 543–73.

# 14
## Aristotle's Divine Cause

*Fred D. Miller, Jr.*

## 1 Introduction

In *Metaphysics* Lambda (book XII), Aristotle argues that there is a substance which is eternal, intelligent, and, in a word, divine. This imperceptible and incorporeal entity, which exists separately from perceptible, material substances, is "the principle on which heaven and nature depend" (7.1072b13–14). The foundation for this doctrine is laid in *Physics* VIII which argues that the eternal movement of heaven is caused by an eternal prime mover which is itself not in motion.[1] Lambda, "the coping-stone of the *Metaphysics*,"[2] has been the subject of extensive interpretation and criticism over the past two millennia. Scholarly debate continues unabated over such questions as: What is the nature of Aristotle's divine mind and can it be understood as a monotheistic god? To what extent does his argument depend upon an obsolete cosmology, which views the sun, moon, and stars as eternal bodies imbedded in spheres revolving eternally about an immovable Earth located in the centre of the universe? Does he commit the logical missteps found in other traditional arguments for the existence of God? Rather than revisiting these familiar questions, however, this essay will focus on an issue fundamental to Aristotle's thesis: In what sense of "cause" is the prime mover supposed to be the cause of motion?[3]

This question must be confronted because Aristotle distinguishes four different ways in there may be a cause in *Physics* II:

> [*Material cause*] In one way, then, that out of which a thing comes to be and which persists, is called a cause, e.g. the bronze of the stature, the silver of the bowl, and the genera of which they are species.
> [*Formal cause*] In another way, the form or model, i.e. definition of the essence, and its genera, are called causes (e.g. of the octave the

relation of 2:1, and generally number), and the parts in the definition. [*Efficient cause*] Again, the primary source of the change or rest: e.g. the person who deliberated is a cause, the father is cause of the child, and generally what makes of what is made and what changes of what is changed. [*Final cause*] Again, in the sense of end or that for the sake of which a thing is done, e.g. health is the cause of walking about. ("Why is he walking about?" We say: "To be healthy", and, having said that, we think we have provided the cause.) The same is true also of all the intermediate steps which are brought about through the movement of something else as the means towards the end, e.g. slimming, purging, drugs, or surgical instruments are means towards health. For all these things are for the sake of the end, though they differ from one another in that some are acts and others instruments. Causes then are perhaps said in this many ways....[4]

Even though Aristotle frequently applies this distinction in other contexts, *Physics* VIII does not raise the question: In which of these ways does the unmoved mover cause motion? In *Metaphysics* Lambda, however, he recognizes the question and takes his predecessors to task for failing to answer it: although some of them recognize that the first principle is the good, "*how* the good is a principle they do not say – whether as end or as mover or as form." (*Meta.* XII.10.1075a38-b1) This presupposes that the prime mover cannot be a material cause like Empedocles' principle of cosmic love, which would seem reasonable to Aristotle because unmovable substances "must be without matter" (6.1071b21, cf. 10.1075b3–4). We would expect Lambda to contain a definitive discussion of whether the prime mover is a formal, efficient, or final cause; but it does so only in passing. It seems doubtful, however, whether he would regard it as a formal cause in the senses he ordinarily recognizes: it is not a Platonic Form (because he denies that the Forms can cause motion: cf. 6.1071b14–19, 10.1075b16–20); it is not an Aristotelian form of a composite substance (because the unmoved mover is "a substance separate from perceptible things", 7.1073a4–5, cf. 3.1070a14);[5] and it is not a form in the sense of knowledge existing in a craftsman's soul (cf. *Meta.* VII.7.1032a32-b22). There remain the final two modes: efficient and final. Is the prime mover either of these? Or both?

## 2   Final cause or efficient cause?

Lambda clearly indicates that Aristotle's prime mover is a final cause: it is that for the sake of which (*to hou heneka*) in the sense of an aim, and, though itself unmoved, "it brings about movement as being loved" (7.1072b1–3). But is it an efficient cause as well? He hints as much in his criticism of Anaxagoras: "Anaxagoras makes the good a principle in the sense of bringing about movement; for Mind brings about movement. But it brings about movement for the sake of something, which must be different from it, except as *we* state the case; for the medical art is in a way health." (10.1075b8–10) This suggests that Aristotle thinks he improves on Anaxagoras's account of the first principle by treating it as both efficient and final cause. This is also implied by his comparison of it to the general of an army (10.1075a13–15) and his description of it as "capable of moving and producing" (*kinêtikon kai poiêtikon* (6.1071b11, cf. 10.1075b31). However, this gives rise to a further question: If Aristotle's prime mover is both an efficient and final cause, how are these two modes of causation related? This is a fair question because Aristotle poses a similar one concerning Empedocles' principle of cosmic love: "Now even if it happens that the same thing is a principle both as matter and as mover, still *being* them is not the same. In which respect then is love a principle?" (10.1075b4–6) By the same token, if Aristotle believes that his divine cause is both efficient and final, which is more fundamental: Is it an efficient cause because it is final, or a final cause because it is efficient?

These issues have perplexed interpreters since antiquity. Simplicius reports, in his commentary on Aristotle's *Physics* (1360,24–1363,24), that the ancient commentators disagree over whether Aristotle's prime mover was the efficient cause as well as the final cause of heavenly motion. He reports that Alexander of Aphrodisias and some other Peripatetics deny that Aristotle believes in an efficient cause of heavenly motion, but Simplicius argues on the contrary that the prime mover is an efficient as well as final cause. He adds that his teacher Ammonius wrote an entire book (unfortunately lost) providing many arguments for this interpretation. Simplicius concedes that Aristotle does not explicitly state that the prime mover is an efficient cause, but he argues that this was Aristotle's view on the basis of circumstantial evidence, including Aristotle's afore-mentioned apparent approval of Anaxagoras' claim that Mind is the cause of motion (cf. *Meta.* I.3.984b20–2). To be sure, Simplicius is less persuasive when he contends that Aristotle's prime mover is on a par with Plato's demiurge who constructed the perceptible universe in the *Timaeus*. But if not as an intelligent designer, in what way is the prime mover supposed to be an efficient cause?

According to W. D. Ross, "The answer is that God is the efficient cause by being the final cause, but in no other way."[6] Ross reasons that the source of movement (*archê tês kinêseôs*) must be either an end which is aimed at or else it must be some sort of propulsive force, which could be either a physical force (e.g. a blow or shove) or a mental force (e.g. an act of will). But Aristotle implies that this god does not move the cosmos by means of either physical force or mental force, so that He can only be a final cause. Ross goes on to describe Aristotle's God as absorbed in self-contemplation, narcissistically aloof and disengaged from the perceptible universe, and yet exerting a powerful influence on it owing to His intrinsic lovableness. Charles Kahn, even more emphatically, maintains that the prime mover is only a final cause: "There is no place in Aristotle's system for a transcendent artisan or potentate. The [prime mover] is not properly an agent at all."[7] This interpretation – that the prime mover is a final cause and incidentally, at most, an efficient cause – has long been dominant among commentators.[8]

A minority (including Enrico Berti and Sarah Broadie) has advanced an opposed interpretation that the unmoved mover is fundamentally an efficient cause.[9] As "unmoved mover" implies, it does not transfer any motion of its own to the moved object.[10] Instead, the divine cause "moves the heaven by a special impulse, not physical, but psychical, like that by which the soul moves the body."[11] Some proponents of this interpretation take the extreme position that the unmoved mover is not a final cause and not an efficient cause.[12] Others grant that Aristotle speaks of the unmoved mover also as a final cause in some sense, but they regard this as only incidental to its fundamental role as efficient cause.[13] The prime mover's causal efficacy derives from its own life-force, its pure actuality understood as activity.

There are then two interpretations, which disagree over whether the divine mind is, more fundamentally, a final cause or an efficient cause when it moves the cosmos. Although each of these interpretations has textual support, both of them encounter theoretical difficulties. This has led some commentators to try to combine the two interpretations by treating the prime mover as a soul or soul-analogue. These interpretations are considered in turn in the following three sections.

## 3   The final cause as metaphorical mover

There seems to be incontrovertible evidence that Aristotle regards the prime mover as a final cause. This is explicit in Lambda 7 with the explanation of how the first cause can move objects without itself being moved. Aristotle's rather tortuous argument (1072a26-b1) may be summarized as follows: A desirable object does not have to be in motion in order to move the faculty of desire. But whether something is the object of desire depends on whether it is the object of thought; for we desire something because we think it is good rather than the converse. Moreover, thought is moved by the object of thought, and substance is the first among the possible objects of thought. Further, the good coincides with that which is desirable for its sake, and the first such object (already identified with substance) is the best. Aristotle next (1072b1–4) heads off the objection that the object of desire must be affected in some way if it is desired.[14] He distinguishes two senses of "that for the sake of which" (*to hou heneka*): the beneficiary (literally, that to whom, *tini*) and the aim (literally, that for which, *tinos*). "That for the sake of which" is also the expression used for final cause in *Physics* II.3.174b33 (quoted above) where an example illustrates the present distinction: If someone walks about for the sake of health, he is the beneficiary, and health is his aim. The beneficiary is moved but the aim is not. Thus the prime mover is the final cause: "it brings about movement as being loved" (1072b3–4). Moreover, Aristotle, here and subsequently, characterizes the prime mover as good and noble (7.1072b4–13, 24–9; 9.1074b34; 10.1075a11–15, 35–9, b8–10) and therefore as an end (8.1074a20).

The thesis that the prime mover is a final cause also figures in the Lambda's argument that there are only as many eternal substances as there are moving celestial spheres (8.1074a17–31). For this assumes that an unaffected substance is an end (*telos*) because it has in virtue of itself attained to the best, and that as an end it will bring about motion.[15] There is, admittedly, a complication in that a subsidiary argument assumes that it is the celestial body which is the end of its own sphere's motion, on the grounds that "every movement belongs to something that is moved" (1074a24–31). However, we should recall the distinction (7.1072b1–4) between two senses of end: the aim and the beneficiary. A celestial motion has two final causes: the celestial body that is moved (the beneficiary) and the prime mover (the aim).[16]

Though Aristotle leaves little doubt that his prime mover is a final cause, some commentators worry that to treat it simply as such is to demote it to a mere "exemplary cause".[17] They can appeal to a passage in *Generation and Corruption* which distinguishes between an efficient cause and a merely final cause. Aristotle contrasts productive agents (*poiêtika*) which possess their form in matter with agents which do not, and maintains that only the former are affected or altered in the process. One example of the former is food, which nourishes the body and is digested in the process. One example of the latter is the medical art which produces health; although the patient's body is cured, the medical art is not affected by the body. Aristotle's main point is that in any causal chain, the first cause must be of the unaffected sort. The crucial passage follows:

> The productive agent is a cause in the sense of that from which the movement begins. But the that-for-the-sake-of-which is not productive (which is why health is not productive except metaphorically). For when the productive agent is present, the patient becomes something, but when the states are there, <the patient> no longer becomes <something>, and forms or ends are states of a sort. [*GC* I.7.324b13–18]

Hence, although health is a final cause, it is a *metaphorical mover*, not a bona fide efficient cause. Aristotle would likewise dismiss the Forms as mere metaphorical movers. Accordingly, he rejects the theory in Plato's *Phaedo* that Forms are causes later on in *Generation and Corruption*:

> If the Forms are causes, why do they not generate continuously rather than sometimes doing so and sometimes not, since there are always Forms as well as thing that partake <of them>? Further in some instances we observe that the cause is other <than the Form>. For it is the doctor who produces health and the person who knows who produces knowledge, even though there is health itself and knowledge itself as well as the things capable of participating <in them>; and the same holds for everything else done in virtue of a capacity. [*GC* II.9.335b18–24]

The point is that even if there were a Form such as health itself, there would still need to be an efficient cause to bring it about that a particular body participated in that Form. In the language of *Generation and Corruption*, if the Form is not an efficient cause it is at best a metaphorical mover.

However, if Aristotle's prime mover is a final cause which merely "brings about movement as being loved" (*Meta.* XII.7.1072b3–4), is it not vulnerable to the same charge: i.e. that it is at most a metaphorical mover? In response one might appeal to Ross' remark that Aristotle's prime mover "is not an end existing merely in the future; He exists eternally and thus differs from a merely imagined and anticipated ideal."[18] This does not settle the issue, however; for Aristotle complains that the mere existence of the Forms would not suffice for them to be movers (6.1071b2–7).[19]

It might be objected that the comparison with health is unfair because the prime mover is not an end in the same way as health. Thomas Aquinas makes this very point:

Now one thing can be the goal of another in two ways: first, as something having prior existence, as the centre of the world is said to be a goal which is prior to the motion of heavy bodies; and nothing prevents a goal of this kind from existing in the realm of immovable things. For a thing can tend by its motion to participate in some degree in something immovable; and the first mover can be a goal in this way. Second, one thing is said to be the goal of another not as something exists actually, but only as existing in the intention of the agent by whose activity it is produced, as health is the goal of the activity of the medical art. An end or goal of this kind does not exist in the realm of immovable things. [*Comm. Aristotle's Metaphysics* 2528.]

Although Aquinas is correct that an actually existing goal differs from one that only exists in the intention of the agent, this distinction does not solve the problem at hand, which is whether the prime mover is a genuine mover. For, as just noted, Aristotle contends that a Form could not be a moving cause even if it did exist. As for Aquinas' analogy between the prime mover and the centre of the universe, it should be noted that according to Aristotle a heavy body moves to the centre of the universe on account of its own nature, which is its internal principle of movement or rest (*Phys.* II.1.192b8–23, *DC* IV.4). And as Aquinas elsewhere remarks, "the nature of physical things is the principle by which each of them carries out the activity proper to it in the order of the universe." (*Comm. Aristotle's Metaphysics* 2634). Finally, it is striking that Aquinas' example of the wrong sort of goal is health as the goal of the activity of the medical art, when Lambda itself compares the prime mover to the medical art which is in a way health (10.1975b8–10, cf. 4.1070b28). Moreover, this analogy suggests a dilemma for the final-cause interpretation. If health is identified with a healthy condition of the body in distinction from the medical art which produces it, it is a merely metaphorical mover. But if health is identified with the activity of the medical art which brings about a bodily condition, then there is an efficient cause, but now this is the activity of the art and not merely its goal. Hence, the comparison with health *qua* medical art implies that the prime mover must be some sort of productive activity over and above a mere aim, however lovable it may be. These sorts of worries lead some commentators to argue that the prime mover must be not merely a final cause but also an efficient cause.

## 4   The efficient cause as untouched toucher

Proponents of the efficient-cause interpretation cite as evidence the above-mentioned argument in Lambda 6 that the prime mover could not be a Platonic Form.[20] The argument is as follows:

> But if there is something which is capable of moving or producing <things>, but does not act (*mê energoun*) in any way, there will not be movement; for it is possible for that which has a capacity not to act. Nothing, then, is gained even if we assume eternal substances, as do those who assume the Forms, unless there is to be in them some principle which brings about change. Neither is this enough, nor is another substance besides the Forms enough. For if it does not act (*energêsei*), there will be no movement. [6.1071b12–17]

This indicates that the prime mover must *act* (*energein*) or else it cannot actually bring about movement. This is what he means when he asserts that its substance or essence (*ousia*) must be actuality and, on this interpretation, an activity (*energeia*).[21] Commentators have also understood Aristotle's prime mover as "pure actuality" in the sense that it involves no potentiality. [22] This seems assumed by his subsequent argument that since the prime mover is eternally in actuality it cannot contain any matter, because matter is a source of potentiality (cf. 1071b20–2).[23]

Aristotle's assumption that an agent can act without being in motion itself requires a distinction between two types of actuality as set forth in *Metaphysics* IX.6.1050a23-b2. In a movement, an agent acts on a patient and thereby produces a product, e.g. a builder (practicing the art of building) assembles materials (e.g. bricks and mortar) in order to make a house. This movement is an event that occurs in the patient. In contrast, other actions involve an agent but no patient and no product other than the action itself, e.g. seeing or contemplating. Here the actuality occurs in the agent itself, e.g. the seeing is in the one who sees and the contemplating is in the one who contemplates. Elsewhere, Aristotle describes movement as incomplete (or imperfect, *atelês*) actuality, because it involves the actualizing of a potential; e.g. in building a potential house, such as bricks and mortar, becomes an actual house (*Meta.* XI.9.1066a20–2 (cf. *Phys.* III.2.201b31–3); *Meta.* IX.6.1048b29; *Phys.* VIII.5.257b8–9; *DA* III.7.431a6–7). In contrast, the act of seeing or contemplating is an actuality in the full or unqualified sense. This is the sort of act that the prime mover performs on the efficient-cause interpretation. What kind of act is this? Lambda 7 has an answer: The mover is a mind or thought (*nous*), and its activity is thinking of thinking (*noêsis*):

> [T]hat which is capable of receiving the object of thought, i.e. the substance, is mind, and it acts (*energei*) when it possesses <the object>; so that the latter rather than the former is the divine <character> which the mind is believed to possess, and contemplating of what is most pleasant and best. [1072b22–4][24]

Eternal motion is thus caused by the prime mover's eternal activity of contemplation.[25] The implication is that the prime mover is the efficient cause of eternal heavenly motion in virtue of its eternal activity of thinking.

Two other passages in Lambda make better sense if the prime mover is understood as an efficient cause as well as a final cause. The first contains an argument that the unmoved mover cannot have any magnitude (7.1073a5–11; *Physics* VIII.10.266a23-b20). "It brings about movement in unlimited time, but nothing limited possess limited power." So, it cannot have a limited magnitude. But an unlimited or infinite magnitude is impossible (as Aristotle argues in *Physics* III.5), so it cannot have any magnitude, since every magnitude is either finite or infinite. The argument depends on the tacit premiss that a causal agent must possess unlimited power (*dunamin apeiron*) if it is to bring about movement through an unlimited span of time. This premiss is intelligible if the agent is an efficient cause: If an efficient cause has limited magnitude, it has limited mass, so that it must exhaust all of its causal power after a certain span of time (see *Physics* VII.5 for details). But it is hard to make sense of this premiss if the agent is a final cause. How long must Don Quixote go on tilting at windmills in order for Dulcinea to be no longer lovable?

The other passage contains an argument that there can be no more prime movers than there are celestial motions (8.1073a23–36). This hinges on the premise that "eternal movement must be brought about by something eternal and a single movement by a single thing", from which it is inferred that "each of these [sc. eternal] motions is brought about by an unmovable eternal substance in virtue of itself". In other words, if there are numerically distinct eternal motions which require an unmoved mover, then each of these motions must have its own prime mover. This assumption seems implausible in the case of a merely final cause, which is the object of knowledge or desire.[26] Why could not "the face that launched a thousand ships" have launched ten thousand ... or a million ... or an unlimited number of ships?

The foregoing passages support the interpretation that Aristotle's unmoved mover is an efficient cause in some stronger sense than being a mere final cause. But how is this possible? How could a substance which is without matter or magnitude operate as a genuine efficient cause? One possible answer is suggested by Aristotle's above-mentioned analogy: "The medical art is in a way health" (4.1070b33, 10.1075b8–10). Aristotle seems to hold that the art of sculpture is the efficient cause of the statue, indeed is more strictly the efficient cause than the sculptor is. Moreover, the medical art is not affected by the body when the latter is cured, so that the art is a sort of unmoved mover (see *Phys.* II.3.195b21–5 and *GC* I.7.324a24-b13).[27] This interpretation, stated so baldly, is seriously incomplete. For (as seen in the previous section) Aristotle emphasizes the causal role of the individual agent when he rejects Plato's Forms as causes in *Generation and Corruption*:

> For it is the doctor who produces health and the man who knows who produces knowledge, even though there is both health itself and knowledge itself as well as the things capable of participating <in them>; and the same holds for everything else done in virtue of a capacity. [*GC* II.9.335b21–4]

Nonetheless, Aristotle goes on to criticize the materialists who omit the "controlling" cause, i.e. the essence or form (335b33–5). For, as he remarks in the *Physics*, the individual can be a cause in a coincidental way: "In one way Polyclitus, in another the sculptor is the cause of a statue, because being Polyclitus coincides with being a sculptor" (*Phys.* II.3.195a33–5). It is *qua* sculptor that Polyclitus is the cause. In specifying the cause we must identify that in virtue of which it is the cause: "a human builds because he is a builder, and he is a builder in virtue of the art of building" (195b23–4). But this in no way nullifies the indispensable role of the individual agent. Hence, if the prime mover is an efficient cause, it must be an individual agent.[28]

Another possible answer may be found in a passage in *Generation and Corruption* which explains how a mover can move something else even though it remains itself unmoved. First, he remarks that "in one way movers touch the things that are movable, and in another way they will not." In the first way the touching is reciprocal:

> Most of the time, to be sure, the thing that touches is touched by the thing that it touches. Almost everything we encounter brings about

movement by being moved, and in these cases it is necessary, and it appears, that the thing that touches is touched by a thing that is touched. However, it is possible, as we sometimes say, for the mover only to touch the thing moved and for the thing that is touched not to touch the thing that touches it. (But because things of the same kind bring about movement by being moved, it is believed that the mover must touch the thing that touches it.) So if something brings about movement without being moved, it will touch the movable object although nothing touches it. For instance, we sometimes say that the person who grieves us touches us, but we do not touch him. [*GC* I.6. 323a25–33]

Here the unmoved mover is characterized as an *untouched toucher*. This suggests a way in which the unmoved mover of the cosmos could be a genuine efficient cause: It touches the outermost sphere of the heavens at its outer surface, but the sphere does not touch it in return.[29] Although Aristotle does not elsewhere speak of the prime mover as "touching" material bodies, it seems implicit in an otherwise puzzling passage in the *Physics* which argues that the unmoved mover must be "at" the outer sphere of the cosmos. "It must be either at the centre or at the circumference; for these are the principles. But the things nearest the mover are moved most quickly, and the movement of the circumference is the quickest. Therefore that is where the mover is." (*Phys.* VIII.10. 267b6–9). The claims that the mover must be "at" the centre or the circumference of the sphere that it moves and that the effects are more pronounced the "nearer" they are to the cause are plausible if it is supposed that the mover must make contact with the moved and thereby produce its effects. This is all rather mystifying if the prime mover is understood to be a mere final cause. Would Don Quixote move more slowly if his beloved Dulcinea were further away?[30] If the prime mover in contrast is viewed as an efficient cause also, there would be a point to saying that it is located "at" the circumference of the cosmos.[31]

This also suggests a way of understanding the vexing Lambda arguments mentioned above.[32] The argument that there are no more movers than there are celestial motions (8.1073a23–36) depends on the assumption that each celestial sphere has its own unmoved mover. This makes better sense if it is supposed that in order to impart motion, each mover must be in direct contact with its respective sphere. For the efficient cause of motion must "touch" the moved object.[33] Since the different spheres are in different locations, each sphere will have a different mover touching it. The other argument, that the prime mover cannot have any magnitude (7.1073a5–11), depends on the assumption that it could not possess the "infinite power" required to produce eternal motion if it had magnitude.[34] This might seem plausible if the prime mover were regarded as analogous to a corporeal efficient cause, which makes an object move by touching it. Such a cause has "limited power" in the sense that it can only produce motion for so long. The unmoved mover might be viewed as a special kind of efficient cause which also touches an object and moves it in virtue of its own unlimited activity. Finally, Aristotle's above-mentioned claim that if the purported prime mover does not *act*, there will be no movement (6.1071b12–17), can be understood in terms of the untouched toucher. Although the prime mover is not itself in motion, it is active (i.e. it thinks); and because it is in contact with the appropriate sort of body (i.e. a celestial sphere), it causes it to it move.

Admittedly, there is no mention of an untouched toucher in Lambda. Nor does Lambda rehearse the argument from the *Physics* that the prime mover is situated at the circumference of the cosmos.[35] It is unclear, also, how a substance without magnitude which is separate from perceptible substances could have any literal contact with them. There is no hint in Aristotle's work of spooky causes such as telepathy or telekinesis. The only example he offers of untouched touching – the person who grieves us touches us without being touched in returned – is regarded by most commentators as irredeemably metaphorical. [36] In order to cash out the metaphor in terms of Aristotelian causality, we must imagine that a person causes us grief only by performing some action or saying something which we perceive and to which we respond emotionally (cf. *DA* II.5.417a2–9). It is unclear how an incorporeal substance can have a comparable affect on a corporeal substance.

Aristotle leaves his commentators in a quandary. If the unmoved mover is a mere final cause, it looks like the metaphorical mover which he dismisses in *Generation and Corruption* I.7. If it is also an efficient cause, its mode of causation is obscure: the only lead is the untouched toucher in *Generation and Corruption* I.6, but it is hard to see how an immaterial extensionless substance could literally "touch" anything. In the face of these difficulties faced by these two interpretations, another interpretation has been proposed which tries to draw on their strengths and avoid their weaknesses.

## 5   Both efficient and final: A cosmic soul?

Aristotle maintains that formal, efficient, and final causes often coincide in the natural world.

For the what and the that-for-the-sake-of-which are one, while the primary source of movement is the same in form as these. For human generates human – and so too, in general, with all things which bring about movement by being moved; and such as are not of this kind no longer belong to natural science, for they bring about movement not by possessing motion or a source of motion in themselves, but being themselves immovable. [*Phys.* II.7.198a24–9]

The natural convergence of causes is manifest in the soul, which *De Anima* describes as the cause and principle of the living body in three senses: as formal cause, final cause, and efficient cause. (II.4.415b8–28) The soul is a formal cause in so far as it is the substance or essence of the living body. "For substance is the cause of the existence of all things, and for living things to exist is to live, and the soul is the cause and principle of this. Further, the actualization is the account of what exists potentially." Soul is also a final cause: "For just as the mind acts for the sake of something, nature acts in the same way also, and the thing for the sake of which it acts is its end. And the soul is this sort of cause in animals according to nature; for all natural bodies are tools of the soul, and just as the bodies of animals are tools, the bodies of plants are too, because they exist for the sake of the soul." Finally, soul is an efficient cause: "Soul is the primary source of movement in place, though not all living things have this capacity. Alteration and growth also occur in virtue of soul; for perception is believed to be a sort of alteration, and nothing perceives which does not partake of soul. The same goes for growth and decay; for nothing decays or grows naturally without being nourished, and nothing is nourished which does not share in life." Given Aristotle's characterization of the soul as formal cause (in the sense of actualization) and as both formal and efficient cause, some commentators (e.g. Aryeh Kosman) view the prime mover along the same lines, that is, as the soul (or quasi-soul) of the cosmos.[37] On this interpretation, *Physics* VIII and *Metaphysics* Lambda are in basic agreement with *De Caelo* when it asserts that "the heaven is ensouled (*empsuchos*) and possesses a principle of movement" (*DC* II.2.285a29–30).[38] Other commentators (e.g. Mohan Matthen) unwilling to go this far treat the prime mover as analogous to a soul, related to the cosmic body as its form so that "Aristotle's universe is a hylomorphic substance."[39]

Aristotle does not describe the cosmos as "ensouled" in *Physics* VIII or *Metaphysics* Lamda. Instead he speaks of the prime mover as itself a mind, a god, and a living being (*Meta* XII.7.1072b26–30). None the less *Physics* VIII analyzes self-motion in a very suggestive way:

> That which moves itself then must possess something that brings about movement but is unmoved and something else that is moved but does not necessarily move anything else; and both of these two things must touch each other or at rate one of them must touch the other. If, then, that which brings about movement is continuous (for that which is moved must be continuous), each will touch the other. So it is clear that the whole moves itself but not because some part of it is the sort of thing that moves itself; rather it moves itself as a whole, both being moved and bringing about movement because one component of it brings about movement and another component is moved. [*Phys.* VIII.5.258a18–25]

Aristotle's purpose here is, in part, to reject Plato's theory that all motion is due to self-moving souls understood as self-movers (cf. VIII..9.265b32–266a1). On the contrary, Aristotle argues here, a putative self-mover is analyzable into two components, of which one is in motion, and the other is an unmoved mover. The mention of "touching" calls to mind the untouched toucher in *Generation and Corruption*. A natural power may be thought of as in touch with the body in which it inheres. It is tempting, then, to suppose that the unmoved-mover component of the whole is related to the moved component in the same way as a soul to its body. Thus, the prime mover is not only a mind. It turns out to be the soul, or something analogous to a soul, of the cosmos.

However, this interpretation seems open to the objection that Aristotle rules out this very analogy in *Physics* VIII.6.259b1–16. He remarks that "we clearly see that there are things that move themselves, for example, the genus of ensouled things and animals." One might think that they originate their own motion entirely by themselves, but this is not strictly true because the animals cannot move continuously. They need to eat food and digest it, breathe, and sleep, which shows that they depend on external causes involving their environment and material entering their bodies. The animal's "prime mover", its soul, is thus nothing like the unmoved mover of the cosmos. To this objection, it might be replied that, although the cosmic prime mover differs in this respect from an animal soul (which may one reason why Aristotle does not call it a "soul"), this can be explained by the different makeup of animals and the cosmos. Animal bodies are composed of terrestrial elements, and they depend on their environment for their continued existence. The cosmic body is composed of ether, an indestructible fifth element, and there is, in fact, nothing outside of the outer sphere of the cosmos.[40] The cosmic prime mover might accordingly be viewed as a sort of super-soul without the limitations of ordinary souls.

However, as this passage continues (259b16–20), it suggests an even more serious objection to the cosmic-soul interpretation. "In all these [sc. living] things the prime mover and cause of self-motion is moved by itself, though in a coincidental way; for the body changes its place, so that the thing which is in the body and moves itself by leverage also changes its place." By "the prime mover" in the body Aristotle clearly means the soul. The soul moves the body in which it is located and thereby moves itself coincidentally. However, Aristotle maintains that the prime mover of the universe is "unmoved and devoid of all change, both without qual-ification and coincidentally" (*Physics* VIII.6.258b13–16; 259b20–31).[41] If the prime mover were to stand to a heavenly sphere like a soul to a body, it would move itself coincidentally "by leverage" in the same way that animal souls move themselves coincidentally.[42]

This sets the stage for the final objection to the cosmic-soul interpre-tation. The soul moves itself coincidentally because it moves the body *in* which it is located. However, Lambda asserts that the prime mover is "separate (*kechôrismenê*) from perceptible objects" (7.1073a4–5; cf. 10.1075a12).[43] For in Lambda 1, he distinguishes three sorts of substance: perceptible and eternal (i.e. celestial bodies, e.g. sun, moon, planets, and stars), perceptible and perishable (i.e. terrestrial bodies, e.g. plants and animals), and immovable (i.e. imperceptible and imperishable) and adds that "some say that this is separable" (1.1069a33–4). Elsewhere in the *Metaphysics,* he distinguishes between physics and first philosophy or science in terms of whether their objects are "separable (*chôrista*) from matter": "Physics deals with objects which are inseparable but not immovable, and some areas of mathematics deal with objects that are immovable but not separable but present in matter, while the first science deals with objects that are separable and immovable." (*Meta.* VI.1.1026a13–16; cf. *DA* I.1.403b12–16). Aristotle speaks of things as "separable" (and "separate") in different senses. The relevant sense here is ontological separability: an unmoved mover can exist without percep-tible matter, but a physical object cannot.[44]

The final objection to the cosmic-soul interpretation is that if the unmoved mover is separate in the ontological sense, it cannot be an efficient cause in the way that a soul is. This is clear from Aristotle's definition of soul in *De Anima*. He defines the soul as "the first actu-alization of a natural body which possesses life potentially" or "of a natural organic body" (II.1 412a27–8, b5–6). The definition of soul thus contains a reference to a natural body, which is defined as a body that possesses a nature, i.e. an internal principle of change or rest which belongs to it essentially and not coincidentally (1.412b16–17; cf. *Phys.* II.1.192b13–32). All natural bodies have such an internal principle, although in the simplest bodies – air, earth, fire, and water – it is very rudimentary, e.g. causing them to rise or fall to their natural places. In living things, the internal principle is its soul, which involves a complex network of faculties, including the nutritive, perceptive, locomotive, and cognitive. This is what Aristotle means when he relates soul to body as form to matter: "The body is not the actualization of the soul, but the soul is the actualization of a body." And he concurs with theorists who believe that the soul does not exist without a body and that it is not a sort of body. "For it is not a body but something belonging to a body, and for this reason it is present in a body, and in a body of a specific sort." (*DA* II.2.414a 18–22) Hence, a given soul cannot fit into any chance body but they must be suited for each other.

This is the way that Aristotle's thesis that the soul is an efficient cause must be understood. On the one hand, the animal is an efficient cause – i.e. the man begets a man – because it has a soul; on the other hand, the soul itself is an efficient cause in virtue of being embodied. The soul is a natural power (or nexus of powers) which enables the animal to act. Unlike the medical art, the soul inheres naturally in the body to which it belongs. In this light, the passage quoted at the beginning of this section needs to be reconsidered:

> For the what and the that-for-the-sake-of-which are one, while the primary source of movement is the same in form as these. For human generates human – and so too, in general, with all things which bring about movement by being moved; and such as are not of this kind no longer belong to natural science, for they bring about movement not by possessing motion or a source of motion in themselves, but being themselves immovable. [*Phys.* II.7.198a24–9]

In the final clause, "such as are not of this kind" refers to unmoved movers. Given the prime mover's separateness from the perceptible cosmos which it moves, it cannot be related to it as a soul is to a body. Indeed, it is outside the purview of physics. For if it exercises efficient causality, it cannot do so in the same way as the internal principle of a natural body.

## 6  Implication for mental causation

Aristotle's divine cause remains an enigma. The three main interpretations on offer all present difficulties. On the first interpretation the
prime mover is a final cause and only incidentally an efficient cause.
But then it looks like a metaphorical mover, a mere exemplary cause
like Plato's Forms which Aristotle dismisses. On the second interpretation, it is a genuine efficient cause, but then there arises the problem of
how an unmoved mover could act as such a cause. If it is purported to
be an "untouched toucher," in what sense does it "touch" a body? Both
interpretations ultimately fall back on unsatisfying metaphors. On the
third interpretation, the prime mover is related as a soul to the celestial
body which it moves. Although this is, for Aristotle, a way in which a
cause can be both efficient and final, the explicit "separateness" of the
prime mover is a stumbling block for this sort of interpretation; for a
soul's efficient causality is fundamentally and inextricably grounded in
its embodiment. The problem of interpreting the divine mind is due
to the difficulty of fitting an incorporeal prime mover into the causal
framework which Aristotle has developed for natural substances.

Given Aristotle's definition of " soul", he could not subscribe to psychological dualism, in the sense that soul and body are substances which
are ontologically independent of each other. That is why he rejects the
Pythagorean view that a soul can leave one body at death and enter
another at birth and that any soul can occupy any sort of body whatever
(*DA* I.2.414a22–7). His psychological theory is fundamentally at variance with that of Descartes, who maintains that body and mind have
distinct essences: extension for body and thinking for mind. Descartes
also contends that the mind could cause the body to move and the body
could give rise to thoughts in the mind, but he is unable to explain satis-
factorily how an immaterial substance could interact with a material
substance. This sort of problem does not arise for Aristotle, because he
views the human mind as an integral part of the embodied human soul
and as attached to the other psychic faculties: the nutritive, perceptive,
and conative. The human mind (except for the productive mind briefly
discussed in *De Anima*) is thus a constituent of the nature of a human
being, which is the internal principle responsible for how humans act
and respond to their environment. When embodied human beings act,
they are exercising the cognitive faculty, so that human mental activity
is an essential part of the efficient cause of human action.[45]

Aristotle's theology, however, is not free of this difficulty. Although
he takes great pains to emphasize that the prime mover is active, that

its activity takes the form of thinking, and that its thinking is akin to (though far superior to) human thinking, he does not provide a satisfactory explanation of how divine mental activity could be an efficient cause of cosmic motion. Aristotle's divine mind might thus be viewed as a precursor of Descartes' human mind. When Aristotle makes problematic claims, they are often, in fact, incompatible with his own general principles.[46] Such a problem arises when he tries to detach divine causation from his hylomorphic theory of substance.[47]

## Notes

1. In Lambda 8, Aristotle argues that 55 unmoved movers are needed to account for the movements of 55 celestial spheres. One of these is the first, the mover of the outermost sphere (*Meta.* XII.7.1073b2–3), which will be referred to as "the prime mover" in this essay.
2. Ross (1924, p. Cxxx).
3. The primary focus of this essay is on *Metaphysics* Lambda, although it is assumed that this book substantially agrees with and depends at critical junctures on conclusions reached in *Physics* VIII. More controversial is the relation of both these works to *De Caelo*, which seems (except for a few passages) to precede Aristotle's discovery of the prime mover. In any case this essay does not rely on *De Caelo*. On the development of Aristotle's theology see Guthrie (1939: xv-xxxvi) and Ross (1936: 94–102).
4. *Phys.* II.3.194b23–195a4 (with labels added in brackets); cf. *Meta.* V.1013a24–35. The translations of Aristotle generally follow the Revised Oxford Translation but are often revised in places with a view to greater precision or consistency with the main text.
5. Ryan (1973) argues that Aristotle did not understand the prime mover as a "pure form". Regarding the interpretation that the prime mover is the form of the cosmos, see section 5 below.
6. Ross (1964, p. 181).
7. Kahn (1985: 185). Assuming Kahn means that the prime mover is not an efficient cause except in so far as it is a final cause, he is in agreement with Ross.
8. See also Guthrie (1981, 252–59); Lear (1988, 295); Natali (1997); Sedley (2000); Bordt (2011).
9. Broadie (1993) and Berti (2000). See also Menn (2012: 443): "Aristotle is not saying that this kind of unmoved mover is only a final cause: it must first produce motion (at least, produce a cognition of itself as good and desirable) as an efficient cause, and only thereby can it act as a final cause."
10. The expressions *mê kinoumenon* (not moving) and *akinêton* (immovable) both mean it does undergo motion wheher caused by itself or by anything else.
11. Berti (2000: 186); cf. Broadie (1993).
12. Giacon (1969); cf. Berti (2000: 186).
13. Berti contends that the prime mover is the final cause *of itself* rather than the heavens (2000: 203, 206). Bordt criticizes this autoerotic interpretation (2011: 104–08).

14. For the assumption underlying this objection compare Plato's *Euthryphro* 10c: "SOCRATES: Is something loved either something changed or something affected by something? EUTHYPHRO: Certainly." 1072b1–3 presents textual difficulties which are discussed in Menn (2012: 461 n. 40).

15. Reading *telos* at 1074a20 with Jaeger and Ross.

16. For this solution, see G. E. R. Lloyd (2000: 265).

17. Broadie (1993: 382). She also objects that proponents of the final-cause interpretation suppose that the celestial spheres have souls which try to imitate the unmoved mover with circular motions, but there is no mention of such "souls" or "imitation" in *Metaphysics* Lambda or *Physics* VIII.

18. Ross (1924: cxxxiv).

19. Judson (1994) argues that if the final cause is good and is desired for its goodness, there is a sense in which it is an efficient cause. Judson distinguishes between two sorts of efficient causes: "energetic" efficient causes, which "involve the transmission of energy or motion (and typically some interaction between agent and patient that involves change to the agent)," and "nonenergetic" efficient causes that do not. He proposes that Aristotle's divine cause is of the nonenergetic variety. It is unclear, however, why the Platonic Forms (including the Form of the Good) would not qualify as a nonergetic efficient cause, even though Aristotle explicitly rejects them at *Meta.* XII.6.1071b12–17. See Tuozzo (2011) for criticism of Judson's proposal.

20. Berti interprets the argument along these lines (2000: 189–90).

21. The verb *energein* is translated "to act" here, in behalf of the efficient-cause interpretation, rather than "to be active" or, even more weakly, "to be actual". In support of "to act" compare *Rhetoric* III.11.1411b24–1412a9 which explains that metaphors are vivid when they signify inanimate objects as acting (*energounta*) like living creatures, e.g. "the arrow flew on eagerly" and "the point of the spear drove furiously through his breastbone".

22. See Bordt (2011: 98). Pseudo-Alexander comments that by "if it does not act, there will be no movement" Aristotle means "if it does not act in a manner involving no potentiality, there will be no eternal movement" (*In metaph.* 689, 1–5).

23. The text is difficult because it mentions "these substances" (*tautas ousias*) possibly anticipating the 55 unmoved movers proposed in Lambda 8 and because it is uncertain based on manuscript evidence whether Aristotle meant to say that the prime mover is an actuality (*energeia*, read by Ross, Jaeger, and Alexandru with manuscript A^b ) or that it exists in actuality (*energeai*, with an iota subscript as in manuscript in E). However the manuscripts agree on *energeia* (actuality) at 7.1072a25.

24. "The former" refers to the capacity to think of an object and "the latter" to its actualization. The translation follows Ross, Jaeger, and Pseudo-Alexander's paraphrase, rather than the manuscripts.

25. Berti suggests that God's "active intervention" in the universe can also include an "act of will"; for "God for Aristotle feels pleasure and he is happy, which implies that he has will" (2000: 201 n. 35).

26. Beere (2003: 17 n. 29) points out the inadequacy of explanations of this assumption in terms of final cause as offered by Ross (1924: 382) and Lloyd (2000: 254).

27. See Menn (2012: 443) and n. 19 for this interpretation. See also Menn (1992).
28. Compare Tuozzo (2011: 457): "For an art to act as an efficient cause is simply a special case of a soul acting as efficient cause." See also *Meta.* XII.5.1071a20–2: "For the individual is the source of the individuals. For while man is the cause of man universally, there is no universal man; but Peleus is the cause of Achilles, and your father of you."
29. See Williams (1982: 115–18) for this interpretation. Admittedly, however, Aristotle does not mention this application here.
30. Compare Graham (1999: 177). Ross dismisses the claim that the prime mover is "at" the circumference as "an incautious expression which should not be pressed" (1949: 181).
31. "At" here translates *en* with the dative. The prime mover cannot literally occupy a place since it has no magnitude. Graham (1999: 177–78) finds difficulties with the argument even on the efficient-cause interpretation.
32. Judson (1994: 167–71) concedes that these two arguments are not easily accommodated by the interpretation (which he favors) that the prime mover is a final cause only in virtue of being a final cause. Judson adds that these arguments "do not seem to be reconcilable with *any* interpretation of the unmoved mover". As argued here, however, the untouched-toucher interpretation makes better sense of these arguments.
33. Compare *Physics* VII.2.243a32–5: "The first mover – *not in the sense of that for the sake of which but in the sense of the source of movement* – is always together with the thing moved. By 'together' I mean that there is nothing between. This holds universally for every mover and thing moved." (The italicized phrase makes clear that togetherness is necessary for the efficient not the final cause.)
34. See Menn (2012: 438–9) on this argument.
35. However, the untouched toucher may be alluded to in *Phys.* VIII.5.258a18–25, discussed in the following section.
36. E.g. Simplicius *In phys.* 1243, 25–8. Natali (2004: 215–16) offers a non-metaphorical interpretation involving a person who outrages us with an outrageous act, but it remains unclear how such a person can *literally* touch us without being touched in return.
37. This interpretation is defended by Kosman (1994) and criticized by Judson (1994).
38. Kosman (1994) sees the three works as in basic agreement. See however note 3 above.
39. Matthen (2001: 197). Matthen also describes the universe as "consisting of the prime mover plus the corporeal universe" (189). Though more nuanced and carefully qualified, Matthen's interpretation is vulnerable to the main objections advanced in this section.
40. See Kosman (1994: 140–01).
41. See Judson (1994: 162–03) for further discussion of this objection.
42. In *De Anima* Aristotle remarks that even if the heaven was moved a self-moving soul, as Plato claims, that soul would be moved coincidentally not essentially (cf. I.3.407b7–8, 406b11–15).
43. Compare *Motion of Animals* 4.699b32: the unmoved mover must be "outside of" (*exô*) what is moved.

44. This may explain Lambda's suggestion that unmovable substance belongs to a "different" science (1.1069b1). See Miller (2012: 308–10) on the different senses of "separable". Aristotle holds that a mathematical object is separable only in thought or by abstraction..
45. In *De Anima* III.5 Aristotle speaks of the "productive" mind as "separable". If he means that a part of the human mind is ontologically separable and acts on the rest of the mind, this raises problems comparable to those discussed in this essay. See Miller (2012) for further discussion.
46. I owe this observation to David Keyt (2013), who points out, also, that the (supposedly empirically confirmed) spontaneous generation is incompatible with the principle that "the actual member of a species is prior to the potential member of the same species" (*Met.* IX.8.1049b18–19).
47. I am grateful to Brian Battiste, Christopher Shields, and the editor for valuable comments on an earlier draft. I also owe a great debt is to fellow members of the Ohio Greek Philosophy Group with whom I studied *Metaphysics* Lambda from October 2009 until June 2011.

# Bibliography

Aquinas, Thomas. 1961. *Commentary on Aristotle's Metaphysics*. Trans. John P. Rowan (Notre Dame: Dumb Ox Books), 1961.

Beere, Jonathan B. 2003. "Counting the Unmoved Movers: Astronomy and Explanation in Aristotle's *Metaphysics* XII.8," *Archiv für Geschichte der Philosophie* 85: 1–20.

Berti, Enrico. 2000. "Unmoved Mover(s) as Efficient Cause(s) in *Metaphysics* Λ 6," in Michael Frede and David Charles (ed.) *Metaphysics Lambda* (Oxford: Clarendon Press), pp. 181–206.

Bordt, Michael. 2011. "Why Aristotle's God is Not the Unmoved Mover," *Oxford Studies in Ancient Philosophy* 40: 91–109.

Broadie, Sarah. 1993. "Que fait le premier moteur d'Aristote? (Sur la théologie du livre Lambda de la 'Métaphysique')," *Revue philosophique de la France et de l'Étranger* 183: 375–411.

Giacon, Carlo. 1969. *La causalità del motore immobile* (Padua: Antenore).

Graham, Daniel. 1999. *Aristotle Physics Book VIII: Translated with a Commentary* (Oxford: Clarendon Press).

Guthrie, W. K. C. 1939. *Aristotle On the Heavens* (Cambridge, Mass.: Harvard University Press).

____ 1981. *Aristotle: An Encounter*, vol. 6 of *A History of Greek Philosophy* (Cambridge: Cambridge University Press).

Judson, Lindsay. 1994. "Heavenly Motion and the Unmoved Mover," in M. L. Gill and J. G. Lennox (ed.) *Self-Motion from Aristotle to Newton*. (Princeton: Princeton University Press), pp. 135–53.

Kahn, Charles. 1985. "The Place of the Prime Mover in Aristotle's Teleology," in Allan Gotthelf (ed.) *Aristotle on Nature and Living Things: Philosophical and Historical Studies*, (Pittsburgh: University of Pittsburgh Press), pp. 183–205.

Keyt, David. 2013. "A Life in the Academy," in Georgios Anagnostopoulos and Fred D. Miller, Jr. (ed.) *Reason and Analysis in Ancient Greek Philosophy: Essays in Honor of David Keyt* (Dordrecht: Springer).

Kosman, Aryeh. 1994. "Aristotle's Prime Mover," in M. L. Gill and J. G. Lennox (ed.) *Self-Motion from Aristotle to Newton* (Princeton: Princeton University Press), pp. 155–71.

Laks, André. 2000. "*Metaphysics* Λ 6," in Michael Frede and David Charles (ed.) *Metaphysics Lambda* (Oxford: Clarendon Press), 207–43.

Lear, Jonathan. 1988. *Aristotle: The Desire to Understand* (Cambridge: Cambridge University Press).

Lloyd, G. E. R. 2000. "*Metaphysics* Λ 8," in Michael Frede and David Charles (ed.) *Metaphysics Lambda* (Oxford: Clarendon Press), pp. 245–73.

Matthen, Mohan. 2001. "The Holistic Presuppositions of Aristotle's Cosmology," *Oxford Studies in Ancient Philosophy* 20: 171–99.

Menn, Stephen. 1992. "Aristotle and Plato on God as Nous and as the Good," *Review of Metaphysics* 45: 543–73.

—— 2012. "Aristotle's Theology," in Christopher Shields (ed.) *The Oxford Handbook of Aristotle* (Oxford: Oxford University Press), pp. 422–64.

Miller, Fred D. 2012. "Aristotle on the Separability of Mind," in Christopher Shields (ed.) *The Oxford Handbook of Aristotle* (Oxford: Oxford University Press), pp. 306–39.

Natali, Carlo. 1997. "Causa mortice e causa finale nel Libro Lambda della Metafisica di Aristotele," *Methexis* 10: 105–23.

—— 2004. "*On Generation and Corruption* I.6," in F. De Haas and J. Mansfeld (ed.) *Aristotle's Generation and Corruption I* (Oxford: Clarendon Press), pp. 195–217.

Ross, W. D. 1924. *Aristotle's Metaphysics: A Revised Text with Introduction and Commentary* (Oxford: Clarendon Press).

Ross, W. D. 1936. *Aristotle's Physics: A Revised Text with Introduction and Commentary* (Oxford: Clarendon Press).

—— 1964. *Aristotle* fifth ed. (London: Methuen).

Ryan, Eugene E. 1973. "Pure Form in Aristotle," *Phronesis* 18: 209–24.

Sedley, David. 2000. "*Metaphysics* Λ 6," in Michael Frede and David Charles (ed.) *Metaphysics Lambda* (Oxford: Clarendon Press), pp. 327–50.

Tuozzo, Thomas. 2011. "How Dynamic Is Aristotle's Efficient Cause?" *Epoche* 15: 447–64.

Williams, C. J. F. 1982. *Aristotle's De Generatione et Corruptione: Translated with Notes* (Oxford: Clarendon Press).

# Index

Ancient and medieval authors are indexed according to their given names.

CPSIA information can be obtained
at www.ICGtesting.com
Printed in the USA
LVHW030334061219
639559LV00005B/284/P